Science, Technology, Policy and International Law

This book presents innovative insights into the intersections between science, technology, and society, and particularly their regulation by the law. Departing from the idea that law and science have similar methods and objectives, the book deals with problems, and solutions, that source from these interactions: concerns on how to integrate scientific evidence into trials, how to best regulate new technologies, or whether technological innovations could improve democratic legitimacy, create new regulatory tools or even new spaces of regulation, and what is the impact on the society. The edited collection, by building on a functionalist and comparatist approach, offers answers to how to best integrate law, science, and technology in policy-making and reviews the current attempts made at the transnational and international levels. Case studies, ranging from emerging technologies via environmental protection to statistics, are complemented by a solid theoretical framework, all of which seek to provide readers with tools for critical thinking in the reassessment of the relationship among theory, practice, political goals, and international regulation.

Justo Corti Varela is an associate professor of public international law and international relations at the National University of Distance Education (Spain) and the deputy dean of the School of Law and is responsible of the Quality and Innovation Policy of the faculty. Qualified in Spanish and in Argentina law, he is a member of the Bar in both countries. Previously, he has been a senior fellow and EU project manager at the Royal Institute for European Studies (Madrid), a visiting professor of Université de Nanterre (Paris 10), a postdoctoral researcher at CNRS (Paris), a visiting scholar at the University College London and at Scoula Superiore Sant'Anna (Pisa), and a member of the judicial office in several jurisdictions. He obtained a PhD in law summa cum laude under the supervision of Prof. Gil Carlos Rodriguez Iglesias, former president of the European Court of Justice (between 1994 and 2003). He also holds an LLM in EU law by Complutense University (Spain), and an LLB in law by the National University of Littoral (Argentina). He holds a Jean Monnet Module on European Climate Law and leads as the main researcher a national project on climate migrations, awarded by the

Spanish Research Agency, coordinating a multidisciplinary research team, including biologists, sociologists, anthropologists, and lawyers. As project manager of the Royal Institute for European Studies, he coordinated eight European projects involving universities and research teams from United States, United Kingdom, China, Germany, France, Belgium, Holland, Denmark, Italy, Portugal, Croatia, Brazil, and Argentina, organizing events, coordinating publications, and managing a multilingual and multicultural research staff. His areas of expertise research are global governance, European and international economic and environmental law, and the new technologies international regulation. Being a leading expert in biotechnological regulation since his PhD, much more recently, he has been involved in the regulation of the climate transition, studying the interactions of rules and proceedings at national, European, and international levels and how they impact on the most vulnerable people. Energy security, climate migrations, climate justice (and injustices), and the new perspectives of the role of law for managing the Anthropocene era are part of his recent interests, pushing his research to a much more holistic vision of societal problems linked to climate change. He has produced two monographs, seven books, and more than 50 chapters, articles, and working papers written in English, French, and Spanish and published with international publishers. He is a member of the board of the Revista de Derecho Comunitario Europeo (Ministry of Presidency, Spain) and the chair of the interest group on bio-law at the European Society of International Law. He teaches at the Diplomatic School of Spain (Ministry of Foreign Affairs) and gives advice, regularly, to national and international institutions on his areas of expertise.

Paolo Davide Farah is a full professor at West Virginia University, Eberly College of Arts and Sciences, John D. Rockefeller IV School of Policy and Politics; founder and director of the West Virginia University, Energy Justice and Just Transition Lab; and founder and coordinator of the Eberly College Interdisciplinary Research Collaborative on Global Challenges and Local Response Initiatives. He is a visiting professor of law at the University of Pittsburgh School of Law; the founder, president, director, principal investigator, and senior research fellow at gLAWcal – Global Law Initiatives for Sustainable Development (United Kingdom); an "internationally renowned professor/distinguished professor of law" (full professor level) at the Beijing Foreign Studies University (BFSU), Law School, Beijing, China; and a senior research fellow at the Institute of International Economic Law (IIEL), Georgetown University Law Center, Washington, DC, USA. He is teaching and researching in law, public policy and public administration, democratic context of public administration, legal and political foundations, international law, climate change, international trade, business and human rights, social justice, sustainable development, and energy and environmental law and policy. Professor Farah is an expert in the interaction among trade, economic globalization, and non-trade concerns, such as sustainable development, energy, environment, and human rights. He has variously taught classes in different institutions on public international law, international economic law and WTO law, European law, comparative law, and Chinese law in Italy (2003–2011), in the UK as a senior lecturer in law, associate professor (2012–2014), and in the USA and China as a visiting professor (since 2008). He acts as the editor-in-chief for the book series Transnational Law and Governance and for the book series Global Law and Sustainable Development (in English), published by Routledge (New York/London). He is the series editor for Global Issues. He was a visiting scholar (2011–2012) at Harvard Law School, East Asian Legal Studies Program. As a scientific director, since 2006, he has been coordinating the Summer Law Institute in China, Executive Education Training Program (www.summerlawinstitute.com), held in China. He was an international consultant and legal advisor for projects implemented for the United Nations Development Program (UNDP), for the Italian Ministry of Economic Development and Commerce, and for the OECD. He has previously worked at the Legal Affairs Division of the World Trade Organization in Geneva and was an associate lawyer of Baker & McKenzie Law Firm, Milan, Italy. Professor Farah has collaborated in different roles with the European Union Chamber of Commerce in Beijing (China), the China–Italy Chamber of Commerce (CICC) in Beijing (China), Freshfields Bruckhaus Deringer International Law Firm in Beijing (China), Assolombarda (Italian Entrepreneurial Association of Lombardy Region, the largest regional Entrepreneurial Association of Confindustria), ANCI (Italian Association for Shoes Producers), Chamber of Commerce in Milan, and Banca Popolare di Milano. From 2018 to 2022, he served as an elected board member of the European Society of International Law (ESIL), and since 2016, he has been the chair of the ESIL Interest Group on International Environmental Law (elected for an additional term until 2024). Professor Farah also served as the vice-chair (2019–2020) and chair (2020–2023) of the American Society of International Law (ASIL) Interest Group on International Environmental Law; the vice-chair (2020–2021) and chair (2021–2023) of the American Society of International Law (ASIL) Interest Group on International Law and Technology. From 2017 to 2020, he was the chair for the ASIL Interest Group on Intellectual Property Law. From 2014 to 2022, Professor Farah was an appointed member of the International Law Association, ILA Committees on Sustainable Development, and the Green Economy in International Trade Law and ILA Committee on Role of International Law in Sustainable Natural Resource Management for Development. Since 2023, he has been an appointed member of the International Law Association – ILA Committee on Submarine Cables and Pipelines under International Law and since 2024 an appointed member of the International Law Association – ILA Committee on Business and Human Rights. Professor Farah has more than 60 peer-reviewed and US law review articles or book chapters, nine books and six journal special issues published or forthcoming, and 20 additional peer-reviewed publications in Italian, French, Spanish, and Chinese. He has presented his work to more than 150 international conferences and workshops. Professor Farah was a guest editor-in-chief for the SSCI *Journal of World Energy Law and Business*, and a guest editor-in-chief for SSCI *Journal Sustainability*. Professor Farah's work has appeared or is forthcoming in such journals as *Arizona State Law Journal*, *Connecticut Law Review*, *UMKC Law Review*, *Oregon Law Review*, *University of Pittsburgh Law Review*, *West Virginia Law Review*, *Georgetown International Environmental Law Review*, *Columbia Journal of Asian Law*, *Duke Environmental Law and Policy Forum*, *Fordham Environmental Law Review*, *Brooklyn Journal of International Law*, *Journal of International Economic Law*, *Journal of World Energy Law and Business*, *Journal of World Trade*, *Leiden Journal of International Law*, *MDPI Sustainability*, *Journal of Cleaner Production*, *Asian Journal of WTO & International Health Law and Policy*, *Legal Issues of Economic Integration*, and *European Energy and Environmental Law Review*. He has coordinated and led, as a principal investigator or major co-principal investigator, externally funded research grants for an overall amount of $2 million. He graduated with a maîtrise in international and European law from Paris Ouest La Defense Nanterre University (France), LLM in European legal studies from the College of Europe in Bruges (Belgium), and a dual PhD in international law from Aix-Marseille University (France) and University of Milan (Italy).

Transnational Law and Governance

Series Editor: Paolo Davide Farah

West Virginia University, USA and gLAWcal – Global Law Initiatives for Sustainable Development, UK

In recent years the concepts of "transnational law" and "governance" have been explored by both scholars and practitioners with the terms taking on new meaning and significance, particularly in light of the ongoing economic crisis and a corresponding critical reappraisal of global institutional structures and governance. This multidisciplinary series aims to provide a home for research exploring these issues.

Transnational law covers a broad theoretical definition which includes studies emerging from disciplines such as international law, comparative law, international economic law and administrative law undertaken by legal scholars but also features extensive research undertaken by scholars from other disciplines, including but not limited to, political sciences, international relations, public administration, sociology, history, philosophy and geography. Governance in particular is now seen as important when we refer to the general stability of the markets, to good faith and other key principles which are fundamental to the notion of a fair market which is responsive to the needs of governments and citizens as well as businesses.

This series features cutting-edge works which critically analyse the relationship between governance, institutions and law from a variety of disciplinary perspectives.

Available titles in this series include:

Sustainability in Public Procurement, Corporate Law and Higher Education
Edited by Dr. Lela Mélon

US Trade Policy, China and World Trade Organization
Nerina Boschiero

Science, Technology, Policy and International Law
Edited by Justo Corti Varela and Paolo Davide Farah

Science, Technology, Policy and International Law

Edited by Justo Corti Varela and Paolo Davide Farah

Routledge
Taylor & Francis Group
LONDON AND NEW YORK

First published 2025
by Routledge
4 Park Square, Milton Park, Abingdon, Oxon OX14 4RN

and by Routledge
605 Third Avenue, New York, NY 10158

Routledge is an imprint of the Taylor & Francis Group, an informa business

British Library Cataloguing-in-Publication Data
A catalogue record for this book is available from the British Library

Library of Congress Cataloging-in-Publication Data
Names: Corti Varela, Justo, editor. | Farah, Paolo, editor.
Title: Science, technology, policy, and international law/edited by Justo Corti Varela and Paolo Davide Farah.
Description: Abingdon, Oxon [UK] ; New York, NY : Routledge, 2025.
Series: Transnational law and governance | Includes bibliographical references and index.
Identifiers: LCCN 2023052376 | ISBN 9781032070216 (hardback) | ISBN 9781032751139 (paperback) | ISBN 9781003472421 (ebook)
Subjects: LCSH: Technological innovations—Law and legislation. | Technological innovations—Law and legislation—European Union countries. | Information technology—Law and legislation. | Science and law. | Evidence, Expert. | Rule of law.
Classification: LCC K487.T4 S369 2024 | DDC 344/.095—dc23/eng/20231117 LC record available at https://lccn.loc.gov/2023052376

ISBN: 978-1-032-07021-6 (hbk)
ISBN: 978-1-032-75113-9 (pbk)
ISBN: 978-1-003-47242-1 (ebk)

DOI: 10.4324/9781003472421

Typeset in Galliard
by Apex CoVantage, LLC

Contents

Contributors

Giovanni Bombelli
He is a full professor at the Catholic University of the Sacred Heart (Milan, Italy). He graduated in philosophy and law and holds a PhD in philosophy of law. He teaches philosophy of law and legal methodology at the School of Law of the Catholic University of the Sacred Heart of Milan and is a member of research associations (Italian Society of Philosophy of Law, CERMEG, Center for Philosophical Studies of Gallarate) and scientific journals (*Theory and Critique of Social Regulation*, *Diachrony*, and others). Furthermore, he belongs to the Steering Committee of the Psychological, Law and Policy Lab (Psylab) of the Catholic University of the Sacred Heart and is a member of the doctoral teaching staff of the doctorate "Person and legal orders" activated at the School of Law of the Catholic University of the Sacred Heart of Milan.

Ciarán Burke
He is a professor and senior research fellow at the Jena Center for Reconciliation Studies at the Friedrich Schiller University, Jena, Germany, and a senior legal officer at the EFTA Surveillance Authority in Brussels. He is a visiting professor at various universities around Europe. He is the former director of research of the Irish Law Reform Commission and also works as a freelance legal consultant.

Alessandra Donati
She is *Référendaire* at the European Court of Justice. She is the editor-in-chief of the *EU Journal of Consumer Law* (REDC). She is a specialist in EU law and environmental and public health law. She is the co-director of the collection Reflex Europe (Larcier). Before joining the Court, she worked as a postdoctoral researcher at the University of Luxembourg and as a senior research fellow at the Max Planck Institute Luxembourg. She worked in two law firms in Italy and France. She holds a PhD in EU law from the University Paris 1 Panthéon Sorbonne.

Alessio Lo Giudice
He is a full professor of philosophy of law and legal theory at the Law Department of the University of Messina (Italy). He is the director of the editorial series L'Europa del pensiero. Collana di Filosofia del diritto, for Castelvecchi

Publisher, and Coordinator of the editorial series Rifrazioni. Studi critici di storia della filosofia del diritto, for ETS Publisher. He is a member of the board of directors of the Scientific Journal *Teoria e Critica della Regolazione Sociale*. He holds a PhD in philosophy of law from the University of Tilburg (the Netherlands) and a PhD in sociology of law from the University of Milan (Italy).

Gemma Hobcraft
She is an experienced barrister practising in regulatory law with a particular focus on health care and human rights. She was previously an Authority member of the Human Fertilisation and Embryology Authority (HFEA). She was the deputy chair of the Authority and also chaired the Ethics and Standards Committee amongst other roles. She was a trustee of Brook (sexual health for young people) and an elected member of the Executive Committee of the Human Rights Lawyers Association (and its bursary officer). She has also lectured in medical law and ethics.

Imad Antoine Ibrahim
He is an assistant professor in environmental law and governance at the Department of Governance and Technology for Sustainability (CSTM), Faculty of Behavioural, Management and Social Sciences (BMS), University of Twente, Enschede, the Netherlands. He is also a senior research associate at gLAWcal, Global Law Initiative for Sustainable Development, Essex, United Kingdom. He has been working on global environmental issues from a legal perspective and their interplay with emerging technologies for the last decade.

Kirk W. Junker
He is a university professor of law and holds the chair in US law at the University of Cologne, where he is also the director of the Environmental Law Center, board chair of the International Masters of Environmental Science Program, and a member of the Global Studies South Center. He is an adjunct professor of environmental law at the Bharati Vidyapeeth Institute of Environment Education and Research, Bharati Vidyapeeth University, Pune, India. He was previously a lecturer at the Faculty of Science, Technology, Engineering & Mathematics at the Open University, UK; a lecturer at the Humanities and Social Sciences Faculty at Dublin City University, Ireland; and an associate professor at the Faculty of Law at Duquesne University, Pittsburgh, USA. Prior to his university positions, Prof. Junker was a practicing trial lawyer with the Pennsylvania Department of Environmental Protection.

Anthi Koskina
She is a professor of law at Collège Idef-PARIS XIII, Athens, Greece, and a research fellow at Athens Public International Law Center (AthensPIL), National and Kapodistrian University of Athens, Greece. She obtained her PhD cum laude on "the right to conduct scientific research," from the National and Kapodistrian University of Athens, Greece, published in 2013 (Nomiki Bibliothiki Eds.). She was the recipient of a fellowship for young researchers, co-funded by the Greek Ministry of Economy and the EU (NSRF 2014–2020),

to conduct research titled "Artificial Intelligence and Space Law." She has been elected to take part in the prestigious International Visiting Professor Program 2020, under the fellowship of the University of Science and Technology of China Fellowship Initiative (Hefei, China). She is collaborating with the National Observatory of Athens, Greece, on space law matters and on environmental and climate change issues. She has published many articles on science, technology, and law; artificial intelligence law; environmental law; and space law – in national and international journals – and participated in several national and international conferences on these topics.

Alexandra Molitorisová
She is a researcher and lecturer at the Faculty of Life Sciences, University of Bayreuth, Germany, and at the Faculty of Law, Masaryk University, the Czech Republic. She graduated in law and jurisprudence from Charles University, the Czech Republic. She practiced law first as a paralegal and later as an associate in international as well as Czech law firms. She was a fellow at Uppsala University and a research assistant at Friedrich Schiller University in Jena, Germany. She regularly advises governmental bodies, European institutions, as well as NGOs (victim support organizations) and other organizations (European Academies' Science Advisory Council).

Antonio Quirós Fons
He is a professor of international law at Universidad Europea de Valencia and has been the associate professor at Universidad Cardenal Herrera CEU and visiting professor at Universidad de Navarra (Spain). He is the director of the PhD program in socio-educational innovation. He holds a PhD in international law from Universidad de Murcia (Spain) and a PhD in canon law from Pontificia Università della Santa Croce, Rome (Italy). He has extensive teaching and research experience in the areas of international law and international relations. He is a member of AEPDIRI, ESIL, and the Learning Research Network.

Mihail Stojanoski
He is an administrator/lawyer at the Istanbul Convention monitoring mechanisms division at the Council of Europe, and a PhD candidate in the field of human rights at the University of Strasbourg. He was the human rights advisor and assistant manager of the European Roma Rights Centre in Brussels and a former case-processing lawyer at the European Court of Human Rights in Strasbourg. He holds an LLM from the Ss. Cyril and Metodius University of Skopje.

Lilla Vukovich
She is a legal officer at the Department for the Execution of Judgments of the European Court of Human Rights and a former case-processing lawyer at the European Court of Human Rights. She was a research specialist for FRANET at the University of Luxembourg. She holds an LLM in intellectual property law from Queen Mary University of London.

Abbreviations

ADS	American Dialect Society
AGs	advocates general
AGGG	Advisory Group on Greenhouse Gases
AFIN	ASEAN Financial Innovation Network
APIX	application programming interface (API) exchange
APP	application
ART	assisted reproductive technologies
ASEAN	Association of Southeast Asian Nations
BTKNEEC	best technical knowledge not entailing excessive costs
CDR	carbon dioxide removal
CEFDW	Convention on the Elimination of All Forms of Discrimination against Women
CFCs	chlorofluorocarbons
CH4	methane
CJEU	Court of Justice of the European Union
CMA	Conference of the Parties serving as the meeting of the Parties to the Paris Agreement
CMP	Conference of the Parties serving as the meeting of the Parties to the Kyoto Protocol
CO_2	carbon dioxide
COP	Conference of the Parties
DDT	dichlorodiphenyltrichloroethane
DNA	deoxyribonucleic acid
DSU	Dispute Settlement Understanding
DTC-GT	direct-to-consumer genetic testing
EBP	evidence-based policy
EC	European Commission
ECB	European Central Bank
ECHR	European Court of Human Rights
ECJ	European Court of Justice
EGC	European General Court
ESCB	European System of Central Banks
ESHRE	European Society of Human Reproduction and Embryology

EU	European Union
FAO	Food and Agriculture Organization
FBI	Federal Bureau of Investigation
FDA	Food and Drug Administration
FinTechs	financial technologies
FSA	Food Standard Agency
FSB	Financial Stability Board
GATT	General Agreement on Tariffs and Trade
GC	General Court
GDP	gross domestic product
GFIN	Global Financial Innovation Network
GHG	greenhouse gases
GMO	genetically modified organisms
HFEA	Human Fertilisation and Embryology Authority
HIV	human immunodeficiency virus
IA	impact assessments
ICANN	Internet Corporation for Assigned Names and Numbers
ICCPR	International Covenant on Civil and Political Rights
ICJ	International Court of Justice
ICM	International Confederation of Midwives
ICT	information and communication technology
ID	identification
IGC	Intergovernmental Committee on Intellectual Property and Genetic Resources, Traditional Knowledge, and Folklore
ILO	International Labour Organization
INDCs	intended nationally determined contributions
IPCC	Intergovernmental Panel on Climate Change
IT	information technology
ITLOS	International Tribunal for the Law of the Sea
IUD	intrauterine device
IVF	in vitro fertilization
KM	kilometres
LDCs	least developed countries
MG	milligrams
MIT	Massachusetts Institute of Technology
MKKP	*Magyar Kétfarkú Kutya Párt*
MMT	methylcyclopentadienyl manganese tricarbonyl (metallic additives in fuel)
MOU	memorandum of understanding
MOX	mixed oxide
MRT	mitochondrial replacement techniques
MS	member states
MSM	men who have sex with men
MST	maternal spindle transfer
MUP	minimum unit pricing

NAS	American National Academies of Sciences
NDCs	nationally determined contributions
NGOs	non-governmental organizations
NICE	National Institute for Health and Care Excellence
NOx	nitrogen oxide
NTCs	non-trade concerns
OECD	Organization for Economic Co-operation and Development
OSCE	Organization for Security and Co-operation in Europe
PA	Paris Agreement
PIN	personal identification number
PGD	pre-implantation genetic diagnosis
PNT	pronuclear transfer
RCT	randomized control trials
RDE	real driving emissions
RegTech	regulatory technology
SAD	social anxiety disorder
SBI	Subsidiary Body for Implementation
SBSTA	Subsidiary Body for Scientific and Technological Advice
SCAAC	Scientific and Clinical Advances Advisory Committee
SEI	Stockholm Environment Institute
SIDS	small island developing states
SPS	Sanitary and Phytosanitary Measures Agreement
SROCC	Special Report on the Ocean and Cryosphere in a Changing Climate
SSK	sociology of scientific knowledge
STS	science, technology, and society
TFEU	Treaty on the Functioning of the European Union
TNAs	technology need assessments
UK	United Kingdom
UN	United Nations
UNEP	United Nations Environmental Programme
UNESCO	United Nations Educational, Scientific, and Cultural Organization
UNFCCC	United Nations Framework Convention on Climate Change
UNICEF	United Nations Children's Emergency Fund
US	United States
USGCRP	US Global Change Research Program
VAAs	voting advice applications
WHO	World Health Organization
WIPO	World Intellectual Property Organization
WMO	World Meteorological Organization
WTO	World Trade Organization

Acknowledgements

The origin of this book was an international call for papers and an international workshop, "Sound Science-Based Regulation in the Post-Truth Era: Domestic and International Rule of Law Under Fire," held at the premises of the Institute for International and European Law, Georg-August University of Göttingen, Germany, on 4–5 April 2019 under the framework of the European Society of International Law (ESIL) Research Forum "The International Rule of Law and Domestic Dimensions: Synergies and Challenges."

The workshop was the first event jointly organized by the ESIL Interest Group on International Environmental Law and Interest Group on Bio-Law, chaired by Professor Paolo Davide Farah and Professor Justo Corti Varela, respectively. We are very grateful to Professor Luis Hinojosa Martinez, for his support and enthusiasm in our proposal and for promoting the idea during his tenure as past ESIL president that joint events among different ESIL Interest Groups would be an enriching experience for the society, and to Professor Peter Tobias Stoll, local organizer of the ESIL Research Forum in Göttingen.

It is notable that among the proposed topics included in our call for papers, there was also "pandemics declaration and implementation of coordinated measures." At that moment, we could not imagine that several months later a worldwide pandemic was going to change our lives and our research interest.

In our discussions for designing the event, our main concern was how the anti-science discourse was disturbing political dialogue in a very different range of fields, given that many of these disruptions could affect the rule of law.

Against the background of a dynamic technological development with new emerging issues such as big data, blockchain technology, artificial intelligence, and cybersecurity, various disciplines of public international law, such as international environmental law, international health law, and international bio-law, are becoming increasingly based on scientific data to face these new challenges. Regulating climate change, human health, human genome, circular economy, pandemics, nanoscience, sustainable development, food safety, and security would not be possible without objective and scientifically sound information. At the same time, achieving harmonized international rules is only possible against the backdrop of common understanding on the scientific realities. Such common positions have been greatly aided by the work of UN agencies and related committees. In these science-based areas, scientific arguments and proceedings are not only a way to achieve political agreements in practice (norms and standards) but also significantly affect interpretation and application of international law. International law creates an "infrastructure" to global risk governance where regulators, stakeholders, and citizens interact. It does not matter whether we are talking about legal regulation (domestic or international), law-backed self-regulation, or self-regulation. In all cases, the rule of law departs from the premise that widely accepted scientific data is a solid foundation on which to construct principles and rules. However, sound science data has been put in doubt. This is partly caused by the diversity of sources and ideology of scientific information. Since the role of science in policy-making is under fire domestically and internationally and scientific data are relativized in the post-truth era, the very foundations of rule of law are undermined.

Our event aimed to address legal aspects of the intersections between sound science and rule of law in both international and domestic contexts, such as:

- Climate change relativism in international and domestic law and its impact on the implementation of Paris Agreements.
- Pandemics declaration and implementation of coordinated measures.
- Effective communication of sound scientific decisions. Social networks and new technological channels. Neutralization of fake news. Legal instruments and practice of international organizations.
- Evaluation of scientific evidence by international courts and tribunals. Impact of post-truth in the production, assessment, and impact of sound science evidence on the decisions.
- Politicization of scientific committees and international scientific organizations. Limits of neutrality and impartiality in the selection of experts. Conflict of interests. Is there an "ideological" scientific background that it is worth evaluating?
- Scientific research and ideology: scientific funding and the impact on the selection of research objectives. Impact on the production of data and expert profiles.
- Ethics and religion in a post-truth context: impact of ethics and religion on the evaluation of scientific data. Is it possible to balance or neutralize scientific data with moral and/or religious believing?
- Rule of law in the post-truth era: influence from domestic to international and vice versa (in environmental, health, and bio-law contexts).
- Principles and proceedings of the rule of law and the scientific methods. Similarities and differences.
- Human rights protection and the rule of law in the context of sound science decline. Positive/negative impact on different rights.
- Historical development of sound science arguments as part of the international/domestic rule of law guarantees. Our standard? Whose standard? Exportation and acceptance in non-Western countries.

- Is sound science gender-neutral? Post-truth and feminism. Rule of law and gender discrimination (in environmental, health, and bio-law contexts).
- Future international legal framework for space resources activities: interactions between international space law and science.

Later, this book has become a joint effort between gLAWcal (Global Law Initiatives for Sustainable Development), United Kingdom, and National Distance Learning University (UNED), Spain. It is a book project that has permitted some of the authors of this book to present the earlier drafts of their chapters in an academic venue, facilitating scholarly exchange, questions, and comments from the public, which benefitted the overall quality of the book. Some of the chapters of this book have been selected through a careful peer-review process from a call for papers which was publicly available in the academic networks provided by the European Society of International Law (ESIL) Interest Group on International Environmental Law, the European Society of International Law (ESIL) Interest Group on International Bio Law, gLAWcal (Global Law Initiatives for Sustainable Development) (United Kingdom), and National Distance Learning University (UNED) (Spain).

As it could happen with call for papers, not all the aforementioned themes have been covered by specific paper presentations, but they have still nourished the conversations and the background of this event and additional future events of our ESIL Interest Groups.

In particular, the earlier drafts of this selected set of peer-reviewed chapters included in this book have been first presented in this workshop, which facilitated scholarly exchange as well as questions and comments from participants, altogether benefitting the quality of the ideas that eventually made it to this book. All the paper presentations had been peer-reviewed and edited to develop and complete the book's overall theme and subdivisions.

We also want to thank the following colleagues who have actively participated in the debates and colloquium, like Professor Chamundeeswari Kuppuswamy (University of Hertfordshire), Belen Olmos Giupponi (University of Portsmouth), Jesse Reynolds (UCLA, University of California–Los Angeles). We are truly thankful to all of them for their comments and suggestions.

COVID-19 represented an important challenge to the whole of humanity, including the community of this publication. We suffered many disturbances in the preparation of the book. However, at the same time, it offered an opportunity to open the approach to new interactions between law and science in a context of increasing anti-science discourses. These pauses allowed authors in revised versions to delve into the magnification that the pandemic was producing on these discourses. Concerning the editors, and in this regard, Professor Paolo Davide Farah played an essential role in unfolding his extended academic network; it was an opportunity for expanding the approach to new directions, permitting, for example, going deeper into theoretical developments and in the multidisciplinary research areas exploring the relations among science, technology, and society (STS) and science technology, society, and law.

During this growing-up period, the research that surrounded the book was enriched by new projects. As a result, in addition to the contributions presented at this event, supplementary peer-reviewed chapters have been included in the book for completing the framework and objectives the book was aiming for. In particular, the book has developed a more accentuated technology angle to the already well-developed science component with the three following contributions and a detailed framework described in the introduction and conclusions of this book: "The Interlinkages Science-Technology-Law: Information and Communication Society, Knowledge-Based Economy, and the Rule of Law" (Chapter 3, by Giovanni Bombelli and Paolo Davide Farah); "Using Flexibility Mechanisms for Addressing Technological and Scientific Developments: Examples from Selected Global Regulatory Frameworks" (Chapter 4, by Imad Antoine Ibrahim), and "Climate Justice in the Anthropocene and Its Relationship with Science and Technology: The Importance of Ethics of Responsibility" (Chapter 11, by Paolo Davide Farah and Alessio Lo Giudice). These chapters are part of the gLAWcal project Emerging Technologies and Their Implications for Sustainable Development (gLAWcal ETIS Project).

gLAWcal (Global Law Initiatives for Sustainable Development) is an independent non-profit research organization (think tank) founded by Professor Paolo Davide Farah, and a gLAWcal scientific committee in place (www.glawcal.org.uk/), through research and policy analysis, sheds a new light on issues such as good governance; human rights; right to water; rights to food; social, economic, and cultural rights; labour rights; access to knowledge; public health; social welfare; consumer interests and animal welfare; climate change; energy; environmental protection and sustainable development; product safety; food safety; and security. All these values are directly affected by the global expansion of world trade and should be upheld to balance the excesses of globalization. In the past ten years, gLAWcal has promoted and successfully organized several events around the world, particularly in Europe, the United States of America, and Asia, partnering with various professional associations, such as the ASIL and the ESIL, and institutions such as the National Distance Learning University (UNED) (Spain). Many of these conferences and workshops have been carefully planned and later developed, having in mind a combination of factors such as the academic impact, advocacy, and the reach out towards the broader audience, with the objectives of academic publication as peer-reviewed books and peer-reviewed journal special issues with various prestigious international publishers. gLAWcal has also established two book series, Global Law and Sustainable Development and Transnational Law and Governance, both published by Routledge Publishing (Taylor & Francis), edited and directed by Professor Farah. gLAWcal also partnered for the series on "global issues" published by Palgrave MacMillan. In addition to these highly scientific and academic results, gLAWcal has also made these publications more accessible with the preparation of additional policy briefs rooted and based on the contents of these journal articles, chapters, and books and available on the website, social media, and addressed and sent to policymakers and civil society representatives. gLAWcal has also lead or contributed to various projects funded by the European Commission, such as the EPSEI Project, or "Evaluating Policies for Sustainable Energy Investments: Towards an Integrated Approach on National and International Stage," funded by the Marie Curie IRSES of the European Union's Seventh Framework Programme under REA grant agreement no. 269327, in consortium with several European, Chinese, and Russian universities and institutions; the LIBEAC Project, or "Liberalism in Between Europe And China," funded by the Marie Curie IRSES of the European Union's Seventh Framework Programme under REA grant agreement no. 317767, in consortium with several European, Chinese, and Japanese universities and institutions; and the POREEN Project, or "Partnering Opportunities between Europe and China in the Renewable Energies and Environmental Industries," funded by the Marie Curie IRSES of the European Union's Seventh Framework Programme under REA grant agreement no. 318908, in consortium with several European and Chinese universities and institutions.

Justo Corti Varela has led several proposals on science–law correlation in the field of climate change, awarded by EACEA, the UNED Deputy Chancellorship for Research, and the Spanish Agency of Research and funded by the NextGenerationEU Fund. This research included the launch of a paper series (European Climate Law Papers) and a book published in Spanish by Tirant lo Blanc Publishers. These activities have been completed by dissemination and transfer actions, in summer courses, specialized seminars, radio programmes, and long-life training courses, where scientists, policymakers, and CEOs interacted. We are particularly grateful for the participation of the head of the Spanish Office on Climate Change (Ministry for Ecological Transition), representatives of Iberdrola, PwC, the National Commission for Markets and Competition, and different NGOs. All these activities inspired many comments and approaches included in this book, and particularly regarding the Erasmus+ programme of the EACEA, there is a specific financial contribution for the preparation, edition, and correction of the initial manuscript.

The book has received financial support from the Department of Public International Law of the National Distance Learning University of Spain and the 2020–2023 Jean Monnet project "European Climate Law" (Ref. 620617-EPP-1–2020–1-ES), chaired by Justo Corti Varela.

In addition, we would like to thank Professor Farah collaborators at gLAWcal (Global Law Initiatives for Sustainable Development) (UK) and the gLAWcal scientific committee members, for their contribution in the last round of peer-review process completed in 2022 as external reviewers and referees for the final approval of this book.

Our gratitude to both institutions for it.

We cannot omit a sincere acknowledgement to all contributors to the book. Both to whom were part of it since the initial workshop and to those that joined it later. Regarding the first group, we would like to thank Prof. Kirk W. Junker (Environmental Law Center at the University of Cologne, Germany),

Alessandra Donati (Court of Justice of the European Union), Antonio Quirós Fons (European University of Valencia, Spain), Mihail Stojanoski (European Court of Human Rights), and Lilla Vukovich (Council of Europe); Gemma Hobcraft (UK Human Fertilisation and Embryology Authority), Ciarán Burke (Friedrich Schiller University, Jena, Germany), and Alexandra Molitorisová (University of Bayreuth, member of the Chair of Food Law, Germany); and Anthi Koskina (IdEF College, Sorbonne Paris North University, France, and National and Kapodistrian University of Athens, Greece). Thanks to all of you for your patience and the several revisions of your chapters. And concerning the second group, we would like to thank Giovanni Bombelli (Catholic University of the Sacred Heart, Milan, Italy), Imad Antoine Ibrahim (Department of Governance and Technology for Sustainability (CSTM), Faculty of Behavioural, Management and Social Sciences (BMS)), and Alessio Lo Giudice (University of Messina, Italy).

Last but not the least, we have to mention the editors' assistants, particularly Cristina García Santos, who gave support with the essential final editing tasks of the book.

This book was published thanks also to the funding and support of gLAWcal, Global Law Initiatives for Sustainable Development (UK); West Virginia University; John D. Rockefeller IV School of Policy and Politics, Department of Public Administration (USA); and the European Climate Law Initiative, National Distance Learning University Law School, Department of Public International Law (Spain).

Paolo Davide Farah
Essex, United Kingdom, and
Morgantown, West Virginia, USA

Justo Corti Varela
Madrid, Spain

With the support of the Erasmus+ Programme of the European Union

Foreword

Science, Technology, Policy and International Law, edited by Justo Corti Varela and Paolo Davide Farah, is a timely and thought-provoking collection of essays that explores the interplay between science, technology, and international law. The book is organized into 13 chapters that cover a range of topics, from the use of smartphone applications in the democratic process to the science-based policy-making process established in the Paris Agreement.

One of the strengths of this book is its interdisciplinary approach. The editors and contributors have backgrounds in law, policy, science, and technology, bringing diverse perspectives to the discussion. This allows for a more nuanced and comprehensive understanding of the issues at hand. The book is divided into 13 chapters, each exploring different aspects of this relationship.

This collection of essays dives deep into the intricate relationship between these three pillars of modern society and their impact on legal frameworks and decision-making. The book is structured meticulously, beginning with an insightful introduction by the editors that sets the stage for the thought-provoking chapters that follow. The diverse and accomplished group of contributors, including legal scholars, scientists, and technology experts, brings a wealth of knowledge and perspectives to the table. The first chapter, "Introduction," provides an overview of the themes and topics covered in the book by outlining the main contents and unveiling the motivations for the edited volume. The subsequent chapters delve deeper into the subject matter, with a range of perspectives and case studies from contributors across the globe.

Several chapters in the book focus on the precautionary principle, a key concept in international law that calls for caution in the face of scientific and technological uncertainty. Alessandra Donati's chapter on the precautionary principle under EU law is particularly relevant in the current "post-truth" era, where scientific evidence is often contested.

Other chapters examine the use of smartphone applications in the democratic process, the soundness of science in determining regulatory change, and the ethics of responsibility in the Anthropocene era.

The book's interdisciplinary approach brings together experts from various fields, including law, science, and ethics. This approach allows for a nuanced examination of the complex issues at the intersection of science, technology, and international law. For example, Chapter 4, which discusses the use of flexibility mechanisms in global regulatory frameworks, draws on insights from both law and science to explore how regulatory systems can adapt to rapid technological change.

Another strength of the book is its focus on practical issues and real-world examples. The contributors offer insights into how science and technology are shaping international law and how legal frameworks can be adapted to better respond to new scientific and technological developments. Chapter 6, which examines the precautionary principle and the burden of proof in international courts, provides a detailed analysis of how courts have applied the principle in cases involving scientific uncertainty.

In an overview of the different chapters, Chapter 2, "Facts Are the Moveable Furniture of the Legal Mind, Not Stones of Science," by Kirk W. Junker, challenges conventional wisdom about facts and their role in legal proceedings. Junker's chapter is a philosophical journey that forces readers to reconsider the fundamental nature of facts and how they interact with the legal system.

Chapter 3, authored by Giovanni Bombelli and Paolo Davide Farah, delves into the interlinkages between science, technology, and law in the context of the information and communication society. This chapter offers a comprehensive view of the knowledge-based economy and the rule of law, shedding light on the complexities of regulating a rapidly evolving technological landscape.

Chapter 4, written by Imad Antoine Ibrahim, explores the use of flexibility mechanisms in global regulatory frameworks to address technological and scientific developments. Ibrahim provides valuable examples and insights into how legal systems can adapt to the ever-changing world of technology.

In Chapter 5, "The Precautionary Principle Under EU Law," Alessandra Donati discusses a "post-modern" principle in a "post-truth" era, offering a critical analysis of the precautionary principle's role in European Union law, especially in an age of misinformation and uncertainty.

Chapter 6 by Justo Corti Varela, "Precautionary Principle and the Burden of Proof in International Courts," explores the weight of the precautionary principle in international legal settings. This chapter provides a compelling examination of how international courts handle complex scientific evidence and the burden of proof.

Antonio Quirós Fons delves into the contentious issue of conscientious objection in Chapter 7, highlighting the delicate balance between sound science and individual freedoms in a thought-provoking discussion.

Gemma Hobcraft, in Chapter 8, explores the soundness of science in regulatory decision-making, using the Human Fertilisation and Embryology Authority and mitochondrial donation as case studies. This chapter addresses the evolving challenges of regulating cutting-edge medical technologies.

Chapter 8 by Mihail Stojanoski and Lilla Vukovich, "The Use of Smartphone Applications in the Democratic Process," examines the integration of technology into the democratic process, offering insights into the potential and challenges of smartphone applications in shaping modern democracy.

Chapter 10, authored by Ciarán Burke and Alexandra Molitorisová, delves into the distinction between procedural and substantive approaches to scientific evidence in legal opinions, offering a comprehensive analysis of the various perspectives and approaches.

Chapter 11, "Climate Justice in the Anthropocene," by Paolo Davide Farah and Alessio Lo Giudice, explores the ethical dimensions of climate justice and its intricate relationship with science and technology in the Anthropocene era.

Anthi Koskina, in Chapter 12, provides a detailed analysis of the science-based policy-making process established in the Paris Agreement of 2015, shedding light on its modus operandi and implications for global climate action.

The book concludes with Chapter 13, where Paolo Davide Farah and Justo Corti Varela offer thoughtful insights and reflections on the overarching themes discussed throughout the anthology.

In sum, this book is a must-read for scholars, policymakers, and anyone interested in the evolving landscape of law and its relationship with the dynamic forces of science and technology. The book provides a valuable interdisciplinary perspective that is both thought-provoking and enlightening, making it an essential addition to the field of legal studies. It challenges preconceptions, encourages critical thinking, and invites readers to contemplate the profound implications of the ongoing convergence of science, technology, and the law in our increasingly complex world.

Professor Belen Olmos Giupponi,
Professor and Head of Law,
University of Portsmouth, United Kingdom

1 Science, Technology, Society, and Law

Paolo Davide Farah and Justo Corti Varela***

Over the years, numerous studies and publications have examined the influence of civic and political values on science and technology, emphasizing their inherent social dimensions and society's role in their production.[1] Science examines the laws of nature. In contrast, technology uses tangible scientific knowledge to create new things, machinery, and inventions. Scientific research is crucial for technological development, and vice versa; technology is essential for the creation of new research instruments.[2] Science contributes to technology in various ways, including serving as a source of innovations, a catalyst for developing new engineering tools and techniques, an enhancer of human skills, and a tool for assessing and evaluating the impact of technology on society. Technology also contributes to science by introducing new scientific

* Paolo Davide Farah, Full Professor, West Virginia University, Eberly College of Arts and Sciences, John D. Rockefeller IV School of Policy and Politics; Founder and Director of the West Virginia University, Energy Justice and Just Transition Lab; Founder and Coordinator of the Eberly College Interdisciplinary Research Collaborative on Global Challenges and Local Responses Initiatives; Visiting Professor of Law, University of Pittsburgh, School of Law; Founder, President, Director, Principal Investigator and Senior Research Fellow, at gLAWcal – Global Law Initiatives for Sustainable Development (United Kingdom). Email Addresses: paolofarah@yahoo.com; paolo.farah@glawcal.org.uk

** Justo Corti Varela, Associate Professor, National Distance Learning University (Spain), Deputy Dean on Quality and Innovation of the Law School. Former visiting professor at Paris Ouest La Defense Nanterre University (France) and visiting scholar at University College London. Chair of the Jean Monnet European Climate Law project. Corresponding Author: jcorti@der.uned.es.

1 Sheila Jasanoff, *A Field of Its Own: The Emergence of Science and Technology Studies*, *in* The Oxford Handbook of Interdisciplinarity (Robert Frodeman (ed.), Oxford University Press 2017); S. Jasanoff & others, Handbook of Science and Technology Studies (SAGE Publications 2001); J. Thompson Klein, Transdisciplinarity: Joint Problem Solving Among Science, Technology, and Society: An Effective Way for Managing Complexity (Springer Science & Business Media 2001); Dana L. Zeidler & others, *Beyond STS: A Research-Based Framework for Socioscientific Issues Education*, 89 Science Education 357 (2005); Steve Woolgar & Javier Lezaun, *The Wrong Bin Bag: A Turn to Ontology in Science and Technology Studies?* 43(3) Social Studies of Science 321 (2013).

2 G. Giacomelli & R. Giacomelli, *Science, Technology and Society*, *in* Non-Accelerator Astroparticle Physics (R. A. Carrigan, G. Giacomelli and N. Paver (eds.), World Scientific 2005).

DOI: 10.4324/9781003472421-1

challenges and providing improved methods for measuring scientific procedures and designs.[3] Views on the relevance of science and technology range from seeing it as a net positive contributor to societal development to being concerned about its potentially negative consequences.[4] Science and technology are connected, but society's role in their application is typically overlooked. Both fields are usually taken for granted as objective truth, rather than considering their political and social dimension and their consequent fallibility of that. Over the years, an entire philosophy of science and technology has developed to better understand the relationships between science, technology, and society. In parallel, new terms such as "technoscience," "science, technology, and society (STS)," and "science and technology studies" have emerged to denote this intricate relationship. These terms encompass a wide range of disciplines, and their collective use implies that science and technology are viewed as human activities and products conducted in a social environment, rather than merely simple applications of knowledge. This new discipline engages in philosophical debates on science, technology, and society, with some focusing on internal aspects such as language and structure, while others focusing on external aspects like history, economy, and politics.[5] Based on this, several scholars across various human eras examined the relationship between science, technology, and society. Among other major concerns, the objectivity and neutrality of these fields have achieved prominence in debates among academics.[6] Indeed, this topic is as relevant now as it was in previous centuries, despite the differences in technological and scientific advancement since then.[7] The STS field has gained importance in the last century, particularly since the 1960s and 1970s, a time characterized by escalating social unrest and activism tackling social issues, such as the environment and civil rights. Growing recognition of the need to address the societal impact of science and technology has led to increased attention on these fields. This attention has resulted in the creation of various committees and organizations, the adoption of new rules regulating the use of science and technology, and an increased academic focus on this issue.[8] Additionally, discussions concerning society's impact on science

3 Harvey Brooks, *The Relationship between Science and Technology*, 23 Research Policy 479–484 (1994).

4 Andrew Webster, Science, Technology and Society: New Directions (1st ed., Bloomsbury Publishing Plc 1992).

5 Wenceslao J. González, *The Philosophical Approach to Science, Technology and Society*, *in* Science, Technology and Society: A Philosophical Perspective (W. J. Gonzalez (ed.), Netbiblo 2005).

6 Kristin Shrader-Frechette, *Objectivity and Professional Duties Regarding Science and Technology*, *in* Science, Technology and Society: A Philosophical Perspective (W. J. Gonzalez (ed.), Netbiblo 2005).

7 Robert K. Merton, *Science, Technology and Society in Seventeenth Century England*, 4 Osiris 360 (1938).

8 See: Stephen H. Cutcliffe, *Science, Technology, and Society Studies as an Interdisciplinary Academic Field*, 11 Technology in Society 419 (1989); Klaus-Heinrich Standke & M

and technology continue to take place, bridging the past, the present, and the future.[9] Indeed, contemporary studies are exploring the intersections of science, technology, and society, including their regulation and the potential societal impacts of technological and scientific advancements.[10] The issues being examined include the relationship between science and technology in the context of blockchain technology,[11] social media, automated vehicles, food, energy security, sustainability, political security, and stability in regions such as the Middle East and Africa, among others.[12] In addition to the Global North, the Global South is also voicing its concerns about how to best regulate and determine the legal framework for producing and governing innovations in science and technology.[13] Generative artificial intelligence models, such as ChatGPT, represent one of the most recent testing grounds where tensions between law and technology emerge.[14] International organizations, such as

---

Anandakrishnan, Science, Technology and Society: Needs, Challenges and Limitations (Elsevier 2013).

9 Gert Verschraegen & others, Imagined Futures in Science, Technology and Society (Routledge 2017).

10 Todd L. Pittinsky (ed.), Science, Technology, and Society: New Perspectives and Directions (Cambridge University Press 2020).

11 Paolo Davide Farah & Marek Prityi, *Public Administration in the Age of Globalization and Emerging Technologies from Theories to Practice Symposium Issue: Blockchain Technology and the Law*, 88 UMKC Law Review 397 (2019); Poshan Yu, Ruixin Gong & Michael Sampat, *Blockchain Technology in China's Digital Economy: Balancing Regulation and Innovation*, *in* Regulatory Aspects of Artificial Intelligence on Blockchain (IGI Global 2022).

12 Heather Christina Lum, Critical Issues Impacting Science, Technology, Society (1st ed., IGI Global 2019); United Nations Commission on Science and Technology for Development, The Role of Science, Technology and Innovation in Ensuring Food Security by 2030: Report: 2017 (UN 2017); Clark Miller, Daniel Sarewitz & Andrew Light, *Science, Technology, and Sustainability: Building a Research Agenda*, 319 Science 424 (2008); Yannis Stivachtis, Science, Technology and Security in the Middle East (*E-International Relations*, 23 May 2019) <www.e-ir.info/2019/05/23/science-technology-and-security-in-the-middle-east/> accessed 18 September 2023; African Union Commission, Science, Technology and Innovation: Strategy for Africa 2024 (STISA 2024).

13 In the past two decades, China has been proactive in regulating new technologies and also in developing innovative approaches on the relations between state and society. See generally, Paolo Davide Farah, *Trade and Progress: The Case of China*, 30 Columbia Journal of Asian Law 51 (2016); Gregory Chin & Ramesh Thakur, *Will China Change the Rules of Global Order?* 33 The Washington Quarterly 119 (2010); on the relations between state and society, see: Paolo Davide Farah & Davide Giacomo Zoppolato, *Public Ownership and the WTO in a Post-Covid-19 Era: From Trade Disputes to a "Social" Function*, 125 West Virginia Law Review (2022); on Energy: Davide Giacomo Zoppolato & Shisong Jiang, *China-MENA Energy Cooperation under the Belt and Road Initiative: Megaprojects, Economic Planning, and a Pragmatic Approach to the "Green" Transition*, 16 The Journal of World Energy Law & Business 143 (2023); Jesse Rodenbiker, *Making Ecology Developmental: China's Environmental Sciences and Green Modernization in Global Context*, Annals of the American Association of Geographers 1 (2021).

14 For an overview of generative AI, see: Anis Koubaa & others, Exploring ChatGPT Capabilities and Limitations: A Critical Review of the NLP Game Changer <doi:10.20944/preprints202303.0438.v1>; on the issues of regulations, *see*: Philipp Hacker, Andreas Engel &

the United Nations, are also examining how society produces is affected, and changes science and technology.[15]

Science and technological fields are rapidly evolving[16] and interacting with the law and its regulations.[17] In this context, various communities have played a role in developing the intricate link, interplay, and "nexus" between science, technology, and law. Indeed, with every scientific and technological discovery, more rules have been developed to regulate these discovery and address any potential risks arising from their use.[18] More recently, science and technology have been used to further develop fields within international law, given the negative human-caused impact on the planet witnessed over the last few decades.[19] In fact, science and technology are seen as reasons for the increased fragmentation of global law along sectoral lines rather than territorial ones.[20] Transnational law transcends state boundaries and is increasingly formed within sectors such as the environmental or finance, rather than within the territory of the modern state. Simultaneously, the rapid scientific and technological developments in this field and others have affected the ability of lawyers and policymakers to keep pace with this progress.[21] This has already impacted, and is expected to continue impacting, the judicial-legal system both locally and globally.[22] Jurists and scientists have both assumed the responsibility of determining the domains of science and technology. Jurists are tasked with determining justice, rather than truth, through their decisions. While scientists, with their expertise in science and technology, might be perceived as aiming at the objective truth, in recent years, tension between justice and truth has become increasingly common and more intense, as has

---

Marco Mauer, Regulating ChatGPT and Other Large Generative AI Models, *Proceedings of the 2023 ACM Conference on Fairness, Accountability, and Transparency* (2023) <https://dl.acm.org/doi/pdf/10.1145/3593013.3594067>; Glorin Sebastian, *Do ChatGPT and Other AI Chatbots Pose a Cybersecurity Risk?: An Exploratory Study*, 15 International Journal of Security and Privacy in Pervasive Computing (IJSPPC) (2023) 1 <http://dx.doi.org/10.2139/ssrn.4363843>.

15 IAEA, ITU, UNESCO, UNOOSA, WIPO, Science, Technology and Innovation and Intellectual Property Rights: The Vision for Development (Thematic Think Piece May 2012).

16 Christopher Freeman and Luc Soete, *Developing Science, Technology and Innovation Indicators: What We Can Learn from the Past*, 38 Research Policy 583, 588 (2009).

17 Simon A. Cole and Alyse Bertenthal, *Science, Technology, Society, and Law*, 13 Annual Review of Law and Social Science 351, 351 (2017).

18 Manfred Lachs, *Thoughts on Science, Technology and World Law*, 86 American Journal of International Law 673, 677 (1992).

19 Lachs, *supra* note 18, at 692.

20 Andreas Fischer-Lescano and Gunther Teubner, *Regime-Collisions: The Vain Search for Legal Unity in the Fragmentation of Global Law*, 25 Michigan Journal of International Law 999, 1000 (2003).

21 Sheila Jasanoff (ed.), Science at the Bar: Law, Science, and Technology in America, vol. 9, IX (Harvard University Press 1997).

22 Phil McNally & Sohail Inayatullah, *The Rights of Robots: Technology, Culture and Law in the 21st Century*, 20 Futures 119, 119 (1988).

occurred in many different periods of history. Both jurists and scientists are criticized for being merely representatives of the elite, known as "experts." Hence, another dilemma arises, with experts and specialists on one hand and an increasingly skeptical general populace on the other, regarding the role of science and technology, as well as truth and justice in contemporary society. Furthermore, law plays a regulatory role in overseeing the use of science and technology. Scientific and technological developments often outpace the law, leaving regulations unable to keep pace with the rapid changes in science and technology. As such, this interaction is quite complex.[23] This phenomenon is well documented in the literature, as it is often extremely difficult to adapt legal frameworks to changing circumstances.[24] The push for legal precision and comprehensiveness easily results in a practical disconnect with these fields.[25] This raises moral and philosophical questions about the role of laws within these fields and whether they can truly promote better transparency and accountability in this context.[26] Due to this, the last few decades have witnessed an increase in scholarly articles addressing the interplay between science, law, and technology on topics such as international economic law, the oceans, national security, anthropology, ethics, and capitalism.[27] Yet, there remains a growing need for research on law, science, and technology from a broader perspective,[28] given the necessity of bridging the existing gap between the law as written and the current state of technology.[29] This is despite the fact that such an inquiry was initiated years ago, when various studies attempted to understand who the actual decision-maker is when science and technology

23 Shirley Johnson, *Science and Technology v. Law, or a Plague on Both Your Houses: Comment*, 47 Denver Law Review 565, 566 (1970).

24 Lyria Bennett Moses, *Agents of Change: How the Law 'Copes' with Technological Change*, 20 Griffith Law Review 763, 763 (2011).

25 Roger Brownsword & Han Somsen, *Law, Innovation and Technology: Before We Fast Forward – A Forum for Debate*, 1 Law, Innovation and Technology 1, 3 (2009).

26 Sheila Jasanoff, *Serviceable Truths: Science for Action in Law and Policy*, 93 Texas Law Review 1723, 1723–1749 (2014).

27 For some seminal books, see: Marie-Claire Foblets & others, The Oxford Handbook of Law and Anthropology (Oxford University Press 2022); Bryan Mercurio & Kuei-Jung Ni, Science and Technology in International Economic Law: Balancing Competing Interests (Routledge 2013); Davor Vidas, Law, Technology and Science for Oceans in Globalisation: IUU Fishing, Oil Pollution, Bioprospecting, Outer Continental Shelf (Brill 2010); Thomas A. Johnson, National Security Issues in Science, Law, and Technology (CRC Press 2007); Christian Lenk & Nils Hoppe, Ethics and Law of Intellectual Property: Current Problems in Politics, Science and Technology (Routledge 2016); David F. Noble, America by Design: Science, Technology, and the Rise of Corporate Capitalism (Oxford University Press 1979).

28 Arthur J. Cockfield, *Towards a Law and Technology Theory*, 30 Manitoba Law Journal 383, 383–416 (2004).

29 Paul Hunton, *The Stages of Cybercrime Investigations: Bridging the Gap between Technology Examination and Law Enforcement Investigation*, 27 Computer Law & Security Review 61, 51 (2011).

are used for decision-making purposes,[30] whether it be scientists, regulators, or the public.[31]

In terms of the interplay between science and law, its study is not a recent phenomenon; in the past, this topic had gained prominence in literature, where authors examined, for instance, the science of law,[32] whether the law is actually a science in itself,[33] how the law behaves towards science,[34] and the impact of science on legal objectivity.[35] In this context, new terms emerged, such as "legal science"[36] and "scientific law,"[37] which have been examined by various scholars,[38] including Kelsen.[39] Both fields are characterized by formal rationality, and they each have their limitations. Decisions made by jurists or scientists are typically the result of careful deliberation and/or consensus among a specific epistemic community, where factors such as culture, history, and institutions influence their development. While science and law are separate fields, they often deal with similar issues, even though one seeks truth while the other seeks justice. In an ideal world, one would expect both fields to coexist in harmony – a world where science is used for drafting sound legislation and for addressing court cases and legal procedures. Justice and truth would proceed hand in hand, mutually supporting each other while working for the greater benefit of humankind. However, the political dimension involved within the two domains shapes both law and science. Thus, tension and conflict arise due to diverging epistemological assumptions and priorities. For example, lawyers and judges make determinations and judgements, even when uncertainty exists, whereas, from a scientific point of view, "fact" has a much higher standard of admissibility in a legal context. New discoveries or scientific facts, even if recognized as truth by the scientific community, are often excluded from legal proceedings due to either a lack of knowledge on the part of legal experts or the simple incompatibility of the new scientific truth with the principles of

30 T. A. Cowan, *Decision Theory in Law, Science, and Technology*, 140 Science (New York, NY) 1065, 1065–1075 (1963).

31 Mads Borup & others, *The Sociology of Expectations in Science and Technology*, 18 Technology Analysis & Strategic Management 285, 287 (2006).

32 Robert D. Taylor, *Ancient Tradition – The Relationship of Science and Law*, *in* Forensic Science and Law (CRC Press 2005).

33 M. C. Roos, *Is Law Science?* 17 Potchefstroom Electronic Law Journal/Potchefstroomse Elektroniese Regsblad 1391 (2014).

34 Kirk W. Junker, *Comparing Law as Science with Science in the Law: Preliminary Thoughts*, 14 Law Forensic Science 82, 83 (2017).

35 Alain Pottage & Martha Mundy, Law, Anthropology, and the Constitution of the Social: Making Persons and Things (Cambridge University Press 2004) 73–114.

36 Junker, *supra* note 34, at 91.

37 Igor Hanzel, The Concept of Scientific Law in the Philosophy of Science and Epistemology: A Study of Theoretical Reason (Springer Science & Business Media 1999).

38 K. N. Llewellyn, *The Theory of Legal Science*, 20 North Carolina Law Review 1 (1941).

39 Peter Langford, Ian Bryan & John McGarry (eds.), Kelsenian Legal Science and the Nature of Law 1–10, vol. 118 (Springer International Publishing 2017) <http://link.springer.com/10.1007/978-3-319-51817-6> accessed 18 September 2023.

justice. While uncertainty and complexity are inherent in the scientific domain, they are typically excluded from the legal system, which prioritizes certainty. In its pursuit of certainty, the legal system establishes rules and issues court ruling based on justice as determined in specific and contingent cases, sometimes relying on standards of proof that loosely mirror those used in science[40] and align with its understanding of "truth."[41] This is further exacerbated by the historical contestation of what constitutes science, particularly by various actors such as religious authorities, which has influenced the adoption of laws. The resulting confusion regarding the nature of science persists to the present day.[42] This situation has prompted calls for bridging the gap between scientists and lawyers, especially since each community tends to prioritize its own goals without adequately considering the impact of their work on the other field.[43] Understanding the position of science within law, and vice versa, requires careful consideration in light of the different epistemological premises of the two domains[44] – law delivering justice while science seeks truth. In fact, bridging this gap is especially difficult given the existing differences between legal reasoning and scientific reasoning. For instance, scientists have access to extensive empirical data, whereas lawyers must present their case to a judge immediately, relying only on the existing evidence.[45] This interplay between law and science is even more complicated now, given that it is occurring in a blockchain and knowledge-based society, where legal regulation and scientific advice should be viewed as complementary to each other.[46]

In terms of the interplay between technology and law, each field often interacts with the other. In fact, this increasing interconnection has resulted in the emergence of new terms, such as "techno-regulation" and "normative technology,"[47] given the need to regulate the use of technology in society and consider various non-technical factors.[48] Technology can support the rule of law by enhancing the ability to reach legal objectives, facilitating access to

40 Lee Loevinger, *Standards of Proof in Science and Law*, Jurimetrics 323, 323–325 (1992).

41 Margaret A. Berger & Lawrence M. Solan, *The Uneasy Relationship Between Science and the Law: An Essay and Introduction*, 73 Brooklyn Law Review 3, 847–856 (2008); Jasanoff, *supra* note 26, at 1724–1730.

42 Robin Feldman, *Historic Perspectives on Law & Science*, Stanford Technology Law Review 1, 1–4 (2009).

43 Micah L. Berman & Annice E. Kim, *Bridging the Gap between Science and Law: The Example of Tobacco Regulatory Science*, 43 Journal of Law, Medicine & Ethics 95, 95–98 (2015).

44 Robin Feldman, The Role of Science in Law (Oxford University Press 2009).

45 Phoebe C. Ellsworth, *Legal Reasoning and Scientific Reasoning*, 63 Alabama Law Review 895, 907–915 (2011).

46 Nico Stehr & Bernd Weiler (eds.), Who Owns Knowledge?: Knowledge and the Law 67–87 (Transaction Publishers 2011).

47 Erica Palmerini & Elettra Stradella, Law and Technology: The Challenge of Regulating Technological Development 14 (Pisa University Press 2013).

48 Mario Biagioli & Marius Buning, *Technologies of the Law/Law as a Technology*, 57 *History of Science* 3, 544–550 (2019).

justice, increasing transparency, and eliminating discrimination. It may also act as a means of enforcing compliance by preventing breaches of the law, such as in the case of minors seeking to access certain websites.[49] Simultaneously, technology has the capacity to negatively affect legal interests and values protected by regulation.[50] Therefore, a legal assessment of technology is essential,[51] particularly its impact on individuals,[52] necessitating the use of legal ethics in its regulation.[53] Moreover, it is becoming increasingly difficult for the law to keep pace with all the technological developments taking place, which could, in turn, exacerbate technology's impact on society and the economy as well as its potential to change the relationship between citizens and the government.[54] Given this dilemma, there is a growing need for research on law and technology, providing a critical evaluation of this interplay in a broader sense,[55] especially considering the interdisciplinary nature of technological developments.[56] Issues to be examined include the historical interplay of law and technology, the role of culture, and the role of international law, among many other things.[57] Indeed, lawyers and scholars have already started examining the legal consequences of new technologies, resulting in new specialties and expertise, as well as new scholarly journals addressing the interplay between law and technology.[58] Because of this, the term "*law and technology*" has been used extensively in the literature to describe this interdependency as both simple and complex, calling for improvements and addressing existing challenges.[59] Suggestions have been made to use a general theory of laws

49 Palmerini & Stradella, *supra* note 47, at 14; James E. Cabral & others, *Using Technology to Enhance Access to Justice*, 26 Harvard Journal of Law & Technology 241 (2012).

50 Cockfield, *supra* note 28, at 384–388.

51 Philip L. Bereano, *Saving Us From Ourselves: The Interaction of Law and Science-Technology: Comment*, 47 Denver Law Review 671, 677 (2021).

52 Nicola Lucchi, The Impact of Science and Technology on the Rights of the Individual, vol. 26 (Springer International Publishing 2016) <http://link.springer.com/10.1007/978-3-319-30439-7> accessed 18 September 2023.

53 Richard Zorza, *Re-Conceptualizing the Relationship between Legal Ethics and Technological Innovation in Legal Practice: From Threat to Opportunity*, 67 Fordham Law Review 2659 (1998).

54 Noel Cox, *The Relationship Between Law, Government, Business and Technology*, 8 Duquesne Business Law Journal 31, 31 (2006).

55 Cockfield, *supra* note 28, at 384–388.

56 Giorgia Guerra, *An Interdisciplinary Approach for Comparative Lawyers: Insights from the Fast-Moving Field of Law and Technology*, 19 German Law Journal 579, 579–580 (2018).

57 Kieran Tranter, *The Laws of Technology and the Technology of Law*, 20 Griffith Law Review 753, 753–760 (2011); Joseph W. Dellapenna, *Law in a Shrinking World: The Interaction of Science and Technology with International Law*, 88 Kentucky Law Journal 809, 809 (1999).

58 Lyria Bennett Moses, *How to Think about Law, Regulation and Technology: Problems with 'Technology'as a Regulatory Target*, 5 Law, Innovation and Technology 1, 1–7 (2013).

59 Daniel J. Gifford, *Law and Technology: Interactions and Relationships*, 8 Minnesota Journal of Law, Science & Technology 571, 571–587 (2007).

in the regulation of technologies to adapt the law to constant technological developments.[60]

The book *Science, Technology, Policy and International Law* presents innovative insights into the role of science in the decision-making process. In times when scientific knowledge and expertise, in general, are constantly in question, it is necessary to reassess the relationship between science and transnational regulations. COVID-19, and the initial slow and contradictory responses to it highlights how policy-making, even when scientific data are presented, tends to underestimate health risks and is built on uncertainty.[61] Mediation among different interests is a key part of decision-making, but when data or science is not used in order to reach equilibrium, negative outcomes can arise. By relying on anti-science rhetoric and cultural absolutism, populist movements sprouted in Europe and across the globe in the last decade. This backlash is not only directed at the political establishment or elite but also at actors shaping and producing scientific knowledge.[62] This loss of confidence and trust in politicians and the scientific community is a clear reflection of the establishment's inability to deal with societal, civic, and sustainability crises in a timely manner.[63] A globalization too focused on economic growth, at the expense of non-trade concerns,[64] has played a role in strengthening the foundation and radicalism of populist political spaces. Economic inequalities, as well as cultural factors, affect the relationship of trust between rulers and the citizenry in almost every aspect of policy-making.[65] At the national and local levels,

60 Gregory N. Mandel, *History Lessons for a General Theory of Law and Technology*, 8 Minnesota Journal of Law, Science & Technology 551, 551–570 (2007).

61 For an overview of initial reactions on the pandemic and the role of uncertainty, see Christopher M. Weible & others, *COVID-19 and the Policy Sciences: Initial Reactions and Perspectives*, 53 Policy Sciences 225 (2020); Paola Rebughini, *A Sociology of Anxiety: Western Modern Legacy and the Covid-19 Outbreak*, 36 International Sociology 554 (2021). On the relations between science and media, see: The Lancet Infectious Diseases, *The COVID-19 Infodemic*, 20 The Lancet. Infectious Diseases 875 (2020); Amy Koerber, *Is It Fake News or Is It Open Science? Science Communication in the COVID-19 Pandemic*, 35 Journal of Business and Technical Communication 22 (2021); Salman Bin Naeem & Rubina Bhatti, *The Covid-19 "Infodemic": A New Front for Information Professionals*, 37 Health Information & Libraries Journal 233 (2020).

62 Niels G. Mede & Mike S. Schäfer, *Science-Related Populism: Conceptualizing Populist Demands toward Science*, 29 Public Understanding of Science 473 (2020).

63 Margaret Stout & Jeannine M. Love, A Radically Democratic Response to Global Governance: Dystopian Utopias (Routledge, Taylor & Francis Group 2016).

64 Countries that strengthen the provision of socioeconomics and cultural rights and promoted the protection of non-trade concerns at a national level witnessed lower level of grassroots populism. For an overview of the progress of China, see: Paolo Davide Farah, *Trade and Progress: The Case of China*, 30 Columbia Journal of Asian Law 51 (2016); Paolo Davide Farah & Elena Cima (eds.), China's Influence on Non-Trade Concerns in International Economic Law (Routledge 2016).

65 Dani Rodrik, *Populism and the Economics of Globalization*, Journal of International Business Policy 1 (2018); Abdul Noury & Gerard Roland, *Identity Politics and Populism in Europe*, 23 Annual Review of Political Science 421 (2020).

science-based decision-making is in crisis; at the international level, and especially in multilateral institutions, it is still the preferred tool for designing effective policies. International experts communicate via a general and mutually agreed-upon language to build effective transnational regulation. However, the lack of accountability and transparency in the work of experts is damaging the further development of science-based decision-making. A more transparent regulatory framework regarding the role of experts could revive the importance of science in designing effective and socially responsive international policies and regulations.[66] This edited collection offers insights on how to best integrate knowledge and science in policy-making and reviews other current attempts at the transnational and international levels. By building on a functionalist and comparatist approach to international law, this book clarifies the role of science in the current transnational governance framework. The case studies span different disciplines and regimes, ranging from emerging environmental protection technologies to statistics. This book is complemented by a new, solid theoretical framework that seeks to reassess the relationship between law and science.

Kirk W. Junker in "Facts Are the Moveable Furniture of the Legal Mind, Not Stones of Science,"[67] breaks down the differences between truth and opinion, the first built upon the burden of proof and the second on the burden of persuasion. We are moving towards an era in which the personal beliefs of both individuals and institutions are considered superior to facts. Beliefs thus gain the same importance as established knowledge, allowing individuals to freely determine their truth based on persuasion. Not limited to this post-truth era, science has been in crisis since the Industrial Revolution with the advent of globalized capitalism.[68] What is different now is that humans increasingly act against rationality and follow fake news and misinformation. As a result, rationality is not the default pattern of behaviour, and many individuals form biased opinions based not on facts but on emotions and intuitions. Kirk W. Junker sheds light on how the very basic notion of fact transitioned from law to the natural sciences. This transition has played a role in positioning the scientific paradigm as the preferred lens through which to understand reality. The production of

66 Alessandra Arcuri & Florin Coman-Kund, Technocracy and the Law: Accountability, Governance and Expertise (Routledge 2021).

67 Kirk W. Junker, *Facts Are the Moveable Furniture of the Legal Mind, Not Stones of Science*, *in* Science, Technology, Policy and International Law (Justo Corti Varela & Paolo Davide Farah (eds.), Routledge 2024).

68 Jean-Francois Lyotard, The Postmodern Condition: A Report on Knowledge 39 (Manchester University Press 1984) 'The "crisis" of scientific knowledge, signs of which have been accumulating since the end of the nineteenth century, is not born of a chance proliferation of sciences, itself an effect of progress in technology and the expansion of capitalism. It represents, rather, an internal erosion of the legitimacy principle of knowledge. There is erosion at work inside the speculative game, and by loosening the weave of the encyclopedic net in which each science was to find its place, it eventually sets them free.'

scientific knowledge is built on replicability and the certainty that a specific phenomenon will occur if the same conditions are met. On the contrary, replicability, as well as being a predefined and immovable approach, is antithetical to law. In fact, law requires finding solutions to different or similar problems based on social and cultural contexts and allows a margin of flexibility in the interpretation of social reality that is excluded from science. A law too tied to the scientific understanding of fact is, in the post-truth era, unable to respond to global challenges. Kirk W. Junker examines the so-called "iGeneration's" role in shaping reality, as well as the role of technology in forming knowledge and challenging the roles of science and law. The author also highlights the relationship between humans and reality and how it is grounded in irrationality. He explains the features of this "irrationality 2.0": the arrogant intentional pursuit of power, the citizen who unintentionally contributes to the proliferation of untruths, and the citizen who has been conditioned to think that truth is not an important category of human thought. How should we counterbalance irrationality? For Kirk W. Junker, the solution lies in using law as a tool to mitigate the features of irrationality, and he finds the courtroom to be a locus where rationality is used to construct social facts. Under this equation, the law should act as the basis of the judgement, while science could help ground the judgement in rationality.

Departing from the same idea of the previous chapter – that is, the evolution from a rationality-based truth to a narrative model of truth (Junker's distinction between truth and opinion) – in "The Interlinkages Science-Technology-Law: Information and Communication Society, Knowledge-Based Economy, and the Rule of Law,"[69] Giovanni Bombelli and Paolo Davide Farah construct a model to understand the complex relationship between science, technology, society, and law. As the first relation under analysis, the authors connect the issue of the democratic deficit with the technology-society nexus. The democratic deficit is a consequence of the lack of adaptability of Western democracy to complex (information) societies. In this context, technology expands the amount of available information and facilitates its accessibility. Yet it decreases the reliability and accuracy of information, giving rise to tensions that challenge the role of information in advancing societal knowledge. By breaking the link between information and knowledge, technology also shifts societies towards technocracy. In this sense, legitimacy in democracy is no longer defined by truth but by the ability of politicians to produce large amounts of information and engage with different sectors of society.

As a second set of relations, the authors assess technology and law. Law is increasingly being reduced to a normative technique, driven by its lateness and

69 Giovanni Bombelli & Paolo Davide Farah, *The Interlinkages Science-Technology-Law: Information and Communication Society, Knowledge-Based Economy and the Rule of Law*, *in* Science, Technology, Policy and International Law (Justo Corti Varela & Paolo Davide Farah (eds.), Routledge 2024).

incompleteness in adapting to and anticipating technological changes. Thus, for the authors, we are witnessing a transition from hard law to soft law, from norms to rules, and from government to governance. At the same time, technology aims to be recognized as a legal framework based on the new "net/web" relationship, applied to new spaces (cyberspace), and based on accountability instead of sovereignty. This new legal structure would operate in the "net" society (interactive, dematerialized, and based on database memory), where cognitive acquisition (hypertextualization of knowledge, cyberculture) simplifies political deliberation to expressions of subjectivism and emotive decisions based on casual and contingent information. As a result, in highly technologized and mass societies, there is a dislocation between information and knowledge, which can no longer be easily identified. Technological and scientific developments are currently affecting legal systems at the national and international levels, and legislators are facing great challenges when it comes to regulating them.

In "Using Flexibility Mechanisms for Addressing Technological and Scientific Developments: Examples from Selected Global Regulatory Frameworks,"[70] Imad Antoine Ibrahim shows that this is mostly due to existing uncertainties, lack of knowledge, and the rapid progress occurring in these fields. The situation is further complicated, as these developments affect all aspects of human society, including the law (and vice versa),[71] and are developed in the global arena, where international law is needed to govern the use of technologies and sciences. It is precisely on the details regarding international law, given the critical role that it is expected to play, that this chapter is focused on. Scholars in recent years have been attempting to provide suggestions and solutions concerning the way emerging technologies and sciences can be regulated. In this context, Ibrahim examines the inability of current law to keep up with technological and scientific development and other issues that arise when trying to regulate them, for example, the fact that new technologies often do not fit in the general framework of existing rules and legal categories. To help solve these problems, the author argues for the use of existing flexibility mechanisms from different global regulatory frameworks when adopting new agreements and instruments addressing technologies and sciences in the international sphere. Ibrahim provides examples of these mechanisms as developed within international financial law. He uses several examples to demonstrate his point. For instance, he analyzes the concept of a sandbox, which allows testing in a safe environment under the supervision of the proper authorities.

70 Imad Antoine Ibrahim, *Using Flexibility Mechanisms for Addressing Technological and Scientific Developments: Examples from Selected Global Regulatory Frameworks, in* Science, Technology, Policy and International Law (Justo Corti Varela & Paolo Davide Farah (eds.), Routledge 2024).

71 Diganth Raj Sehgal, Relationship Between Law, Science, and Technology in Modern Society (*Pleaders*, 3 March 2021) <https://blog.ipleaders.in/relationship-law-science-technology-modern-society/>.

Another example is the use of Article XX of GATT in international trade law, which allows the restriction or control of technological developments in justified cases. In the case of international climate change law, Ibrahim describes how the success of the Paris Agreement was also due to its mechanism to ease implementation and compliance via non-binding commitments.[72] Similarly, in international water law, flexibility mechanisms exist in the context of amendment and review procedures or for joint management institutions.[73]

Alessandra Donati, in "The Precautionary Principle Under EU Law: A 'Post-Modern' Principle in a 'Post-Truth' Era,"[74] shifts the focus to how law is being formed in the post-truth era. Donati seeks to explain the precautionary principle from a philosophical standpoint. The author frames this principle as an example of a post-modern legal framework. Alessandra Donati begins with an assessment of the core characteristics of modern law (systematic, general, universal, and stable) and post-modern law (disorder, complexity, indeterminacy, and relativism). This change could also be seen in the increasing decline of multilateralism as the expression of modern law. Both efficiency and fragmentation, instead of coherence and consistency, are, for the author, a radical change in perspective in post-modern law. Consensus decision-making is not able to keep up with the fast-paced changes of post-truth reality; therefore, other deliberation methods are preferred. This could also be seen in the lack of precision, clarity, and the vagueness of post-modern law, as in the case of the precautionary principle or the predominance of non-binding, often empty, contents of political principles. Based on the author's reconstruction, these political principles continue to guide the decision-making process. Political dimensions have always played a role in shaping and producing science and technology, not just in the post-truth era. Alessandra Donati highlights how the precautionary principle links different regimes and disciplines and, most importantly, broadens the focus of law by including social and ethical considerations resulting from dialogue and exchanges.

After reviewing the precautionary principle from a theoretical perspective, Justo Corti Varela, in "The Precautionary Principle and the Burden of Proof in International Risk Regulation Trials,"[75] analyzes how the principle is interpreted and applied by international courts. More specifically, Justo Corti investigates how a "modern" legal institute – i.e. the burden of proof – is affected by post-modern law. By designing a socially responsive burden of proof,

72 United Nations, Paris Agreement (2015), Art. 15(1).

73 Heather Cooley & Peter H. Gleick, *Climate-Proofing Transboundary Water Agreements*, 56 Hydrological Sciences Journal 711 (2011).

74 Alessandra Donati, *The Precautionary Principle Under EU Law: A "Post-Modern" Principle in a "Post-Truth" Era, in* Science, Technology, Policy and International Law (Justo Corti Varela & Paolo Davide Farah (eds.), Routledge 2024).

75 Justo Corti Varela, *The Precautionary Principle and the Burden of Proof in International Risk Regulation Trials, in* Science, Technology, Policy and International Law (Justo Corti Varela & Paolo Davide Farah (eds.), Routledge 2024).

international courts help clarify the relationship between these apparently contradictory realms. Despite not yet being recognized as a customary principle of international law,[76] the use of the precautionary principle in international law is possible in cases of scientific uncertainty.[77] Corti studies it as a decision-making tool for procedural decisions in judicial trials, such as the burden or assessment of proof.[78] The adjudicatory application of the precautionary principle could contradict the classical *actori incumbit probatio*. To resolve this contradiction, the following solutions have been explored within international case law, where the lack of explicit wording in the procedural rules permits international courts to modulate the precautionary principle according to the circumstances: a call for collaboration in the production of evidence, a shift in the burden of proof, or a reduction of the standard of proof. All three of these solutions have been analyzed in both interim orders and substantive proceedings occurring before international courts. Corti concludes in his study that the acceptance of the precautionary principle does not yet extend beyond administrative risk management.

Sound science-based decision-making should also integrate ethics in order to be effective. Moral dilemmas can arise, especially in fields related to

76 Discussion has been particularly intense in WTO case law, where, due to the lack of official recognition in its treaties, it would be applicable only when it can be demonstrated that the precautionary principle was a general principle of customary international law, something that "appears less than clear." See Appellate Body Report, European Communities – Measures Concerning Meat and Meat Products (Hormones) WT/DS26/AB/R; WT/DS48/AB/R (16 January 1998) hereafter AB EC-Hormones, paras. 123 and 124; and, Panel report EC-Biotech Products, paras. 7.73 and 7.89. Beyond the WTO, only an award of the Permanent Court of Arbitration has recognized it clearly, in the Iron Rhine Railway case (Reports of International Arbitral Awards, vol. XXVII, pp. 35–125, para. 59). In EU law, it has been recognized as "EU" general principle (see case C-180/96, ECLI:EU:C:1998:192, para. 99–101; and case C-157/96, ECLI:EU:C:1998:191 para. 62–64). International literature agrees that it is an "emerging" principle: David Freestone, *Caution or Precaution:"A Rose By Any Other Name . . ."*? 10 Yearbook of International Environmental Law 25 (1999); or that, at least, it starts to be an international custom: Philippe Sands & Jacqueline Peel, Principles of International Environmental Law (Cambridge University Press 2012). This idea of a principle in progress has been incorporated in the Seabed Dispute Chamber of ITLOS (see Advisory Opinion of 1 February 2011, para. 135).

77 Elizabeth Fisher, Risk Regulation and Administrative Constitutionalism (Bloomsbury Publishing 2007).

78 Caroline E. Foster, Science and the Precautionary Principle in International Courts and Tribunals: Expert Evidence, Burden of Proof and Finality, vol. 79 (Cambridge University Press 2011). For the distinction between "administrative" and "adjudicative" burdens of proof in the application of the precautionary principle, see Panel Report Japan – Measures Affecting Agricultural Products, WT/DS76/R, (27 October 1998) hereafter PR Japan – Agricultural Products, para. 8.13 and Panel Report Japan – Measures Affecting the Importation of Apples, WT/DS245/R (15 July 2003), para. 8.41. For other "archetypical versions" of the precautionary principle ("uncertainty does not justify inaction," "uncertainty justifies action," and "shifting the burden of proof"), see Lavanya Rajamani & Jacqueline Peel, The Oxford Handbook of International Environmental Law (Oxford University Press 2021) ch 18.

individual rights, such as health, reproduction and sexuality. To what extent should the law intervene in this context? Antonio Quirós Fons, in "The Precautionary Principle and the Burden of Proof in International Risk Regulation Trials,"[79] investigates ethical concerns and the role of law. Antonio Quirós Fons reviews how conscientious objection paved the way for a discussion in the international community about how far positive laws could regulate human behaviour. After reviewing how the conscientious objection was included under Article 18 of the International Covenant on Civil and Political Rights (ICCPR), Antonio Quirós Fons analyzes the institutionalization process of this right. The inclusion of this right based on religious grounds, at an international court (European Court of Human Rights, or ECHR), and then at a constitutional level, emphasizes the importance of adapting to changing circumstances. Conscientious objection shares commonalities with reproductive services in the sense that both are characterized by a strong ethical dimension. The decision to perform or not to perform an abortion procedure, along with other hotly debated issues in health care, such as euthanasia, is often left to the physicians. While opting out for physicians should be allowed in principle, procedures should be greatly improved and rationalized. Opt-outs should not hinder, slow down, or affect patients' decisions. To achieve this, the author suggests that the refusal process should be streamlined, and suitable replacements must be readily and easily available for patients. For Antonio Quirós Fons, an ecological approach could strengthen individual rights and, in the same time, promote biodiversity.

Gemma Hobcraft, in "Assessing the Soundness of Science to Determine Reactive and Proactive Regulatory Change: Human Fertilisation and Embryology Authority, Mitochondrial Donation, Treatment Add-Ons, and Future Challenges for Regulation,"[80] expands the analysis of the relationship between science and law by specifically addressing assisted reproduction. Innovations in the reproductive field are not easily received by international and national legislation. Along with difficulties in regulating these aspects from a legal standpoint, cultural and ethical considerations lead the debate. International documents are scarce, fragmented, and politically motivated.[81] National laws and regulation, therefore, fill this gap. Gemma Hobcraft investigates the example of the United Kingdom and how the main regulator in charge of this task – the Human Fertilisation and Embryology Authority (HFEA) – is backed

79 Antonio Quirós Fons, *The Precautionary Principle and the Burden of Proof in International Risk Regulation Trials*, *in* Science, Technology, Policy and International Law (Justo Corti Varela & Paolo Davide Farah (eds.), Routledge 2024).

80 Gemma Hobcraft, *Assessing the Soundness of Science to Determine Reactive and Proactive Regulatory Change. Human Fertilisation and Embryology Authority, Mitochondrial Donation, Treatment Add-ons and Future Challenges for Regulation*, *in* Science, Technology, Policy and International Law (Justo Corti Varela & Paolo Davide Farah (eds.), Routledge 2024).

81 Guido Pennings, *International Evolution of Legislation and Guidelines in Medically Assisted Reproduction*, 18 Reproductive BioMedicine Online S15 (2009).

by scientific data to craft its regulations. Specific sub-committees, such as the Scientific and Clinical Advances Advisory Committee (SCAA), have been established to keep up with advancements, not only in science but also in ethics. Science-based policymaking is even more relevant in contexts such as add-ons, where the shift from research to treatment took some time. In the final section of the chapter, Gemma Hobcraft critically assesses potential challenges related to human fertilization and embryology, such as privacy, genetic testing, and treatment for non-UK nationals. The diverging approach taken by the HFEA (proactive in the case of add-ons and reactive in the case of mitochondrial donation) highlights the difficulties faced by an independent agency in integrating science within a regulatory framework. Gemma Hobcraft suggests that regulations should be both proactive and reactive to accommodate further scientific research while simultaneously integrating ethical considerations. Her chapter also highlights how science is assessed not only by experts but also by governments in formulating policy.

This collection then transitions from science to the impact of emerging technologies on decision-making. Mihail Stojanoski and Lilla Vukovich, in "Use of Smartphone Applications in the Democratic Decision-Making Process,"[82] analyze how technology is poised to change consumers' behaviour. E-voting not only impacts consumers' behaviour but also influences the deliberation process. Smartphones are essential and convenient daily tools for most of the population. Not only could they influence voting, but they are also already influencing how citizens receive political information. While e-voting has been on the agenda of the European Union since 2004, little progress has been made in this regard. The post-COVID-19 pandemic and its experience could speed up the adoption of e-voting at a larger scale, to reduce the spread of viruses. Mihail Stojanoski and Lilla Vukovich analyze several examples, both in the United States (West Virginia) and Europe (Estonia and Switzerland), where e-voting has been experimented with. Recent advances in technology, such as distributed ledger technology and biometrics, have made these examples possible. These issues continue to arise, ranging from privacy concerns via cyber-attacks to the involvement of third parties in the national voting process. Mihail Stojanoski and Lilla Vukovich highlight the downsides and benefits of e-voting.

The relation between science and law is clarified from a more practical perspective by Ciarán Burke and Alexandra Molitorisová in "Procedural versus Substantive Approaches to Scientific Evidence in the Opinions of Advocates-General."[83] More specifically, the authors analyze how evidence

82 Mihail Stojanoski & Lilla Vukovich, *Use of Smartphone Applications in the Democratic Decision-Making Process, in* Science, Technology, Policy and International Law (Justo Corti Varela & Paolo Davide Farah (eds.), Routledge 2024).

83 Ciarán Burke & Alexandra Molitorisová, *Procedural versus Substantive Approaches to Scientific Evidence in the Opinions of Advocates-General, in* Science, Technology, Policy and International Law (Justo Corti Varela & Paolo Davide Farah (eds.), Routledge 2024).

is used and evaluated in the European Court of Justice (ECJ). Evidence is the point of contact and, often, conflict between law and other disciplines.[84] Ciarán Burke and Alexandra Molitorisová critically investigate this relation by building on the division between questions of fact and questions of law and how, in certain areas such as the proportionality analysis in the ECJ, the two apparently separated worlds blend together. The assistance of the Advocates General (AGs) regarding evidence is essential for the proper functioning of the Court. AGs are called upon when novel questions of law or cutting-edge scientific evidence are involved. Ciarán Burke and Alexandra Molitorisová propose an analytical framework based on core and shared characteristics of AGs' opinions in light of EU law. So far, AGs have been principally involved in providing impact assessments of EU measures to the ECJ by using mostly statistics and econometrics. By offering an interpretation of notions or statutory terms, AGs help clarify and determine the factual circumstances of a case. Ciarán Burke and Alexandra Molitorisová also emphasize that AGs assist adjudicators in assigning weight and significance to specific evidence. Due to the growing complexities and technicalities in law, and considering the diminishing clear division between questions of law and questions of fact, the involvement of AGs' is urgently needed to aid the ECJ.

Climate change is a global phenomenon. Therefore, Paolo Davide Farah and Alessio Lo Giudice, introduce the concepts of climate justice and globalization in their chapter titled "Climate Justice in the Anthropocene and Its Relationship with Science and Technology: The Importance of an Ethics of Responsibility," within the context of law, science, and technology.[85] The authors argue that globalization provides the necessary hermeneutical horizon for developing an analysis of the potential political, social, and economic transformations caused by climate change. They demonstrate how the relationship between the concept of the Anthropocene[86] – with climate change as its most apparent effect – and the call for justice allows for the inclusion of political considerations, such as the impacts of climate change, within the

84 William Twining, *Evidence and Legal Theory*, 47 The Modern Law Review 261, 264 (1984): "If one looks at law as a discipline in these terms, it is hardly surprising that its relationship both with other disciplines and with the world of affairs is perennially problematic. . . . The primary task of the jurist is to study the assumptions underlying the discipline of law: many of those assumptions lie at key points of contact between the world of learning and the worlds of practical affairs. . . . Understanding law is dependent on understanding much else besides."

85 Paolo Davide Farah & Alessio Lo Giudice, *Climate Justice in the Anthropocene and Its Relationship with Science and Technology the Importance of an Ethics of Responsibility*, *in* Science, Technology, Policy and International Law (Justo Corti Varela & Paolo Davide Farah (eds.), Routledge 2024).

86 Paul J. Crutzen & Eugene F. Stoermer, *The "Anthropocene" (2000)*, Paul J. Crutzen and the Anthropocene: A New Epoch in Earth's History 19 (2021); Paul J. Crutzen, 'Geology of Mankind' [2016] Paul J. Crutzen: A pioneer on atmospheric chemistry and climate change in the Anthropocene 211; Anu Valtonen, Outi Rantala & Paolo Davide Farah (eds.), Ethics and Politics of Space for the Anthropocene (Edward Elgar Publishing 2020).

legal system. This particular political interpretation aligns with the advocacy for climate justice, which is understood in the broadest sense as a conceptual strategy rooted in social movements, global civic politics, and political activism concerning climate change, environmental protection,[87] and intergenerational equity. Indeed, to prevent the reduction of this claim to a mere outcome of ideological critique against capitalism, the concept of climate justice must be supported by a rational and ethical model. The thesis of this chapter posits that the concept of an ethics of responsibility, inspired by Hans Jonas's well-known philosophy, where future generations play a leading role,[88] could serve as a promising rational foundation for the advocacy of climate justice. The ethics of responsibility, which attains full significance only within a global perspective, would also align with principles established through the study and analysis of the dynamics between science, technology, and society.

Anthi Koskina, in "The Science-Based Decision-Making Process as Established in the Paris Agreement (2015),"[89] explains how evidence-based decision-making entered the international community's jargon, thanks to environmental law. Since the 1992 Earth Summit, science has been used to construct and legitimize the use of multilateralism for environmental protection purposes. Principle 15 of the Rio Declaration on Environment and Development posits: "[L]ack of full scientific certainty shall not be used as a reason for postponing cost-effective measures to prevent environmental degradation." Following declarations made under the premises of the United Nations Framework Convention on Climate Change (UNFCCC) acknowledged even more directly the link between science and law. For example, it recognizes how the Kyoto Protocol centres on the role of non-state actors[90] and science in both reviewing and guiding the development of the environmental protection regime.[91] Following this line of reasoning, Anthi Koskina investigates how the

87 Neil Carter, The Politics of the Environment: Ideas, Activism, Policy (Cambridge University Press 2018).

88 On the scholarship of Hans Jonas on environmental ethics: Theresa Morris, Hans Jonas's Ethic of Responsibility: From Ontology to Ecology (State University of New York Press 2013); Lewis Coyne, Hans Jonas: Life, Technology and the Horizons of Responsibility (Bloomsbury Publishing 2020); Vittorio Hösle, Filosofia della crisi ecologica (Einaudi 1992); Maria Loredana Furiosi, Uomo e natura nel pensiero di Hans Jonas (Vita e Pensiero 2003); Paolo Becchi, La vulnerabilità della vita. Contributi su Hans Jonas (La Scuola di Pitagora 2008); Karl-Otto Apel, Paolo Becchi & Paul Ricoeur, Hans Jonas: il filosofo e la responsabilità (Albo Versorio 2004).

89 Anthi Koskina, *The Science-Based Decision-Making Process as Established in the Paris Agreement (2015)*, *in* Science, Technology, Policy and International Law (Justo Corti Varela & Paolo Davide Farah (eds.), Routledge 2024).

90 Art. 5 Kyoto Protocol: Methodologies for estimating anthropogenic emissions by sources and removals by sinks of all greenhouse gases not controlled by the Montreal Protocol shall be those accepted by the *Intergovernmental Panel on Climate Change*.

91 Karin Bäckstrand & others, *Non-State Actors in Global Climate Governance: From Copenhagen to Paris and Beyond*, 26 Environmental Politics 561 (2017).

Paris Agreement, concluded in 2016, attempted to establish a new framework grounded in science. The decision-making process of the Paris Agreement highlighted how, at each stage, the common language of negotiators was science. Policymakers used law to balance the need to counteract the negative effects of climate change with economic, social, and cultural development. Anthi Koskina sees the multilateral environmental framework as a clear attempt to integrate science to the fullest extent in the context of policymaking. The sharing of scientific data, good practices, and experiences, as facilitated by the Paris Agreement, also has implications at the national and local levels. Koskina concludes by examining how the decision-making process of the Paris Agreement could positively influence member states encouraging them to design environmental policies based on science.

In summary, these contributions underscore the importance of addressing the topic of science and technology in the context of recent events and subject matters, including COVID-19, politics (especially populism), globalization, economics, culture, and the environment. They also emphasize the crucial role of law, particularly in regulating the interplay between science and technology. This can be observed through various aspects such as the flexibility mechanisms mentioned previously, the application of legal principles like the precautionary principle, the significance of international courts and regulatory authorities in governing science and technology, and the adoption of a pro-human rights approach to these issues. Finally, these contributions also delve into the role of ethics, morals, and practical considerations surrounding technology and science.

2 Facts Are the Moveable Legal Furniture of the Mind, Not the Stones of Science

Kirk W. Junker[*1]

1 Introduction: A Few Words about the Truth

We are discussing the role of law in science-based regulation in the post-truth era. The theme is fraught with words that carry heavy weights of meaning. In the thematic title alone, we have the words "science" and "law," but inextricable from these words are "truth," "fact," "rationality," and "reality." Each of these is an entire world of discourse that spans disciplines, cultures, and time. All these terms have multiple usages and meanings that change over time – that is the nature of language. These associated words will only be considered here insofar as they address our theme of sound science-based regulation in the post-truth era. All these terms are abstractions and therefore are given their existence and meaning by human beings. While linguists and communication scholars know that words are never labels for things,[2] these words, which give meaning to abstractions, are most certainly not labels for material things. They are social constructions. However, that does not mean that the intent of one person can just change the meaning of these abstractions at will. Despite their nature being humanly created abstractions, one cannot just wish them away. It is because a person cannot wish things away, even if they are social things and not material things, that those things have the quality of being real. Insofar as they are real, their socially constructed nature is not a reason to rush to absolute relativism or arbitrary values, as some shallow criticisms have suggested. It explains instead that not only the meanings of party politics and economic budgets but so too things like truth and fact and rationality and even science must be socially negotiated. Their meanings are not fixed, and the

* Kirk W. Junker is Vice Rector for Sustainability, Director of the Environmental Law Center, and holds the Chair in U.S. law at the University of Cologne. Corresponding Author: kwjunker@yahoo.com

1 Thanks to Alessandro Galli, lawyer, legal translator, and lecturer at the University of Padua, for the informative discussion and explanation regarding the etymology and use of "*factum*."

2 See Ferdinand de Saussure, Course in General Linguistics (first published 1916, Roy Harris, transl., Duckworth 1993); Ludwig Wittgenstein, Philosophical Investigations 3–30 (3rd edn, G. E. M. Anscombe, transl., MacMillan 1958); Kenneth Burke, Language as Symbolic Action: Essays on Life, Literature and Method (University of California Press 1966). Burke famously goes so far as to say that things are the symbols of words.

DOI: 10.4324/9781003472421-2

people of each age and place, simply by using language in social existence, either maintain or change the meanings. So the questions facing us today are questions regarding social constructions – how have they changed, in which direction they are changing, and if we anticipate change that is not to our liking or advantage, what the practices and institutions of law do about it. One must pay close attention to the creation and use of the words as markers for when and why social needs arise. In that sense, much of that which follows is written "backwards," so to speak, to unpack the meanings of our topic. The histories of how, when, and why the meanings of particular words are created and used in language can tell us quite a bit about how we can discuss an era.

We begin with the daunting task of discussing the word "truth." At least one meaning of truth that we use today in English can trace its pedigree back to the foundations of that which is now recognized as Western philosophy in fourth-century Greece.[3] Closely associated with Western philosophy was the concept of what we today call "ancient science." As regards the topic of science, although we would find that Enlightenment science differs significantly from ancient science,[4] both stand confidently upon the same foundation that distinguishes αλήθεια (aletheia), which is commonly translated as "truth," from δόξα (doxa), which is commonly translated as "opinion." That notion of truth concerns the abstract relations of abstract ideas, such as 2 + 2 = 4, which is a different concept from facts, as we shall see later. In the scientific sense, whether something can be called "true" is determined by the use of logic or reasoning. By "logic" or "reasoning," I do not mean just generally interchangeable terms for thinking. I mean these terms as used by philosophers themselves:

> Logic is the study of the methods and principles used to distinguish good (correct) reasoning from bad (incorrect) reasoning.[5] . . . Reasoning is a special kind of thinking in which inference takes place, in which conclusions are drawn from inference.[6] . . . Inference is a process by which one proposition is arrived at and offered as the basis of one or

3 We tell the story of the West today because of the current presence, if not dominance, of Western culture. African philosopher Philip Higgs notes that African philosophy addresses several different notions of philosophy, including "professional" philosophy, which is Western philosophy. Phillip Higgs, *The Revision of Western Rationality and Philosophy in Africa*, 20(2) Journal South African Philosophy 116–133 (2001). Other cultures of the East or South, of course, have other traditions of thought.

4 Merrilee Salmon et al., Introduction to the Philosophy of Science 12–13 (Prentice-Hall 1992).

5 Irving M. Copi, Introduction to Logic 3 (5th edn, Collier MacMillan 1978). In general use, specialist use and general use are often conflated and made indistinct from each other. So for example, in general use, English speakers may use "organic," when buying groceries, to mean food grown without pesticides, but a chemist restricts "organic" to mean only that a substance is carbon-based. Likewise, although in general language we may conflate the meanings of fact and truth, for a careful consideration of science-based regulation in the post-truth era, investigators must be careful to give each its precise meaning. The precise meanings will open up a role for law in the discussion.

6 *Id.* at 5.

> more other propositions, accepted as the starting point of the process. Propositions are either true or false.[7]

This was the method of scientific knowledge construction in the truth era. In the post-truth era, however,

> [w]hen the writer Claire Fox arrived at a girls' high school in the United Kingdom for a debate, she expected the girls to challenge some of what she had to say. . . . When the girls disagreed with her, she was shocked when they began crying and saying "You can't say that" instead of presenting rational arguments for positions.[8]

Using social scientific evidence consistent with this representative anecdote, the following shall examine how it could have come to be that people could invite a speaker to "debate" in such a mode. In a broader context, this episode raises the question of why we should care to reason logically. The best answer remains the foundational necessity of reason described by Epictetus:

> When one of his audience said, "Convince me that logic is useful," he said, Would you have me demonstrate it? "Yes." Well, then, must I not use a demonstrative argument? And, when the other agreed, he said, How then shall you know if I impose upon you? And when the man had no answer, he said You see how you yourself admit that logic is necessary, if without it you are not even able to learn this much – whether it is necessary or not.[9]

The ability and need to reason were certainly characteristic traits of the truth era. They may no longer be valued in the post-truth era and are instead treated as specialist practices reserved for scientists. Too often, lawyers and other persons regard science as a set of practices by and for specialists only, and even worse is the fact that science is often regarded as an instrumental set of practices by specialists that can be taken off the shelf and applied to political, social, economic, or legal problems and then put away again as those other practices

7 *Id.* at 6. Copi reminds us, however, that "the process of inference is not of interest to logicians, corresponding to every possible inference is argument, and it is with these arguments that logic is chiefly concerned. An argument in this sense, is any group of propositions of which one is claimed to follow from the others, which are regarded as providing support grounds for the truth of that one." Copi, 7. See, Wesley C. Salmon, The Foundations of Scientific Inference 17–21 (University of Pittsburgh Press 1966).

8 Jean M. Twenge, iGen: Why Today's Super-Connected Kids Are Growing Up Less Rebellious, More Tolerant, Less Happy – and Completely Unprepared for Adulthood . . . and What That Means for the Rest of Us 153–154 (Atria 2017).

9 Epictetus, Discourses (William Abbott Oldfather, transl., Loeb Classical Library 1928). The capitalization is Oldfather's.

then continue on their way. On the contrary, science is a way of understanding the world.

1.1 *Marking an Era*

The notion of marking an era is relevant to our discussion because we are considering what it could mean for science and law to be in a moment of time that has been given a new label – the "post-truth" era. The use of "post" has become a rather standard way to show change or movement of an era, perhaps even progress. In a relatively short period of human history, the English language has recognized "post-modern"[10] (and its "-ism"), "post-structural" (and its "-ism"), and now "post-truth," which, if patterns follow, will soon be followed by its own "-ism." Naming any era serves to both recognize that change has occurred from a previous era and cement that change into time. Before there was "post-modernity," as Bruno Latour pointed out, the adjective "modern" has been used to designate "a new regime, an acceleration, a rupture, a revolution in time."[11]

Several observations from the marking of other eras apply to this discussion. First, our marking of the beginning and ending of a period is tentative and subject to change in the future. Second, the characteristics or events that are said to mark a period can be selected differently by other generations to suit their own understandings. Martin Heidegger described our experience of individual beings as "*Geworfenheit*" or "thrown-ness." We are thrown into life in a particular time and a particular language and culture, and if we are not critical and reflective, we may believe that these particular attributes are somehow universal in time and space. This is an extremely important point to be made in intellectual history. The newest generation, known as the iGeneration (also known as Generation Z), is thrown into the patterns of such phenomena as influencers and social media platforms, for example, and understandably takes that as "normal" (literally, the measure), just as we all are thrown into a pre-existing world at a particular moment in its evolution. It can therefore be difficult for us to understand previous eras because those people were thrown into different moments, with different social and intellectual structures in place and different social and intellectual tools to use.

When we are not careful, we project ourselves onto other eras as we try to understand them, their motivations, and their expressions of meaning. Michel Foucault provides a philosophical treatment and critique of dogmatic structural readings of history and philosophy, portraying continuous narratives as naive ways of projecting our own consciousness onto the past. For present

10 Despite associations of the term with art, it is relevant to knowledge production. See Jean-François Lyotard, The Postmodern Condition: A Report on Knowledge (Geoff Bennington and Brian Massumi, transl., University of Minnesota Press 1984).

11 Bruno Latour, We Have Never Been Modern 10 (Catherine Porter, transl., Harvard University Press 1991).

purposes, there is no better example of Foucault's point than the notion of "fact." As science historian David Wootton notes, "[w]e take facts so much for granted that it comes as a shock to learn that they are a modern invention."[12] As we will see later, "fact" has been with us for some time, but as a different concept in the past.

Insofar as we mark eras, there is an implication – itself a manifestation of a time-bound attitude – that each new era marks not only change but also progress over a preceding era. A sense of irreversibility underpins notions of progress in general and underpins a certain type of rational progress in specific. All these points are being called into question by natural and social phenomena today.[13]

The intellectual tools that we build to address the world that we encounter both enable and limit our encounter. Finally, when discussing eras and the change of eras, those tools themselves can change, not just the objects that we encounter with those tools. We begin with the notion of truth, but the truth era is not characterized by the notion and use of "truth" alone. Associated with truth, and some would say built upon it, are opinion (as a dialectical opposite), rationality, and fact.

1.2 Distinguishing Truth from Opinion

The Western notion of truth as accuracy or agreement begins most notably with the event of Plato's writing. In the Western intellectual tradition, we are familiar with the Athenian criminal trial, conviction, and execution of Socrates, as described by Plato. As the story goes, Chaerephon asked the oracle of Apollo, a prophetess at Delphi, whether there was a wiser man in Athens than Socrates, and she replied that there was not. Chaerephon relayed that assertion to Socrates, but Socrates was certain that this could not be correct, because there was so much about the reality of daily life that he did not know. So he set for himself the task to disprove the "hypothesis" announced by the prophetess. To accomplish his goal, Socrates employed a research method known today to every courtroom lawyer. Plato wrote: "After a long consideration, [Socrates] at last thought of a method of trying the question."[14] This dialectic practice consisted of allowing interlocutors to question propositions to determine if they were true or false, and to test whether the conclusion

12 David Wootton, The Invention of Science: A New History of the Scientific Revolution 254 (Harper Collins 2015).

13 See, George G. Iggers, ***Rationality and History***, ***in*** Developments in Modern Historiography 19–39 (Henry Kozicki (ed.), Palgrave 1993), which is the text of a lecture presented by Iggers at East China Normal University in 2007.

14 Plato, Apology 21b (Hugh Tredennick, transl, in *The Collected Dialogues of Plato*, Edith Hamilton and Huntington Cairns (eds.), Bollingen Series LXXI, Princeton 1961); see comment by Benjamin Jowett, trans. *Internet Archive*, January 1, 1970, archive.org/details/Apology-Socrates/page/n1.

could be inferred from the true evidence. The evidence made the proposition testable and limited the warrant of the conclusion. And upon questioning politicians, poets, and craftsmen through this method, the answers that Socrates received demonstrated to him that while all these Athenians might have posited some demonstrable and useful truths about their field of specialization, none could distinguish these truths based upon evidence and rational argument from their own opinions, which were conclusions lacking evidence, rational argument, or both.

On trial for failing to pay heed to the gods and corrupting the minds of the young, Socrates explained the dialectic method by which he tested the prophetess's hypothesis among the Athenians. He then said to the citizens who were to judge him:

> [The] professional experts seem to share the same failing which I had noticed in the poets. I mean that on the strength of their technical proficiency they claimed a perfect understanding over another subject, however important, and I felt that this error more than outweighed their positive wisdom.[15]

Later at trial, after explaining his dialectic method in response to the charges against him, Socrates then turned his dialectic method to interrogate the testimony of his accusers. But at trial, his "trying the question" as a method of inquiry was conducted under the state's authority to force his interlocutors to answer, and the form of his questions was very much leading the witness to simple yes-or-no answers. Today, cross-examination formally mimics this form in many common-law courts around the world and is informally employed in civil law and other jurisdictions as well.

Politics were not absent from the trial of Socrates. Thucydides put the trial in historical context when he reported that near the end of Athens's war with Sparta, when it was apparent that Athens would lose, intense civil strife was present in Athens. When the war ended, after a short period of oligarchical dictatorship, the old democratic order was restored. But Socrates had been critical of some of the democratic activities and was friends with some persons, such as Alcibiades, Critias, and Charmides, who were now on the outside of those persons who were on the inside of political power. Those political activities and associations, coupled with Socrates's unrelenting insistence upon evidence to warrant inferences, may well have contributed to his demise.[16]

15 Plato, Apology, 22d-e.

16 Melvin Rader, The Enduring Questions; Main Problems of Philosophy 10–11 (3d edn, Holt, Rinehart & Winston 1976). Upon reading the *Apology*, one is struck by how often Socrates acknowledges that he must defend himself against the underlying feeling of the Athenians that he is annoying them with his questions and by the suggestion that they have invented other concrete charges against him just to stop his bothering them with his pursuit of truth through rational questions. One needs only to translate his term for knowledge to "*scientia*" in Latin

In retrospect, the politics are too often omitted from the story. As a result, planted already at the inception of this Western distinction of truth from opinion, we find a sanitizing effort to de-politicize the production of knowledge. The truth of that knowledge, according to Plato, originates in the ability of a person to understand the basis of his or her own beliefs, and in the ability to distinguish those beliefs, based upon evidence and a reasoning process by which the conclusion is inferred, from the opinions for which one has no evidence or reasoning.

1.3 Characterizing Rationality

If we want to commit a bit of Whiggish etymology, we can begin with the relation of λόγος (*logos*) to mathematics. In surviving texts, we know that Euclid identified numbers that he called "irrational" numbers ἄλογος (*alogos*). To our understanding today, he might have been using ἄλογος in the sense of "unsayable" numbers or in the sense of "unreasonable" numbers. Mathematicians assume *alogos* was used in the sense of unsayable numbers. In the "Ἠθικὰ Νικομάχεια" (*Nicomachean Ethics*), Plato's student Aristotle wrote that our τέλος (*telos*) or ultimate end or purpose is *logos*, which is eventually translated into English as "rationality." His characterization of the human is *not* that we are always rational but that we are most human when we are rational.[17] Historically, three axioms were used to establish rationality: identity, the excluded middle, and noncontradiction. Noncontradiction is the axiom most fitting to this discussion, and among several formulations that Aristotle provides for the meaning of "noncontradiction," the most apt for the law is "contradictory statements are not at the same time true."[18] Λήθη (*Lethe*) means, in translation, "oblivion," "forgetfulness," or "concealment." The word ἀλήθεια (*aletheia*) is variously translated as "unclosedness," "unconcealedness," "disclosure," or "truth." The literal meaning of the word *aletheia* is "the state of not being hidden; the state of being evident." It is fitting to note that in the history of these words, *alogos* preceded *logos*, that is, the word that we translate as "irrationality" preceded the word we translate as "rationality" and that "truth"

---

and then "science" in English to recognize the similar annoyance and anger felt by others for the persons who tell them to follow the "inconvenient truth" (Al Gore), or simply "the science" (Greta Thunberg).

17 Renowned nineteenth-century philologist Eduard Zeller said that "[t]he most important feature of the Aristotelian teleology is the fact that it is neither anthropocentric nor is it due to the actions of a creator existing outside the world or even of a mere arranger of the world, but is always thought of as immanent in nature." (1883, §48). Eduard Zeller, Outlines of the History of Greek Philosophy (13th ed., rev by Wilhelm Nestle, L. R. Palmer, transl., Noonday Press 1955).

18 Aristotle, Metaphysics (Book Gamma, 6, 1011b14). Although he did not name it as a principle of reasoning, Aristotle's teacher, Plato, made use of it by name in his cross-examination proofs, asserting, for example, that Meletus, Socrates's accuser, was contradicting himself. Plato, *Apology*, *supra* note 14, 27a.

was not introduced in its positive form but as a disclosure from the primary state of concealedness. In his 1931–1932 lecture course called "On the Essences of Truth," Heidegger lectured carefully on the word "*aletheia*," stating that the proper translation is thus "*Unverborgeneheit*" (unconcealedness).[19] Heidegger later said that Plato initiated the decline of *alethia* into "correctness" and "truth-as-agreement."[20] Translation practice is always an interpretive step, but when it makes such a cultural interpretation of abstract practices, it must be scrutinized. Thus, one must consider that the "foundation" that we are recognizing from the concept of truth fit a different era of thinking, and we need a different concept, perhaps unrelated to truth and neither post-truth nor even anti-truth, but different. The positive sense of the meaning of truth as agreement or accuracy was further developed by Aristotle, which we call "non-contradiction." This sense was carried forward and is our sense today. The practice of law uses the non-contradiction meaning of the scientific method of truth when witnesses and evidence are examined.[21]

Like the word "truth," there are several meanings and usages of the word "rationality."[22] Sociologist Max Weber is usually credited with having identified the difference between value rationality and instrumental rationality.[23] Legal philosopher John Rawls applied Weber's two kinds of rationality explicitly to

19 Martin Heidegger, Gesamtausgabe (Collected Works) XXII 25 (Frankfurt, Klostermann 1975).

20 *Id.* at XXXIV.

21 The practice of law also uses a moral sense of truth when legislating norms. Only if and when the speaker knows the difference but intentionally deceives his or her audience does morality enter the discussion of truth. Truth is relevant to morality insofar as one is capable of knowing the truth but intentionally contradicting it. I am concerned in this chapter, however, only with the former use, not the latter use. See Kirk W. Junker & Konrad Ott, *More Than Just Doing What's Right: Ethics in Science, in* Science and the Public (Kirk W. Junker (ed.), Milton Keynes, The Open University Press 1998).

22 When it comes to the English word "rationality," one is again reminded of difficult problems in the translation of terms and the translation of intellectual tools from language to language, culture to culture, ancient to modern, and discipline to another discipline. The Greek word *logos* is translated as "rationality," but that is a selected one meaning from many, none of which are one-to-one correspondences to any English words. Unlike some of the translation of ancient texts, the translation of *logos* is so obviously problematic in contemporary English that it often includes an explanation (like this one). "The most important discovery of the ancient Greeks is the idea of *Logos* that makes up the crucial problem and the postulate connecting ancient Greek culture together with European culture. We translate *Logos* in English usually as reason, or *rationality*. These terms, however, do not cover the whole semantic field of *Logos*. The main problem does not concern the translation, but is related to the difference of human self-understanding and understanding of the world. Generally speaking, *Logos* can be reason and language, ground of things and order of Being, discourse and discursive rationality. The semantic focus depends on the semantic interrelations within a concrete context." Georgia Apostolopoulou, *From Ancient Greek Logos to European Rationality* 2(7) Wisdom 118 (2016) (emphasis added.)

23 See, Max Weber, Economy and Society 24–26, 399–400 (Guenther Roth and Claus Wittich (eds.), University of California Press 1978).

law.[24] Insofar as positive law uses a notion of "truth," it is a use built upon the Aristotelian rational notion that if anything is accepted through some social or scientific method as true, its opposite (a contradiction) cannot be true. We find examples of that sense of truth in the law when there is a private obligation not to express known untruths in writing or speaking, and when the consumer is legally protected against advertising that is intended to mislead him or her, and even when criminal penalties are demanded against those who tell lies while under oath in a courtroom because it is an affront to the rational sense of public order. All these are based largely on a societal norm in support of rationality, which weaves its way back to the principle of non-contradiction.

A further point made by Aristotle is relevant to this consideration of law and science in the post-truth era – rationality is not a matter of choice but rather is a pattern of habit,[25] which, like other habits, we sometimes practice and sometimes do not practice. But when we do, we just do it without any critical reflection, having been socialized to treat it as natural or normal.[26] This characterization of rationality is supported by neuroscience still today[27] and by Nobel Prize–winning economics.[28] Nowhere does Aristotle reduce the human to a rational essence or define humans as purely rational. To understand what he would have meant, we must come to terms with the meanings of his language, as philologists understand them, and the less-than-exact matching of his language with even modern Greek, let alone modern English.

Given that rationality may thus be considered as the manifestation of a habit, custom, or pattern, we must ask a new and different question: Can the pattern itself be intentionally established, and if so, how can it be intentionally

24 John Rawls found just patterns of social action in his A Theory of Justice, and Justice as Fairness: A Restatement (Belknap Press 2001).

25 Aristotle. Metaphysics, Books X–XIV (W. D. Ross, transl, *in* The Complete Works of Aristotle, The Revised Oxford Translation, Jonathan Barnes (ed.), Bollingen Series LXXL.2 1984).

26 Aristotle, Nicomachean Ethics (1104a 27–31, W. D. Ross, transl, rev. by J. O. Urmsorn, *in* The Complete Works of Aristotle, The Revised Oxford Translation, Jonathan Barnes, ed., Bollingen Series LXXL.2 1984). Aristotle indicated in *Nicomachean Ethics* 1.13 "that one element in the soul is irrational and one has a rational principle" and that they are "by nature inseparable, like convex and concave in the circumference of the circle." Aristotle mentions the potential of humans to be rational in other texts as well, including Περὶ ζῴων μορίων (*The Parts Animals)*, 686a, and Πολιτικά (*Politics*), 1253a1–18. We must remain precise on both what he says rationality means and how humans are associated with it, regardless if we are going to accept or reject it.

27 Javier Bernacer & Jose Ignacio Murillo, *The Aristotelian Conception of Habit and Its Contribution to Human Neuroscience*, Frontiers in Human Neuroscience (2014) <www.ncbi.nlm.nih.gov/pmc/articles/PMC4217383/>.

28 In 2017, behavioral economist Richard Thaler won the Nobel Prize for his work that demonstrated that humans do not make rational economic choices, contrary to assumptions of "free" market supporters. Thaler concluded that, instead, economic choices of individuals need to be "nudged" – by private interests driven by profit, or by the state driven by public interests. Cf., Paul Kennedy, The Rise and Fall of Great Powers: Economic Change and Military Conflict from 1500 to 2000 (Random House 1987).

established? Minimally, according to Aristotle, one *can* intentionally choose between using πίστεις ἄτεχνοι (*pisteis atechnoi* or inartificial proofs) or πίστεις ἔντεχνοι (*pisteis entechnoi* or artificial proofs).

> As for proofs, some are inartificial others artificial. By the former I understand all those which have not been furnished by ourselves but were already in existence, such as witnesses, tortures, contracts, and the like; by the latter, all that can be constructed by system and by our own efforts. Thus we have only to make use of the former, whereas we must invent the latter.[29]

One might see a resemblance in this distinction from today's commonly uttered distinction between "objective" proofs that are to be accepted because their evidence is external to the person and "subjective" proofs, which are not to be accepted because their evidence is internal to the person. But these artificial and inartificial proofs are not to be confused with rational and irrational proofs.

The context in which he wrote was the context of knowing that the geometry of Pythagoras and Euclid held that there were abstract, static truths available for our description of the world. But in the *Nicomachean Ethics*, he says that the irrational element of the soul is itself twofold: the sense in which one "pays heed" to his or her father or friends, and as the absence of "the rational" in mathematics.[30] Today we would associate the former with *logos* as irrational thoughts or acts that are logical or without foundation in reason, and the latter with *logos*, as in irrational numbers. Because there are these multiple foundations, we can see that a sense of rationality today that would be purely mathematical only selects part of the potential concept. The other – a social concept – provides other foundations, such as that in law when Socrates is charged with failing to pay heed to the gods.

Plato's narrative of the events in the *Apologia* provided the structure of dialectic reasoning that would become known as the basis of the scientific method. Thus, a foundation stone was laid in the social construction of knowledge in Western culture – one must distinguish truth from opinion through the method of cross-examination, as presented by Socrates, not in natural science, but rather in a court of law. The method itself was that of *logos.* Linguistically, we also know that the Greek word "*logos*" would be culturally and linguistically translated to English today as both "logic" and "speech" (as in the word "dialogue"), and "*logos*" was translated into Latin as "*rationalis*," and "*rationalis*" was translated into English as "rationality."

29 Aristotle, Rhetoric (Book I, John H. Freese, transl., Harvard University Press, Loeb Classics 1926).

30 Aristotle, *supra* note 26, at I.1102b 29–33. W. D. Ross, the translator, himself has difficulty translating this passage and tells the reader in a footnote that λόγον ἔχειν means (1) "possess reason," (2) "pay heed to," "obey," or (3) "be rational" (in the mathematical sense).

Eventually, the Greek word *alogos* was translated into Latin as *irrationalis.* Relying heavily upon Aristotle and the interpretation of truth as agreement, Cicero emphasized in his *De inventione* that *factum* must be developed from that which is known to be true.[31] That which was known to be true was distinguished from that which was opinion, and the process through which to make the distinction was rational inquiry. The mathematical sense of "irrational" is first attested in English in 1551, and the mathematical sense of "rational" in English comes only after "irrational," in 1570.[32]

Despite these linguistic issues, the continuous use of this concept of rationality, based upon this concept of truth, can be said to lay a foundation for rationality in human social experience, including law. For example, the Romano-canon tradition developed a complex evidentiary system during the Middle Ages that included "irrational proofs," such as inflicting wounds on an accused person because the wounds were believed to heal if one was innocent, but not heal if one was guilty. In England, only in 1215 were irrational proofs banned and replaced by rational inquiry and the critical sifting and evaluation of available evidence offered by witnesses and weighed by professional judges.[33] Presumptions in any dispute, made prior to the introduction of any proof or evidence, have played a role in law throughout history. Even after the English ban on irrational proofs and the European Enlightenment, we know that still as recently as the seventeenth century, presumptions were attached to the identity of the witness, without rational inquiry. Problems of credibility and trust in English "gentlemanly culture" were not solved solely through rationality. If English gentlemen had an annual income of £280 or more, their propositions would be presumed to be true.[34] The propositions of women, servants, and other dependents, by comparison, were presumed not to be true, just as they would have been presumed not to be true in ancient Greek legal proceedings. While the process of law has methods for inferring valid conclusions from true propositions, the norms of law, even during the truth era, tolerated some non-truths. Institutionalized, legally permitted non-truth more recently included advertising and marketing that permits non-truths called "puffery" in the law of contracts.[35]

31 Cicero, De Inventione, (*On Invention*) viii–ix (H. M. Hubbell, transl., Jeffrey Henderson, ed., Harvard University Press, Loeb Classics 1949). To a lesser degree Cicero was also relying upon Aristotle in his *Rhetoric ad Herennium.*

32 Oxford English Dictionary, irrationality, n. (*OED Online*, Oxford University Press 2020) <www.oed.com/view/Entry/99593>.

33 Barbara J. Shapiro, A Culture of Fact: England, 1350–1720 8 (Cornell University Press 2003), citing R. C. von Caenegem, *The History of European Civil Procedure, in* Encyclopedia of Comparative Law 13, 16 (Tübingen 1972).

34 Steven Shapin, A Social History of Truth; Civility and Science in Seventeenth-Century England (University of Chicago 1995).

35 Peter J. Henning, *The Difference Between Puffery and Fraud*, New York Times (10 October2011)<https://dealbook.nytimes.com/2011/10/10/the-difference-between-puffery-and-fraud/>.

Even if one is sceptical of progress and the biases ingrained in Western cultures, when one looks at the various methods of valuing and proving truth, it would be difficult for us today to claim that rationality did not enlighten previous methods, especially those by the trials of duels or burning flesh. And despite such questionable cultural features as the presumption of truth due to the status of "gentlemen" on one hand, truth became cemented through rationality during the European period of history known today as the Enlightenment, which included the legal step to ban irrational proofs on the other hand.

Trial by rational discourse simply using the principle of non-contradiction provided the opportunity for predictability and fairness, as well as a far more transparent application of a rule of law to facts presented. Indeed, as will be discussed in Part 2 of this chapter, *infra*, it was the trial by rational discourse that created the need for events with particulars to be characterized as "facts." In the same paragraph in which Aristotle formulated the principle of noncontradiction, he made clear that "consequences follow from the denial of this belief"[36] (in the principle of noncontradiction). If we follow the construction of facts from rationality, and rationality from truth, we must then ask: In an era that labels itself "post-truth," what will the consequences to the concepts of rationality and fact be?[37]

1.4 Facts

In this narrative of the truth era, truth was built from non-contradiction, rationality from truth, and facts from rationality. The concept of fact does not begin with natural phenomena and was, if anything, a rather late arrival in natural philosophy, having become a well-established concept elsewhere before it was adopted by the community of naturalists,[38] according to legal historian Barbara Shapiro and science historian David Wootton. For our purposes, it is of particular interest to note that the "elsewhere" where the notion of "fact" was developed was the field of law, which also contributed to the broader demarcation of an era. And with the introduction of this last element – fact – to our construction of knowledge in the truth era, we introduce an element that cannot be derived from reason alone. While truth can be tested and proven through reason alone, Wootton reminds us that "[o]ur knowledge of contingent matters, of matters of fact, depends on evidence: testimony, experience, documents."[39] If that list looks like one that a lawyer would use, it is because it *is* a list that a lawyer would use. It is the law, not science, that needed, and therefore invented, the notion of the fact to make it possible to make judge-

36 Aristotle, *supra* note 18, at Book Gamma, 6 1011b14–15.

37 The Latin *animal rationale* is the translation of ζῷον λόγον ἔχον, a term that Aristotle wrote about in *The Parts of Animals*, S86a27H1, as well as in *Politics*, 125341–18.

38 Shapiro, *supra* note 33, at 2.

39 Wootton, *supra* note 12, at 253.

ments on past *events*, not on the existence of material *things*. The practices of law use "fact" to mean acts that change from time to time and place to place, called "particulars" at some points in history, as opposed to the law itself, which is generally the same rule for all persons.[40] English takes the word "fact" from the Latin "*factum*." The word "*factum*" was already in general use in classical Latin before Cicero, and it was also used in a specific legal sense. An example is the Latin "*actio in factum*" as opposed to the "*actio in ius*." As a noun, "*factum*" has a range of different meanings, including both "fact" and "action" (human conduct), as well as the result of an action (something that has been done/made/accomplished). The criterion underlying the "*actio in factum*" in early and classical Roman law appears to have been the need to allow citizens to take legal action based on the occurrence of a "fact" which was not (or had not yet been foreseen as) deserving legal consideration or protection according to statutory law. From this perspective, it is not dissimilar from the distinction between "actions at law" versus "suits in equity" in the early stages of English law.

The historical record of human thought indicates that before there was modern science, the practices of law invented the notion of a "fact" to distinguish *acts that were done* (deeds) from the persistent rules that are independent of any deeds.[41] In no small part through the agency of Francis Bacon, English lawyer turned scientist, science borrowed and changed the meaning of facts from descriptions of actions or events to descriptions of things or abstract statements of the laws of the universe. Bacon provided the bridge that enabled the notion of fact to migrate from law to science, with his

> emphasis on experiment, the connection between "fact" and the new-style natural history, the nature of scientific witnessing, and the role of observational aids such as the telescope and microscope. [Unsurprisingly] the conditions of scientific investigation, experiment, and decision making . . . resembled . . . those of the law court.[42]

Although, when speaking in common usage, one might say that "F = ma" is a fact in science because it is a "law" of physics, one would still distinguish a fact in the practices of law from the laws themselves.

> Kepler had lots of facts, and della Porta had one or two, but neither had the word "fact" in the modern sense. Where does that word come from?

40 I say "generally" because, as a cultural phenomenon, law extends only to adults who are mentally competent and within the geographic boundaries of that particular jurisdiction.

41 One may note that before anyone could say whether humans are "progressing," the concept of "progress" needed to be invested with meaning. That was done through literature, not natural science. Georges Sorel, The Illusions of Progress 125–128 (University of California Press 1972). "No medieval natural philosopher had a view of natural science as making progress." Wootton, *supra* note 12, at 575. Today, of course, it is regarded as orthodoxy to say that science does make progress.

42 *Id.* at 4.

> In 1778 Gotthold Lessing wrote a little essay on the German word for "fact" [which is] *Tatsache*: "The word is still youthful," he said. "I remember perfectly the time before anyone used it."[43] But the word itself, at least in English, French and Italian is not new. Its source is the Latin verb *facio*, "I do." *Factum*, the neuter past participle, means that which has been done.[44]

Isaac Newton relied upon the concept of fact that had been established by law for his use in explaining physical sciences. He also borrowed from the courts the worldview that along with functioning according to laws, the universe may be thought of as orderly.[45] Only after the notion of fact migrated from law to natural science have natural science practices become regarded as the primary practices by which we produce knowledge. However, this rarefied status of science as an exclusive knowledge producer has not been sufficient to relegate evidence-free belief to a subservient position. Instead, we make the error of treating science as only a specialty area of technology, limiting it to the work of men and women who are working out the mathematics of the universe like taking apart a great wristwatch, as William Paley famously maintained in 1802. When we relegate science to the mathematics of the technological details, we leave the space in which to answer larger questions to evidence-free, non-scientific, or even anti-scientific beliefs and opinions. Science is a worldview about the nature and meaning of bodies and forces, not only the technical calculations about those bodies and forces. As Enlightenment thinking expanded into all areas of Western thought, fact changed from referring to events of the social world to the accuracy of propositions about the material world's "stones of science."

Today, to distinguish juvenile from adult abilities to testify in court, we even use the simple test of whether the witness understands the difference between telling the truth and telling a lie. These litmus paper distinctions allow only two possibilities in the controlled situation of legal testimony – truth and untruth. Thus, they do not help beyond the courtroom, such as when voters choose among candidates for office. Moreover, informed, intelligent discussion is difficult, if not impossible, if everything is seen through only these two possible frames. The real harm is not that one candidate or opinion carries the day through truth or lies or halfway in between but that we, as beings capable of rationality, have devalued rationality to a point where we do not use truth or untruth as a determining factor.

So much have we become conditioned into the natural science worldview of facts that we seem even to believe that the material of nature itself produces

43 Gotthold Ephraim Lessing, Lessings Leben (Vol. 3, 1793) 177–178 (*Ueber das Wörtlein "Thatsache"*); *Grimms Wörterbuch* gives 1756 as the date for the first use of *Thatsache.*

44 Wootton, *supra* note 12, at 283, citing Thomas Browne, Pseudoxia Epidemica 3 (1646).

45 James E. McGuire, *Predicates of Pure Existence: Newton on God's Space and Time*, *in* Philosophical Perspectives on Newtonian Science 91–108 (Phillip Bricker & R. I. G. Hughes (eds.), MIT Press 1990).

facts, rather than recognizing that we produce facts regarding our experience of material nature. Consequently, today it comes as a surprise to many to learn that the notion of fact was created in law, not in the natural sciences. That noted, it is perhaps then not surprising that without reflection, some persons might think that the material objects of nature give those human-created facts more "facticity" than the human-created facts that concern social objects or relations. Furthermore, as historian Barbara Shapiro reminds us, "fact," in the legal context, did not even mean an established truth but rather an alleged act, the occurrence of which was in dispute.[46]

For fact or any other concept to become a pattern or habit, a society needs to have used the concept sufficiently to make it commonplace. The resolution of dispute requires third parties to resolve issues of fact and issues of law. The common law made clear, through its institutions, that these were separate legal functions. It manifested the distinction by giving each of two different institutions one of these two roles. For professional judges, determining issues of law was part of their training. But for issues of fact, there needed to have been a steady supply of laypersons capable of serving on juries. At this point, we can observe a common notion of fact that would contribute to science as a way of life, not just an instrumentality. A sufficient supply of jurors

> could only have been possible if there had already been a widespread experience and familiarity with legal institutions and the language of fact and methods of fact determination so that for the English public, the creation of matters of fact was simply part of the "furniture of the mind."[47]

Thus, the lay jury is a good example of how a society participates in the creation and maintenance of legal institutions and, in turn, how those legal institutions are capable of contributing to a society's knowledge production, such as when they determine that which is necessary and sufficient to make a fact count as a fact.

As mentioned earlier, it was only *after* the notion of fact was established and institutionalized in law that it was borrowed and used in natural science, although when a person is thrown into the world today, the order might seem to have been the reverse. In addition to the pervasive power of the ideology of science reduced to materialism, the act of translation may have contributed to the association today of facts with things. According to David Wootton, the Latin word *res* (thing) was very often translated into English as "fact." But as Wootton points out, consistent with the logician's use of the word "truth,"

46 Not long after Lessing introduced the word "*Tatsache*" to German to refer, literally, to the thing that had been done, German courts began using the word in the same way as the English courts used "fact."

47 Shapiro, *supra* note 33, at 9.

"[a] thing exists without words, but a fact is a statement, a term in a discourse. Things are not true, but facts are. Things and facts are not the same."[48] Prior to borrowing the notion of fact from the law and elsewhere, science could speak of particulars as compared to general things, but it could not speak of facts.

For evidence of cultural change over time *in law*, we can return to the simple example of the lay jury. From ancient times until that of the common-law courts today, the jury provides an indication of how the use of evidence in culture changes over time. This change in legal evidence parallels the use of evidence by historians.[49] Until the eighteenth century, it was thought that one should be an eyewitness to events in order to be a better historian, just as it was earlier the case that jurors should have witnessed, or at least know of, the events that they were meant to be judging. With the Enlightenment ideas of progress and its epistemology, both historians and courts became persuaded that one is a better observer of particular events from which to infer facts if one is further away from having personally experienced those particulars. Only persons who are thoroughly indoctrinated in notions of the human as neutral observers of things cannot be at least a little puzzled by the idea that the uninformed is a better witness than the directly informed. Yet in common law, we have gone, for example, from lay juries being persons who knew the parties or who had witnessed the events in question to being people who must be able to say they know nothing of the parties or events in order to qualify as jurors. This latter quality is that of the neutral and disinterested fact judgement machine, rather than a person with values invested in the outcome of the dispute.

When we talk about truth in the historical context of an era and truth in the social contexts of science or law, we must be careful not to conflate "truth" with "fact." Facts are contingent and changeable – that is their nature. As we construct the frameworks of our intellectual and cultural dwellings, we are reminded that facts are the moveable furniture of the legal mind, not the stones of materialist science. Once we make clear the distinction between truth and fact and the relationships of each to law and science separately, then we can begin to appreciate the notion that law has had, and may continue to have, a significant role to play in the shaping of fact in a post-truth era. Thus, the questions become: How are facts understood differently in an era of post-truth? And in what ways will law contribute to that understanding and meaning?

1.5 Reality

Another operative term must be explored: "reality." Like "fact," "reality" cannot be derived from reason alone. As a corrective to the industrially conditioned

48 Wootton, *supra* note 12, at 255.

49 See, Christopher Carey, *Artless 'Proofs in Aristotle and the Orators*, 39 Bulletin of the Institute of Classical Studies 95–106 (1994).

notion that materiality constitutes reality, sociologists Peter Berger and Paul Luckmann maintain that "reality" does not rely upon materiality but is a quality appertaining to phenomena that we recognize as being independent of our own volition. This characterization of reality is fully consistent with Aristotle's inartificial proofs. But in addition, that same characterization addresses how true premises in the law can be constructed without relying only upon materiality. Simply stated, things – including social things – are real when we cannot simply "wish them away." Valid facts are inferred from these true premises regarding social things. Reality includes material and social realities. The nature of things is not limited to the things of nature. Law belongs to social realities. The need for the law to judge behaviour was responsible for inventing the human concept of fact in order to describe human behaviour from other times and places and represent it in a courtroom. Only after the Enlightenment did we reverse the relationship of the social and the material and consequently come to expect physical evidence, such as lie detector tests or DNA, in order to prove that which had occurred at another place and time.

Berger and Luckmann add that "knowledge" is the confidence we have that phenomena are real. So even when our realities are socially constructed, they exist independently from us, with particulars of the real being known as "facts," which are as real as realities about material. In both the material and social worlds, the realities are constituted by the meanings that we give to these material things and social events, meanings that no one person can wish away.

When it comes to method, Berger and Luckmann state that at one end of the spectrum, we have philosophers whose way of talking about and investigating reality will question everything, and at the other end of the spectrum, we have what they call the "man in the street" who exercises the extreme opposite comportment towards reality by ***never*** questioning the nature of reality and instead follows the pre-established habits of behaviour into which he is thrown, until there is a crisis. According to Berger and Luckmann:

> The ***sociological*** understanding of "reality" and "knowledge" falls somewhere in the middle between that of the man in the street and that of the philosopher. The man in the street does not normally trouble himself about what is "real" to him and about what he "knows" unless he is stopped short by ***some sort of problem***.[50]

It would seem that we are currently experiencing that "***sort of problem***" when we feel compelled to label our entire era as "post-truth." When addressing such issues as science-based regulation in a particular era, using law to look at law provides no outside reference point from which to gain a perspective. Justice

50 Peter L. Berger & Thomas Luckmann, The Social Construction of Reality: A Treatise in the Sociology of Knowledge 14 (Anchor Books 1966). (Emphasis added.)

Susanne Baer of the Federal Constitutional Court of Germany maintains that for interdisciplinary treatment of law, our point of perspective should come from sociology.[51] In defining acute problems of human existence such as the climate crisis, some parts of the world may see poverty, religion, or dictatorial preferences as the cause for the effect of climate inaction. But that is not the case in Australia, Canada, the United States, and other Western countries that have failed to act and yet which would like to characterize themselves as cultures that carry forward Enlightenment scientific thinking. In those cultures, there must be other reasons.

Berger and Luckmann's middle position from their field of sociology says that even the everyday reality that persons practice as habit can and should be interrogated with the aim of finding out how everyday things achieve the status of unquestioned reality or what they call "objective facticities." Their position in the sociology of knowledge is most like that of lawyers in legal practice and therefore should be used by lawyers to understand the construction of social facts, including those we call "science." Like the sociology of knowledge, the law does not leave the construction of facts, reality, and knowledge unexamined. The law works with and serves all persons, not just specialists. Thus, it is appropriate to use the sociological construction of reality to best fit legal practice to the society it serves.

1.6 Science

This social construction from truth to rationality to facts to reality brings us, at the conclusion of this truth-era discussion, to science. Ancient categories were concerned with characterizing knowledge by the methods through which we could acquire that knowledge – τέχνη (*techne*), which we translate into English as "art," ἐμπειρία (*empeiria*), which we commonly translate into English as "experience,"[52] and ἐπιστήμη (*episteme*), which we translate as "knowledge." Plato's Socrates favoured *episteme* over *empeiria*.[53] Plato's Socrates, in the *Phaedrus* dialogue, maintains that a *techne* must also have a rational principle (*logon*) by which it applies the things it applies to explain what they are by nature. He refuses "the name of art (*techne*)" to anything (*pragma*) irrational (*alogon*)" (465a).[54] While in the *Politics*, Aristotle states that human beings are

51 Susanne Baer, Rechtssoziologie: Eine Einführung in die interdisziplinäre Rechtsforschung (An Introduction to Interdisciplinary Legal Research) 24 (Nomos 2011).

52 Kirk W. Junker, *Rhetoric Demonstrates the Foundation of Law as Techne, Not Empeiria*, *in* Philosophy, Art and Technology 99–114 (K. Boudouris (ed.), Ionia Publications 2011).

53 *Ibid.*

54 Plato, *Phaedrus*, 465a., *in* The Platonic Political Art: A Study of Critical Reason and Democracy (John R. Wallach (ed.), Penn State University Press 2001). Wallach states that this statement situates the knowledge of a *téchne* on an abstract rational plane that appears nowhere in other dialogues.

by nature political animals,[55] we can find an even broader assertion in his *Metaphysics*, however, which he opens with the fundamental premise that "[a]ll human beings by nature desire knowledge."[56] Latin translators of Aristotle's "*episteme*" used the term "*scientia*." Most of Europe received Aristotle through Latin translation before any of the ancient Greek texts were ever recovered.[57] For Aristotle, geometry would have been characterized as *episteme*, but mechanics was *techne*, an art or "practical knowledge."

Based upon these distinctions in the production of knowledge, generations encountered the natural world. With the Enlightenment, the mathematization of that encounter, and the greater presence of Latin in learned culture, English began to refer to those practices as natural science, not natural philosophy.[58] Natural science was further and further restricted to a mathematic encounter of nature, which in turn engendered specialization. This process enabled science to be seen as a specific, mathematized, and mechanical set of specialized practices, only applicable when called upon, rather than as the way in which the human encounters nature through knowledge. The more specialized science became, the less that nonspecialists could claim knowledge, and consequently, when science is called upon, it is generally, by Berger and Luckmann's man or woman "in the street," accepted or rejected based upon its authority (*ethos*), not its rationality (*logos*) or knowledge (*episteme*).

An important point that contributed to the specialization of the knowledge called "science" occurred during a meeting of the British Association for the Advancement of Science, in 1833, when William Whewell suggested the word "scientist" in English for the first time to describe those persons who were present, by analogy with "artist." "The term previously used was 'natural philosopher' or just 'philosopher.'"[59] But eras are not marked by clean breaks with the past. Physics degrees at Oxford and other top universities around the world are still referred to as degrees in natural philosophy. In addition, many cultures still award a doctor of philosophy (PhD) degree to graduates in mathematics, chemistry, or physics. Today, in various languages, things other than the *natural* sciences are nevertheless called "*Wissenschaft*," "*wetenschap*," "*science*," "*scienzia*," and so forth. English, the language of Newton and Bacon, seems to have gone the most extreme in limiting the usage of "science" to natural sciences, thereby implying, at least linguistically, that knowledge outside the material world is not possible. The specialization of science has evolved to the point in the English language where the usage of the word "science" means only the natural sciences,

55 Aristotle, Politics, 1253a1–18.

56 Aristotle, Metaphysics, 980a1.

57 Olaf Pedersen, *Tradition and Innovation, in* A History of the University in Europe 457 (Walter Rüegg, general editor, Vol. II, Universities in Early Modern Europe 1500–1800, Hilde de Ridder-Symoens, ed.).

58 Scott Montgomery, The Scientific Voice (The Guilford Press 1996).

59 *Dictionary of the History of Science* (W. F. Bynum et al. (eds.), "scientist," Princeton 1981) 381, citing W. Whewell, Quarterly Review 51 (1834) 59f.

and if we wish to include things that are social, as a matter of usage, we must then say "social sciences" and not just "sciences" alone.

It was not long after sociologists explained the social construction of reality that they turned their focus on science as a big part of that socially constructed reality.[60] At first, sociologists were only looking to explain narratives of those times when science goes wrong, by using a sociology of knowledge. Not long thereafter, however, they turned to explain the sociological factors influencing successful science as well, such as why one interpretation succeeds and another does not, due to social particulars.[61] The focus on unsuccessful science was featured in the USA, and the focus on successful science was featured in the UK, where David Bloor contrasted the two as the "weak" sociology of scientific knowledge and the "strong" programme in the sociology of scientific knowledge (SSK).[62] SSK is not a programme to attack science or to relativize knowledge, both of which are common superficial criticisms from persons on the outside who have not read the work.[63] Philosophers, too, began to turn attention towards social constructions in science,[64] as did linguists and lawyers.[65] Looking back on SSK, Sheila Jasanoff concluded her book *Science at the Bar* by saying:

> Finally, the rationales for public preference for specific types of legal procedures and, more generally, the relationship between legal process, scientific authority, and political culture deserve more systematic investigation. A few empirical studies carried out in the 1970s provided suggestive if inconclusive evidence that the level of public satisfaction with the legal process rises when the participants "control the process of evidence presentation themselves while a third party controls the result. . . . Constructivist analyses of science, technology, and the law could provide a framework for probing the cultural and institutional foundations for such preferences.[66]

60 Ludwik Fleck, a Polish physician and biologist, had already created foundational theory for such inquiry in 1935, but until his work was translated into English in 1979, it received little notice. Ludwik Fleck, Entstehung und Entwicklung einer wissenschaftlichen Tatsache. Einführung in die Lehre vom Denkstil und Denkkollektiv (Schwabe und Co., Verlagsbuchhandlung, Basel 1935); T. J. Trenn & R. K. Merton, Genesis and Development of a Scientific Fact (University of Chicago Press 1979).

61 See Harry M. Collins, *The Seven Sexes: A Study in the Sociology of a Phenomenon, or the Replication of Experiments in Physics*, 9 Sociology 205–224 (1975).

62 David Bloor, Knowledge and Social Imagery (Routledge 1976).

63 See, Barry Barnes & David Edge, Science in Context: Readings in the Sociology of Science (The Open University Press 1982).

64 Bruno Latour & Steve Woolgar, Laboratory Life: The Construction of Scientific Facts (Sage 1979); Bruno Latour, Science in Action: How to Follow Scientists and Engineers Through Society (Harvard University Press 1987).

65 Most notably, Sheila Jasanoff, who is both a linguist and a lawyer and who founded the Program on Science, Technology, and Society at Harvard University.

66 Sheila Jasanoff, Science on Trial, Law Science and Technology in America (Harvard University Press 1995).

Referring back to the preceding discussion of facts, it was noted that it can only be possible to have lay juries determine the facts of a dispute "if there had already been a widespread experience and familiarity with legal institutions and the language of fact and methods of fact determination"[67] in a given culture. It is thus a necessary cultural phenomenon of the entire culture to agree upon the ways in which facts are constructed in order to produce knowledge, or what Berger and Luckmann would call "intersubjectivity."[68] It cannot remain only the specialized knowledge of some. "If as 'agents' knowledge' we allow only verbal statements of the agents themselves – axioms, hypotheses and the like – then beyond any shadow of doubt we handicap our understanding: we count as knowledge very much less than the culture knows."[69]

Dialectically, "post-truth" seems to be needed as a word to help explain things like populism, power politics, and irrationality – practices that may not accept truth values or that may accept truth values but make invalid inferences from truths. If the latter, then the era may be more accurately termed an "irrational" era or a "post-rational" era. Furthermore, the prefix "post" suggests that we are past truth and it is not coming back. But even as we saw non-truth elements in law during the truth era, there are truth elements during the post-truth era. There are cyclical elements to history, and consequently, just as we have neo-classical, renaissance, neoliberal, neo-modern, and neo-colonialism, so too may we have neo-rationalism. Although we might not be post-truth (that is, forever past the time when truth held a particular meaning), something has changed, as evidenced by the fact that this label has stuck. "Post-truth" was *Oxford Dictionaries* Word of the Year for 2016, for example. Oxford explained that its method for choosing the word was a spike in the recorded frequency of use.[70] Usage, not definition, has elevated the label of "post-truth" to its status. Yet when the history is told of the present, sufficient evidence indicates that we will not have been post-truth (yet).

2 The Post-Truth Era?

To say that the era is "post-truth" does not mean there is not a role for truth in law, science, or elsewhere. It also does not mean that truth does not retain some of the functions and meanings that it has had before.

2.1 Marking a Generation

If we follow the same pattern for the construction of facts in the post-truth era, as I offered for the truth era, and we allow that the post-truth era identify

67 Shapiro, *supra* note 33, at 9.
68 Berger & Luckmann, *supra* note 50, at 23–25.
69 Barnes & Edge, *supra* note 63, at 6.
70 *Word of the Year 2016*, Oxford Languages <https://languages.qup.com/word-of-the-year/2016/>.

and label itself in reference to the truth era, then it makes sense to look at the post-truth era through a similar structure. First, then, we will consider post-truth and thereafter the facts construed in post-truth. But before we do, a few words need to be said about the notions of era and generation.

In addition to naming and delineating the ages, we name and delineate smaller periods in our lives by the name "generations." To the geologist, an *era* is shorter than an eon and longer than a period. But in modern common usage, an *era*, although of indeterminate length, is generally regarded as longer than a year and, instead of being marked by time, is marked by a distinctive character or events. There is an additional difference between the era and the generation. An "era" is an age, whereas a *generation* is the process of that which has been generated.

The events that mark the truth era could include the legal presumption of truth for any statement made by "gentlemen" in the courtroom or puffery in advertising to which a contracting party is not bound. In not so many years, the thinking that dominates the culture in the West has passed from the post–World War II "Baby Boomer" generation to Generation X to the Millennials, and now already the Millennials are somewhat passé. Young workers and university students are the next generation – the iGeneration.[71] Like the late sixteenth-century generation of Gutenberg's printing press,[72] the iGeneration is heavily characterized by communication technology – the entirety of their lives has taken place during the existence of the smartphone – hence part of the reason for being called the "iGeneration."[73]

When it comes to the relationship between ages and generations, there is a relationship between this generation and how this era will be named and characterized in history, especially with regard to how it thinks and makes decisions. We need to know this because, in 2019, the iGeneration already comprised 32 per cent of the world population.[74] These societal trends are not limited to the West. More than half of India's population is under 25 years old, that is, 600 million people, or nearly 8 per cent of the world's population. No country has more young people. "No matter how poorly placed they

71 See Twenge, *supra* note 8, at 7–8; Larry D. Rasen, *Welcome to the iGeneration! Here's How to Define the Generation Born into New Millennium Technology*, Psychology Today (27 March 2010) <hites.//www.psychologytaday.com/us/blog/rewlred-the-psychology-lechnology/2010 03/welcome-the-Igereration>.

72 See Sven Birkerts, The Gutenberg Elegies: The Fate of Reading in an Electronic Age (Faber and Faber 1994).

73 The birth year span of iGen is 1995 to approximately 2012, although "any generational cut-off is arbitrary." The same generation is often labelled "Generation Z," but since, when asked, the previous generation rejected being labelled "Generation Y," naming the next generation "Z" is not quite right. When asked, young persons have also expressed that they do not want to be named as successors to an older generation. Twenge, *supra* note 8, at 6.

74 Anne Gherine, *Gen-Z, Is About to Outnumber Millennials. Here's How That Will Affect the Business World, Inc.* (22 August 2018) <www. inc, convanne-gherini/gen-z-is-nboul-to-outnumber-millennials-heres-how-that-will-affect-business-world. Html>.

find themselves now," writes Delhi journalist Snigdha Poonam, "they make up the world's largest ever cohort of like-minded young people, and they see absolutely no reason why the world shouldn't run by their rules." The effect, Poonam says, will be to "change our world in ways we can't yet imagine." "This new generation is motivated: it combines the cultural values of the traditional Asian family with the life goals of the American teenager."[75] This connection of East to West should sound alarm bells in even the simplest study of resource distribution for the basic reason that the Earth cannot sustain the resource consumption of the US teenager if extended to other populations. Back in 1970, Paul Ehrlich made a very fitting comparison, based upon Indian, Indonesian, and US consumption rates at that time:

> The birth of every American child is fifty times more of a disaster than the birth of an Indian child. If you take consumption of steel as a measure of overall consumption, you find that the birth of an American child is 300 times more of a disaster for the world than the birth of an Indonesian child.[76]

Thus, we would be wise to focus our basic question on the associations made by the iGeneration in the East and in the West to develop a meaning for the concepts of truth and the process of rational inference if we want to address the role of science in law. The point was made earlier that eras are marked not by time but by characteristics and events. The characteristic that marks the East, represented by the newest Indian generation (Indians are 17.7 per cent of the world population and soon to be the majority of the world population)[77] and the West, represented by the newest US generation, is technology. The fact that 600 million Indians are heavily influenced by media representations of US teenage culture may well yield a greater impact on the Earth's resources than the US teenagers themselves. Thus, while the US resource-intensive lifestyle is unsustainable, that unsustainability is multiplied many times over by exporting that lifestyle through social media. The iPhone is not just a medium; it is the defining characteristic of the generation.

The iGeneration occupies not only the role of university students and young working adults but also the role of the dominant world demographic age group; how the iGeneration thinks is the way of the future, and that includes how the

75 Jan Jack, *India Has 600 Million Young People – and They're Set to Change Our World*, The Guardian (13 January 2018) *in* book review of *Dreamers: How Young Indians Are Changing the World* <www.theguardian.com/commentistree/2018/jan/13/india-600-million-young-people-world-citles-Internet>.

76 Paul Ehrlich, *Listener*, 215 (30 August 1970).

77 To put this in perspective, the total number of humans currently living was estimated to have reached 7.3 billion people as of March 2020 and 7.6 billion as of July 2020. It took over 200,000 years of human history for the world's population to reach 1 billion, and only 200 years more to reach 7 billion.

iGeneration thinks about law, science, and what they will count as knowledge. We cannot begin to talk about the specific facts or ideas, such as the precautionary principle, free speech, or biotechnology, if, unlike the English population, who supplied juries with any number of fungible jurors, the majority of the population has a different basic understanding of what constitutes truth or facts and a different relationship towards rationality. And research shows that the iGeneration *does* have such a different basic understanding. Psychologist Jean Twenge has been observing statistical trends from four nationally representative surveys of 11 million Americans since the 1960s. She reports that:

> Around 2012, I started seeing a large, abrupt shift in teens' behaviors and emotional states. All of a sudden, the line graphs look like steep mountains (from which) rapid drop-offs erased the gains of decades in just a few years (bringing) traits to all-time highs. In all of my analyses of generational data – some of it going back to 1930 – I had never seen anything like it. . . . A pattern emerged: many of the large changes began around 2011 or 2012. That was exactly when the majority of Americans began to own smartphones.[78]

In reflecting upon this observation, it is important to note that Twenge is a scientist and is in no way an enemy of social media or communication technology – but she maintains that they have created a new cognitive order. The rapid drop-offs that Twenge references are the loss of teenagers who read books and magazines for a significant percentage of their time and, importantly, a statistically corresponding drop in standardized university entrance examination scores. Also corresponding, but in inverse proportion, are the number of hours of social media used daily by the same teenagers.

Twenge confirmed her statistically prompted hypothesis of a causal link between academic decline and smartphone use by conducting personal interviews. During interviews with a nationally representative sample of the subject age group, Twenge found that those interviewed expressed preferences for social media over face-to-face time with friends. For example, a particular Texas high school student said, "I would rather be on my phone in my room [alone] watching Netflix than spend time with my family. . . . I think [my generation] likes our phones more than we like actual people."[79] From her statistical observations, hypothesis, and confirmation through interviews, Twenge concluded that when it comes to the iGeneration, "[t]he life experiences they have every day are radically different from those of their [truth era] predecessors,"[80] including the facts that they are slower to mature,[81] have overwhelming inter-

78 Twenge, *supra* note 8, at 4.
79 *Id.* at 2.
80 *Id.* at 5.
81 *Id.* at 41.

net use time, show a marked decline in time of person-to-person social interaction, have a sharp rise in mental health issues,[82] have a sharp rise in their interest in safety, demonstrate a decline in civic involvement, and form political views independent of party. At the same time, these iGeneration members are more tolerant of sex, relationships, religion, and issues of equality.

If we couple Berger and Luckmann's notion of the construction of facts with Twenge's overwhelming evidence of a change in the conditioning upon which facts are constructed, we arrive at the following distinction in non-vetted situations. In Berger and Luckman's original formulation, we might have a situation, for example, where husband notices that wife always wears the same blue T-shirt on Saturdays. "There she goes again," he says to the children. The children see Mom wearing the blue T-shirt and objectify the fact named by Dad – there she goes again wearing the same blue T-shirt on Saturday. Then Mom stops wearing the same blue T-shirt on Saturdays. Husband and children no longer say, "There she goes again wearing that same blue T-shirt on Saturday," and with that, the commonplace belief based upon true premises and observed fact comes to an end. By comparison, in the social construction of a post-truth era's reality, husband notices that wife always wears the same blue T-shirt on Saturday. He tweets, "My wife always wears the same blue T-shirt on Saturdays." Two hundred people read the tweet and believe that she always wears her blue T-shirt on Saturdays. Then Mom stops wearing the blue T-shirt on Saturdays. Husband and children no longer say it, but 200 other people continue to do so, and this gets reposted exponentially without review, retractions of errors, vetting for truth, or even knowing Mom. Were this limited to the clothing that a family member wears, there would likely be little harm done. But this is the method through which many people claim to get their true premises or even their factual conclusions for consumer behaviour, voting, and a sense of what is real. In other words, when the social construction of realities was limited to real-time communication at arm's length, the creators could change the realities with the same persons present. As soon as communication occurs beyond arm's length, we *cannot* take back what was said even when we *want* to take it back.

Sociologists explain that once we construct social realities, they become objectified and reified after they leave the control of the creator. In short, we

82 While Twenge's work focuses on the USA, she notes that "[r]esearchers around the world are documenting many of the same trends, with new studies constantly appearing." (12). "[D]epression and anxiety [in the USA] have risen at an unprecedented rate, and . . . twice as many young teens commit suicide as a few years ago" (293). For example, *The National Mental Health Survey of India, 2015–16* indicates that mental health in India is also trending in this direction. Ministry of Health and Family Welfare, Government of India, *The National Mental Health Survey of India, 2015–16* (2016) <www.nimhans.ac.in/sites/default/filesul97/NMHSReportl.pdf>. More specifically, in the *Indian Journal of Psychiatry*, it has been proposed that developmental loneliness be re-characterized as a disease and not only a symptom. The *Journal* reports that "[e]very one of us has a need to be related to others. This need is essential for our development as a human being. . . . By the same token, developmental deficits . . . often lead to developmental loneliness."

cannot take them back even if we want to. That means, when tweets can reach a million persons instantaneously, no matter how untrue their premises or invalid their conclusions, an immediate fact-check cannot correct public perceptions. In addition, as Berger and Luckmann point out, it is precisely because subjective meanings can go beyond the persons creating them that they can achieve the sense of objective facticity.[83] Mass campaigns practicing non-truth in the past were attacked for their non-truth character – now non-truth is the standard, the norm by which other practices are judged. It is the ubiquity of the phenomenon, not its existence, that enables a post-truth era. It is now a custom.

The UN's Sustainable Development Goal 3.4 is that "[b]y 2030, we reduce by one-third pre-mature mortality from non-communicable diseases through prevention and treatment and promote mental health and well-being." Yet reports from the United States, Europe, and India indicate that mental health is trending in the opposite direction at the same time as we witness the rise of the "post-truth era." The World Health Organization 2017 Report on India indicates a disturbing increase in social anxiety disorder (SAD). SAD manifests its onset most commonly in adolescence.[84] When coupled with the corroborating evidence of Twenge's interviews in the United States, one is struck by the fact that the most common manifestation of SAD is *avoiding speaking with others.*

In the *Sunday Express* of India, Nithan Shah, professor of new media and co-founder of the Centre for Internet and Society in Bengaluru, in reaction to a post regarding a 2019 Pakistani–Indian armed border conflict, wrote:

> I had to do a double take when the post flashed on my feed. It was a post filled with armchair bloodlust, calling for war and justifying it through emotional bullshit. . . . The post came from an unexpected source. It was shared in a group that generally has *rational*, fairly academic and measured discussions about politics and *everyday life*.[85]

(Recall that the sociologists Berger and Luckmann characterize reality as *everyday* reality.) Shah writes further:

> When we talk of information overload and the constant engagement with social media streams, we often talk about people doing strange things that they would not do in real life – if there is a real life that can

83 Berger & Luckmann, *supra* note 50, at 89.

84 The same World Health Organization 2017 Report on India states that SAD and depression are the "two diagnostic categories that constitute common mental disorders; . . . The burden of depression in India is high. The burden of depression, in terms of disability adjusted life years, increased in India by 67% between 1990 and 2013." That same report, however, concludes by stating that "depression is largely preventable and treatable."

85 Nishant Shah, *Digital Native: How an Information Overload Affects What You Forward*, Centre for Internet & Society <cis-indin.org/raw/nishant-shah-march-10-2019-indian-express-digital-native-how-an-information-overload-affects-what-you-forward>. (Emphasis added.)

> be separated from the digital domains. . . . Researchers have pointed out that one of the most dramatic effects of information saturation is the suspension of emotional guards. Information overload sometimes leaves the subject in an emotional state that resembles victims of mental abuse. It leads to such a state of stress and tension, that many people just give in to the onslaught of information and follow the patterns rather than resisting or questioning it. . . . This emotional state can be easily controlled – towards making political choices, buying things we don't want, towards attacking people, communities, countries.[86]

2.2 *From Truth to Truthiness*

Truthiness practices are limited neither to politics nor to intentional non-truth. Once made commonplace, non-truth practices become the repeated habits and customs that replace the customs and habits of the truth era. And through these other uses, customs, and habits, non-truth evolves into other habits, which still nevertheless establish their identities in their relationships to truth, even if those relationships feature rejecting the notions that maintain the truth era. Evidence that post-truth understands itself dialectically in relation to truth is exhibited by the term "truthiness." The American Dialect Society (ADS) named "truthiness" its sixteenth annual word of the year for 2005, explaining that "truthiness refers to the quality of preferring concepts or facts one *wishes or believes to be true*, rather than concepts or *facts known to be true*."[87] As political satirist Stephen Colbert put it: "I don't trust books. They're all *fact*, no heart."[88] In these simple statements, much has been said. Characterizing the truth era, Berger and Luckmann said that reality is reality precisely because one cannot make it go away by wishing it to be otherwise. In contrast to this wish are what the ADS called "facts known to be true." Knowing – the production of knowledge – in the truth era, was the process of inferring valid conclusions from true premises. Truth is not established by trust relationships alone. Colbert's critique juxtaposes trust with knowing. Returning to the truth era structure of establishing facts through rationality and establishing rationality from truth, to understand the post-truth era, we would need to understand what, if not rationality, one can establish from truthiness. Could truthiness, a trust relationship of wishes, thus provide a post-truth basis from which one could claim to establish facts, after observing particulars of events? Or is it just the same as the Athenians' evidence-free opinions against which Socrates established the method of examination still used in courts today?

86 *Ibid.*
87 American Dialect Society, *Truthiness Voted 2005 Word of the Year* (6 January 2006) <www.americandialect.org/truthiness_voted_2005_word_of_the_year> (Emphasis added.)
88 *Ibid.* (Emphasis added.)

In 2006, the *Merriam-Webster Dictionary* also selected "truthiness" as its Word of the Year, based on a reader poll. "We're at a point where what constitutes truth is a question on a lot of people's minds, and truth has become up for grabs,"[89] said *Merriam-Webster* president John Morse. And in 2009, the BBC Online magazine asked its readers to nominate things to include on a poster to represent important events in the first decade of the new century. A panel of five independent experts selected from the readers' submissions. The readers submitted the word "truthiness," the panel agreed, and "truthiness" appeared in the poster.[90] This surface foam is carried along by an audience conditioned to accept it, no matter how preposterous it might sound in isolated emphasis.

We have changed from practices that express the use of "truth" as accuracy, based upon non-contradiction, to celebrating practices that are contrary to that practice. Truthiness is one such practice. Truth-era persons hid their non-truthful behaviour and felt guilt, shame, or fear of social or legal retribution. Post-truth persons celebrate their ability to exercise belief in evidence-free opinions. Truth-era persons shamed others with the phrase "might does not make right." Post-truth persons defend their might or wealth as making right – "we create our own reality," said the post-truth manifesto (in section 2.5, *infra.*). That defence has social impact. When confronted with disparate distribution of wealth, truth-era people revolted. In the post-truth era of 2020, when people are confronted with a situation in which 2,153 billionaires owned 60 per cent of the world's wealth,[91] instead of revolting, they ask how they can join the 2,153.

At consequence is society's relationship to the establishment and maintenance of the process of distinguishing truth from opinion and the value placed upon actions that are based upon facts that are established by truths, after that distinction is made. Confirmation bias – the practice of consciously or unconsciously seeking out information that confirms one's already held views – adds repetitiveness (rather than evidence) to opinions, therefore making them appear to be that much more believable.[92] The phrase "fake news" has been made commonplace not only in English language vocabulary but also in non-English-speaking cultures as well.[93] The usage works as follows: When the President of the United States says "fake news," the audience is to

89 Adam Gorlick, *Colbert's 'Truthiness' Pronounced Word of the Year* (8 December 2006) AP/Houston Chronicle.

90 *A Portrait of the Decade*, BBC News (14 December 2009) <news.bbc.co,uk/2/hi/uk_news/magazine/8406898.stm>.

91 Oxfam, *World's Billionaires Have More Wealth than 4.6 Billion People* (20 January 2020) <www.oxfam.org/en/press-releases/worlds-billionalres-have-more-wealth-46-billion-people>.

92 David Lazer et al., *The Science of Fake News*, 359(6380) Science 1094–1096 (2018).

93 All Languages Tuition and Translating, *'Fake News' So Ubiquitous that Germans Use the Anglicised Term Instead of the German Translation* <http://alllanguages.co.uk/2017/02/28/fake-news-anglicised-german-translation/>.

understand that a lie has been told about him in the media, but essentially he means to assert that he has the power to disagree with not only validly inferred facts but also to deny simple truth-as-accuracy premises, beginning on the first day of his presidency regarding something that is the perfect example of truth-as-accuracy: counting the number of persons who were present at his inauguration ceremony. "Fake news" is another practice that is contrary to the truth-era notion of truth-as-accuracy. "Fake news" appears to be a characterization of something as untrue but, as used by populist politicians, means, in truth-era terms, "I have an opinion that differs from the facts established by rational inference from truth." One should note that all this attention to "truthiness" preceded the rash of populist political leaders and the popularity of their term "fake news." In other words, "truthiness" contributed both to making populism possible and making aspersions of "fake news" popular, not the other way around.[94]

2.3 Rationality amid Crisis

Returning to our topic of the post-truth era, specifically to discuss the "how?" and, if possible, the "why?" of the turning away from the truth era, we are faced with asking why potentially rational animals would not practice science to implement social change in time of crisis. We demonstrated that we can exercise rationality when COVID-19 was deemed a crisis worldwide and most cultures willingly responded in ways that disrupted normal lives.[95] As of this writing, COVID-19 caused nearly seven million deaths worldwide. Yet UN Secretary-General Guterres has characterized climate change as a crisis, and we have done nearly nothing, despite the fact that the WHO predicts that climate change will kill 3.5 million people *every year* by the end of the century,[96] thereby demonstrating that we do not always exercise rationality. Being potentially rational means that we are not always rational. At present, we learn through natural sciences, however, that when we fail to be rational, we endanger our own lives and, even more so, those of future generations.

If we then ask why we, as potentially rational animals, would not practice science to implement social change to save ourselves, changes that could occur

94 See Kirk W. Junker, *News Is Not Always Truth and Truth Is Not Always News*, Bonner Rechtsjournal (special edition 01–2017) 18–24 (2017).

95 It must be noted, however, that even with the COVID-19 virus pandemic, there are those who claim either that the science is a "hoax" or that the economy is more important than life itself, as when the lieutenant governor of Texas, Dan Patrick, called for social distancing measures to be eased in Texas because "[t]here are more important things than living." The Independent (22 April 2020) <www.independent.co.uk/news/world/americas/coronavirus-texas-dan-patrick-fox>.

96 Vulnerable Group of Twenty, *New Health Data Shows Unabated Climate Change Will Cause 3.4 Million Deaths Per Year by Century End* (12 November 2022) <https://www.v-20.org/new-health-data-shows-unabated-climate-change-will-cause-3.4-million-deaths-per-year-by-century-end>.

through the establishment and implementation of legal norms, we hear excuses of inconvenience, economic expediency, the failure to perceive personal impact, or information overload, none of which is commensurate with, or proportional to, the measurable and demonstrated threat, *if* rationality were a matter of choice. But as Aristotle pointed out, rationality is a pattern, habit, or custom, not a conscious choice. Thus, legislation that says "use science" has two serious weaknesses. First, science is not a commodity to be taken from the shelf and "used" instrumentally. Second, our potential to be rational does not make the use of science inevitably obvious. How and when are the patterns of habit formed? Many patterns are formed as humans mature. What patterns do psychologists observe in the iGeneration? The answer is that many iGeneration patterns are formed by social media enabled through communication technology. Long before we called ourselves post-modern, let alone post-truth, Marshall McLuhan pointed out that, contrary to the electrical engineer's sender-message-receiver model of communication, the medium *is* the message.[97]

2.4 *What, Indeed, Is the Matter with Fact(s)?*

> "Let us assay our plot; which, if it speed,
> Is wicked meaning in a lawful deed
> And lawful meaning in a lawful act,
> Where both not sin, and yet a sinful fact.
> But let's about it."[98]

Perhaps we are neither post-truth nor post-rational, but our construction of patterns that enable rationality has changed, and thus, the proportion of time when we are rational by habit, compared with the proportion of time when we are not rational, has shifted. Patterns of rationality in law and regulation may contribute to scientific practices in a post-truth era. In basic logic, "reasoning is a special kind of thinking in which inference takes place, in which conclusions are drawn from premises."[99] If the premises can be true, the conclusions are valid.[100] If the premises include contingencies, they nevertheless establish facts. Valid conclusions, reasoned from true facts, were in turn constructed from

97 Marshall McLuhan, Understanding Media (Mentor Books 1964).

98 William Shakespeare, All's Well That Ends Well (Helena's conclusion to Act III, Scene vii, 1623).

99 Copi, *supra* note 5, at 5.

100 Reasoning in this sense relies both upon the notion that the premise can be proven true or false, and that the evidence from which the premise can produce facts is observable. As such, the phrase "emotional reasoning" is a non-sequitur. Emotions remain within the realm of persuasion by pathos, not logos. The notion of making choices based upon personal feelings is regarded by lawyer Greg Lukianoff and psychologists Jonathan Haidt and Jean Twenge as a cause of psychological problems among the iGeneration: "Emotional reasoning is now accepted as evidence." Twenge, *supra* note 8, at 252 citing Greg Lukianoff & Jonathan Haldt, *The Coddling of the American Mind*, The Atlantic (September 2015).

truth in its simplest mode – accuracy.[101] An expression of disbelief based upon opinion is a non-response to a valid inference.[102] When Donald Trump encountered the valid conclusions of climate change, he offered only an irrelevant response – "I don't believe it."[103] One can refute the inference with superior evidence that leads to the construction of other facts, but from the perspective of the truth era, one could not have countered facts with evidence-free opinion. Seen through the values of the truth era, one can only say that that response is an attempt to shift the focus from "you have provided truths from which one may validly infer facts" to "there are no truths, so this is a matter of evidence-free opinion only." But there are facts (at least these count as facts in the truth era): "Under the current circumstances, it is a fact that dangerous climate change will occur within several decades. [Therefore,] a worldwide reduction of emissions is necessary in order to prevent irreversible climate change."[104]

As noted earlier by Barbara Shapiro, in order for the lay jury to be able to determine particular facts in a particular dispute, the society needs to have enough persons to constitute juries that have the same notion of how any fact is determined. And while that is particularly true in a court of law, it is more commonly obvious in politics. When campaigning for Brexit, then UK foreign minister Boris Johnson advertised on the side of a red London bus: "We send the EU £350m a week: let's fund our NHS instead." But then afterwards, when the UK Statistics Authority challenged this claim, it was found that by "no honest calculation can Britain's net payment to the European Union be estimated as £350m a week. Nigel Farage admits it. So does the *Daily Mail*. Even Johnson admits it."[105] And by the time they admitted it, the damage was done. Like the story earlier regarding Mom's blue T-shirt – once

101 Truth can be moral, as when the Christian Bible says that Jesus said, "I am the way, the truth and the life," or a-moral, as in the scientific sense that truth is accuracy.

102 Inference is a process by which one proposition is arrived at and affirmed on the basis of one or more other propositions as accepted as the starling point of the process. Copi, *supra* note 5, at 6. See also Trevor Melia, *The Rhetorical Functions of Presuppositions from the Point of View of the Sociology of Knowledge* (1965) Unpublished doctoral thesis on file with the author.

103 In December of 2015, during the same annual UN Conference of the Parties (COP) of the Framework Convention on Climate Change, the UN called for a special report. In response, 91 authors from 40 different countries produced a report of the IPCC which contains over 6,000 scientific references. Il is called "A Special Report on Global Warming of 1.5°C (SR 15)" and was published by IPCC on October 8, 2018. At the United Nations' 48th meeting session of the IPCC, the IPCC fulfilled the request by the UN to "deliver the authoritative, scientific guide for governments" to deal with climate change. Nevertheless, when asked what action the United States would take in response to this scientific report, US president Donald Trump answered, "I don't believe it." "I don't believe it – Trump on climate report" BBC World News (26 November 2018) <https:/fwwow.bbc.com/news/av/world-us-canada-46324405/-don-t-believe-il-trump-on-climate-report>.

104 *Urgenda Foundation v. State of the Netherlands*, Supreme Court of the Netherlands Decision 4.1–4.8 (2019).

105 John Litchfield, *Boris Johnson's £350m Claim Is Devious and Bogus. Here's Why*, The Guardian (18 September 2017) <www.theguardian.com/commentisfree/2017/sep/48/boris-johnson-350-million-claim-bogus-foreign-secretary>.

the statement is released, repeated, and retweeted, fact-checking and correction will not change opinions that were not formed on true premises from the beginning. Attitudes had been formed, based on this truthiness, and votes were aligned accordingly. Recalling the characteristics of the truth era, we are all familiar with the oath for witnesses in the court of law from popular culture in which one must "swear to tell the *truth*, the *whole truth* and *nothing but the truth*."[106] These three terms sound like variations on a theme when a film quickly includes the oath as an empty ceremonial speech while the viewing audience eagerly waits to get to the facts of the witness's testimony. But each of the three elements is a different aspect of what we mean by the word "truth." The first part asks the witness: Insofar as you can tell the difference between truth and not truth and will make a choice between the two, do you promise to choose truth? That is truth understood as Aristotle's notion of agreement or accuracy of description. But when we get to the second and third iterations, we have moved far beyond descriptive accuracy to senses of appropriateness and context.

When Boris Johnson put the figure of 350 million pounds on the side of the bus, the Statistics Authority said it failed the test of truth as descriptive accuracy, but even if it had been descriptively accurate, what more needs to be said to tell the *whole* truth (on the side of a bus)? And as to the third iteration – "nothing but the truth" – what other statements did he or his followers assert that were untrue in order to give the simple bus-sized tweet more context? This media-reported public indifference to the principle of non-contradiction can lead to characterizing the era as post-truth. In such a society, one cannot use a rational process from true premises to infer valid conclusions. Many in the UK, for example, used truthiness, resonating with other evidence-free allegations, to act. Thus, in 2016, these same persons in the UK voted by popular referendum to leave the European Union (EU), many of whom (said those who so voted) for economic reasons. Yet the economic loss caused by leaving the EU has been conservatively estimated to cost the UK 3.9 per cent of gross domestic product (GDP), and it could be as high as 9.3 per cent of GDP. Nevertheless, buoyed by the truthiness that Brexit was still economically a good idea, Conservative Party members voted Johnson to be their new party leader in July 2019, despite his having admitted that his claim that the EU cost the UK 350 million pounds per week was false.[107]

But law is not politics, and in law, at a basic level of rational processes from which valid inferences can be made from true premises, how might the

106 Cf., Shapin, *supra* note 34. In the Apology, Socrates also maintains that "from me, you will hear the whole truth" and "I assure you that I am going to tell you the whole truth." Plato, *supra* note 14, at 17b and 20d.

107 Boris Johnson, *My Vision for a Bold, Thriving Britain Enabled by Brexit*, The Telegraph (15 September2017)<https://telegraph.co.uk/politics/0/boris-johnson-vision-for-brexit-bold-thriving-britain/>.

post-truth era consider the courtroom trial? When former Trump campaign chairman Paul Manafort was sentenced to seven and a half years in prison on federal charges of fraud, among other things,

> U.S. District Judge Amy Berman Jackson brushed aside Manafort's pleas for leniency and rebuked him for misleading the U.S. government about his lucrative foreign lobbying work and for encouraging witnesses to lie on his behalf.[108] . . . "It is hard to overstate the number of lies and the amount of fraud and the extraordinary amount of money involved" in the crimes, Jackson told Manafort. Judge Jackson made clear the case against Manafort had nothing to do with Russian election interference and she scolded Manafort's lawyers for asserting that their client was charged only because prosecutors couldn't get him on crimes related to potential collusion with the Trump campaign. She said they were evidence that Manafort had spent a considerable portion of his career "gaming the system." He undermined the American political process by concealing from the public and Congress that he was working on behalf of Ukraine – and earning millions of dollars that he never reported to the IRS, she said. "Court is one of those places where facts still matter," she said.[109]

Note that while Karl Rove's career gaming the system, as described next, freely continued in the political sphere, when Manafort's gaming the system went to court, the judge relied upon the truth-era structure of facts to decide.

2.5 *Creating Other New Realities*

When looking for evidence of change in our relation to truth and the construction of reality, we may well begin with politics. In the October 2004 issue of the *New York Times Magazine*, a journalist reported the following exchange between him and an "unnamed [US President G. W. Bush] administration official." During a reception, the unnamed official said to the journalist that "guys like [the journalist] are in what [they] [the Bush administration] call the reality-based community," which he defined as people who "believe that solutions emerge from your judicious study of discernible reality."[110] Mistaking where the unnamed official was headed with his provocation, the journalist nodded and said something about enlightenment principles and empiricism.

108 Eric Tucker & Chad Bay, *Court Is Where the Facts Still Matter*, Associated Press (14 March 2015).

109 *Ibid.*

110 Ron Suskind, *Faith, Certainty and the Presidency of George W. Bush*, The New York Times (17 October 2004) <www.nytimes com/2004/10/17 magazine/faith-certainty-and-the-presidency-of-george- w.bush.html>.

The unnamed official cut the journalist off: "That's not the way the world really works anymore." He continued:

> We're an empire now, and when we act, we create our own reality. And while you're studying that reality – judiciously, as you will – we'll act again, creating other new realities, which you can study too, and that's how things will sort out. We're history's actors . . . and you, all of you, will be left to just study what we do.[111]

This encounter between a representative of the national executive administration and a reporter was a clear display that not only had something changed in this relationship between government and news media but also that something had changed in the government's attitude towards established truths, from which valid conclusions can be inferred. What had changed with this encounter was *not* that a government for the first time was inventing news or facts. *Nor* of course was it the first time that a government did so with the intention to represent as true that which was untrue. What *was* new was that the government would admit rejecting the truth-era processes and openly celebrate its own creation of reality. If one is looking for a "post-truth manifesto," this lecture to the reporter was it. Lying to the fourth estate was openly and cynically boasted about in order to be celebrated by one's tribal support group. From such an event, the civil society that intersubjectively creates realities was invited to normalize the celebration of lying.

Era-defining events like these are some of the clear steps towards post-truth that can be found. It is now regarded as clear that the administration official was Karl Rove, the unelected senior adviser and deputy chief of staff for George W. Bush, the president of the United States, whose administration fabricated the notion that Iraq maintained "weapons of mass destruction" as a pretext for invading Iraq in 2003. And if the event was the post-truth manifesto, Rove is the manifesto's author. Rove had practiced for this event since at least 1970, when he used a fake identity card to gain access to the Chicago campaign headquarters of Alan Dixon, a politician running for the office of state treasurer in Illinois for the party opposed to Rove's own party. Rove stole 1,000 sheets of Dixon campaign stationery and began using it to circulate forged "invitations" in Chicago's red-light district and soup kitchens, promising "free beer, free food, girls and a good time for nothing" for all comers at Dixon's headquarters. In 1972, Rove quit university studies to become an active participant in the infamous Richard Nixon presidential campaign that included the burglary of the Democratic National Committee headquarters in the Watergate office building.[112] This resulted in an FBI investigation of

111 *Ibid.*

112 Nicholas Lehman, *The Controller Karl Rove Is Working to Get George Bush Re-elected, But Has Bigger Plans*, The New Yorker (12 May 2003).

Rove. Then, in 1973, when he campaigned to be the National Chairman of the College Republicans, Rove produced a version of the College Republican Constitution that differed from the one used by others, including his opponent. He then challenged the credentials of others who followed the standard organizational constitution. There is no doubt that this senior adviser to the US president was a harbinger of post-truth, if not anti-truth, and he was rewarded by his circle of society for those practices.

2.6 *Science Revisited*

One of the most frequent and damaging consequences of treating science as only a specialist instrument is the misguided belief that scientific knowledge must provide certainty, and when it does not provide certainty, we are free to insert any belief or opinion we have without regard for evidence or the process of valid inference. It is difficult to say where and how this belief started. Some research says it is in schoolbooks.[113] Neurobiologist Steven Rose reports that even when students come to university with such a belief, it is usually dispelled the first time they must write and conduct their own experiment.[114] It might also be an idea planted to enable a political agenda. In a past era, science would have needed to assert its promises and products so as to be accepted as an alternative to religious or political authority. But science has its own legitimacy now, so we must ask who demands certainty and why.

2.6.1 *Integration of Science in Law*

If the misguided expectation of certainty is a problem, some solutions can be found in socially constructed legal tools, such as assigning the burden of proof to one party or another in a dispute, or setting a presumption in favour of, or against, a party in dispute. In the practices of law, laws can be certain, but facts are always contingent. To say that one disagrees with a fact does not make sense. One can say that premise is false because it contains contradictions. Or one could say that the fact concluded cannot be rationally inferred from the premises. Science may demand more evidence to increase its confidence in the fact to be inferred, but law must work within the confines of time that a sense of justice demands. A person cannot sit in prison awaiting trial for years because the prosecution believes that more research is necessary. As the maxim says, "justice delayed is justice denied." Therefore, tools are needed to enable law to proceed without the benefit of an excessively long (and complete) evidence-gathering process. In resolving disputes, law, therefore, makes frequent use of presumptions that have not been, or that cannot be demonstrated to be, true when a decision must nevertheless be made.

113 Noel Cunningham, *Review of Certainty in Irish Science School Curriculum* (Dublin City University 1998). Unpublished manuscript on file with author.

114 Interview by author of Steven Rose (Open University 1996). Notes on file with author.

Historically, when scientists have insufficient evidence upon which to form true premises, they will claim that "more research is necessary." But in law, when a person's life, liberty, or property are at issue, a fair decision must be taken even when more research would be helpful to produce true premises from which to infer valid conclusions. Science can proceed the same way. To say that no action is possible because there is insufficient evidence to form true premises is to ignore the processes that law uses all the time. Uncertainty in the truth of the premises does not mean that no valid facts can be inferred. Uncertainty simply means we must set the burden of proof before we have complete evidence or use presumptions before we have complete evidence.

Consequently, for the phrase "uncertainty in science" to sound like doubt and therefore portend inaction, an audience is required who is conditioned by expectations, just like the jury seasoned to the "language of fact," as described earlier by Barbara Shapiro. While it is possible that one might be distrustful of science itself or of government that uses facts to make and enforce law, a more likely motivation than distrust is the motivation of calls to action or inaction, based upon religion, upon short-term instrumental rationality to obtain strength over enemies,[115] or upon economic advantages.[116]

Before a dispute can be adjudicated, a practical process of presenting and considering the propositions of the parties must be established. Who goes first? The party that wants the state to do something – put a person in prison, levy a fine, force performance of a contract, or pay damages for a crushed automobile – must go first. In the case of private activities that may harm the public, such as polluting air or water, we force the would-be polluter to carry the burden of proof in obtaining a permit to emit solids, liquids, gases, radiation, etc. that will harm the public. Certainty is not a determining factor – a judgement on the permit application must be made. Arguments alleging that laissez-faire economic practices should continue until the state has scientific certainty to prove environmental harm to the public are intentional distractions by the polluters to buy themselves more time. Waiting for certainty is neither part of legal practice nor part of science.

As a concept for the production of knowledge, the burden of proof does even more. The common image of the goddess *Dikē* holding the scales of justice is misleading. Using the tool of burden of proof, if the moving party who carries the burden of proof fails to carry the burden, when he, she, or it finishes presenting his or her evidence, the judge may rule without hearing a word from the defendant. That is a different knowledge production concept than just weighing the evidence. That leads us to the second legal tool, the presumption.

115 In the *Gorgias* dialogue, Polus, the interlocutor of Socrates, insists that the evil man is happier than the good man if the evil man can obtain his desires and exercise his powers and not be caught. Plato, Gorgias, 473–475.

116 Donald A. Brown, American Heat: Ethical Problems with the United States' Response to Global Warming (Rowman & Littlefield 2002).

Presumptions are also socially determined. One presumption in some systems is that the person accused of a crime is presumed to be innocent until and unless the state can prove him or her to be guilty. That is the reason that the criminal defendant need not present evidence in some systems after the state has presented its evidence. It may also be presumed that children do not have the capacity to conclude contracts but adults do have the capacity. Such presumptions could be overcome, but there would be an additional legal tool needed, from which to remove the presumption. Thus, presumptions can often be determinative of the outcomes of the dispute.

There is one final general point to be made before turning our attention to specific cases. At this moment in history, one often hears or sees the word "anti-science." Words are invented because there is a social need. What could possibly be the need for such a word? Persons against science or who "don't believe in science" were dismissed as Luddites in the truth era. In the post-truth era, with the moniker "anti-science," such persons are treated as having a legitimate voice in public debate and permitted to flaunt untrue premises, irrational inferences, and invalid conclusions. Like populism and fake news, anti-science is enabled by truthiness.

2.6.2 *Specific Cases of Science in the Law*

The following cases from several jurisdictions are not meant to be conclusive on the law itself but to illustrate some examples of science being integrated into the law. In doing so, the cases demonstrate that the post-truth era appears not to have yet reached the courtroom. It remains to be seen whether this means law simply needs to catch up with the post-truth era or if it means the institutions and practices of law will force the post-truth era to continue to characterize itself in terms of truth, even if as *post*-truth. The famous 1964 defamation case in the United States, *New York Times v. Sullivan*, sets the stage for the role of truth in the production of legal knowledge. There, the US Supreme Court stated: "There is no constitutional value in false statements of fact. Neither the intentional lie nor the careless error materially advances society's interest in 'uninhibited, robust, and wide-open' debate on public issues."[117]

Functioning as a working laboratory for testing social fact, law historically maintained its ability to distinguish facts that true premises rationally infer from opinion that has no rational basis. Even within that distinction, however, there have been conceptual shifts as to what constitutes evidence in litigation. Of particular interest are the rules that accept scientific evidence in litigation, such as from the *Frye* case standard and the *Daubert* case standard in the United States. The original position was announced in the 1923 case of *State v. Frye*, in which lawyers were faced with the question of

117 *New York Times Co. v. Sullivan*, 376 U. S. at 270 (1964).

what it means to "know" something in law. The First World War had just ended, and as is so often the case in the aftermath of war, technology shifted to the forefront of cultural attention both because ideological topics were worn out and because the extra emphasis on technological research during wartime inevitably produces invention. Thus, rather than infer facts from the rational testimony of a witness under oath, parties wanted to increase their confidence in the knowledge produced by using a new and simple piece of technology that measured a person's systolic blood pressure and heart rate while answering questions.[118] The question for the court was whether the results of such a test should be accepted as scientific evidence that could distinguish truth from lying, which in turn raised the more abstract question of what constitutes science.

In 1923, the answer to that question was that science is whatever scientists generally agree science is. Thus, to know whether a lie detection device could produce scientifically trustable results, one needed only to ask other scientists. In effect, the *Frye* court was, unfortunately, treating science as a set of specialized practices reserved only for those trained in those practices, thereby leaving law to "trust" the ethos of scientists, as a group, rather than to interrogate the science itself. It is not clear whether that reservation treated science as knowledge based upon experience (*empeiria*) or as deference to science as some special type of knowledge, since both are permitted. In a two-page opinion, the *Frye* court wrote:

> The rule is that the opinions of experts or skilled witnesses are admissible in evidence in those cases in which the matter of inquiry is such that inexperienced persons are unlikely to prove capable of forming a correct judgment upon it, for the reason that the subject matter so far partakes of a science, art, or trade as to require a previous habit or experience or study in it, in order to acquire a knowledge of it. When the question involved does not lie within the range of common experience or common knowledge, but requires special *experience* or special *knowledge*, then the opinions of witnesses skilled in that particular *science*, *art*, or *trade*[119] to which the question relates are admissible in evidence.

118 In the *Frye* decision, Associate Justice van Orsdell explained, "It is asserted that blood pressure is influenced by change in the emotions of the witness, and that the systolic blood pressure rises are brought about by nervous impulses sent to the sympathetic branch of the autonomic nervous system. Scientific experiments, it is claimed, have demonstrated that fear, rage, and pain always produce a rise of systolic blood pressure, and that conscious deception or falsehood, concealment of facts, or guilt of crime, accompanied by fear of detection when the person is under examination, raises the systolic blood pressure in a curve, which corresponds exactly to the struggle going on in the subject's mind, between fear and attempted control] of that fear, as the examination." *Frye v. United States*, 293 F. 1013 (D.C. Cir. 1923) 1013.

119 These categories closely track the truth-era foundational distinctions made by Plato of *empeiria*, *episteme*, and *téchne*.

> Numerous cases are cited in support of this rule. Just when a scientific principle or discovery crosses the line between the experimental and demonstrable stages is difficult to define. Somewhere in this twilight zone the evidential force of the principle must be recognized, and while courts will go a long way in admitting expert testimony deduced from a well-recognized scientific principle or discovery, the thing from which the deduction is made must be sufficiently established to have gained general acceptance in the particular field in which it belongs.[120]

The method, then, to answer the question "What counts as science?" was to ask scientists if they generally agreed. If they did, a lawyer must accept that the method of knowledge production was unassailable. The facts offered by an expert were based upon true premises of the observable world, interpreted through the method of science. In 1975, US Federal Rule of Evidence 702 echoed the *Frye* court's reasoning by permitting that:

> If scientific, technical or other specialized knowledge will assist the trier of fact to understand the evidence or to determine a fact in issue, a witness qualified as an expert by knowledge, skill, experience, training, or education, may testify thereto in the form of an opinion or otherwise.[121]

Under this standard, even though the methods of science were unassailable, it is the trier of fact (either judge or jury), and not the scientist, who decides the case. As Barbara Shapiro noted regarding the English lay jury during the Enlightenment, that trier of fact needs to have come from a society that regards the establishment of fact in a way that is generally understood, so that the juries can be relied upon to maintain civil society through the standards of law. Thus, citizens are not simply to defer to the authority of a scientist and let him or her determine the outcome of the dispute. Moreover, the conclusions of fact by legal method may include the conclusion drawn by scientists or other persons with special knowledge or experience, but the law must also interpret the relevance of that conclusion to the applicable rule of law. The rule of evidence in law allows the judge or a jury to understand and contribute to the production of knowledge. Here, of course, there would be a distinction between a court's scientist advising the judge, which is more common in civil law systems, and scientists as expert witnesses in common-law systems,

120 *Frye*, 1014.

121 Note that the rule integrates the two different, and at times competing, chief schools of epistemology – rationalism (expert by knowledge) and empiricism (expert by experience). Moreover, the rule also recognises the ancient distinctions among knowledge (*episteme*), skill (*téchne*), and experience (*empeiria*).

where they are called to testify as an advocate and support the interpretation of knowledge by one party in the case.[122]

Because premises are to be true, critics often mistakenly claim that only one conclusion of fact can be drawn from the premises. If there are conflicting conclusions, can a judge decide? The famous case of *Daubert et al. v. Merrell Dow Pharmaceuticals Inc.*[123] raised the issue of whether the drug Bendectin (Doxylamine/Dicyclomine/Pyridoxine) caused birth defects in the children of mothers who ingested Bendectin during pregnancy. Justice Blackmun, writing for the majority of the US Supreme Court, interpreted US Federal Rule of Evidence 702 as follows:

> Faced with a proffer of expert scientific testimony, the trial judge must determine whether the expert is proposing to testify to 1.) scientific knowledge that 2.) will assist the trier of fact to understand or determine a fact in issue. Many [f]actors will bear on the inquiry and we do not presume to set out a definitive checklist or test. But some general observations are appropriate.[124]

The court found that the criteria of "fit, "testability and falsification," "reliability," and "validity" must be used to determine if a practice qualifies as science.[125] The concept summarized in the *Daubert* case has explicitly been adopted by Canada and further used as the basis of a new scientific evidence standard in the law of England and Wales. Furthermore, *Daubert* is treated as a "standard" by the American Society for Testing and Materials, an international organization that provides documents' standards worldwide.

The issue of whether opinions constitute science has impact in educational settings and, as such, is clearly not just a specialized topic but one for all of civil society. Can law be a tool to resist and repel opinion or irrational ideology, or does it just contribute to, and further express, unfounded opinions and ideology? In 2004, when religious believers tried to have religion taught as part of

122 An exception to this division occurred in 1976 when a neutral "science court" was proposed by a US White House Task Force on Anticipated Advances in Science and Technology, headed by physicist Arthur Kantrowitz. See Arthur Kantrowitz, *Science*, 653–656 (20 August 1976). The proposal was that a panel of impartial scientist-judges would preside over an adversary proceeding in which scientific expert would testify and scientist-advocates would cross-examine them, solely to decide the disputed technical questions, leaving political, ethical, and other questions for subsequent consideration. It seems ironic that when Jimmy Carter, an engineer, became president, the task force was dissolved, and the science court never tried. Barry Casper & Paul Wellstone, *Science Court on Trial in Minnesota, in* Barnes & Edge, *supra* note 63, at 282–289, 282–283.

123 *Daubert v. Merrell Dow Pharmaceuticals*, 509 U.S. 579 (1993).

124 *Daubert*, 593.

125 See Kenneth R. Foster & Peter W. Huber, Judging Science: Scientific Knowledge and the Federal Courts (MIT Press 1999) citing the case of *Daubert v. Merrell Dow Pharmaceuticals, Inc.*, 509 U.S. 579, 600 (1993).

science lessons in a US public school district, a federal court ruled that religious belief is not science and that religious belief does not have equal knowledge status with the science of evolution. Specifically, the Dover Area School District board in Pennsylvania required science teachers to read a statement to students in biology class at Dover High School. The statement maintained that since evolution is a "theory," it is on equal cognitive status to religious creationism (also called "intelligent design") and that, therefore, science alone cannot determine the facts of human origin, but "[t]he school leaves the discussion of the origins of life to individual students and their families,"[126] as if the origin of life is a matter of personal opinion. Consistent with their own education and training, the science teachers refused to read the statement in science classes, and the parents of 11 students filed a lawsuit, asking the court to enjoin the school district from forcing biology teachers from reading the statement in science classrooms. Law was required to determine whether these religious beliefs constituted science. After a trial on the evidence, the court reasoned at length and decided in favour of the parents. The court did not explicitly cite either the *Frye* case or the *Daubert* case but in fact employed some of the reasoning of each of those previous cases in determining whether "intelligent design" qualified as "science":

> For the reasons that follow, we conclude that the religious nature of intelligent design would be readily apparent to an objective observer, adult or child. The writings of leading intelligent design proponents reveal that the designer postulated by their argument is the God of Christianity. The overwhelming evidence at trial established that intelligent design is a religious view, a mere re-labelling of creationism, and not a scientific theory.
>
> After a searching review of the record and applicable case law, we find that intelligent design is not science. We find that intelligent design fails on three different levels, any one of which is sufficient to preclude a determination that intelligent design is science. They are: (1) intelligent design violates the centuries-old ground rules of science by invoking

126 The more complete text read: "State Academic Standards require students to learn about Darwin's theory of evolution and eventually to take a standardized test of which evolution is a part. Because Darwin's Theory is a theory, it is still being tested as new evidence is discovered. The Theory is not a fact. Gaps in the Theory exist for which there is no evidence. A theory is defined as a well-tested explanation that unifies a broad range of observations; Intelligent design is an explanation of the origin of life that differs from Darwin's view. The reference book *Of Pandas and People* is available for students to see if they would like to explore this view in an effort to gain an understanding of what intelligent design actually involves. As is true with any theory, students are encouraged to keep an open mind." "The school leaves the discussion of the origins of life to individual students and their families. As a standards-driven district, class instruction focuses upon preparing students to achieve proficiency on standards-based assessments." *Kitzmiller v. Dover Area School District*, 400 F. Supp. 2d 707 (M.D. Pa. 2005) 709.

> and permitting supernatural causation; (2) the argument of irreducible complexity, central to intelligent design, employs the same flawed and illogical contrived dualism that doomed creationism in the 1980s; and (3) intelligent design's negative attacks on evolution have been refuted by the scientific community. . . . It is additionally important to note that intelligent design has failed to gain acceptance in the scientific community, it has not generated peer-reviewed publications, nor has it been the subject of testing and research.
>
> Expert testimony reveals that since the scientific revolution of the 16th and 17th centuries, science has been limited to the search for natural causes to explain natural phenomena. Our conclusion today is that it is unconstitutional to teach intelligent design as an alternative to evolution in a public school science classroom.[127]

This court decision, arrived at through a trial based upon rule-bound evidence, standards of procedure, and socially agreed norms, produced a clear outcome in which specific acts could be judged not to be science. The decision distinguished science from religion. It was sufficient to prevent religion from being taught in the science classroom as an alternative to evolution. By comparison, the science of evolution has not fared as well with some legislators. In Turkey, for example, in September 2018, the government removed the teaching of Darwinian evolution from its science schoolbooks.[128]

The most common interference in scientifically determined legislation, especially in matters concerning the environment, comes from economic interests. In the name of jobs or growth, politicians make short-term choices consistent with the span of their political lives, rather than science-determined choices consistent with the span of human life, let alone generations of human life. In the same year that Donald Trump announced that climate change was a matter of opinion, the Dutch Urgenda Foundation took legal action on behalf of 886 citizens against the Dutch government to hold it accountable for contributing to dangerous climate change.[129] The Dutch political

127 *Kitzmiller*, 735.

128 Rachel Jolley, *It's an Outrage that Turkey Is Ditching Darwin from Science Textbooks*, New Scientist (12 September 2018) <www.newscientist.com/article/2179351-its-an-outrage-that-turkey-is-ditching-darwin-from-science-textbooks/#ixzz6TJYNNWfv.>.

129 Also in 2015, 21 youth plaintiffs represented by the non-profit organization Our Children's Trust filed a suit against the United States and several executive branch officials, asserting that the United States government violated the plaintiffs' rights by encouraging and allowing activities relating to greenhouse gas emissions that significantly infringed upon their right to life and liberty. With no advisory jurisdiction in any US Court, the US Courts are very conservative in recognizing *locus standi* among public law litigants. Similar past lawsuits have been dismissed by US courts, and although in this case, *Juliana v. the United States*, the US District Court judge did not dismiss the case, ruling that access to a clean environment was a fundamental right, one month after *Urgenda* was decided, in January 2020, a US Court of Appeals Ninth Circuit panel reversed the District Court and dismissed the case on the

administration had planned only a 17 per cent reduction in greenhouse gases (GHG). In the first instance, the District Court of The Hague ruled that the government must cut its GHG emissions by at least 25 per cent by the end of 2020 (compared to 1990 levels). That ruling would have required the government immediately to take more effective action on climate change. The government appealed.

An appeals court in The Hague upheld the order to the Dutch government to accelerate carbon emissions cuts.[130] Appellate judges ruled that the severity and scope of the climate crisis demanded that GHG emissions be reduced at least 25 per cent below 1990 levels by 2020. When the ruling was announced, news agencies reported similar cases were being planned around the world in Norway, New Zealand, the UK, and Uganda.[131] The Dutch government then appealed to the Dutch Supreme Court. In December 2019, the Dutch Supreme Court held that Dutch courts have the power to enforce compliance with international treaties against a national government.[132] In so ruling, the Supreme Court upheld the 2018 Court of Appeal decision which found that the state has a duty of care to protect its citizens from climate change in accordance with its obligations under the European Convention for the Protection of Human Rights and Fundamental Freedoms. That decision is claimed by the Urgenda Foundation to have inspired further climate change litigation in Belgium, Canada, Colombia, Ireland, Germany, France, Norway, and against the EU.

Among the EU cases, the cities of Madrid, Paris, and Brussels brought before the European General Court (EGC) an action for annulment of Regulation 2016/646, which set the nitrogen oxide (NOx) emission limit just at 168 mg/km (milligrams per kilometre of vehicle travel).[133] In the opinion, the justices said the original particulate matter limit of 80 mg/km must be maintained and that the 2016 relaxation of vehicle emission limits in Regulation 2016/646 was illegal, and that the provisions of the Real Driving Emissions (RDE) Regulation (2016/646) that set the NOx emission limit must be annulled. The city government's actions had been based upon

grounds that the plaintiffs lacked standing to sue. In March 2020, attorneys for the plaintiffs filed a request for rehearing before the 9th US Circuit Court of Appeals *en banc*. *Juliana v. the United States*, 18–36082.

130 Marjan Minnesma, the director of the Urgenda campaign that brought the case, made a particular point of noting that the climate issue ought to be based upon science and legislated by politicians, but because it is not, citizens must instead rely on the tool of litigation and the decisions of judges, based upon science.

131 Arthur Neslen, *Dutch Appeals Court Upholds Landmark Climate Change Ruling*, The Guardian (9 October 2018) <www.theguardian com/environment/2018/oct/09/dutch-appeals-court-upholds-landmark-climate-change-ruling>.

132 Case 19/00135 (Engels) *De Staat Der Nederlanden v. Stichting Urgenda* ECLI:NL:HR:2019:2007.

133 Case T-339/16 *Ville de Paris v. Commission* ECLI:EU:T:2018:927 (Joined Cases T-339/16, T-352/16 and T-391/16.)

peer-reviewed scientific research and conclusions that, among other things, demonstrated the existence of automobile exhaust and industrial pollutant particles in the hearts of urban residents.[134] Buoyed by these decisions, other Dutch non-governmental organizations (NGOs) reintroduced a claim against Dutch Royal Shell that had previously been dismissed,[135] requesting full environmental restoration. In 2021, the District Court of The Hague ordered Royal Dutch Shell to reduce its emission by net 45 per cent by 2030 in comparison to levels in 2019 – although without assertion of any unlawful conduct by the defendant.[136]

These cases illustrate a further point to be made about the integration of science in law. Too often, legal solutions are conceptualized as new regulations and legislation. Both of those legal tools are filtered through the less-than-transparent political process, however. If law is conceptualized as litigation, then we have the situation of lawyers trying cases before judges, all of whom are educated in the law, and tried in open court. This is not just a shift from legislation to litigation as a process but is also a shift from agents who are politicians to agents who are judges and lawyers.

These court decisions all serve to demonstrate that the courtroom provides a social forum in which we can decide scientific facts and the actions that we will take based upon scientific facts. Contrary to the bias of materialist thinking that is unfamiliar with the history of ideas, in particular the history of those ideas that constructed the concepts of rationality and fact, we determine the status of knowledge socially, not materially.

Before concluding these case studies, however, one should consider ways in which science can be effectively employed in creating sources of law, such as treaties, statutes, and regulations, rather than waiting for dispute resolution. For example, science has been concretely integrated into the law employed by the UN Framework Convention's Intergovernmental Panel on Climate Change (IPCC), beginning in nearly the same year as the *Daubert* decision in the United States. The IPCC receives the collective conclusions of the world's scientists from all participating countries and then meta-analyzes the truth of the premises and the inferences drawn. The UN does not conduct its own scientific investigations but instead relies upon the fact that scientists from the entire world community are invited to agree or disagree with one another. IPCC scientists check the science, and then the IPCC's conclusions are accepted by the United Nations Framework Convention on Climate Change

134 Gonzalez-Maciel et al., *Combustion- and Friction-Derived Magnetic Air Pollution Nanoparticles in Human Hearts*, Environmental Research, Elsevier (29 June 2019) <ora.ox.ac.uk/objects/uuid:e60a6ac3-80fo-4a83-bb14.50431d5e7e61.>.

135 *Akpan v. Royal Dutch Shell plc* (2013) Case No. ECLNL:RBDHA:2013:BY9845 <https://uitspraken.rechtspraak.nl/inziendocument?id=ECLI:NL:RBDHA:2013:BY9845>.

136 *Milieudefensie et al v. Royal Dutch Shell plc* (2019), Case No. C/09/571932/HA ZA 19–379 (English version) <https://uitspraken.rechtspraak.nl/inziendocument?id=ECLI:NL:RBDHA:2021:5339>.

(UNFCCC) Secretariat as the facts from which to conduct the actions of the UNFCCC Secretariat and its Subsidiary Body for Implementation (SBI) and its Subsidiary Body for Scientific and Technological Advice (SBSTA). It is important to pause and reflect on this method of knowledge production: unlike the political use of science in domestic legislation and regulation, the UNFCCC actively seeks to de-politicize science by inviting all states to participate and by conducting none of its own primary research. If some states conduct scientifically faulty or politically determined non-scientific research, their submissions to the SBSTA and IPCC will be compared to that of other states that conduct scientific research.

2.7 *Concealed Again? – A History of the Present*

Faced today with an onslaught of unchecked "information" sources that unhesitatingly blur the truth-era borders that separated news, opinion, entertainment, and advertisement,[137] people from all walks of life complain that they do not know who or what to believe, and that gives them stress and anxiety.[138] Truth is in crisis when we *cannot* distinguish truth from untruth, *choose not* to distinguish truth from untruth, or fall into a pattern and custom of behaviour where the distinction is irrelevant. Remedies that lie in knowledge (science) exist, and they are not restricted to seeking refuge in a concept of science that is either only a measurement of the material world or restricted to a set of specialist information to which we have no access, and therefore must accept or reject as facts without the ability to judge the truth of its premises, the rationality of its reasoning, or the validity of the inferences. A social fact is no less a fact than a fact related to material existence, but it is neither constituted by material things nor a matter of opinion.[139] Unclear use of language and unclear thinking tend to conflate facts with truth, and truth with things, especially when understood as material things. As Wittgenstein states in his *Tractatus Logico-Philosophicus*, "[t]he world is the totality of facts, not of things. The world is determined by the facts."[140]

The era began to shift when, for years, cultural theorists assured us that language did not fix meaning as tightly and neatly as the mechanics of symbolic

137 The number of hours per day that people spend on social media is in inverse proportion to the number of hours spent reading printed text or consulting information authorities. Jean M. Twenge, *Internet: Online Time – Oh, and Other Media, Too, in* Twenge, *supra* note 8, at 49–68.

138 Cf. Indian Ministry of Health and Family Welfare, *supra* note 82 and Shah, *supra* note 86, with Twenge, *supra* note 8, at 4.

139 As explained by Peter Berger and Paul Luckmann, a social fact is any social phenomenon that you cannot wish away. It exists without you – it is a fact. "Jennifer is married to Marcel" is a social fact. It is capable of being proven true or false and is not dependent for its truth or falsity on the material world. See Berger and Luckmann, *supra* note 50, at 13

140 Ludwig Wittgenstein, Tractatus Logico-Philosophicus 1.1 (David Pears & Brian McGuinness, transl., Kegan Paul 1922).

logic might lead us to believe. Was that a crack in the edifice of the truth era that should be repaired or celebrated? Then, sociologists of scientific knowledge wanted to convince us that, while the material world does what it does, we humans, in doing what we do, might only be seeing the natural world insofar as we can, through our limited and human interpretations, which does not equal human practices that are as precise, fixed, and mathematically sound as the material world itself. Is that another crack in the truth era edifice to be repaired or an opportunity to be celebrated? The result of these cracks, it seems, is, rather than having humanized natural science by adjusting our thinking to the real limits of language and science, we have instead become conditioned to accept political factions who are "anti-science," "opinion-based," or "faith-based," as being capable of governing through the intentional creation of post-truth realities.[141]

A person can unintentionally contribute to the problems of not knowing how to establish facts through re-tweeting and participating in clickbait for profit and thus conflating information, commercial advertising, and entertainment. Communication scholars indicate that large discourse communities who believe that social media is a "news" source are quick to proliferate opinions due to the group communication methods.[142] In addition to the intentional deceiver and the uncritical group-joiner, there is also the citizen who has been *conditioned* to think that truth is not an important category of human thought. Conditioning is understood from the perspective of the person being conditioned. Repeated exposure to even the most banal event, like a pop song that is played over and over, is conditioning. Conditioning is a form of patterned behaviour, of habit. Hannah Arendt reminded us, after having witnessed the 1963 trial of Adolf Eichmann first-hand, that when it comes to evil, we may be looking not at cunning sociopaths but at persons of average, mundane, common stupidity, relying upon cliché, motivated by personal promotion, and unable or unwilling to think for themselves, whose behaviour is simply banal.[143]

We have also learned that it is hubris to treat human history as being a story of irreversible and inevitable progress. The Western narrative holds that we exited from dark ages through an enlightening scientific worldview. That worldview included limiting legal facts to be inferred from true premises in rational discourse. But it would be naive and unwarranted to believe that we are incapable of returning to the dark by abandoning our ability to base our practices upon valid inferences of fact from true premises. It is the consequence of which Aristotle wrote when he said that there are consequences to a failure to

141 Frazier, Kendrick, *Science Wars' Veteran Latour Now Wants to Help Rebuild Trust in Science*, 42(1) Skeptical Inquirer 7 (2018).

142 A very good example of WhatsApp being confused with providing news can be found in the article of Julio Ribeiro, *Fake News Is Correct*, The Indian Express (9 March 2019) <indianexpress.com/article/opinion/columns/the-fake-news-is-correct-56 17651/>.

143 Hannah Arendt, Eichmann in Jerusalem: A Report on the Banality of Evil (Viking Press 1963).

follow the principle of non-contradiction. We might profit from re-acquainting ourselves with why medieval Western humans came to embrace testable truths over unverifiable opinions, because today, humans have reverted to talking about simple opinion in areas in which we already have inferred valid facts from true premises, as when the president of the United States presented with the rational facts of climate change inferred from scientific truths responded, "I don't believe it."[144] That is no different from not "believing" that the Earth is a sphere because there is a little group of people with an irrational opinion to the contrary – the Flat Earth Society. Moreover, when faced with a rational choice and we instead do that to which we are otherwise accustomed, even if harmful, we not only fail to exercise rationality by choice but also demonstrate that although we have developed its use based upon custom and habit, we have not developed it as a custom or habit with equal or superior pull to other customs or habits of behaviour.[145]

One of post-modernism's most insightful tools, self-reflexivity, reminds us that the tradition that criticizes the truth-era culture, from Nietzsche and Heidegger to Horkheimer and Foucault, itself has roots in the Enlightenment. These critiques nevertheless offer important correctives of an Enlightenment unaware of its contradictions and social constructions. "A chastened idea of the Enlightenment, and with it, as its essential constituent part, a chastened rationalism, still have meaning today."[146] Foucault argues that the contemporary study of the history of ideas, although it targets moments of transition between historical worldviews, ultimately depends on continuities that break down under close inspection. The truth era had inconsistencies and non-truth moments, such as presumptions of truth based upon being characterized as "a gentleman." The post-truth era also has and will have inconsistencies in which it behaves as the truth era. For a society really to be post-truth, it would need a moniker and behaviour with no mention whatsoever of the word or idea of truth. Labelling ourselves instead as "post-truth" and making observations of our behaviour in their relation to truth demonstrate that we still have some meaning of truth as the social and psychological anchor by which we assess our behaviour. To that end, television theatrics aside, courtrooms can still function to establish facts, inferred through reasoning from valid premises.

3 Conclusions: What Is the Role of Law in the Post-Truth Era?

While writing this chapter, when looking for a date in history, I clicked on the *Encyclopedia Britannica*, and the response was "Truth Needs a Champion – Will

144 BBC, *supra* note 104.

145 See John H. Bodley, Cultural Anthropology: Tribes, States, and the Global System (Rowman & Littlefield 2017).

146 Iggers, *supra* note 13.

You Donate?" Lawyers can ask the same question of themselves: Will law or lawyers donate to truth, as accuracy-based science, in the post-truth era? Private law can offer protection for individuals through actions for slander, libel, and other speech-related torts and intellectual property violations, but these traditional private legal actions are part of dispute resolution, not legislation or the making of administrative regulations. Litigation, not politics or the marketplace, offers a forum and a process for testing the truth of propositions. The legislative-regulatory process could not produce the responsible climate control that the Urgenda Foundation citizens accomplished through dispute resolution in the 2019 before the Dutch Supreme Court, nor what Luisa Neubauer and the other young applicants did before the German Federal Constitutional Court in 2021.

Science is a way of thinking, not a thing or a commodity that is only instrumentally "applied" like a consumer product. A fully post-truth era, functioning as a non-truth era, could have nothing to do with science, the practice of which depends upon at least some notion of truth as accuracy. But the post-truth era is – so far – only a non-truth generation, with a rather different mentality from those that preceded it. Law has historically preceded science in establishing the concept of fact. Only with Enlightenment science did science begin using the concept of fact, and it did so by borrowing from law. As noted earlier, the questions have become: "How are facts understood differently in an era of post-truth, and in what ways will law contribute to that understanding and meaning?" Among all the concepts discussed in this chapter, facts are the main concern of the lawyer. If we consider that the fact has both a truth element and a contingency that is dependent on the particulars of events, we could look to either one to determine which has changed in the new era. One might think that, of course, the truth element cannot have changed, and since the other part is based upon changeable contingencies, therein must lie the change in the post-truth era. But the reverse seems instead to have occurred. The social particulars change, but the concept of a social contingency has not changed. Instead, we have quite surprisingly changed the underlying concept of truth. The invention of "alternative facts" by politicians is not just a function of a strong political intention – it is made possible because of the conditioning of the audience to allow different information foundations, namely, truthiness instead of truth. Here, one is reminded by the word "information" that an audience and a society are formed when they are informed. That information need not be formal instruction or even instruction at all. It can just be following a pattern of habit, whether a pattern of rational behaviour or a frequent look at social media. Law in the truth era incorporated matters of fact, understood to be based upon a distinction of truth from opinion in a context of non-contradictive rationality.

In both science and law, we use knowledge to make choices and take actions, or we ignore knowledge and ride as passengers on the bus. For industrial societies, the supreme luxury is to ignore the production of knowledge and rather just do one's specialized job while passively treating knowledge as an optional consumer good. This presents an opportunity and a burden for lawyers – the courtroom was and remains a forum in which rationality is used to construct social facts, including the social facts of science. Our conception of social fact has been based upon Enlightenment-era legal thinking, with law-making, adjudication, and enforcement dependent upon rational decisions. It may turn out to be the most important, if not the last wall to fall, if we are to resist the conditioning of society to accept irrationality, alternative facts, and beliefs as the bases for social action. We know, of course, that law can be ideological – there is no doubt about that. But law can also check the irrational ideologies of politics, economics, and beliefs about the world through the same method of cross-examination that separated truth from opinion 25 centuries ago.

The Aristotelian idea of irrationality was that it was episodic in each of our individual lives. During the truth era, rationality was regarded as the basis upon which education, science, progress, and democratic government could function. We now seem to be seeing, in the post-truth era, that the proportion of rational to irrational has reversed, first perhaps in individual lives, but now as the marker of an "era" (or at least a generation) in the collective value expressions of many cultures. If our notion of history is in any manner cyclical, rather than being only a rising line of progress, then we might say, like with a disruptive child, "he's just going through a phase." Indeed, we might be relying upon some cyclical return to rationality in the future.

Civil society is not prepared to make rational choices when citizens are overwhelmed by smartphone isolation with immediate and widespread distribution of an indistinguishable blur of entertainment-advertising-fact. We have substantial scientific evidence not only of irrational behaviour but also scientific evidence of the stress and anxiety caused by the post-truth patterns of behaviour. We will need to decide whether the post-truth era, founded upon something like truthiness, is essentially a different era or is just the opinion-mongering against which Socrates established his method of inquiry that we still use in litigation practice today in the courts of the world. If it is something new, law – and presumably science – will both need to accommodate this something new in structuring that which is accepted as knowledge. If it is not something new, then the courts can continue to function as the laboratory for applying the truth-era methods, including the establishment of facts that constitute knowledge. In large part, the answer will not be determined by top-down law-making or top-down science lectures about science's own practices. The intersubjective nature of social reality demonstrates that the realities determined by a society contribute not only to the particulars of contingencies but also to the methods of knowledge production itself. East and West, research and observation, indicate that the newest generation may well produce knowledge differently. We should not forget that rationality itself, as Aristotle told us, is also a process of following patterns, but to an end that we know, and our legal systems are based upon it.

3 The Interlinkages Science-Technology-Law

Information and Communication Society, Knowledge-Based Economy, and the Rule of Law

Giovanni Bombelli and Paolo Davide Farah***

1 The Problem and a Brief Analysis Outline

This contribution attempts to address some aspects of the circular and complex relationship between science, technology, society, and law in the post-truth era, with particular regard to the idea and models of "society" and the "rule of law."[1]

In a very concise manner, this chapter focuses on several interrelated points. At an introductory level, attention is paid to some modern (and post-modern) relationship patterns between science, society, and law. This focus aims to highlight the historical-conceptual landscape and the philosophical roots of the current interaction between science and law. Specifically, science is considered in light of its technological applications, while law is viewed concerning its "classical" regulative function and, more broadly, its role within society as a whole.

Following this explanatory introduction, some general remarks about the relationship between technology and society are proposed. These remarks introduce the principal arguments of Robert Dahl regarding the legal sphere and the political-institutional dimension. From this perspective, this contribution focuses on the crisis of democracy (the so-called democratic deficit);[2] the problems of functioning as well as legitimization underlying Western society

* Giovanni Bombelli, Full Professor, Università Cattolica del Sacro Cuore, Milan (Italy).

** Paolo Davide Farah, Full Professor, West Virginia University, Eberly College of Arts and Sciences, John D. Rockefeller IV School of Policy and Politics; Founder and Director of the West Virginia University, Energy Justice and Just Transition Lab; Founder and Coordinator of the Eberly College Interdisciplinary Research Collaborative on Global Challenges and Local Responses Initiatives; Visiting Professor of Law, University of Pittsburgh, School of Law; Founder, President, Director, Principal Investigator and Senior Research Fellow, at gLAWcal – Global Law Initiatives for Sustainable Development (United Kingdom). Email Addresses: paolofarah@yahoo.com; paolo.farah@glawcal.org.uk

1 B. Tamanaha, On the Rule of Law: History, Politics, Theory (Cambridge University Press 2004).

2 R. Celikates, R. Kreide & T. Wesche, Transformations of Democracy: Crisis, Protest and Legitimation (Rowman & Littlefield International 2015).

DOI: 10.4324/9781003472421-3

as a whole.[3] This crisis should also be considered in light of the idea of "information society and knowledge-based economy," which is sometimes discussed within the philosophical-legal debate and synthesized by the concept of "network society."

Next, an observation concerning the "technology-models of society-law" circle is offered. Addressing the increasing tensions between social models and patterns of law, these remarks highlight aspects of transformation within the legal sphere resulting from the implementation of technology and the consequent diffusion of new societal models. In particular, this discussion covers patterns of regulation, the concept of "norm," and, ultimately, the classical idea of "rule of law" dating back to the origins of modernity.

Furthermore, this framework encompasses relevant anthropological and cognitive reflexes. The ongoing relevance of technology, especially when considered as a particular articulation of scientific knowledge closely related to the post-truth age, modifies fundamental anthropological-cognitive dimensions (i.e. language, memory, corporeity) and, therefore, the ability to understand or conceptualize politics and law.

Finally, some conclusive remarks emphasize both the Western conceptual-historical bases of the "science-technology-society (politics, law)" discourse and the future necessity of addressing the sociological-cultural scenarios, that strongly differ from those of Western societies.

2 Patterns of Relations in "Science-Technology-Society-Law": An Overview

Through modernity and post-modernity, the relationship in "science-technology-society" has developed according to several different models, each involving different concepts of law. From a philosophical-legal perspective, three fundamental patterns can be outlined: (a) *the "hard" paradigm*, (b) *the "pragmatic" model*, and (c) *the "post-modern" framework*.

The most suitable way to deepen the understanding of these patterns is to refer to a methodological grid. This grid relies on three closely related conceptual lenses: *truth* (regarding the epistemological profile, which includes the idea of science), *society* (the sociological analysis based on the idea of society), and *law* (concerning the legal approach and the concepts of "state" and "law" or "rule of law"). The combination of these two levels – general patterns and the trinomial truth-law-society – allows for a better grasp of the articulation of "science-technology-society" in order to sketch conceptual models.

1 The *"hard" paradigm* refers to a very strong epistemological premise: the idea of "truth." It dates back to the origins of modernity, the fundamental

3 M. Crozier, S. P. Huntington & J. Watanuki, The Crisis of Democracy: On the Governability of Democracies (New York University Press 1975).

historical passage between the eighteenth and the nineteenth centuries (i.e. the Enlightenment and idealism movements),[4] and is rooted in a substantial idea of "reason (rationality)" as it pertains to the enforcement of the social role of technology.

The consequent equation between "reason" and "truth" entails the possibility of building both a "scientific republic" (i.e. Francis Bacon's idea of a scientific academy inspired to the concept of "New Atlantis"[5] and its recent reinterpretation elaborated by Michael Polanyi[6] and Robert Merton[7]) and a rational-scientific model of society. The ultimate goal is the creation of a "knowledge-based society," which in turn relies on a rational anthropological model.

Legal and political projections then become clear. Within the modern framework of law and the political-institutional dimension, these projections are to be understood as expressions of a rationality-based truth. This is the philosophical core underlying the modern model of the "state" and the conceptual basis of "rule of law."

2 The *pragmatic model* developed around the middle of the last century and was based on different premises regarding both its epistemological horizon and its social-legal corollaries.

Science is no longer a question of truth but one of social impact. Thomas Kuhn's well-known analysis marks this transition as "normal science" to "post-normal science." Normal science operates within a theoretical-pragmatic and historically conditioned framework, which can be radically changed only by an epistemological revolution, leading to the "post-normal" model of scientific knowledge.[8] Notably, the idea of "truth" remains, but its nature fundamentally changes. Scientific investigation no longer aims at "rational" (hence "true") knowledge but at a "contextual" model of knowledge closely connected to its performative and persuasive force.

Furthermore, it should be noted that this process appears to have significant similarities to, and may parallel, the increasing development of pragmatism within the contemporary philosophical debate (though this is from a different perspective compared to Peirce's pragmatism[9]), involving a different

4 I. Kant, Critique of Pure Reason [1781] (Cambridge University Press 1999); F. G. W. Hegel, The Phenomenology of Spirit [1807] (The University of Notre Dame Press 2019).
5 F. Bacon, The New Atlantis and the Great Instauration (Wiley Blackwell 2017).
6 M. Polanyi, *The Republic of Science: Its Political and Economic Theory*, 1 Minerva 54–74 (1962).
7 R. Merton, Social Theory and Social Structure (The Free Press 1968).
8 T. Kuhn, The Structure of Scientific Revolutions (University of Chicago Press 1962).
9 C. S. Peirce, *What Pragmatism Is*, 15(2) The Monist 161–181 (1905).

pattern of society. Society is no longer a "rational" ideal but rather a mere "space of social transactions" in a pragmatic manner.

Accordingly, law and politics, or rather, the dimensions of "regulation" become increasingly pragmatic. The idea of law as a "normative technique," which is also embraced by some classical legal philosophers (for instance, the Kelsenian idea of law "as a specific social technique")[10], evolves into "legal realism." The polarity between "law in books" and "law in action," established within the American version of realism, paradigmatically marks the progressive shift to a different conceptualization of regulation.[11] In the final analysis, the "state" and the "rule of law" are to be considered as the product of balancing different forces, serving as the categorial horizon that gives way to a merely pragmatic/factual approach.

3 The *post-modern framework* implies a further transition, which can once again be understood through the aforementioned perspectives.

At a philosophical level, post-modernism,[12] which emerged in the second half of the last century, signifies the slow and apparently unstoppable decline of the idea of "truth," including the modern equation between "reason" and "truth." In other words, it marks the transition from a strong to a narrative model of truth. Post-modernism logically entails a post-truth position, which should be considered its conceptual evolution.

This theoretical framework legitimizes and intersects the epistemological debate, particularly regarding the nature, methodological approach, and content of scientific investigation. Science becomes a *narrative dimension*.

The crisis of the epistemological horizon splits the science–technology couple, making space for the performative force of technology. Consequently, Bacon's, Polanyi's, and Merton's models of scientific knowledge leave space for different patterns of the science–society relation. It is not by chance that Tallacchini describes the new scenario through the idea of "co-production" between the scientific community and the legal/political apparatus.[13]

Law and politics suffer because of this conceptual shift. Additionally, they progressively lose their "technical nature" and their regulative role, ultimately becoming merely narrative dimensions.[14] Within the post-modern and post-truth era, the broad concept of regulation, encompassing its classical-modern

10 H. Kelsen, *The Law as a Specific Social Technique*, 1(5) University of Chicago Law Review 9, 75–97 (1941).

11 R. Pound, *Law in Books and Law in Action*, 44 American Law Review 12–36 (1910).

12 J. F. Lyotard, La condition postmoderne. Rapport sur le savoir (Les Editions de Minuit 1979).

13 M. Tallacchini, *Scientific Evidence and Environmental Rule-Making: The Co-production of Science and Law, in* Scientific Evidence in European Environmental Rule-Making 3–15 (A. Biondi, et al. (eds.), Kluwer Law International 2003).

14 J. Derrida, De la grammatologie (Editions de la Minuit 1967).

articulations (i.e. "state" and "rule of law"), becomes only a performative or convincing "narration."

The *reticular model* of the interlinkages science, technology, and law develops the theoretical sequence of the post-modern/post-truth era and, at the beginning of the twenty-first century, characterizes the "liquid" societies.[15] Its definitive epistemological rejection of the idea of truth, along with the contemporary fulfilment of the post-modern orientation, entails a fragmented social model. Far beyond classical sociological functionalism,[16] under the pressure of the ongoing implementation of new technologies, society and law can be interpreted as a "net."[17]

The web society (i.e. network society) differs from the modern pattern of law, which was based on a hierarchical legal order, and implies a reticular normative framework that takes the functionalist orientation to extremes. Through the transformation of subjects and norms, the notion of "governance" synthesizes and emphasizes an approach to social processes based on a management dimension.

3 On the Technology–Society Connection

The conceptual framework outlined in the previous section has highlighted the types of interaction among three levels: patterns of scientific knowledge, models of society, and concepts of law.

To sum up, the model of science (i.e. technology) is closely and circularly interwoven with a certain idea of society and, consequently, with a certain legal and political-institutional apparatus. In other words, a specific model of scientific knowledge implies a corresponding model of technology. A post-truth pattern of science implies a corresponding model of technology.

The point here is the role played by the most relevant output of scientific knowledge: technology. The increasing role of technology within the contemporary sociological-legal order represents a well-known and accepted fact. We all experience this process daily, which signifies an inescapable and hegemonic trend.

In particular, attention must be paid to information and communications technology (ICT), often equated with technology in general. Given their interconnection, ICT can be viewed as the "heart" of the so-called information society – an ambiguous term akin to other expressions used in this context, such as "communication-based society" and "knowledge-based society."

This contribution does not delve into a detailed analysis of this sociological-legal process (or "technomedial process"). The focus here is on deeply understand

15 Z. Bauman, Liquid Modernity (Polity Press 2000).

16 N. Luhmann, Soziale Systeme. Grundriß einer Allgemeinen Theorie (Suhrkamp 1984).

17 F. Ost & M. van De Kerchove, De la pyramide au réseau? Pour une théorie dialectique du droit (Publications des Facultés universitaires Saint-Louis 2002).

how and to what extent these dynamics have involved and modified what we traditionally call "law." By employing methodologically hybrid conceptual lenses, incorporating sociological and philosophical-legal perspectives various aspects of the relationship between ICT and law will be explored.

First, as initially mentioned, attention will be directed towards some legal-institutional "applications" of ICT, specifically concerning the "crisis of democracy" and the issues associated with the functioning or non-functioning of representative-democratic systems regarding deliberative processes and decision-making.

Secondly, it is necessary to explore the ambiguities related to the use of technology, which entail theoretical implications regarding the conceptualization of law (including the idea of the "rule of law").

Finally, the close relationship between the social role of technology and the anthropological dimension is discussed. At the anthropological level, the ongoing interweaving in the ICT–sociological context entails radically different frameworks for understanding the subjective dimension and for addressing new global scenarios.

4 Democratic Deficit and the Ideal "Information and Communications Society and Knowledge-Based Economy"

There is no need to dwell on the dysfunctions and pathologies of contemporary democratic systems. The so-called democratic deficit, which occasionally plagues the "post-modern" (or "post-industrial") society, raises questions about some crucial points, particularly the legitimacy crisis and the inadequate functionality of representative mechanisms. After all, in the rich debate about democracy, it is no coincidence that Crouch has proposed the dangerous yet realistic term "post-democracy" to indicate the increasing concentration of power in the hands of a professionalized political *élite*.[18]

From this perspective, the "classical" outlook discussed by Robert Dahl remains important. The American author is neither a computer scientist nor a philosopher of law; rather, he is a political scientist. In this sense, his work appears paradigmatic as it anticipates contemporary political issues (while also discussing potential solutions). The key points of his argument will now be examined, with particular focus on his landmark work, *Democracy and Its Critics*.[19]

Thirty years ago, Dahl identified four issues regarding contemporary democratic systems: the questionable nature of the majority principle, the formal/substantive nature of the democratic process, the expansion of the polyarchy (i.e. the broadening of decision-making bodies), and finally, the selection of *élites* (drawing on the works of Gaetano Mosca and Vilfredo Pareto).

18 C. Crouch, Post Democracy (Polity Press 2004).
19 R. A. Dahl, Democracy and Its Critics (Yale University Press 1989).

From this perspective, Dahl concludes his extensive analysis by emphasizing the relevance of "polyarchy" (a form of power invested in multiple people)[20] and questions the practicability of democracy within complex societies, or, using another term, the space for the "guardians' government." Dahl highlights a crucial point: the gap between *élites* and common people, which can be closed by implementing "telecommunications" (in Dahl's terminology) with the goal of creating a "minipopulus" (i.e. a selected microcosm of the public).

According to Dahl, the pathologies of contemporary democracies can be cured through new technologies. They play a decisive role in building the context for a "deliberative democracy,"[21] similar to Rousseau's concept of "direct democracy".

Dahl's analysis is very useful. Its two key elements (insufficient legitimation of democracy and social implementation of the technological devices) remain the basis of contemporary analyses on the topic. In other words, the idea is that technology offers concrete possibilities to close the gap between law and society. The interaction could be beneficial for both technology and law, where the former could gain social legitimation, and the latter could improve its standard of efficiency.

The expression "information-based society" summarizes the point just mentioned and entails a twofold meaning. On one hand, it identifies the aforementioned necessity to revitalize democratic institutions. On the other hand, it implies (and at the same time legitimates) the problematic equation "technology = society" to implement a "knowledge-based society" (addressed in more detail in Section 6). This point is questionable. Regardless of the rhetorical emphasis given to the "law–technologies" relationship, the evocation of a "knowledge-based society" elicits two levels: (1) functional and (2) theoretical.

1 Regarding the functional level, the widespread use of technology seems increasingly reasonable in light of common practices at the legal-institutional level: for instance, the proliferation of databases, the implementation of virtual civil trials, and so on.

These processes legitimize the broad call for extending the law–technology nexus. The ambitious goal is to improve the functionality of democratic systems in at least two directions. First, one direction is to optimize the political-institutional apparatus. Both social networks and web communities promise to create space for a richer and more articulated circulation of opinions and to elevate the political debate.

20 See also R. A. Dahl, Polyarchy: Participation and Opposition (Yale University Press 1971).
21 N. Rao (ed.), Representation and Community in Western Democracies 68–92 (MacMillan 2000).

Secondly, this process should be understood as the premise for the modernization of Western democracies, providing them with functionality and political legitimation, inspired by the so-called "deliberative (participative) democracy."[22] Moving from the importance given to "virtual (electronic, technetronic) democracy,"[23] the goal is to implement e-government models to make electoral systems more functional, guarantee the transparency of the decision-making processes, and improve participation in democracy.

Once again, the point is very questionable. As is well-known, many recent experiences with e-governments[24] need to be critically reviewed, especially in the light of a certain "technological utopianism" underlying the current and past debate.[25]

2 Regarding the theoretical level, the dynamics just described aim at a more profound objective: the *transformation* of the entire society into an "information society." Drawing on Section 2 of this contribution, we can appreciate the distance between the "information-based society" and the "knowledge-based society." The crucial point is the current identification or superimposition sometimes established between the concepts of "information" and "knowledge." There is no direct and proportional relationship between the mass of data carried by technologies and the level or degree of knowledge regarding political decisions and the public debate on specific issues (i.e. bioethics, energy policies, etc.).

In short, "information" is *not* equivalent to "knowledge." The relationship is much more complex: "information" is neither the premise nor the condition of "knowledge." This is a decisive point because the current emphasis on this connection implies an in-depth rethinking of the classical conceptual "democracy–truth" relationship [26] and could be interpreted as the first step towards the construction of a technocracy.

22 Z. Chappell, Deliberative Democracy: A Critical Introduction (Palgrave Macmillan 2012); M. A. Neblo, Deliberative Democracy between Theory and Practice (Cambridge University Press 2015).

23 D. Barney & A. Feenberg, Community in the Digital Age: Philosophy and Practice (Rowman & Littlefield 2004). In particular, Part III; L. Scheer, La démocratie virtuelle (Flammarion 1994).

24 For a comparative perspective, see M. H. Hattingh, et al., Responsible Design, Implementation and Use of Information and Communication Technology 3–60, *19th IFIP WG 6.11 Conference on e-Business, e-Services, and e-Society, I3 E 2020 Skukuza, South Africa, April 6–8, 2020: Proceedings, Part II* (Springer 2020).

25 H. P. Segal, Imagining Tomorrow: History, Technology and the American Future. "The Technological Utopians" (MIT Press 1986).

26 J. Nida-Rümelin, Demokratie und Wahrheit (Beck 2006); J. L. Nancy, Vérité de la démocratie (Galilée 2008).

5 Observatory: Technology, Law, and Models of Society

At this level, we must take a closer look at the technology–law circle, especially considering the resulting conceptualization of the models of society. Regardless of the classical and important distinction between "information technology law" (cyberlaw) and "legal informatics,"[27] the point of discussion is the analysis of any aspects of the ongoing transformation of law and societal patterns under the pressure of technology.

The basic idea is that this process compromises a certain and traditional idea of "law" and, more broadly, "legal normativity." Going step by step, it is first necessary to consider the immediate experience and then the conceptual perspective.

We can start with a simple phrase: technology ***anticipates*** (pre-empts) law. It is a common experience that technology (including information technology) spreads out and settles within the market and broadly within society ***before*** law. Medicine, bioethics, and the environment are the fields wherein technological modifications raise questions, which only ***later*** require legal intervention. In other words, law plays only a ***regulative*** role in the face of many social processes, which have ***already*** been technologically defined and produced.

Law is always late, and it only episodically guides or plans technological transformations.

This sociological-legal observation highlights a conceptual aspect: the fundamental change in our understanding of law and its social environment.

The shift is from a "classical" scheme, which attributed a directive function to the legal system, to a very different pattern where law acts as a mere regulatory factor.

The ***hard law–soft law*** pair[28] synthesizes this historical (and ongoing) transition. As previously suggested, the modern horizon was based on a holistic-philosophical ***hard*** vision of law as a legal order. The basic ideas of "reason" and history (paradigmatically: the Hegelian idea of "ethical state") served as the guiding principles within the long era of legal codes and the construction of the concept of the "legal system."

This gives way to another completely different scenario. Law is no longer the expression of a worldview but just a ***soft*** set of rules. Its goal is not the governance of the social processes, beginning with a legitimation dynamic and through a complex framework of norms, but rather the mere regulation of heterogeneous transactions or phenomena (aside from technology, another example is offered by the European regulation of the "migration question").[29]

The conceptual difference between "government" and "regulation" generates an important corollary regarding the ***typology*** and ***nature*** of legal norms.

27 For a short review, see E. A. Salami, A Brief Overview of Legal Informatics (2017) <https://ssrn.com/abstract=2966201> or <http://doi.org/10.2139/ssrn.2966201>.

28 L. Selden, Soft Law in European Community Law (Hart 2004); U. Mörth, Soft Law in Governance and Regulation: An Interdisciplinary Analysis (Elgar 2004).

29 G. Bombelli, *Migrations and Security. The Problematic Circularity 'Philosophy, Law and Politics'*, 6(1) Revista de Estudios en Seguridad Internacional 1–17 (2020).

The development of IT and legal informatics is characterized by an increasing number of "technical rules,"[30] which are becoming the principal typology within Western legal orders. These rules act as a sort of buffer: in this perspective, privacy is a good example belonging to the traditional idea of "rule of law," which is to be distinguished from the idea of "rule by law."[31]

The legal models underlying current privacy regulation are always in progress (for example, see the *General Data Protection Regulation*: a regulation of the European law adopted on 14 April 2016, which became enforceable on 25 May 2018). In particular, these legal models seem directly connected to the increasing new technological possibilities of violation in the personal sphere. This means that the decline of the conceptual horizon represented by a philosophical-legal understanding of social processes make these rules essentially punctual, self-referential, and operational. That is why we still lack a general discipline of privacy in a technological era.

It is important to note that a distinction between "norm" and "rule" has been established. This is the decisive point closely related to the evaluation of the legal value of technological processes. The idea of "norm" has traditionally been elaborated upon in light of a global interpretative framework of social processes and law. In this framework, the concept of "rule" pertains to a contingency logic designed to establish "limits." This shift is a symptom of the slow but inexorable transition from a legal order traditionally based on "norms" to a different pattern dominated by "rules." A "norm" is traditionally the expression of the "meaning" and complexity of sociality, while the concept of "rule" appears to be a merely functional dimension.

Niklas Luhmann's outlook is fundamental. It highlights the progressive emergence of a functional model of law: in other words, law should be understood as a bundle of functions. Further, he points out, at the turn of the 1970s and 1980s, that his model of society paradigmatically entails a functional representation of the legal sphere. Luhmann's functional perspective,[32] which in some ways can be compared to Talcott Parsons' model,[33] has been expounded upon in light of the emerging field of cybernetics (the forerunner of the contemporary technological transformations). Moving from these technological innovations, the entire society can be conceptualized as a "system" based on the equilibrium among many sub-systems (i.e. law, economics, religion, etc.), and the legal sphere becomes a sub-system composed of calculable rules.[34]

The point here is the direct connection between the massive process of technologization and the modification of the concept (nature) of law. In this

30 See J. E. Cohen, Configuring the Networked Self: Law, Code, and the Play of Everyday Practice (Yale University Press 2012).

31 M. Tushnet, *Rule of Law or Rule by Law?*, 22(2) Asia Pacific Law Review 79–92 (2014).

32 N. Luhmann, Soziale Systeme. Grundriß einer allgemeinen Theorie (Suhrkamp 1984).

33 T. Parsons, The Structure of Social Action. A Study in Social Theory with Special Reference to a Group of Recent European Writers (McGraw-Hill Book Company 1937).

34 See also N. Luhmann, Rechtssystem und Rechtsdogmatik (Verlag 1974).

way, law itself becomes a mere "normative technique" more and more subordinated to other dimensions (i.e., the hybrid techno-economics): the logical condition for technocracy is implemented, and the transformation of law into instrumental rationality is complete. In other words, law becomes a "set of technical rules" in the sense suggested earlier.

But nowadays, we can observe a further complication of the technology–law relationship. On one hand, technology appears more and more unlikely to be interpreted through traditional legal categories ("legal order," "norm," and so on); on the other hand, information technologies gradually aim at interpreting themselves from a legal perspective, and in turn, they transform into a conceptual scheme.

We now analyze these two separate aspects in the following paragraphs. Regarding the first, we can consider the "internet case." Regardless of the many sociological reflections of the "web" (from its emancipatory potentialities to possible forms of technological totalitarianism), it is well-known that the debate focuses on the *legal nature* of the internet with regard to two fundamental positions.

According to the first position, the internet evolves as an "anarchic" dimension. Due to its deconstructed architecture, it is a space without rules and cannot be compared to a legal order. On the contrary, the second orientation relies on the idea that cyberspace creates a sort of specific legal structure (perhaps a new model of "sovereignty", even if outside the common understanding of "legal order"). Furthermore, there is a third position which considers the internet a social organization equipped with a reticular basis radically different from a pyramidal structure.

These remarks allow us to grasp the second point: the conceptual relevance of the new technologies. The implementation of IT reduces law to a normative technique. Also, at a conceptual level, it brings about the development of interpretative models based on the metaphor/category of the "Net."

The increasing sociological accreditation of the internet implies the possibility of conceiving the whole society as a "net," hence the idea of "network (web) society." In this way, post-industrial societies should be understood as a great and disarticulated "net" of relations and transactions, made up of "knots" (subjects, actions) within a legal scheme of soft rules.

This is the most important point. The "network (web) framework" is grounded in a *soft* or *light* model of society and law, as mentioned earlier, and is synthesized by the concept of *governance*.[35] The distance between the

35 G. De Búrca & J. Scott (eds.), Law and New Governance in the EU and in the US (Hart 2006). Especially Part I concerning the relations among new governance, law, and constitutionalism as it pertains to the technological reflexes of this concept; Suzor, Lawless: the Secret Rules that Govern Our Digital Lives (Cambridge University Press 2019). In particular, Part I and chapter 11; R. Radu, Negotiating Internet Governance (Oxford University Press 2019) chs. 2–4.

classical notion of "government" and the concept of "governance" highlights the loss of relevance of traditional philosophical-legal categories such as "state," "sovereignty," and, ultimately, "rule of law": in other words, a model based on accountability without sovereignty.[36]

6 Post-Truth Age, Technology, and Some Anthropological-Political Reflections

Beyond the legal and political-institutional sphere, the implementation of IT involves many other levels and identitarian processes.

Aside from the "traditional" technologies, the new technological applications (in particular, information technology) are not neutral. The epistemological horizon underlying the social implementation of technology, which is based on a post-modern or post-truth model of knowledge, entails significant anthropological modifications and makes the concept of the "information society" much more problematic.

From this point of view, social networks and web communities are a good example. They allow for a focus on some *cognitive processes* implied by the new technologies and a better understanding of the modification of knowledge modeling as well as the concept of an "information (knowledge)-based society." It is necessary now to look at three fundamental anthropological dimensions: language, memory, and the idea of "corporeity."

Within the language dimension, the transition from "communication" to "interaction" is decisive. The wide diffusion of virtual environments (chat rooms, forums, blogs) has produced the shift from a traditional linguistic model, which was based on direct relation and dialogue, to another one. This new model is dominated by the creation of a barrier among interlocutors: taking the form of mere interaction, the technological devices set aside the usual ways of communicating.

A similar transformation occurs in the second dimension: memory. We can grasp this point by highlighting two models of memory. First, the traditional model of memory: the "experience-based memory" or "semantic memory." The traditional model relies on experiential contests; direct experience is the premise for elaborating on memories and transmitting them to future generations. Second, new technologies imply a new structure for mnestic functions: from semantic memory to "database memory." Memory is no longer a fabric of experiences but merely becomes a storage of information.

Finally, the virtual revolution impacts the idea of "corporeity." Internet users are not required to have direct (physical) involvement in the world. Virtual environments create space for different identities (nicknames) and memberships, allowing users to change communities, which leads to two conflicting orientations: virtualization and referentiality.

36 De Búrca & Scott, *Id.* at Epilogue.

Virtualization implies a progressive process of dematerialization, within which the technological interaction makes the physical traits of relationships (face, body posture, voice, etc.) irrelevant. At the same time, virtual interaction is frequently unsatisfactory and elicits a desire for real and personal relationship. In other words, there is a shift from the "virtual community" to the "real community."

As discussed earlier, the anthropological mutations produced by new technologies (language, memory, corporeity) call into question cognitive modifications: the changes in how thinking and speaking involve different ways conceiving things and persons. Accordingly, we must focus on the mental mechanisms underlying these dynamics, both in terms of the construction of knowledge models and the concept of an "information (knowledge)-based society."

Regardless of the superficial phenomenologies concerning the circulation of data, the conceptual point can be explained by comparing the model of knowledge originating from the Enlightenment with the post-modern model.

The scientific community clearly exemplifies the first model. Although it is essentially an "open" model, scientific investigation develops within a structured framework. The sharing of a universal methodology, as well as the realization of a comprehensive model of knowledge (i.e. the ideal of "encyclopaedia"), makes the scientific community a strongly structured dimension: a "scientific republic."

A very different model of knowledge seems to emerge, one based on a fluid, dynamic, and non-hierarchical structure. Wikipedia is a good illustration of this model. Separate from the framework expressed by the modern "scientific republic," the pattern of knowledge (or perhaps information) encapsulated within Wikipedia has two fundamental traits.

Firstly, Wikipedia offers a completely fragmented set of "data (information)"; grounded in non-linear hypertextual browsing, the concept of "hypertext" synthesizes a disarticulated model of knowledge. Secondly, in light of this particular structure, knowledge is always in progress. Wikipedia is "open" in a double meaning. The framework of data is continually evolving; there is no definitive level because the limit of the acquired information is to be understood in an asymptotic manner. Moreover, Wikipedia represents the output of "democratic cooperation" without hierarchical order. As knowledge is a communal endeavour, it is never definite and complete.

In other words, a reticular model of knowledge develops as a parallel process to the implementation of a reticular social model. At an epistemological-cognitive level, knowledge is no longer conceived as a comprehensive and structured system but rather as merely a "net" of information, as described by Lévy in his concept of "cyberculture."[37]

37 P. Lévy, L'intelligence collective. Pour une antropologie du cyberspace (La Découverte 1994); A development in D. De Kerckhove, Connected Intelligence: The Arrival of the Web Society (Somerville House Publ 1997).

It is also important to pay attention to this notion in order to clarify the concept of an "information (knowledge)-based society." According to Levy, "cyberculture" encompasses practices and mental aptitudes developed within the "cyberspace." In this way, the French author establishes a close relationship between "virtual" and "cyberculture." These two concepts embody the technological articulation of the modern-philosophical model and rely on a "universal semantic system." Specifically, this implies a paradigm without a logical center or pivot. More precisely, the reticular system of knowledge underlying the cyberculture entails a new Cartesian tree of knowledge, evolving through the process of *hypertextualization*.

The anthropological-cognitive aspect of these dynamics, as synthesized through Levy's analysis,[38] is closely intertwined with collective decision-making processes and the conceptualization of the "information-based (knowledge-based) society."

The case of "political deliberation" is paradigmatic. The ongoing implementation of reticular and fragmented patterns of knowledge determines the symmetric diffusion of analogous models of "decision-making"; the cognitive level feeds back into the decisional dimension. Fundamental moments of political deliberation, such as reflection, assessment, and choice, progressively become the expression of subjectivist and emotive decisions based on casual and contingent information (*not* knowledge), and in the absence of global philosophical perspectives.

The legitimation and functionality crises of democracy are natural corollaries of this process, revealing the ambiguity of the formula "information-based (knowledge-based) society." Between "information" and "knowledge," there is no superimposition or identification. This is why Levy's outlook is not convincing. Information (and the concept of an "information-based society") is rooted in a reticular, non-hierarchical scheme or series of data, while knowledge (and the notion of a "knowledge-based society") belongs to historical models and epistemological premises vastly different from our highly technologized and mass societies.[39]

7 Concluding Remarks

To avoid misunderstandings, it is necessary to reiterate the following important point. The previous analysis has not questioned technological development itself, particularly when considered as a model of scientific knowledge. In

38 See also P. Lévy, Qu'es-ce que le virtuel (La Découverte 1995).

39 More information about this point can be found at Philip G. Altbach, *Globalization and Forces for Change in Higher Education*, *in* The International Imperative in Higher Education 7–10 (Philip G. Altbach (ed.), Global Perspectives on Higher Education. SensePublishers 2013) <https://doi.org/10.1007/978-94-6209-338-6_2>.

this respect, the ongoing opposition between the "condemnation" and "glorification" of the science–technology relationship appears meaningless.

Technology plays an unavoidable role, meaning that understanding the evolution of new scenarios becomes crucial. More precisely, the present (and future) relationship between technology (science) and law should be examined in light of different conceptual horizons. The evolving global scenario involves both technology and law. Accordingly, close consideration of scientific-technological impact on the legal-institutional level and its deliberative dimension is necessary.

To sum up, three key points need to be underlined. These points concern the *political-institutional* level, the *cognitive* dimension, and the *Western nature* of these processes.

The *political-institutional* level refers to the radically new interaction between technological and political processes. Once again, this passage should be considered in light of its effects on political legitimization and consent mechanisms, which are the key to the "rule of law." Due to the crisis of traditional political mediation (such as the role of parties), the progressive individualization of deliberative processes encompasses an anthropological mutation (defined as a crisis of "network" and "citizen") as well as a different conceptualization of law and politics.

Regarding the cognitive profile, beyond the previous considerations, the massive recourse to and implementation of technologies should be emphasized. This could imply two closely related fatal processes: *sociological homogenization* and demagogic *politics.*

Sociological homologation is driven by the ongoing confusion between information (information-based society) and knowledge (knowledge-based society). The technological circulation of a vast amount of information, focused only on the widespread availability of data, does not necessarily lead to the development of a corresponding level of knowledge. On the contrary, the diffusion of the *same* data through the *same* technological devices and channels flattens cultural horizons, limits the diversity of opinions, and reduces the range of decisional criteria.

Political demagogy relies on this substratum.[40] The implementation of new technologies could serve as a significant vehicle to exacerbate the negative symbiosis between information and knowledge, along with its populist corollaries, fostering a direct relationship between governors/rulers and governed/citizens.[41]Simultaneously, it creates a present (and especially future) disturbing scenario dominated by the tension between the necessity to adopt

40 P. Roberts-Miller, Demagoguery and Democracy (The Experiment 2017).

41 C. R. Kaltwasser et al., The Handbook of Populism (Oxford University Press 2017); C. Mudde & C. R. Kaltwasser, Populism. A Very Short Introduction 1–6 (Oxford University Press 2017); B. Moffitt, The Global Rise of Populism: Performance, Political Style and Representation (Stanford University Press 2016).

complex decisions and the temptation to streamline the decision-making processes. Are we truly in a "post-democracy" age or, as some authors suggest, a "neo-democracy"?[42]

Finally, it is essential to consider the *Western* historical-cultural context of these processes. The implementation of a specific pattern of science (and technology) traces back to the philosophical roots of our cultural model. The "science–technology" pair is deeply embedded in the cultural origins of the Western model, specifically within the complex interplay of philosophy, politics, and law established in ancient Greece.

We can fully appreciate the recent issues concerning democratic models only by considering the role played by technology (including its scientific-epistemological foundations) within this Western framework, particularly in comparison to different cultural models now prevalent in our countries.

In conclusion, regarding the encompassing of law and the political-institutional dimension, the classical category of the "rule of law" is under fire for many reasons, not only by internal (i.e., Western) factors, such as epistemological transitions, modifications of social models (the "ideas" of society), and the progressive implementation of different paradigms of law. The "rule of law" is also called into question by the unavoidable comparison with very different cultural and normative models, which developed without a concept of "science" or a model of technology influencing the social, as well as the legal, model.

42 K. Von Beyme, From Post-Democracy to Neo-Democracy (Springer 2018).

4 Using Flexibility Mechanisms for Addressing Technological and Scientific Developments

Examples from Selected Global Regulatory Frameworks

*Imad Antoine Ibrahim**

1 Introduction

Historically, regulating science was a difficult task, given that the term itself was not clearly defined, where the confusion remains nowadays to a certain extent in various fields.[1] Although rules tackling the science of each century existed, the main literature on the topic emerged in the nineteenth and twentieth century, where the law was used to describe modern science,[2] resulting in the term "regulatory science."[3] The history of science is connected with that of technology, given the interdependence between these two fields.[4] The interplay between law, science, and technology is becoming increasingly complicated as scientific and technological developments are affecting all aspects of human societies. Examples of this interplay include, inter alia, food labels, passports, bank cards, door security locks, etc.[5] Given this interdependent relation, the law impacted, and is still impacting, the development of science and technology and vice versa.[6] In this context, research plays a significant role in the further development of science and technology, increasing their

* Imad Antoine Ibrahim, Assistant Professor, University of Twente, Faculty of Behavioural, Management and Social Sciences, Department of Governance and Technology for Sustainability, Twente University, The Netherlands and gLAWcal—Global Law Initiative for Sustainable Development (United Kingdom). PhD in Law at Sant'Anna School of Advanced Studies; Institute of Law, Politics and Development, Pisa, Italy, Master in European Interdisciplinary Studies, from the College of Europe, Bruges, Belgium, Bachelor in Law from the Lebanese University "Filiere Francophone de Droit," Beirut, Lebanon.

1 Isaiah Berlin, *History and Theory: The Concept of Scientific History*, 1(1) History and Theory 1–10 (1960).

2 Jane E. Ruby, *The Origins of Scientific "Law"*, 47(3) Journal of the History of Ideas 341 (1986).

3 Sheila Jasanoff, *What Is the Regulatory Science? Concept and History in United States and in Japan – Interview with Professor Sheila Jasanoff –*, 39(1) Clinical Evaluation 1, 1–2 (2011).

4 George Sarton, *The History of Science*, 26(3) The Monist 321, 336 (1916).

5 Alex Faulkner, Bettina Lange & Christopher Lawless, *Introduction: Material Worlds: Intersections of Law, Science, Technology, and Society*, 39(1) Journal of Law & Society (2012).

6 Diganth Raj Sehgal, Relationship Between Law, Science, and Technology in Modern Society (*Pleaders*, 3 March 2021) <https://blog.ipleaders.in/relationship-law-science-technology-modern-society/>.

DOI: 10.4324/9781003472421-4

independence and interdependence as fields.[7] Trade as well plays an important role in furthering technological and scientific developments and independence.[8] Moreover, there is a growing legal literature on the interdependence and interplay between the three sectors from a theoretical and practical perspective, where lawyers and scholars are seeking to dissect all the relevant issues.[9] In fact, regulations are expected to play a great role in the management of scientific and technological developments,[10] while these fields have already and are currently pushing towards the evolution of the law to keep up with the fast developments occurring.[11]

Still, this task remains a very challenging one for regulators and policymakers as technological and scientific developments question the boundaries of law[12] and technical expertise of the various courts.[13] Hence, there is an uneasy relationship between law on one hand and science and technology on the other that has been taking place since the scientific and technological

7 The importance of research generally and in this context resulted in calls for considering the existence of a right to research. See Arjun Appadurai, *The Right to Research*, 4 Globalization, Societies and Education 167 (2006); Michael Gibbons & Ron Johnston, *The Roles of Science in Technological Innovation*, 3 Research Policy 220 (1974).

8 United Nations Economic and Social Council, Economic and Social Commission for Asia and the Pacific, Committee on Information and Communications Technology, Science, Technology and Innovation. Second session, Bangkok, 29–31 August 2018; Item 4 (b) of the provisional agenda: Policy issues for science, technology and innovation: leveraging technology and trade for economic development: Leveraging technology and trade for economic development; Note by the secretariat. ESCAP/CICTSTI/2018/7. Sebastian Pfotenhauer, *Trade Policy Is Science Policy*, XXX Issues in Science and Technology (2013) <https://issues.org/sebastian/>.

9 Rafael Dean Brown, *Property Ownership and the Legal Personhood of Artificial Intelligence*, 30(2) Information & Communications Technology Law 208–234 (2021); Erica Palmerini, *The Interplay Between Law and Technology, or the RoboLaw Project in context*, *in* Law and Technology: The Challenge of Regulating Technological Development 7, 11–12 (Erica Palmerini & Elettra Stradella (eds.), Pisa University Press 2013); Andrew Murray, Information Technology Law: The Law and Society (Oxford University Press 2013); Susan Haack, Evidence Matters: Science, Proof, and Truth in the Law (Cambridge University Press 2014); Mireille Hildebrandt, Smart Technologies and the End(s) of Law: Novel Entanglements of Law and the End(s) of Law (Edward Elgar Publishing 2015).

10 James W. Curlin, *Saving Us from Ourselves: The Interaction of Law and Science-Technology*, 47 Denver Law Review 651, 652 (1970); Jon Truby, Rafael Brown & Andrew Dahdal, *Banking on AI: Mandating a Proactive Approach to AI Regulation in the Financial Sector*, 14 Law and Financial Markets Review 110 (2020) (calling for a balanced regulation of technology in the finance industry).

11 Roger Brownsword, Law, Technology and Society: Reimagining the Regulatory Environment (Routledge 2019).

12 Mihalis Kritikos, *What If Technologies Shaped the Law? [Science and Technology Podcast]* (European Parliamentary Research Service) <https://epthinktank.eu/2018/06/08/what-if-technologies-shaped-the-law-science-and-technology-podcast/>.

13 Riikka Koulu, Law, Technology and Dispute Resolution: The Privatisation of Coercion (Routledge 2019).

revolution in the last centuries.[14] In particular, science and technology have a great impact on international law for different reasons, such as globalization of the impact of science/technology due to international trade and international movement of people, despite the little acknowledgement of these effects. In fact, international law has very few treaties addressing science and technology directly or indirectly.[15] These include, for instance, certain agreements in the general framework of the multilateral trade system, such as the Agreement on the Application of Sanitary and Phytosanitary Measures.[16] In this context, the ends of international law, the means available to pursue them, as well as the nature and structure of this field have been changed by science and technology.[17] Moreover, new challenges have also emerged as a result,[18] as science and technology play an important role in the development of nations.[19]

To that end, this chapter focuses on the regulation of science and technological developments at the international level, given the important role international law is expected to play in this regard. The author is seeking to answer the following question: How can the international community address the challenges of regulating science and technology, given the current uncertainties, lack of knowledge, and rapid progress occurring in these fields? The author will argue that existing global regulatory frameworks include flexibility mechanisms that were incorporated to address similar or other challenges witnessed in different sectors such as finance, climate change, trade, and transboundary freshwaters. These mechanisms can be incorporated within new international agreements and instruments addressing emerging technologies and sciences while considering the particularities of these fields. Like that, challenges such

14 Margaret A. Bergert & Lawrence M. Solan, *The Uneasy Relationship Between Science and Law: An Essay and Introduction*, 73 Brooklyn Law Review 847, 847–852 (2008). More on science and technological revolution, See James E. McClellan III & Harold Dorn, Science and Technology in World History: An Introduction (3d ed., John Hopkins University Press 2015); Paul L. Gardner, *The Roots of Technology and Science: A Philosophical and Historical View*, *in* Shaping Concepts of Technology: From Philosophical Perspective to Mental Images 13–20 (Marc J. De Vries & Arley Tamir (eds.), Springer 1997); Paul L. Gardner, *The Relationship Between Technology and Science: Some Historical and Philosophical Reflections. Part I*, 4 International Journal of Technology and Design Education 123 (1994).

15 Joseph W. Dellapenna, *Law in a Shrinking World: The Interaction of Science and Technology with International Law*, 88 Kentucky Law Journal 809, 831–832 (1999/2000); Aqib Aslam et al., Globalization Helps Spread Knowledge and Technology Across Borders (*IMFBlog*, 9 April 2018) <https://blogs.imf.org/2018/04/09/globalization-helps-spread-knowledge-and-technology-across-borders/>; William Sims Bainbridge, *Science and Technology Globalization*, *in* Handbook of Science and Technology Convergence 621, 621–629 (William Sims & Bainbridge Mihail C. Roco (eds.), Springer 2016).

16 The WTO Agreement on the Application of Sanitary and Phytosanitary Measures (SPS Agreement), adopted in 1995.

17 Dellapenna, *supra* note 15, at 832.

18 *Id.* at 842.

19 Manfred Lachs, *Thoughts on Science, Technology and World Law*, 86 American Journal of International Law 673, 676 (1992).

as uncertainties, lack of knowledge, and rapid progress can be tackled. The author will examine this argument in practice in the context of specific flexibility mechanisms developed within international financial law, international trade law, international climate change law, and international water law.

The chapter will first examine the inability of the law to keep up with the scientific and technological developments that are occurring at an extremely rapid pace.[20] Based on the preceding information, the author will call for incorporating flexibility mechanisms from various regulatory frameworks within future agreements and instruments addressing science and technology. Flexibility in this context provides states with a much-needed margin of appreciation to apply the adopted international rules in the context of constant changes and developments in the fields of science and technology, creating uncertainties or rendering these rules inadequate or insufficient. The chapter then addresses selected flexibility mechanisms with specific legal fields. These mechanisms are: (1) Article XX of the General Agreement on Tariffs and Trade (GATT); (2) compliance mechanisms within the Paris Agreement; (3) regulatory sandboxes for the regulation of financial technologies; and (4) flexibility mechanisms within international water law. The selected flexibility mechanisms have been examined in detail in the literature, given the impact and relevance of each one of them in their fields.[21] Moreover, each of these examples provides different means for addressing the relation between science and technology on one hand and regulation on the other.

2 Current Challenges Facing the Regulation of Scientific and Technological Development

This section will address the inability of the law to keep up with scientific and technological changes, given the nature of the law and the rapid progress that is occurring.

2.1 The Law Is Unable to Catch Up With Scientific Progress

The issue of rapid scientific development and the need for its regulation is not new. In the past, science was considered to be developing very fast.

20 See for example, Jon Truby & Rafael Brown, *Human Digital Thought Clones: The Holy Grail of Artificial Intelligence for Big Data*, 30 Information & Communications Technology Law 140 (2021) (discussing the rise of digital thought clones and the inability of regulation to keep up).

21 See for instance, Jan Klabbers, *Jurisprudence in International Trade Law: Article XX of GATT*, 26 Journal of World Trade 63 (1992); Christina Voigt, *The Compliance and Implementation Mechanism of the Paris Agreement*, 25 Review of European, Comparative & International Environmental Law 161 (2016); Hilary J. Allen, *Regulatory Sandboxes*, 87 The George Washington Law Review 579 (2019); Alena Drieschova, Mark Giordano & Itay Fischlendler, *Governance Mechanisms to Address Flow Variability in Water Treaties*, 18 Global Environmental Change 285 (2008).

This led institutions like the church to claim a right to regulate it for moral and ethical reasons, claiming the possession of superior knowledge of morality.[22] Science had a great impact on the Industrial Revolution, resulting in the adoption of regulations to that end. New regulations were also adopted in the twentieth century, and currently, discussions concerning the adoption of rules tackling the fourth Industrial Revolution are ongoing.[23] Moral claims still persist, but in the context of states and the international community seeking to adopt ethical science and regulating it via various legal frameworks such as international human rights law.[24] There are many other aspects where regulations are needed in the context of science, such as its risks and promises, its global governance, etc.[25] In fact, there is a great intersection between science and law taking place between scientists and lawyers, which have different vocabularies. In many instances, a clash occurs between them on the interpretation of various scientific events and rules,[26] while some scholars even classified the law as a science which was subject to great criticism.[27]

Currently, regulators and the various economic actors are seeking to adopt regulations addressing science. Yet these rules become out of date or irrelevant by the time they are implemented.[28] This is further complicated in the transboundary context as companies operate across borders requiring

22 Mary Warnock, *The Ethical Regulation of Science*, 450 Nature 615 (2007).

23 Cormac Ó. Gráda, *Did Science Cause the Industrial Revolution?*, 54 Journal of Economic Literature 224 (2016); Michael C. Jensen, *The Modern Industrial Revolution, Exit, and the Failure of Internal Control Systems*, 48 The Journal of Finance 831 (1993); Anne Marie Engtoft Larsen, Podcast: Regulation for the Fourth Industrial Revolution (*World Economic Forum*, 31 January 2018) <www.weforum.org/agenda/2018/01/podcast-regulation-for-the-fourth-industrial-revolution/>.

24 Ana Nordberg et al., *Cutting Edges and Weaving Threads in the Gene Editing Evolution: Reconciling Scientific Progress with Legal, Ethical, and Social Concerns*, 5 Journal of Law and Biosciences 35 (2018). The international community has considered that everyone has a right to enjoy the benefits of scientific progress and imposed on obligations on states concerning the protection and diffusion of science within Article 15 of the International Covenant on Economic Social and Cultural rights, among many other things. Moreover, various documents have been adopted globally addressing the right to science, most recently General Comment No. 25 (2020) on science and economic, social and cultural rights (Article 15 (1) (b), (2), (3), and (4) of the International Covenant on Economic, Social and Cultural Rights).

25 See, Daniel J. Rozell, Dangerous Science: Science Policy and Risk Analysis for Scientists and Engineers (Ubiquity Press 2020); Yury Sayamov, *Global Governance of Science: Wishful Thinking or a Life Necessity in the Context of International Relations and Their Philosophy*, *in* Marketing Initiatives for Sustainable Educational Development 246–263 (Purnendu Tripathi & Siran Mukerji (eds.), IGI Global 2018).

26 U.S. Department of Justice, Office of Justice Programs, National Institute of Justice, *National Conference on Science and the Law: Proceedings* 1–100 (July 2000; NCJ 179630).

27 M. C. Roos, *Is Law Science?*, 17 Potchefstroom Electronic Law Journal 1391 (2014).

28 Daniel Malan, The Law Can't Keep Up with New Tech. Here's How to Close the Gap (*World Economic Forum*, 21 June 2018) <www.weforum.org/agenda/2018/06/law-too-slow-for-new-tech-how-keep-up/>.

the establishment of global frameworks.[29] In fact, the regulation of scientific development is extremely difficult, given the inability to foresee the scientific changes that may occur. Such changes affect any legal distinction made through rules generating new types of legal issues and challenges.[30] Moreover, drawing policies and laws based on science faces, in many instances, public concerns, in particular, a lack of trust in scientific facts, such as in the case of environmental science[31] or, more recently, COVID-19 and the science behind vaccination.[32] Already, nations face unequal distribution of scientific knowledge and innovation, affecting societies' development, especially in developing countries. Besides, the emergence of proper regulations for tackling scientific progress hinders scientific dissemination, as the majority of scientific knowledge is transferred from developed to developing countries.[33] Also, there is a need to bridge a gap between law and science, as lawyers and scientists often do not engage with each other since scientists consider that lawyers do not have the capacity to assist them effectively, while lawyers do not recognize the role of scientists when drawing public policies. Numerous scientists do not focus on translating their research findings into policy and law, viewing this task as someone's else role, and have little incentives to do so from a professional perspective. In contrast, lawyers and policymakers are seeking to use science to support their arguments without regard to new evidence, as the focus is on strengthening their position, resulting in a narrow and limited understanding of the research that is being conducted by scientists.[34] In this context, other factors also play a role, mainly political ones, as well as the level of acceptable risk a society is willing to tolerate.[35] This is despite the need for sound regulation of science, given the public distrust of science and in the context of the need to regulate risks, including scientific ones.[36]

29 White & Case Technology Newsflash, *Law & Technology: Risks and Opportunities from the Tectonic Forces at Work* (18 June 2018) <www.whitecase.com/publications/insight/law-technology-risks-and-opportunities-tectonic-forces-work>.

30 Lyria Bennett Moses, *Why Have a Theory of Law and Technological Change?*, 8 Minnesota Journal of Law, Science & Technology 589, 602–605 (2007).

31 Nikolaous Voulvoulis & Mark A. Burgman, *The Contrasting Roles of Science and Technology in Environmental Challenges*, 49 Critical Reviews in Environmental Science and Technology 1079 (2019).

32 Regi Jose et al., *Public Perception and Preparedness for the Pandemic COVID 19: A Health Belief Model Approach*, 9 Clinical Epidemiology and Global Health 41 (2021).

33 Maru Mormina, *Science, Technology and Innovation as Social Goods for Development: Rethinking Research Capacity Building from Sen's Capabilities Approach*, 25 Science and Engineering Ethics 671 (2019).

34 Micah L. Berman & Annice E. Kim, *Bridging the Gap between Science and Law: The Example of Tobacco Regulatory Science*, 43 Journal of Law, Medicine & Ethics 95, 95–98 (2015).

35 Christopher Carrigan & Cary Coglianese, *The Politics of Regulation: From New Institutionalism to New Governance*, 14 Annual Review of Political Science 107 (2011); Paul Slovic, *Perception of Risk*, 236 Science 280 (1987).

36 Geoffrey C. Kabat, *Taking Distrust of Science Seriously*, 18 EMBO Reports 1052, 1052–1055 (2017); Morning Future, *Living in the Risk Society: Ulrich Beck's Lesson* (18 March 2020) <www.morningfuture.com/en/2020/03/18/ulrich-beck-risk-society/>.

All these factors resulted in a situation where the law is unable to catch up with the scientific developments taking place, especially as numerous issues were noticed when attempting to regulate these developments. These include, inter alia,

> **(3)** the inherent imprecision of law for regulating complex and rapidly evolving scientific research; (ii) the difficulties of enforcing legal restrictions on an activity that is international in scope; (iii) the limited predictability of the consequences of restricting specific branches of scientific research; (iv) inertia in the legislative process; and (v) the susceptibility of legislators and regulators to inappropriate factors and influence.[37]

In this context, Merchant and Pope argued for the use of non-traditional legal tools, such as norms and voluntary standards developed by scientists for the regulation of scientific research that is deemed problematic.[38]

2.2 *The Law Is Unable to Catch Up With Technological Development*

The law and the legal institutions constantly face technological changes that must be addressed,[39] where numerous questions have risen about the ways the law should regulate technology.[40] Yet the law has not been able to regulate efficiently emerging technologies, especially as these technologies are advancing rapidly.[41] Such rapid development contradicts the way rules are established over centuries in contrast to current technological changes that are occurring over decades and years.[42] Current estimates highlight that the law is at least five years behind when it comes to the regulation of new technologies, as the regulator is forced to catch up with new technological development all the time.[43] Legal scholars have also struggled in the analysis of the impact of technological changes on the legal field, similar to other

37 Gary E. Marchant & Lynda L. Pope, *The Problems with Forbidding Science*, 15 Science Engineering Ethics 375 (2009).

38 *Ibid.*

39 Kieran Tranter, *The Laws of Technology and the Technology of Law*, 20 Griffith Law Review 754 (2011).

40 Lyria Bennett Moses, *How to Think about Law, Regulation and Technology: Problems with "Technology" as a Regulatory Target*, 5 Law, Innovation and Technology 1 (2013); Truby, Brown & Dahdal, *supra* note 10, at 110 (regulation of technology transforming the finance sector).

41 See references to regulatory inertia with digital technologies in Jon Truby, *Decarbonizing Bitcoin: Law and Policy Choices for Reducing the Energy Consumption of Blockchain Technologies and Digital Currencies*, 44 Energy Research & Social Science 399 (2018).

42 Vivek Wadhwa, Laws and Ethics Can't Keep Pace with Technology (*MIT Technology Review*, 15 April 2014) <www.technologyreview.com/2014/04/15/172377/laws-and-ethics-cant-keep-pace-with-technology/>.

43 Julia Griffith, A Losing Game: The Law Is Struggling to Keep Up with Technology (*JHTL*, 12 April2019)<https://sites.suffolk.edu/jhtl/2019/04/12/a-losing-game-the-law-is-struggling-to-keep-up-with-technology/>.

scholars from other fields, such as history and philosophy.[44] Regulators are making an effort to understand and effectively use emerging technologies, such as data science, to increase the efficiency and effectiveness of regulations.[45] This is important, as regulations should not hinder innovation,[46] although in many places nationally and globally, there are calls for slowing down innovation when the risks outweigh the benefits on the basis of the precautionary principle.

Still, technological progress constantly poses challenges for the law, as new technologies do not fit in the general framework of existing rules and legal categories. This creates great uncertainty that is intensified as a result of the often-ambiguous legal concepts and provisions. Moreover, new technologies may affect the reasons for which a law was adopted in the first place by changing the circumstances and the facts, impacting the effectiveness of existing regulations.[47] Because of this, many see the courts and judges as the principal agent to interpret existing rules in the light of technological developments,[48] while others see the emergence of new theories on law and technology as the way forward.[49] New technologies may also challenge the scope of existing rules, requiring changes to include conducts that were not initially covered within these rules. All these situations require an adaptation or reinterpretation of the existing laws. Yet there are situations where new technologies result in the need to repeal existing rules as the *raison d'être* no longer exists or that rule is no longer enforceable. In these cases, there is a need for new rules to address the technological developments.[50] Examples of changes or new rules that need to be adopted concern, for instance, the use of new technologies in policing, posing a new set of challenges and questions in the fields of constitutional law, human rights, etc.[51]

In this context, various suggestions were made to address these challenges. For instance, Brownsword proposed the re-invention of the law via a new understanding of legal responsibilities establishing the rule of law, resulting,

44 Meg Leta Jones, *Does Technology Drive Law? The Dilemma of Technological Exceptionalism in Cyberlaw*, 2018 Journal of Law, Technology & Policy 249, 256 (2018).

45 Kate McEntaggart, Julien Etienne & Simona de Paolis, *The Use of Emerging Technologies for Regulation Main Findings and Roadmap* 6 (BEIS Research Paper Number 2020/041).

46 World Economic Forum, *Agile Regulation for the Fourth Industrial Revolution a Toolkit for Regulators* 4 (December 2020).

47 Lyria Bennetter Moses, *Adapting the Law to Technological Change: A Comparison of Common Law and Legislation*, 26 UNSW Law Journal 394 (2003).

48 William Sowers, *How Do You Solve a Problem Like Law-Disruptive Technology?* 82 Law and Contemporary Problems 193, 193–200 (2019).

49 Lyria Bennett Moses, *Why Have a Theory of Law and Technological Change?* 8 Minnesota Journal of Law, Science & Technology 589 (2007).

50 Moses, *Id.* at 394.

51 Markus Naarttijärv, *Legality and Democratic Deliberation in Black Box Policing*, Technology and Regulation 35 (2019).

among many things, in a restructuring of legal institutions.[52] Other ways to address the interplay between law and technology are through the establishment of groups of experts and stakeholders, such as technologists, political actors, and academics.[53] Hence, a flexible approach to their regulation is needed, especially as COVID-19 highlighted the need for rapid innovation while adopting flexible regulations, considering the uncertainties.[54] It is also in this context that terms such as *regulatory technology* (RegTech) emerged, with the aim of using technology to realize regulatory objectives,[55] while a greater focus on the interplay between law and technology is taking place among legal scholars.[56]

3 Using Existing Flexibility Mechanisms from Various Regulatory Frameworks

There are various reasons for which flexibility mechanisms are needed within international law. These include, inter alia, the lack of information about future events, the changes in states' preferences, and potential shifts in politics at the domestic level. In this context, flexibility mechanisms are very important as they allow the parties to manage any risks emanating from joining the agreement, acting as insurance policy and permitting its revision, updating, and renouncement in case the costs of commitment are too high.[57] Yet selecting a flexibility mechanism that suits an agreement is very challenging, as a balance must be made between having mechanisms that can be used easily and others that are very difficult to deploy when needed.[58] Flexibility tools include "unilateral reservation and declaration clauses; entry into-force requirements; limitations on territorial application; duration provisions; amendment and revision procedures; and rules governing suspension, withdrawal, and termination."[59] Currently, there is a lack of an actual global regulatory framework on science

52 Roger Brownsword, *Law Disrupted, Law Re-Imagined, Law Re-Invented*, Technology and Regulation 10 (2019).

53 Nihit Goyal, Michael Howlett & Araz Taeihagh, *Why and How Does the Regulation of Emerging Technologies Occur? Explaining the Adoption of the EU General Data Protection Regulation Using the Multiple Streams Framework*, Regulation & Governance 1, 3 (2021).

54 World Economic Forum, *supra* note 46, at 4.

55 Australian Government, *Productivity Commission, Regulatory Technology* 4 (Information Paper, October 2020).

56 Roger Brownsword, Eloise Scotford & Karen Yeung, The Oxford Handbook of Law, Regulation and Technology (Oxford University Press 2017); Brownsword, *supra* note 11; Jon Truby, *Governing Artificial Intelligence to Benefit the UN Sustainable Development Goals 2020 Sustainable Development*, 28 Sustainable Development 946 (2020).

57 Laurence R. Helfer, *Flexibility in International Agreements*, *in* Interdisciplinary Perspectives on International Law and International Relations: The State of the Art 175 (Jeffrey L. Dunoff & Mark A. Pollack (eds.), Cambridge University Press 2012).

58 *Id.* at 176.

59 *Id.* at 177.

and technology, where these elements are being addressed through different fields, be it, for instance, climate change, genetic resources, etc.[60] Hence, what is lacking is a comprehensive global framework on science and technology, where efforts are underway for the development of such framework.[61] Because of that, the author is arguing that selected flexibility mechanisms that exist within other legal fields should be incorporated within this new framework to address the constant developments and changes that are taking place in the scientific and technological fields while simultaneously applying the provisions of any agreement established to that end. The following sections will address specific flexibility mechanisms from various global regulatory frameworks, which can be replicated to address the rapid and continuous development of science and technology.

4 Selected Flexibility Mechanisms Within Specific Legal Fields

This section will examine flexibility mechanisms included within international financial law, international trade law, international climate change law, and international water law.

4.1 Article XX of the General Agreement on Tariffs and Trade

The progressive development of the multilateral trade system took place since the Second World War with the establishment of the GATT agreement.[62] Various trade rounds occurred over the years, resulting in the 1990s in the greatest reform of the system with the establishment of the World Trade Organization (WTO) and its agreements. Further rounds occurred since then, like the 2001 Doha Round, and major achievements were made.[63] The other agreements adopted besides GATT are the General Agreement on Trade in Services,[64] the Agreement on Trade-Related Aspects of Intellectual Property Rights,[65] the

60 Gary E. Marchant, Braden R. Allenby & Joseph R. Herkert (eds.), The Growing Gap Between Emerging Technologies and Legal-Ethical Oversight: The Pacing Problem (Springer 2011); Abbe E. L. Brown, Intellectual Property, Climate Change and Technology: Managing National Legal Intersections, Relationships and Conflicts (Edward Elgar Publishing 2019); Michael Halewood et al., *Plant Genetic Resources for Food and Agriculture: Opportunities and Challenges Emerging from the Science and Information Technology Revolution*, 217 New Phytologist 1407 (2018).

61 Kenneth W. Abbott, *An International Framework Agreement on Scientific and Technological Innovation and Regulation*, *in* The Growing Gap between Emerging Technologies and Legal-Ethical Oversight: The Pacing Problem 127–156 (Braden R. Allenby, Joseph R. Herkert & Gary E. Marchant (eds.), Springer 2011).

62 World Trade Organization, *The General Agreement on Tariffs and Trade* (GATT 1947) <www.wto.org/english/docs_e/legal_e/gatt47_01_e.htm>.

63 World Trade Organization, *History of the Multilateral Trading System* <www.wto.org/english/thewto_e/history_e/history_e.htm>.

64 World Trade Organization, *supra* note 62.

65 Agreement on Trade-Related Aspects of Intellectual Property Rights, signed in 1994.

SPS Agreement,[66] and the Agreement on Technical Barriers to Trade.[67] All these agreements include provisions providing flexibility or waivers for member states that are parties to the multilateral trade system, including the GATT agreement, and in particular its Article XX.[68]

According to Article XX of the GATT agreement, states members to the multilateral trade system can restrict trade, be it import or export of products, as well as raising or reducing tariffs, as long as the measures taken are justified through this provision. The circumstances mentioned are associated with the need to take measures to protect public morals and the preservation of human, animal, and plant life or health.[69] States are also entitled to take measures related to the importation or exportation of gold or silver as well as those to secure

> compliance with laws or regulations which are not inconsistent with the provisions of this Agreement, including those relating to customs enforcement, the enforcement of monopolies . . ., the protection of patents, trademarks and copyrights, and the prevention of deceptive practices.[70]

States are allowed to adopt trade-restricting measures related to products of prison labour[71] and to protect national treasures of artistic, historic, or archaeological value.[72] Likewise, measures can be adopted to conserve exhaustible natural resources only if restrictions on domestic production and consumption are also imposed simultaneously,[73] as well as in "pursuance of obligations under any intergovernmental commodity agreement which conforms to criteria submitted to the CONTRACTING PARTIES and not disapproved by them or which is itself so submitted and not so disapproved."[74] Finally, states are entitled to adopt measures

> involving restrictions on exports of domestic materials necessary to ensure essential quantities of such materials to a domestic processing industry during periods when the domestic price of such materials is held below the world price as part of a governmental stabilization plan.[75]

66 SPS Agreement, *supra* note 16.

67 Final Act Embodying the Results of the Uruguay Round of Multilateral Trade Negotiations, April 15, 1994, 1867 U.N.T.S. 14, 33 I.L.M. 1143 (1994).

68 Jeffrey Kucik & Eric Reinhardt, *Does Flexibility Promote Cooperation? An Application to the Global Trade Regime*, 62 International Organization 477 (2008).

69 World Trade Organization, *supra* note 62, at Art. XX (a) & (b).

70 *Id.* at Art. XX (c) & (d).

71 *Id.* at Art. XX (e).

72 *Id.* at Art. XX (f).

73 *Id.* at Art. XX (g).

74 *Id.* at Art. XX (h).

75 *Id.* at Art. XX (i).

Other measures include those necessary to acquire or distribute products that face short supply in general or locally.[76]

In the case of new scientific and technological developments, there may be a need to restrict their use or control it for various reasons, mainly the presence of great uncertainties, given the lack of understanding of their impact on society in general. This is why there are calls for the regulation of emerging risks in technologies and sciences.[77] These risks are mainly affecting humans, society, and the environment. However, the question of regulating risks is very challenging, given the limited knowledge, deep uncertainty, and the inability to use traditional technocratic models to calculate the risks.[78] On one hand, there is a need to protect states and citizens, and on the other hand, innovation must not be hindered. Hence, regulators face a very challenging task as they must regulate in a context where the techno-scientific knowledge that is incomplete and uncertain is rapidly evolving and changing. Moreover, they must tackle political challenges resulting from the need to address the social, cultural, and value dimensions of innovation in science and technology.[79] It is worth mentioning that scientific expertise can be used for the regulation of new technologies, and vice versa.[80] Yet one has to keep in mind that expertise is not necessarily neutral, as it is influenced by many aspects (origin, field of expertise, personal opinions, personal bio, etc.).[81]

Given this reality, a provision like Article XX of the GATT may be useful for other regulatory frameworks seeking to adopt measures for protecting various legitimate interests from the risks posed by the constant technological and scientific developments. This is especially the case when it comes, for instance, to the protection of public morals and ethics, where various concerns have been voiced in this regard by scholars and experts.[82] It is also the case

76 *Id.* at Art. XX (j).

77 Jaime Bonnín Roca et al., *When Risks Cannot Be Seen: Regulating Uncertainty in Emerging Technologies*, 46 Research Policy 1215 (2017); Jonathan Wolff, *Risk and the Regulation of New Technologies*, *in* Risks and Regulation of New Technologies 3–18 (Tsuyoshi Matsuda, Jonathan Wolff & Takashi Yanagawa (eds.), Springer 2021).

78 Maria Weimer & Luisa Marin, *The Role of Law in Managing the Tension between Risk and Innovation: Introduction to the Special Issue on Regulating New and Emerging Technologies*, 7 European Journal of Risk Regulation 469 (2016).

79 Maria Weimer, Risk Regulation in the Internal Market: Lessons from Agricultural Biotechnology (Oxford University Press 2019).

80 Maria Weimer & Gaia Pisani, *Expertise as Justification: The Contested Legitimation of the EU 'Risk Administration'*, *in* Regulating Risks in the European Union: The Co-production of Expert and Executive Power 167, 171 (Maria Weimer & Anniek de Ruijter (eds.), Hart 2017).

81 Katharina Rietig, *'Neutral' Experts? How Input of Scientific Expertise Matters in International Environmental Negotiations*, 47 Policy Sciences 141 (2014); Karin Ingold & Muriel Gschwend, *Science in Policy-Making: Neutral Experts or Strategic Policy-Makers?*, 37 West European Politics 993 (2014); Marilyn Strathern, *Laudable Aims and Problematic Consequences, or: The 'Flow' of Knowledge Is Not Neutral*, 33 Economy and Society 550 (2004).

82 Lambèr Royakkers et al., *Societal and Ethical Issues of Digitization*, 20 Ethics and Information Technology 127 (2018). See in general, Paolo Davide Farah & Elena Cima (eds.), China's

when it comes to the need to preserve human, animal, and plant life or health, as scientific and technological developments may affect them positively or negatively.[83] Based on this, states can consider adding a provision within international agreements similar to Article XX of the GATT or even including further elements within such provisions where states may take measures restricting or controlling the use of emerging technologies and scientific developments for valid reasons mentioned in the provision. It is worth mentioning that the international trade system involves other provisions and practices related to the regulation of science and technology.[84] It is worth mentioning that states may use such a provision to hide unjustified discrimination measures against innovations similarly to many cases filed before the WTO where the parties use Article XX of the GATT as a way to justify measures protecting their products.[85] Hence, cases must be filed before international tribunals in such instances.

4.2 Compliance Mechanisms Within the Paris Agreement

The development of the international climate change regime occurred over decades of efforts and negotiations at the international level, where science played a significant role in proving the human impact on the climate and human responsibility in present global warming.[86] The efforts culminated in the 1990s with the adoption of the United Nations Framework Convention on Climate Change in 1992 and its Kyoto Protocol in 1997.[87] Since then, various Conferences of the Parties (COPs) took place with the aim of the progressive development of international climate change law, resulting in the adoption

---

Influence on Non-Trade Concerns in International Economic Law (Routledge 2016); Panagiotis Delimatsis, *Protecting Public Morals in a Digital Age: Revisiting the WTO Rulings on US – Gambling and China – Publications and Audiovisual Products*, 14 Journal of International Economic Law 257 (2011).

83 See for instance, Violeta Sima et al., *Influences of the Industry 4.0 Revolution on the Human Capital Development and Consumer Behavior: A Systematic Review*, 12 Sustainability 4035 (2020).

84 See for instance, Alessandra Guida, *Are WTO Decisionmakers Regulating Technological Risks or Are Technological Risks Steering WTO Biotechnology Legal Decisions?* Risk Analysis (2021); Jacqueline Peel, Science and Risk Regulation in International Law 171–263 (Cambridge University Press 2011).

85 World Trade Organization, Committee on Trade and Environment, GATT/WTO Dispute Settlement Practice Relating to GATT ARTICLE XX, Paragraphs (b), (d) AND (g); WT/CTE/W/203; 8 March 2002, pp. 3–46; Brandon L. Bowen, *The World Trade Organization and Its Interpretation of the Article XX Exceptions to the General Agreement on Tariffs and Trade, in Light of Recent Developments*, 29 Georgia Journal of International and Comparative Law 182 (2000).

86 Julia Kreienkamp, *The Long Road to Paris: The History of the Global Climate Change Regime* (Global Governance Institute; Policy Brief; November 2019).

87 United Nations Framework Convention on Climate Change signed in 1992; Kyoto Protocol to the United Nations Framework Convention on Climate Change, signed in 1998.

of the Paris Agreement in 2015.[88] The new agreement was hailed as a great achievement in the international arena, breaking new grounds in climate policy, especially when it comes to acknowledging the role of domestic politics in tackling climate change.[89] This agreement includes flexibility mechanisms as a result of the rigid approach adopted in previous climate change conventions, mainly the Kyoto Protocol, which failed to address global warming, as states did not implement its provisions.[90] This rigidity is also the same reason for which the Copenhagen conference on climate change failed, as the various nations were not willing to make the necessary compromises.[91]

The parties to the Paris Agreement established a mechanism to ease implementation and compliance.[92] The mechanism is a committee that is "expert-based and facilitative in nature and function in a manner that is transparent, non-adversarial and non-punitive."[93] The committee must consider the national capabilities and circumstances of the various nations.[94] The information to be used by the committee to assess a state's compliance with the agreement are mentioned in Articles 4 and 13. Parties, in accordance with Article 4(2), shall "prepare, communicate and maintain successive Nationally Determined Contributions (NDCs) that it intends to achieve."[95] The details related to this obligation are further laid out within Article 4, where a distinction in terms of responsibility was made between developed countries and developing ones, least developed countries (LDCs), and small island developing states (SIDS) that were granted flexibilities.[96] The NDCs in this context can be adjusted at any time by the parties.[97] The information that must be provided includes, inter alia, "a national inventory report of anthropogenic emissions by sources and removals by sinks of greenhouse gases."[98] Developed countries are expected to provide information related to finance, technology transfer, and capacity-building, while developing countries must declare what

88 Imad Antoine Ibrahim, Thomas Deleuil & Paolo Davide Farah, *The Principle of Common But Differentiated Responsibilities in the International Regime of Climate Change, in* China's Influence on Non-Trade Concerns in International Economic Law 146–157 (Paolo Davide Farah & Elena Cima (eds.), Routledge 2016).

89 Robert Falkner, *The Paris Agreement and the New Logic of International Climate Politics*, 92 International Affairs 1107 (2016); Jon Truby, *Using Bitcoin Technology to Combat Climate Change*, Nature Middle East (2018).

90 Amanda M. Rosen, *The Wrong Solution at the Right Time: The Failure of the Kyoto Protocol on Climate Change*, 43 Politics & Policy 30 (2015).

91 Daniel Bodansky, *The Copenhagen Climate Change Conference – A Post-Mortem*, 104 The American Journal of International Law 1 (2010).

92 United Nations, Paris Agreement (2015), Art. 15(1).

93 *Id.* at Art. 15(2).

94 *Ibid.*

95 *Id.* at Art. 4(2).

96 *Id.* at Art. 4.

97 *Id.* at Art. 4 (11).

98 *Id.* at Art. 13.7. (a).

kind of support they need.[99] The information is provided in the context of an "enhanced transparency framework for action and support, with built-in flexibility"[100] to developing countries while considering the circumstances of LDCs and SIDSs.[101] Examples of transparency arrangements include "national communications, biennial reports and biennial update reports, international assessment and review and international consultation and analysis."[102] Further rules are also stipulated in this provision.[103] Moreover, COPs "shall periodically take stock of the implementation of this Agreement . . . in a comprehensive and facilitative manner, considering mitigation, adaptation and the means of implementation and support, and in the light of equity and the best available science."[104]

States comply with international treaties under various conditions. Domestic institutions may play an important role in ensuring compliance, especially when domestic leaders have no incentive politically to comply with a given treaty. Time is also very relevant is this regard as a state may take time to sign and ratify a treaty, during which they can violate the provisions of the convention. Moreover, the design of an international treaty and the influence of international actors affect states' compliance.[105] In that sense, the signature and ratification of international treaties do not guarantee compliance with its provisions by the various states,[106] as international agreements regulate states' behaviour in various fields, such as economic, social, and environmental aspects.[107] Indeed, even if states declare support for international law, it is very difficult to measure such support in practice through compliance with the various treaties signed and ratified.[108] The question of compliance gained further complexity in recent years with the marked decline of national sovereignty; the concomitant proliferation of international regimes, institutions, and non-state actors; the collapse of the public–private distinction; the rapid development

99 *Id.* at Art. 13.9 & 13.10).
100 *Id.* at Art. 13(1).
101 *Id.* at Art. 13(2).
102 *Id.* at Art. 13 (4).
103 *Id.* at Art. 13.
104 *Id.* at Art. 14 (1).
105 Carmela Lutmar, Cristiane L. Carneiro & Sara McLaughlin Mitchell, *Formal Commitments and States' Interests: Compliance in International Relations*, 42 International Interactions 559 (2016).
106 Olga Avdeyeva, *When Do States Comply with International Treaties? Policies on Violence Against Women in Post-Communist Countries*, 51 International Studies Quarterly 877 (2007).
107 Beth A. Simmons, *Compliance with International Agreements*, 1 Annual Review of Political Science 75 (1998).
108 Mark A. Pollack, *Who Supports International Law, and Why?: The United States, the European Union, and the International Legal Order*, 13 International Journal of Constitutional Law 873, 877–878 (2015).

of customary and treaty-based rules; and the increasing interpenetration of domestic and international system.[109]

States currently have different capabilities at the various levels, while there are many other factors that affect their ability to invest in emerging technologies and comply with international agreements either applicable to these technologies or addressing them in specific aspects. Hence, all these elements, in addition to the factors mentioned earlier, but also other factors, such as economic competitiveness and natural security and ethical issues, further complicate the possibility of states to comply with international rules applicable to emerging technologies.[110] For these reasons, a compliance mechanism that is similar to the one established under the Paris Agreement must be implemented within international agreements addressing emerging technologies so that states sign, ratify, and comply progressively with these agreements, taking into account all the aforementioned elements.

4.3 Regulatory Sandboxes for the Regulation of Financial Technologies

Financial technologies (FinTechs) have caused disruption in the financial sector through the provision of innovative products and services facilitating transactions and removing intermediaries. It also resulted in the emergence of start-ups and non-financial companies challenging traditional financial institutions, such as banks.[111] The main difference between FinTechs and finance is the purpose. Finance is seeking efficiency, while FinTechs are seeking solutions to reduce human work.[112] Yet there are various risks emerging due to the introduction of FinTechs which require regulation through specific mechanisms, while the regulator must have the capacity and expertise to supervise these technologies. It is in this context that flexibility is needed to foster innovation in this field while protecting the society and financial markets at large.[113]

Regulatory sandboxes are one of the many mechanisms that are being used to that end. It allows the testing of FinTech products and services in a safe environment under the control of financial services authorities. In such an

109 Harold Hongju Koh, *Why Do Nations Obey International Law?*, 106 The Yale Law Journal 2599, 2604 (1997).

110 Scott A. Jones, *Trading Emerging Technologies: Export Controls Meet Reality*, Security and Human Rights 1 (2021); Patrick Lin, *Ethical Blowback from Emerging Technologies*, *in* Military Ethics and Emerging Technologies 56–70 (Timothy J. Demy et al. (eds.), Routledge 2014).

111 Mark Fenwick, Steven Van Uytsel & Bi Ying, *Regulating Fintech in Asia: An Introduction*, *in* Regulating FinTech in Asia: Global Context, Local Perspectives 1, 1–4 (Mark Fenwick, Steven Van Uytsel & Bi Ying (eds.), Springer 2020).

112 Valerio Lemma, FinTech Regulation: Exploring New Challenges of the Capital Markets Union 3–4 (Palgrave Macmillan 2020).

113 Douglas W. Arner, Evan Gibson & Janos Barberis, *FinTech and Its Regulation in Hong Kong*, *in* Research Handbook on Asian Financial Law 431, 451 (Douglas W. Arner et al. (eds.), Edward Elgar Publishing 2020).

environment, the risks of these FinTechs are managed, and the rules that usually apply are temporarily suspended to test the new products and services on selected volunteer customers.[114] In other words, it is a "framework set up by a financial sector regulators to allow small scale, live testing of innovations by private firms in controlled environments (operating under a special exemption, allowance, or other limited, time-bound exception) under the regulator's supervision."[115] The term *sandbox* comes from the technological field and was initially used to test web products and software projects. The first regulatory sandbox was established in the United Kingdom, based on which regulators globally followed suit, where countries such as Singapore, Australia, France, and others have established their own domestic regulatory sandboxes.[116] The participants in a sandbox have a determined period of time based on which they can test their services and products to figure out if their solutions have positive effects on the customers and markets. Regulators in this context have an important role to play as they must determine if these solutions violate existing regulations or whether regulations need to be relaxed.[117] Given that FinTech crosses political borders, international entities such as the Financial Stability Board (FSB) are calling for international cooperation. There are also calls for a global sandbox to harmonize FinTech rules across jurisdictions.[118] A Global Financial Innovation Network (GFIN) was established to that end, creating a "Global Sandbox Program."[119] Moreover, regional sandboxes are being proposed in the European Union[120] and in Latin America.[121] Meanwhile, ASEAN Financial Innovation Network (AFIN) developed a regional sandbox titled the API Exchange (APIX).[122] Hence, it is only a matter of time

114 Jon Truby, *Fintech and the City: Sandbox 2.0 Policy and Regulatory Reform Proposals*, 34 International Review of Law, Computers and Technology 277, 277–278 (2020).

115 Jayoung James Goo & Joo-Yeun Heo, *The Impact of the Regulatory Sandbox on the Fintech Industry, with a Discussion on the Relation between Regulatory Sandboxes and Open Innovation*, 6 Journal of Open Innovation: Technology, Market and Complexity 1, 3 (2020).

116 Elizaveta Gromova & Tjaša Ivanc, *Regulatory Sandboxes (Experimental Legal Regimes) for Digital Innovations in BRICS*, VII BRICS Law Journal 10, 15–18 (2020).

117 Goo & Heo, *supra* note 115, at 3.

118 Luke G. Thomas, *The Case for a Federal Regulatory Sandbox for Fintech Companies*, 22 North Carolina Banking Institute 257 (2018).

119 Global Financial Innovation Network, *Our Members* <www.thegfin.com/members>.

120 European Commission Proposal for a Regulation of the European Parliament and of the Council Laying Down Harmonised Rules on Artificial Intelligence (Artificial Intelligence Act) and Amending Certain Union Legislative Acts (2021/0106) (COD) COM (2021) 206 Final ['EC Proposal'].

121 Diego Herrera & Sonia Vadillo, *Regulatory Sandboxes in Latin America and the Caribbean for the FinTech Ecosystem and the Financial System* 13–14 (Discussion Paper N° IDB-DP-573, 2018).

122 UNSGSA Fintech Working Group and CCAF, *Early Lessons on Regulatory Innovations to Enable Inclusive Fintech: Innovation Offices, Regulatory Sandboxes, and RegTech* 28 (Office of the UNSGSA and CCAF: New York, NY and Cambridge, UK, 2019) <www.unsgsa.org/sites/default/files/resources-files/2020-09/UNSGSA_Report_2019_Final-compressed.pdf>.

before the Global Sandbox Program of GFIN plays a role in the international legal arena along with other international sandboxes that may be created.

Regulation is an important element in the innovation process, which occurs through agenda-setting, legislation, compliance, and enforcement of the rules. In this context, there are various types of regulations, as the latter can occur through information, self-regulation, co-regulation, standardization, market-based instruments, and prescriptive regulatory actions.[123] Yet emerging technologies and sciences require a margin of flexibility to develop where experimentation is a must also for the sake of the legislator. Indeed, the legislator is facing the need to regulate emerging technologies and sciences that have high technological and scientific nature while having a limited knowledge of these elements, which results in great uncertainties, where errors, especially design errors, can occur at any moment.[124] For this reason, there is a need to experiment with the new technologies and sciences instead of applying rigid rules to them to prevent harm, especially as each country has already traditional rules in place addressing general damage occurring from any activity.[125] To address this need, various types of regulatory structures were suggested and are being implemented, including regulatory sandboxes. Other suggestions involve the adoption of adaptive regulation, outcome-based regulation, risk-weighted regulation, etc.[126]

A sandbox approach to emerging technologies and sciences allows the constant evolvement of regulations,[127] especially as nations are already experimenting with these elements[128] and as various stakeholders must be involved in the regulatory process, mainly regulators, private business leaders, researchers, and civic actors.[129] Regulatory sandboxes also offer a great alternative to the adoption of the precautionary principle by legislators who are overly cautious,

123 Jacques Pelkmans & Andrea Renda, *How Can EU Legislation Enable and/or Disable Innovation* 11–15 (European Commission, July 2014).

124 Araz Taeihagh, M. Ramesh & Michael Howlett, *Assessing the Regulatory Challenges of Emerging Disruptive Technologies*, Regulation and Governance 1, 1–6 (2021).

125 Ryan Muldoon, *Don't Ban New Technologies – Experiment with Them Carefully* (The Conversation, 22 August 2019) <https://theconversation.com/dont-ban-new-technologies-experiment-with-them-carefully-120277>.

126 William D. Eggers, Mike Turley & Pankaj Kamleshkumar Kishnani, The Future of Regulation: Principles for Regulating Emerging Technologies (*Deloitte*, 19 June 2018), <www2.deloitte.com/us/en/insights/industry/public-sector/future-of-regulation/regulating-emerging-technology.html>.

127 Tarun Khanna, When Technology Gets Ahead of Society (*Harvard Business Review*, 2018) <https://hbr.org/2018/07/when-technology-gets-ahead-of-society>.

128 Nima Elmi, Here are 4 Technology Trends from Emerging Economies (*World Economic Forum*, 9 September 2020) <www.weforum.org/agenda/2020/09/here-are-4-technology-trends-from-emerging-economies/>.

129 Camino Kavanagh, New Tech, New Threats, and New Governance Challenges: An Opportunity to Craft Smarter Responses? (*Carnegie Endowment for International Peace*, 28 August 2019) <https://carnegieendowment.org/2019/08/28/new-tech-new-threats-and-new-governance-challenges-opportunity-to-craft-smarter-responses-pub-79736>; Mirjana Stankovic, Can

which affects innovation and limits economic growth and social progress.[130] In that sense, regulatory sandboxes balance two values: security and innovation.[131] Such regulatory sandboxes can be incorporated within international agreements addressing technological and scientific progress, allowing the pioneers in these fields to experiment their new ideas in a safe environment.

4.4 *Flexibility Mechanisms Within International Water Law*

The development of international law applicable to transboundary surface water and groundwater occurred in the last few decades. Based on this, two international conventions are currently in force: the 1997 Convention on the Law of the Non-Navigational Uses of International Watercourses and the 1992 Convention on the Protection and Use of Transboundary Watercourses and International Lakes. Moreover, a nonbinding instrument addressing solely transboundary aquifers was adopted in 2008 and titled the Draft Articles on the Law of Transboundary Aquifers. In addition to these, several nonbinding instruments were established by the International Law Association.[132] Moreover, numerous basin-specific water agreements were formed over the last few decades, addressing the shared water resources between countries. These treaties are extremely hard to adopt, given the amount of effort required in the negotiation process and compromises that states need to make to ensure their successful adoption as well as implementation. To that end, these treaties were considered as rigid instruments that cannot be updated when needed, which was criticized.[133] In this context, several flexibility mechanisms were suggested, where some of them are being implemented within basin-specific agreements.

Regulators Keep Up with Emerging Technologies? (*The Startup*, 10 March 2020) <https://medium.com/swlh/can-regulators-keep-up-with-emerging-technologies-c53448bcbd64>.

130 Daniel Castro & Michael McLaughlin, Ten Ways the Precautionary Principle Undermines Progress in Artificial Intelligence (*Information Technology & Innovation Foundation*, 4 February2019)<https://itif.org/publications/2019/02/04/ten-ways-precautionary-principle-undermines-progress-artificial-intelligence>.

131 Bob Violino, Security vs. Innovation: IT's Trickiest Balancing Act (*CIO*, 10 February 2020) <www.cio.com/article/3521009/security-vs-innovation-its-trickiest-balancing-act.html>.

132 Stephen C. McCaffrey, The Law of International Watercourses (3d ed., Oxford University Press 2019); Gabriel Eckstein, The International Law of Transboundary Groundwater Resources (Routledge 2017). These include the 1966 the Helsinki Rules on the Uses of the Water of International Rivers; The 1986 Seoul Rules on International Groundwaters; the 1989 Bellagio Draft Treaty or the "Draft Agreement Concerning the Use of Transboundary Groundwaters" and the 2004 Berlin Rules on Water Resources.

133 Frank A. Ward, *Forging Sustainable Transboundary Water-Sharing Agreements: Barriers and Opportunities*, 15 Water Policy 386 (2013); Rafael Emmanuel Macatangay & Alistair Rieu-Clarke, *The Role of Valuation and Bargaining in Optimising Transboundary Watercourse Treaty Regimes*, 18 International Environmental Agreements: Politics, Law and Economics 409 (2018).

These mechanisms include amendment and review procedures and joint management institutions.[134] For instance, an amend-and-review provision within a technology/scientific agreement allows the updating of the agreement to consider the developments and changes taking place in the scientific and technological fields. Moreover, joint management institutions allow the various stakeholders, mainly states, to address any topic pertaining to science and technology, such as risks and taking the appropriate measures in the regard.[135] Flexible water allocation can occur based on information such as flow percentage during a specific period of time. Specific provisions related to extreme circumstances apply during, for instance, droughts to address unexpected situations. Amendment-and-review procedures are needed, given the constant changes that occur over time in a water basin, such as variances in climatic and hydrological conditions. Joint management institutions play a crucial role, especially when the conditions of the water basin change.[136] Framework agreements on the basis of which future water agreements, protocols, and instruments addressing specific aspects of water management may also be adopted.[137] Flexibility mechanisms can help preserve water agreements when unforeseen events cause harm to states party of an agreement, as they may want to deviate from the agreement in case the harm is not addressed. States in this context choose the mechanism that suits best their purpose,[138] through procedural rules and institutional mechanisms,[139] to ensure just water sharing,[140] given the expected changes in water variability as a result of factors such as climate change.[141]

In the context of emerging technologies and sciences, flexible provisions and open regulatory frameworks are of utmost importance, given the need to understand the characteristics and complexities surrounding the developments

134 Heather Cooley & Peter H. Gleick, *Climate-Proofing Transboundary Water Agreements*, 56 Hydrological Sciences Journal 711, 714 (2011).

135 See for instance, Eyal Benvenisti, *The Legal Framework of Joint Management Institutions for Transboundary Water Resources*, *in* Management of Shared Groundwater Resources: The Israeli-Palestinian Case with an International Perspective 407–428 (Eran Feitelson & Marwan Haddad (eds.), Springer 2001).

136 *Id.* at 714–716.

137 Alistair Rieu-Clarke, *Transboundary Water Governance and Climate Change Adaptation: International Law, Policy Guidelines and Best Practice Application* (United Nations Educational, Scientific and Cultural Organization, Paris, France, 2015).

138 Stephen C. McCaffrey, *The Need for Flexibility in Freshwater Treaty Regimes*, 27 Natural Resources Forum 156, 157–160 (2003).

139 Patricia Wouters & Sergei Vinogradov, *Reframing the Transboundary Water Discourse: Contextualized International Law in Practice*, 29 Review of European, Comparative & International Environmental Law 385, 387 (2020).

140 D. Marc Kilgour & Ariel Dinar, *Flexible Water Sharing within an International River Basin*, 18 Environmental and Resource Economics 43 (2001).

141 Lucia De Stefano et al., *Climate Change and the Institutional Resilience of International River Basins*, 49 Journal of Peace Research 193, 196 (2012).

taking place as well as the uncertainties and the frequent changes.[142] Such flexibility is needed to tackle the complicated task of governing scientific and technological developments, where various suggestions were made in this regard, such as the use of concepts like tentative governance and adaptive governance.[143] More specifically, flexible provisions are needed to "1) keeping pace with change; 2) designing 'fit-for-purpose' regulatory frameworks; 3) tackling regulatory enforcement challenges and 4) addressing the transversal and transboundary dimensions of these technologies" and scientific developments.[144] The legal mechanisms suggested to provide such flexibility include, inter alia, "innovations for expediting rulemaking; issue-specific legislative initiatives; specialized courts; sunset clauses; periodic reviews; independent institutions; adaptive management and principles based regulation."[145]

The flexibility provisions within international water law and basin water agreements can be used for addressing emerging technologies and scientific developments. For instance, the inclusion of amendment-and-review procedures within international agreements and instruments applicable to emerging technologies and scientific developments can play a significant role in constantly updating these mechanisms, given the constant and rapid changes.[146] In this context, Mandel calls for a specific system of governance based on data gathering and evaluation for the constant modification of the system on the basis of scientific understanding.[147] Such system must allow for an incremental change in governance.[148]

5 Conclusion

Technological and scientific developments changed the life of human beings in the last century and are expected to play a greater role currently and in the

142 Sofia Ranchordás, *Innovation-Friendly Regulation: The Sunset of Regulation, the Sunrise of Innovation*, 55 Jurimetrics 201 (2015).

143 Stefan Kuhlmann, Peter Stegmaier & Kornelia Konrad, *The Tentative Governance of Emerging Science and Technology – A Conceptual Introduction*, 48 Research Policy. 1091 (2019).

144 OECD iLibrary, *Shaping the Future of Regulators: The Impact of Emerging Technologies on Economic Regulators: Executive Summary* <www.oecd-ilibrary.org/sites/db481aa3-en/index.html?itemId=/content/publication/db481aa3-en>.

145 Gary E. Marchant, *The Growing Gap between Emerging Technologies and the Law*, *in* The Growing Gap Between Emerging Technologies and Legal-Ethical Oversight: The Pacing Problem 19, 28–30 (Gary E. Marchant, Braden R. Allenby & Joseph R. Herkert (eds.), Springer 2011).

146 See in general, Stephen E. Draper, *Administration and Institutional Provisions of Water Sharing Agreements*, 133 Journal of Water Resources Planning and Management 446 (2007).

147 Gregory N. Mandel, *Emerging Technology Governance*, *in* Innovative Governance Models for Emerging Technologies 44, 59 (Gary E. Marchant, Kenneth W. Abbot & Braden Allenby (eds.), Edward Elgar Publishing 2013).

148 Roger Brownsword & Morag Goodwin, Law and the Technologies of the Twenty-First Century: Text and Materials 385 (Cambridge University Press 2012).

future, given their rapid and constant development. They have played, and are currently playing, a major role in economic growth, where states are seeking to design policies resulting in sustainable economic growth and global competitiveness.[149] In that sense, the prosperity of societies depends on the constant evolution and progress of these fields, taking into account socio-political factors.[150] It is in this context that there are calls for a new contract between technology and sciences on one hand and society on the other.[151] This is because of the many concerns related to the impact of science and technology on society, as these fields must be used correctly.[152] Hence, there is a need to meet technological and scientific challenges through various means,[153] given their great impacts mainly in terms of learning and communication.[154]

Regulations in this regard at the international and national level are required to tackle technological and scientific developments in the context of uncertainty and lack of understanding of the progress occurring in these fields.[155] Various types of regulations mentioned previously are and will be used to this end as new innovative regulatory instruments emerged over the last decades.[156] The role of regulation has not been studied in the literature sufficiently in the past, which is why the last decade witnessed a growth in academic articles and studies on the topic of law, science, and technology,[157] given the limits of these fields and the need to address these limits and the shortcomings,[158] in particular in the international sphere.[159] The main issues

149 Sefer Sener & Ercan Sarıdogan, *The Effects of Science-Technology-Innovation on Competitiveness and Economic Growth*, 24 Procedia Social and Behavioral Sciences 815 (2011).

150 Rajendra Prasad, *Science and Technology: Impact on Society*, 2 Social Scientist 18, 18–25 (1974).

151 World Conference on Science, *Toward a New Contract between Science and Society* (Executive Summary of the Report of the North American Meeting held in advance of the World Conference on Science; Kananaskis Village, Alberta (Canada), 1–3 November 1998).

152 George Fitzgerald, The Affects of Science and Technology Are Already Here (18 May 2018) <https://web.colby.edu/st112a2018/2018/05/18/the-affects-of-science-and-technology-are-already-here/>.

153 Angel Gurría, *The Impact of Scientific and Technological Advances and Innovation* (12 September 2017) <www.oecd.org/science/impact-of-scientific-and-technological-advances-and-innovation.htm>.

154 Mickeel Allen, *Technological Influence on Society* (*BCTV.org*, 7 November 2019) <www.bctv.org/2019/11/07/technological-influence-on-society/>.

155 Jurgen Schmandt, *Regulation and Science*, 9 Science, Technology, & Human Values 23, 23–25 (1984).

156 Jonathan B. Wiener, *The Regulation of Technology, and the Technology of Regulation*, 26 Technology in Society 483 (2004).

157 Encyclopedia.com, *Science, Technology, and Law* <www.encyclopedia.com/science/encyclopedias-almanacs-transcripts-and-maps/science-technology-and-law>.

158 Sintia Radu, The World Wants More Tech Regulation (*US News*, 15 January 2020) <www.usnews.com/news/best-countries/articles/2020-01-15/the-world-wants-big-tech-companies-to-be-regulated>.

159 Amitai Etzioni & Oren Etzioni, *Should Artificial Intelligence Be Regulated?* XXXIII Issues in Science and Technology (2017) <https://issues.org/perspective-artificial-intelligence-regulated/>.

that require regulation are "safety, privacy, competition, and honesty,"[160] with the end goal of protecting the public interest.[161]

Given the need for regulations, the author is arguing for the use of flexible mechanisms within international law to address the risks and uncertainties of scientific and technological developments tackled within international treaties and instruments. The author provides examples of selected flexibility mechanisms from existing global regulatory frameworks. These are (1) Article XX of the GATT agreement, (2) compliance mechanisms within the Paris Agreement, (3) regulatory sandboxes for the regulation of financial technologies, and (4) flexibility mechanisms within international water law. The author, through these selected examples, highlights the importance of existing flexibility mechanisms to the adoption of future global agreements and instruments for the regulation of emerging technologies and sciences.

160 Roger Mcnamee, Big Tech Needs to Be Regulated. Here Are 4 Ways to Curb Disinformation and Protect Our Privacy (*Time*, 29 July 2020) <https://time.com/5872868/big-tech-regulated-here-is-4-ways/>.

161 Mark MacCarthy, The Tech Industry Needs Regulation for Its Systemically Important Companies (*Brookings*, 8 December 2020) <www.brookings.edu/blog/techtank/2020/12/08/the-tech-industry-needs-regulation-for-its-systemically-important-companies/>.

5 The Precautionary Principle Under EU Law

A "Post-Modern" Principle in a "Post-Truth" Era

*Alessandra Donati**

1 Introduction[1]

> At one time, we had truth and lies. Now we have truth, lies, and statements that may not be true, but we consider too benign to call false. . . . This is post-truth. In the post-truth era, borders blur the distinction between truth and lies, honesty and dishonesty, fiction and non-fiction.[2]

In 2016, the word *post-truth* was named the international Word of the Year by *Oxford Dictionaries.* This decision was justified by the fact that the use of this construction "has seen a spike in frequency . . . in the context of the EU referendum in the United Kingdom and the presidential election in the United States."[3] For the *Oxford Dictionaries*, "post-truth" designates a circumstance where "objective facts are less influential in shaping public opinion than appeals to emotion and personal belief."[4] With this definition, *Oxford Dictionaries* "underline that the prefix 'post' is meant to indicate not so much the idea that we are 'past' truth in a temporal sense (as in 'post-war') but in the sense that truth has been eclipsed – that it is irrelevant."[5] The facts can always be "shaded, selected, and presented within a political context that favors one interpretation of truth over another."[6] If this phenomenon is not new, then it has roots that go back thousands of years to the debates over the impossibility of reaching an objective truth. In the past three decades, the concept of "post-truth" has seen an uptick, namely, in the United States and in Europe. This increase is linked to the explosion both at the industrial, political,

* Alessandra Donati is *Référendaire* at the European Court of Justice. Corresponding Author: alessandra.donati@curia.europa.eu

1 Oxford Dictionaries, *Post-truth* <www.lexico.com/en/definition/post-truth>.

2 Ralph Keyes, The Post-Truth Era (St. Martin's Press 2004).

3 Oxford Dictionaries, *Press News* (2016) <www.oxforddictionaries.com/press/news/2016/12/11/WOTY-16>.

4 Oxford Dictionaries, *supra* note 1.

5 Lee Mcintyre, Post-Truth 5 (MIT Press 2018).

6 *Id.* at 6.

DOI: 10.4324/9781003472421-5

and media level of science denial, accompanied by the setting-up of explicit post-truth strategies aimed at producing doubts on the available scientific evidence on major environmental and health risks, such as tobacco, nuclear energy, acid rain, ozone hole, climate change, vaccines, etc.[7] As revealed by an internal memo written by a tobacco executive in 1969: "doubt is our product since it is the best means of competing with the 'body of fact' that exists in the minds of the general public."[8]

Aside from being marked by emotions and personal beliefs as well as by the production of doubts on scientific facts, post-truth society is also characterized by "uncertainty"[9] and "risks."[10] Here lies the paradox of the post-truth society. The more that industries, politicians, and the media strive to create doubts on scientific data to deny the need to act to tackle the major environmental and health risks threatening the planet, the more such risks increase, and the science is genuinely unable to provide a scientific certainty about the existence and extent of such risks. As René-Jean Dupuy pointed out,[11] until recently, people lived as if the Earth had been inexhaustible, the sea incorruptible, the human species immortal. The certainty of progress was based on invulnerable humanity. Suddenly, the linear ascent was broken. Absolute faith in man's ability to master nature and technology was replaced by a progressive acceptance of the limited nature of scientific knowledge. Science is the place of doubt; science generates uncertainty. A society of uncertainty, contemporary society is also, in the words of the German sociologist Ulrich Beck, the "risk society."[12] The risks that threaten our society are not only linked to natural disasters but are also mostly generated by society itself. For Beck, modernization is now operating against itself through the induced effects it causes, particularly in terms of ecological and/or technological risks. Progress, together with wealth, generates risks: pollution, industrial disasters, deforestation, loss of biodiversity, pandemics, etc. The preservation of the planet through the control of these risks thus becomes a necessity. This is why the German philosopher Hans Jonas considers that the power that science and technology confer on humankind brings with it a new responsibility – that of preventing the risk of major damage to the environment and public health to pass on a living Earth to future generations.[13]

7 Naomi Oreskes & Erik M. Conway, Merchants of Doubt: How a Handful of Scientists Obscured the Truth on Issues from Tobacco Smoke to Global Warming (Bloomsbury 2010).

8 Mcintyre, *supra* note 5, at 25.

9 Louis Chauvel, Le destin des générations: Structure sociale et cohortes en France au XXe siècle (PUF 2002).

10 Ulrich Beck, Risk Society: Towards a New Modernity (SAGE Publications Ltd 1992).

11 René-Jean Dupuy, L'humanité dans l'imaginaire des Nations 71 (Éditions Julliard, coll. Conférences, essais et leçons du Collège de France 1991).

12 Beck, *supra* note 10.

13 Hans Jonas, Le principe de responsabilité. Une éthique pour la civilisation technologique (Cerf 1995).

It is in this context that the analysis of the precautionary principle must be placed. *Precaution* can be defined as a principle of anticipated action, which in a context of risk and uncertainty for the environment and public health requires competent authorities to anticipate the traditional time for the adoption of a measure to protect the environment and public health.[14] This means that decision-makers shall not wait until the risk is certain, from a scientific point of view, but shall act before, when the risk is only uncertain. From this perspective, the precautionary principle entails a significant change in the time management of risks. Although it is one of the most evoked principles, its meaning and effects are not unequivocally conceived, and the precautionary principle remains highly controversial. The more the precautionary principle is invoked, the more its legal meaning and effects raise debates and provoke confusion.[15] On the one hand, the precautionary principle is considered as "a principle particularly necessary in our time"[16] and a key tool to protect environmental and health conditions on Earth by the adoption of timely protective measures.[17] On the other hand, for some, precaution is a "scaring principle"[18] which may "kill the law,"[19] and for others, it is "anti-science principle" which is a vector of "technophobia."[20] These diverging interpretations can be explained if we consider that the precautionary principle is not an easy subject matter to grasp and understand.[21] Analyzing the precautionary principle requires understanding the role of law in the current and future society: Where is the law going? ("*Où va le droit?*")[22] What can the law do? ("*Que peut le droit?*")[23] How should the law evolve to tackle the emerging risks for the environment and public health?[24]

14 Alessandra Donati, Le principe de précaution en droit de l'Union européenne (Bruylant 2021).

15 Nicolas Molfessis, *Préface*, *in* Prévention, précaution et responsabilité civile. Risque avéré, risque suspecté et transformation du paradigme de la responsabilité civile 9 (Daphné Tapinos, L'Harmattan 2008).

16 Eric Naim-Gesbert, *Droit général de l'environnement* 90 (Lexis-Nexis 2014).

17 Mireille Delmas-Marty, *Préface, Le principe de précaution et le paradoxe de l'anthropocène, in* Principe de précaution et métamorphose de la responsabilité 15 (Luca D'Ambrosio, Geneviève Giudicelli-Delage & Stefano Manacorda (eds.), Collection de l'Institut des sciences juridiques et philosophiques de la Sorbonne 2018).

18 Gérald Bronner & Étienne Gehin, *L'inquiétant principe de précaution* 177 (PUF 2010).

19 Jean-Philippe Feldman, *Le projet de loi constitutionnelle relatif à la Charte de l'environnement*, 15 Recueil Dalloz 970–972 (2004).

20 Dominique Lecourt, *Technophobie*, Cités. 15 (2000).

21 Eric Naim-Gesbert, *Lumières du principe de précaution. À propos de la résolution du 1er février 2012 de l'Assemblée nationale*, Revue Juridique de L'Environnement 203 (2013).

22 Mireille Delmas-Marty, *Où va le droit? Entre pot au noir et pilotage automatique, le droit peut-il nous guider vers une mondialité apaisée?* 14 La Semaine Juridique 677–684 (2018).

23 Mireille Delmas-Marty, Résister, responsabiliser, anticiper (Éditions du Seuil 2013).

24 Émilie Gaillard, *Le principe de précaution en droit civil français: dynamiques systémiques de métamorphoses, in* Principe de précaution et métamorphose de la responsabilité 120 (Luca

In the context of evolution, the core claim of this chapter is that, to understand the definition and implications of the post-truth society, it is necessary to analyze the theoretical framework under which the concept of post-truth emerged: post-modernism.[25] The concept of post-modernism is not new and, in the last century, has been applied to art, architecture, music, literature, and many other creative endeavours. In the last 30 years, post-modernism specifically grew out of literary criticism in many colleges and universities in Europe and in the United States as a result of Jean-François Lyotard's influential book *The Postmodern Condition*.[26] As the philosopher Michael Lynch considers, due to the diversity of its expressions and the breadth of its manifestations, "pretty much everyone admits that it is impossible to define post-modernism."[27]

If it is difficult to provide a comprehensive definition of *post-modernism*, it can be argued that one of its foundational concepts lies in Derrida's[28] theory of "deconstructing" literature. For Derrida, it is impossible to rely on the idea that an author knows what he or she "meant" in a text, so we must deconstruct the term and examine it as a function of the political, social, historical, and cultural assumptions behind it. The same idea of deconstruction is also embraced by sociologists, philosophers, political scientists, and others who consider that it should apply not just to literary texts but also far more broadly in relation to all human behaviours, since, in a sense, everything could be interpreted as a text and deconstructed.[29] Even from the law perspective – as it will be demonstrated in this chapter – from the late 1970s onwards, we have witnessed the progressive deconstruction of the traditional paradigm of modernity because it was incapable of describing or facing the challenges of the contemporary era.[30] These transformations are of such magnitude that one may speak of the "genetic mutation" of contemporary society.[31] This evolution is reflected in the questioning of the primacy of reason, leading to a corresponding loss of confidence in science and disillusionment with the idea of progress. The emphasis is now on disorder, complexity, indeterminacy, and relativism, which are seen as the main characteristics of the "post-modern condition."[32]

The notion of truth is now under scrutiny. According to post-modernism, there is no such thing as objective truth, because any profession of truth is

---

D'Ambrosio, Geneviève Giudicelli-Delage & Stefano Manacorda (eds.), Collection de l'Institut des sciences juridiques et philosophiques de la Sorbonne 2018).

25 Diego Han, *From Post-Modernity to Post-Truth Society*, Journal of Comparative Studies 1–19 (2018).

26 Jean-François Lyotard, The Postmodern Condition (Manchester University Press 1979).

27 Michael Patrick Lynch, True to Life: Why Truth Matters 34–35 (MIT Press 2004).

28 Jacques Derrida, De la Grammatologie (Éditions de Minuit 1967).

29 Mcintyre, *supra* note 5, at 124–125.

30 Hassan Abdelhamid, *Les paradigmes post-modernes et la démarche pluraliste dans la recherche juridique*, *in* Méthodologie du pluralisme juridique 139 (Ghislain Otis (ed.), Karthala 2012).

31 Gustavo Zagrebelsky, Le droit en douceur (Il diritto mite) 35 (Economica 2000).

32 Lyotard, *supra* note 26.

nothing more than a reflection of the political ideology of the person who is making it. This means that there could be many truths, rather than just one, for any act of deconstruction.[33] Therefore, if it cannot be argued that post-truth – to be understood as the manipulation or the production of truth for achieving a predetermined purpose – is a consequence of post-modernism, one may consider that post-modernism represents the theoretical framework under which post-truth takes its roots. Indeed, by deconstructing the traditional absolute, science-based notion of truth in many different and subjective conceptions of truth, which are no longer necessarily linked to scientific knowledge, post-modernism offered a theoretical justification to those willing to "create" *ad hoc* truths serving their own interests and purposes.

Under the theoretical framework of post-modernism, the analysis of the precautionary principle is utterly significant since it can be defined as a "paradigmatic principle" of post-modern law. Indeed, as this chapter will demonstrate, the precautionary principle is a post-modern principle because it shares the same features of flexibility and complexity which belong to post-modern principles.[34] The definition of *precaution* as a post-modern one is not new in legal scholarship.[35] However, what is new is the methodology adopted in this chapter in order to demonstrate the post-modern nature of the precautionary principle. By comparing the characteristics of the precautionary principle with those traditionally attributed to post-modern principles, I will prove that the precautionary principle is indeed a post-modern principle. To do so, in Section 1, I will explore the rationale for the transition from a modern to a post-modern law, while in Section 2, I will explain why the precautionary principle can be considered as a "paradigmatic principle" of post-modern law. To carry out this demonstration, a choice has been made to focus on the precautionary principle under European Union law ("EU law"). Two reasons explain this delimitation of the scope of work. The first reason is the post-modern nature of EU law. As indicated by Jacques Chevallier, EU law is a privileged place of emergence of the new figures of the legal post-modernity.[36] Marked by pluralism, because of the modalities of the European construction and its institutional equilibrium, EU law is a complex, dynamic, and flexible system

33 Mcintyre, *supra* note 5.

34 V. in this regard: Jacques Chevallier, *Vers un droit post-moderne? Les transformations de la régulation juridique*, 3 Revue du droit public et de la science politique 659–690 (1998); François Ost F. & Michel Van De Kerchove, De la pyramide au réseau? Pour une théorie dialectique du droit (Publications des Facultés universitaires Saint-Louis 2002); Mireille Delmas Marty, Pour un droit commun (Éditions du Seuil, coll. "La librairie du XXe siècle 2004); Mireille Delmas Marty, Le pluralisme ordonné (Éditions du Seuil, coll. "La couleur des idées" 2006); Edgar Morin, Introduction à la pensée complexe (Éditions du Seuil 2005).

35 V. for an example: Nicolas De Sadeleer, Environmental Principles. From Political Slogans to Legal Rules (Oxford University Press 2002).

36 Chevallier, *supra* note 34, at 672.

crossed by contradictory logics.[37] Considering these characteristics, EU law seems to be a good field of choice for the study of the precautionary principle, which is characterized by the same flexibility, plurality, and complexity. The second reason is the importance that EU law has devoted to the precautionary principle.[38] Thanks in particular to the work of the Court of Justice of the European Union ("CJEU"), it is under EU law (more so than under other legal systems) that precaution has been shaped like a key principle of risk management.[39] It is, therefore, towards EU law that we should turn to study this principle.

2 From Modern to Post-Modern Law

The changes going through both society and the law are of such a scale that it has led some authors to consider that Western societies left a first ***modernity*** to enter into a *post-modernity*.[40] In this regard, it is important to note that the emergence of the precautionary principle matched with the advent of the post-modern theory in the late 1970s that undermined the modern foundations of law.

2.1 The Characteristics of Modern Law

The concept of modernity refers to a series of beliefs.[41] First of all, modernity is marked by a conviction in the power of *reason* in contrast to submission to the laws of nature that defined traditional societies.[42] Secondly, modernity is based on a strong acceptance of the virtues of *science*, which allows man to take control of nature.[43] Finally, modernity is characterized by an absolute faith in the utopia of unlimited *progress* based on the continuous improvement of standards of living.[44]

In terms of the law, modernity is reflected in the process of *rationalization* conducted under the sign of *secularization* and *unification* of law.[45] On the one hand, while traditional law was closely linked to religion and the authority of the law corresponded to the divine will, modern law is being secularized, acquiring its autonomy and transforming itself into a specific normative mechanism. On the other hand, if traditional law was characterized by pluralism (both in terms

37 *Ibid.*
38 Baptiste Bonnet, *Le dialogue des normes et des juges et le principe de précaution*, 6 RFDA 1078–1083 (2018).
39 *Ibid.*
40 Jacques Chevallier, L'État post-moderne (4th ed., LGDJ 2014).
41 Chevallier, *supra* note 34, at 661–664.
42 *Ibid.*
43 *Ibid.*
44 *Ibid.*
45 *Id.* at 664–665.

of the sources of law and legal status), modern law is becoming unified. The state establishes itself as the sole source of law "by substituting itself, or at least by superimposing itself on pre-existing legal systems."[46] The state is becoming, in Hans Kelsen's words, the "total legal order," which integrates and brings everything back to it.[47] The process of rationalization entails profound changes in the attributes of modern law, which becomes *systematic*, *general*, and *stable*. First, the law is systematic because it is presented as a coherent and ordered whole, where norms are united by logical and necessary relationships.[48] Second, the law is general because it is constructed through abstract concepts and general rules whose content (linear and straightforward) can be predetermined.[49] Finally, the law is stable because legal norms are enacted in a long-term perspective; they are ensured by a certain permanence that gives the law a high degree of predictability.[50] The metaphor developed to express the characteristics of modern law is that of the *pyramid*.[51] The pyramid represents the hierarchical nature of modern law. As Hans Kelsen states, a legal system "is not an intricate set of norms in force, one beside the other, but a pyramid or hierarchy of norms that are subordinate to one another, higher or lower."[52]

2.2 *The Transformations of Post-Modern Law*

From the late 1970s onwards, we have witnessed the progressive deconstruction of the paradigm of modernity because it is incapable of describing the contemporary era or facing its challenges.[53] As François Ost states, "the world has started to move."[54] This evolution is reflected in the questioning of the primacy of reason, leading to a corresponding loss of confidence in science and disillusionment with the idea of progress. The emphasis is now on disorder, complexity, indeterminacy, and relativism, which are seen as the main characteristics of the "post-modern condition."[55] The changes that are taking place in post-modern society also affect the law.[56] Post-modern law is not radically opposed to modern law. The rise of post-modern law does not mean the end of modern law but the process of gradually affirming new conceptions of

46 *Ibid.*
47 Hans Kelsen, Théorie pure du droit 393 (Dalloz 1962).
48 Jacques Chevallier, Le droit en procès 11–13 (PUF 1983).
49 François Ost & Michel Van De Kerchove, Le système juridique entre ordre et désordre 102 (PUF, coll. "Les voies du droit" 1988).
50 *Ibid.*
51 *Ibid.*
52 Kelsen, *supra* note 47, at 266.
53 Abdelhamid, *supra* note 30, at 139.
54 Ost & Van De Kerchove, *supra* note 34, at 13.
55 Lyotard, *supra* note 26.
56 François Moderne, *Légitimité des principes généraux et théorie du droit*, 4 RFDA 722–742 (1999).

law.[57] The relationship between post-modern law and modern law must not be posed in terms of substitution but coexistence, or more precisely, of entwining.[58] In this sense, post-modernity can be considered as a process of adapting modern law to the new context of contemporary societies.[59] While modern law had been built according to a pyramid of ordered norms, post-modern law is built in a ***network***.[60] A ***network*** is an open structure where different elements interact, integrate, and are conditional on each other.[61] The circular nature of post-modern law supersedes the hierarchical nature of modern law.[62] The state loses its monopoly in the elaboration of the law to the benefit of a plurality of non-state actors. This phenomenon – called regulatory pluralism – is based on the recognition that the law exists alongside a variety of lesser normative orderings.[63] This means that under post-modernity, governments no longer monopolize regulation, which is not monolithic but rather an "unsystematic collage of inconsistent and overlapping parts."[64]

The role of the state in this pluralistic regulatory space can vary. At one extreme, the state can be an active director, and non-state actors may be commanded by law to assist in the regulatory process. A less state-centred approach would see the state acting as a facilitator or a monitor of corporate social control exercised by non-governmental institutions. At the other extreme, the role of the government would be one of a passive observer, where regulatory functions are performed to a greater extent by non-state institutions. In such a context, the boundaries between law and other disciplines are becoming blurred, and powers interact.[65] The knowledge of the law, which in the past claimed its methodological purity, is now more the result of contextualized experience (learning process) than of ***a priori*** axioms.[66] This does not mean that post-modernity marks the transition from order to disorder but that the "new order" established by post-modernity is based on diversity rather than uniformity: rigidity gives way to flexibility, verticality to horizontality, hierarchy to coordination.[67]

57 *Ibid.*
58 Chevallier, *supra* note 34, at 682.
59 *Ibid.*
60 Ost & Van De Kerchove, *supra* note 34, at 14.
61 Sabino Cassese, Lo spazio giuridico globale 21–25 (Laterza 2003).
62 Baldassare Pastore, Interpreti e fonti nell'esperienza giuridica contemporanea 25 (Cedam 2014).
63 Marc Galanter, *Justice in Many Rooms: Courts, Private Ordering and Indigenous Law*, 13(19) Journal of Legal Pluralism and Unofficial Law 1–47 (1981).
64 Julia Black, *Decentring Regulation: Understanding the Role of Regulation and Self-Regulation in a Post-Regulatory World*, 54 Current Legal Problems 103–146 (2001).
65 Ost & Van De Kerchove, *supra* note 34, at 14.
66 *Ibid.*
67 Chevallier, *supra* note 34, at 674.

3 The Identification of Precaution as a Post-Modern Principle

The definition of precaution as a post-modern principle may raise some of the following questions: Are there other principles of post-modern law? Or is the precautionary principle the only option? The answer to these questions is not easy, since no catalogue of post-modern principles exists. The definition of a particular principle as a post-modern one is, therefore, a matter of interpretation and demonstration. In this regard, two different approaches can be retained.

Under the first approach, all directing principles (and especially those of environmental law), including the precautionary principle, can be considered as being post-modern principles. This is the position defended by Nicolas de Sadeleer, who states that the precautionary principle, as well as the preventive principle and the polluter-pay principle, are, as directing principles of environmental law, post-modern principles.[68] To carry out his demonstration, Nicolas de Sadeleer compares directing principles (as an expression of post-modern law) to general principles of EU law (as a manifestation of modern law). Under the paradigm of modern law, and to build a rational system of law, the general principles of EU law have a twofold function. On the one hand, by filling the gaps in the law, the general principles ensure the *completeness* of the legal system.[69] On the other hand, by allowing the application of legal norms deemed essential in the absence of written rules, the principles guarantee the *coherence* of the legal system.[70] General principles make it possible to order the law and to develop it according to unitary inspirations. Under post-modern law, marked by more flexibility and fluidity, directing principles have no structuring purpose but constitute a mechanism for guiding public action.[71] These principles are not used to complement or rationalize the legal system but to achieve public policy objectives by balancing competing interests. They create links; they indicate the way to follow by leaving to their receivers the responsibility of implementing them. The post-modern nature of directing principles is, for Nicolas de Sadeleer, particularly evident under environmental law, which "bears the marks of post-modernity."[72] Indeed, the factors leading to post-modernity have been felt much more sharply in the field of the environment than in other disciplines: nuisances, originally specific as to location and time, have become diffuse and sustained. The ecological crisis that was once local has become planetary. For this reason, the number of institutional actors dealing with environmental risks has increased tremendously, in turn, multiplying the number of regulations. As a result, "rather than being a strongly

68 De Sadeleer, *supra* note 35, at 236.

69 François Moderne, *Légitimité des principes généraux et théorie du droit*, Revue française de droit administratif. 739–742 (July–August 1999); De Sadeleer, *supra* note 35, at 236–238.

70 *Ibid.*

71 De Sadeleer, *supra* note 35, at 258.

72 *Id.* at 251.

hierarchical system based on ideas of order, simplicity, and unity, environmental law is flexible, its structure unsettled, and its outlines uncertain."[73] It is, in other words, a post-modern law.

The second approach that I defend in this chapter is narrower in its scope. I don't deny that EU environmental law – and the same reasoning could be applied *mutatis mutandis* on a larger scale to EU law as a whole – "bears the marks of post-modernity" and that directing principles have a different purpose than the general principles of EU law. However, I consider that the precautionary principle is a "paradigmatic principle" of post-modern law because, much more than other directing principles, it is *flexible* and *complex*.

3.1 *The Flexibility of the Precautionary Principle*

The flexibility[74] of post-modern law is a consequence of its pragmatic nature; unlike modern law, which was marked by a high degree of abstraction and generality, post-modern law is characterized by a concern for efficiency and by a "willingness to act on reality."[75] It is built in a factual way according to specific issues. For this to happen, the law must not be rigid and static, but it needs to be open and allow itself to evolve and take form over time. This is why post-modern law is conceived as both a *smooth* and *adaptable* law. It is in this context that the smoothness and adaptability of the precautionary principle will be analyzed.

3.1.1 *The Smoothness of the Precautionary Principle*

According to Mireille Delmas-Marty, the smoothness of the precautionary principle is linked to its *vague*, *soft*, and *gentle* nature ("*un principe flou, mou et doux*").[76]

3.1.1.1 THE PRECAUTIONARY PRINCIPLE: A "VAGUE" PRINCIPLE

The vague nature of a principle is generally perceived as a result of the lack of precision in the law.[77] The texts create areas of uncertainty and

73 *Ibid.*

74 The idea of flexibility has been widely criticized by international law scholars as it may pose threats to the unity of the system and engender opportunistic behaviors. For an interesting contribution shedding lights on this debate, see: Laurence Helfer, *Flexibility in International Agreements*, *in* Interdisciplinary Perspectives on International Law and International Relations: The State of the Art 175–196 (Jeffrey Dunoff & Mark Pollack (eds.), Cambridge University Press 2012).

75 Chevallier, *supra* note 34, at 677.

76 Delmas-Marty, *supra* note 22, at 677.

77 Mireille Delmas-Marty, Le flou du droit (PUF, coll. "Les voies du droit" 1986).

indeterminacy without indicating the conditions for the application of the norm.[78] The vagueness of the law is thus accompanied by a margin of appreciation granted to the receivers of the norm, who are required to interpret and implement it.[79] The existence of these margins of flexibility (discretionary power of the decision-makers and margin of interpretation of the judge) does not affect the legality of the norm. It remains legal, even if its normativity is *diffuse* or even *multiple*, insofar as the legislator, the decision-makers, and the judge participate in the work of determining its content. It is the complexity of the situations to be resolved that precludes an abstract and general determination of the content of these principles.[80] In such cases, the definition of their meaning is not intrinsic to the legal *text* but refers to the *context* and to the interpretation given to it by the recipients of the norm, who have a margin of appreciation for this purpose.[81]

These considerations can be extended to the precautionary principle. The norms on which the principle is based are limited to mentioning it without defining its content and conditions of implementation.[82] Article 191 § 2 of the Treaty on the Functioning of the European Union (TFEU) – which lays down the main principles of EU environmental law – merely provides that the Union's environmental policy shall be based on the precautionary principle. Similarly, secondary legislation does not specify what precautionary measures are but merely refers to them.[83] Even regulation no. 178/2002 setting forth the general principles and requirements of food law – which to date is the only secondary legislation to define this principle – does not indicate the actual content of the precautionary principle.[84] This implies that it is not possible to deduce precisely the obligations arising from the precautionary principle. In the absence of predetermination in the text of the law, the meaning of this principle depends mainly on the interpretation given to it by the decision-makers and the judge, who co-determine the scope of this principle.[85]

78 Chevallier, *supra* note 34, at 677–679.
79 Delmas-Marty, *supra* note 77, at 15.
80 Mireille Delmas-Marty, Pour un droit commun 139 (Editions du Seuil, coll. La librairie du XX siècle 2004).
81 Antoine Jemmaud, Les règles juridiques et l'action (Dalloz 1993).
82 Elisabeth Fisher, *Opening Pandora's Box: Contextualizing the Precautionary Principle in the European Union, in* Uncertain Risks Regulated 23–24 (Michelle Everson & Ellen Vos (eds.), Routledge-Cavendish 2012).
83 *Ibid.*
84 Regulation (UE) no. 178/2012 of the European Parliament and of the Council of 28 January 2002 laying down the general principles and requirements of food law, establishing the European Food Safety Authority and laying down procedures in matters of food *safety* OJ L 31 2002, 1–24.
85 Chevallier, *supra* note 34, at 678.

3.1.1.2 THE PRECAUTIONARY PRINCIPLE: A "SOFT" PRINCIPLE

Softness refers to the non-binding nature of the legal norm.[86] Post-modern law is considered a soft law since the legal norm loses its mandatory character compared to modern law, and its application depends, "no longer on submission, but on the adherence of the recipients."[87] In this sense, post-modern law seems to fall under a "non-authoritarian legal direction of conduct."[88] The texts "indicate objectives that it would be desirable to achieve, set guidelines that it would be appropriate to follow, formulate recommendations that it would be good to respect," but they do not specify the binding force of the norm.[89]

The precautionary principle can be considered a soft principle whose legal force has long been controversial.[90] It was considered that, to the extent that the content of the precautionary principle is not precisely determined, this principle could not be imposed on its recipients.[91] The precautionary principle had thus been interpreted as being a political principle that guides the action of public decision-makers without producing legal effects.[92]

Today, however, a large majority of the doctrine recognizes that the precautionary principle is a binding legal principle.[93] The flexibility of its content and its low degree of precision are no longer seen as obstacles to the recognition of its binding force. While public decision-makers retain considerable flexibility in choosing how to implement it, the fact remains that the precautionary principle does have legal effects.[94] Nevertheless, although recognized, the binding force of the precautionary principle remains weak and limited to the procedural dimension.[95] A careful reading of the secondary legislation containing a reference to the precautionary principle shows that the binding force of this principle must be interpreted as an ***obligation to take it into account***.[96] Indeed, in these texts, whether it concerns the cross-border

86 Delmas-Marty, *supra* note 22, at 677.

87 Chevallier, *supra* note 34, at 677–678.

88 Paul Amselek, *L'évolution générale de la technique juridique dans les sociétés occidentales*, Revue du droit public 287 (1982).

89 Chevallier, *supra* note 34, at 677–678.

90 Agathe Van Lang, Droit de l'environnement 107 (4e ed., PUF 2016).

91 De Sadeleer, *supra* note 35, at 308–309.

92 Ludwig Krämer, *General Principles of Community Environmental Law and Their Translation into Secondary Law*, 3–4 RAE 355–362 (1999).

93 Nicolas De Sadeleer, EU Environmental Law and the Internal Market 41 (Oxford University Press 2014); Chris Hilson, *Rights and Principles in EU Law: A Distinction Without Foundation*, 15(2) MJ 193–216 (2008); Gerd Winter, *The Legal Nature of Environmental Principles in International, EC and German Law*, *in* Principles of European Environmental Law 19–22 (Richard Macrory (ed.), Europa Law 2004).

94 Naim-Gesbert, *supra* note 16, at 91.

95 Alessandra Donati, Le principe de précaution en droit de l'Union européenne 191 (Bruylant 2021).

96 Regulation no. 1946/2003 of the European Parliament and of the Council of 15 July 2003 on transboundary movements of genetically modified organisms, OJ 2003 L 287, pp. 1–10; Directive no. 2001/18/CE of the European Parliament and of the Council of 12 March 2001

movement or deliberate release of genetically modified organism into the environment, or waste management, toy safety, or the placing on the market of food or biocidal products, the obligation for decision-makers to apply the precautionary principle is conceived as an obligation to take it into account. Such an obligation has procedural content. As the General Court points out, compliance with procedural obligations "constitutes the primary *raison d'être* of the precautionary principle."[97] This is explained by the fact that the precautionary principle applies to prevent the occurrence of uncertain risk. In this context, it is difficult, if not impossible, to predetermine the factual elements that decision-makers will face in each case, and thus the content of the actions they will have to implement. Uncertainty does not allow prognostics based on experience or a cause-and-effect relationship. The law is not in a position to establish every possible answer under uncertain assumptions. Given the impossibility of setting the substantive content of the precautionary principle in advance, it is preferable to set general objectives (in this case, the protection of the environment and public health) and the procedural obligations with which decision-makers will have to comply in order to achieve them.

As Isabelle Pingel states, "the recognition of procedural obligations is one of the manifestations of a phenomenon known as *proceduralization*."[98] Proceduralization is linked to the post-modern nature of law. In a complex and plural world, procedures are mechanisms for simplifying reality and facilitating decision-making by identifying, for each individual case, the minimum basis to be respected in order to guarantee the soundness of the decision.[99] However, the use of procedural obligations still maintains both risks and consequences.[100] Are substantive rights protected better or worse by the aims of these procedural guarantees? Does the proceduralization of the precautionary principle operate to the detriment or to the benefit of the substance of such a principle?

The answers to these questions define the extent of the risks and consequences of the recognition of procedural obligations. On the one hand,

---

on the deliberate release into the environment of genetically modified organisms OJ L 106 2001, pp. 1–39; Directive no. 2008/98/CE of the European Parliament and of the Council of 19 November 2008 on waste, OJ 2008 L 312, pp. 3–30; Directive no. 2009/48/CE of the European Parliament and of the Council of 18 June 2009 on the safety of toys, OJ L 170 2009, pp. 1–37; Regulation (CE) no. 178/2002 *supra*; Regulation no. 528/2012 of the European Parliament and of the Council of 22 May 2012 concerning the making available on the market and use of biocidal products.

97 GC, 11 September 2002, *Pfizer Animal Health vs Conseil*, T-13/99, EU:T:2002:209, points 170–172.

98 Isabelle Pingel, *L'invention par l'Union européenne de principes européens de la procédure administrative, in* Les principes communs de la procédure administrative: essai d'identification 38 (Pascale Gonod & Hervé Ascensio (eds.), Mare & Martin 2019).

99 Niklas Luhmann, La légitimation par la procédure (Les Presses de l'Université Laval, Cerf 2002).

100 Rostane Mehdi, *La démocratie administrative en droit de l'Union européenne, jouvence ou illusion?, in* Mélanges Sudre 463 (LexisNexis 2018).

procedural obligations could be seen as an obstacle to the implementation of the substance. Subordinating the application of the precautionary principle to the fulfilment of procedural obligations would thus mean focusing more on the form than on the substance of this principle. According to Franck Michelman, this would have the undesirable consequence that a decision would no longer be analyzed in terms of the substantive search for the good but as an adaptation to its procedural content.[101] Therefore, the risk would be to empty the precautionary principle of its substantial content by reducing it to a succession of steps to be followed and procedural limits to be respected.

On the other hand, the procedure could be seen as a guide to the substance for at least two reasons. First, as Joana Mendes points out, the procedure facilitates control of the choices made by decision-makers.[102] Insofar as the obligation to take account of the precautionary principle has a procedural content, it enables the CJEU to carry out a more in-depth verification of the way in which this principle is applied. Second, as Joana Mendes also points out, the procedure rationalizes the action of the decision-makers.[103] Specifically, it allows the collection and organization of the information needed to manage uncertain risks, and it structures the decision-making process. From this perspective, procedural obligations are a lever for strengthening the coherence, completeness, and clarity of decisions based on the precautionary principle. The oscillation between a procedure to the benefit and a procedure to the detriment of the substance depends on the way in which the procedural obligations are implemented in each specific circumstance. Therefore, in order to understand whether the procedural content of the precautionary principle constitutes a brake or a lever for its substantial application, it is not possible to provide a general and abstract conclusion, but it is necessary to analyze how the procedural obligations deriving from this principle are implemented in each specific case when such a principle is applied in EU law.

3.1.1.3 THE PRECAUTIONARY PRINCIPLE: A "GENTLE" PRINCIPLE

As stated by Mireille Delmas-Marty, the gentle nature of a principle expresses the absence or difficulty of imposing a sanction when a legal norm is violated.[104]

101 Frank Michelman, *Le juge et la décision politique. Approche procédurale du politique, in* Démocratie et procéduralisation du droit 49–80 (Philippe Coppens & Jacques Lenoble (eds.), Bruylant 2000).

102 Joana Mendes, *Administrative procedure, Administrative Democracy, in* Droit comparé de la procédure administrative, Comparative law of the administrative procedure 235 (Jean-Bernard Auby, Bruylant 2016).

103 Joana Mendes, *Executive rule-making: procedures in between constitutional principles and institutional entrenchment, in* Research handbook on EU administrative law 374 (Carol Harlow, Païvi Leino-Sandberg & Giacinto Della Cananea (eds.), Edward Elgar Publishing Limited 2017).

104 Delmas-Marty, *supra* note 22, at 680.

Precaution is a gentle principle insofar as it is not easy to punish its violation; decision-makers enjoy wide discretion in its application.[105] This is due to the scientific and political complexity of the choices decision-makers face. In a context of high scientific technicality and, politically, very sensitive cases, such as those characterizing the precautionary principle, the judge refuses to substitute his assessment of factual elements for that of the decision-makers and limits his control.[106] As stated by Advocate General Jean Mischo in the case of 12 December 2002 *Commission of the European Communities/Kingdom of Denmark*, "the greater the scientific uncertainty, the broader the discretion of the Member States."[107] Since the available scientific data does not provide a definitive basis for risk decision-making and the existence or scope of risk remains uncertain, it is up to decision-makers, in the exercise of their discretion, to decide on the timeliness and modalities of the precautionary measure.[108]

This limitation of control concerns, first of all, the action for annulment, which is the most frequent means of challenging the legality of precautionary measures.[109] In this case, the Court of Justice restricts the object and intensity of its control. As it pertains to the object, the Court confines itself to verifying only the precautionary measure adopted by the decision-makers, meaning, that the scientific opinions on which the implementation of such a measure was based are excluded from the scope of judicial review.[110] Indeed, they are considered as preparatory acts excluded from the field of the action for annulment.[111] Regarding the intensity of the control, the Court generally makes a limited audit and checks to make sure the decision-makers have not misused their powers or made a manifest error of assessment, or whether they have manifestly exceeded the limits of their discretion.[112] In the context of liability proceedings before the Court of Justice, the non-contractual liability of the European institutions for breach of the precautionary principle is retained only in very exceptional cases.[113] Even if the number of cases filed is not available, to date there is only one case (*Animal Trading Company e.a. v. Commission* of 16

105 European Commission, *Communication of the Commission on the precautionary principle*, COM 1 final, 15 (2000).

106 GC, 17 February 1998, *Pharos SA vs Commission of the European Communities*, T-105/96, EU:T:1998:35, point 69.

107 Opinion of the Advocate General J. Mischo in the case CJEU 23 September 2003, *Commission of the European Communities vs Kingdom of Denmark*, C-192/01, EU:C:2003:492, point 103.

108 European Commission, *supra* note 105, at 15.

109 Estelle Brosset, *Le juge de l'Union et le principe de précaution: état des lieux*, 4 RTDE 737–757 (2015).

110 Jacopo Alberti, Le agenzie dell'Union europea 259–269 (Giuffré 2018).

111 CJEU 11 November 1981, *International Business Machines Corporation vs Commission of the European Communities*, C-60/81, EU:C:1981:264, points 10–15.

112 CJEU 14 July 1998, *Safety High Tech*, C-341/95, EU:C:1998:353, point 54.

113 GC 12 April 2013, *Du Pont de Nemours (France) SAS e.a. vs European Commission*, T-31/07, EU:T:2013:167; GC 16 September 2013, *Animal Trading Company e.a. vs*

September 2013) in which a European institution (in this case, the Commission) has been ordered to compensate the applicant for the damage suffered.[114] It is indeed difficult for the applicant to prove the basis of the non-contractual liability.[115] On the one hand, the violation of the precautionary principle must result in decision-makers' clear and serious disregard of the limits imposed on their discretion.[116] Given the scientifically and politically complex nature of the issues that characterize the precautionary principle, this is not easy to prove. On the other hand, the claimant must demonstrate the existence of a direct causal link between the institution's conduct and the occurrence of the damage and must establish that the damage allegedly suffered is current and certain.[117] However, the causal link and the realization of damage are difficult to demonstrate because, when the decision-makers act based on the precautionary principle, there is only a risk of a causal link and risk of injury.

Flexible in its three dimensions of vague, soft, and gentle, the precautionary principle is also seen as an adaptable principle.

3.1.2 The Adaptability of the Precautionary Principle

Post-modern law is adaptable since it is a law in motion. While modern law was relatively stable, post-modern law is a transitional law, where different norms – with a limited life expectancy – are adopted one after the other and often overlap.[118] The precautionary principle could be considered as an adaptable principle since it is both *interactive* and *evolving*. It is an interactive principle because its content is not determined in advance but adapts to the characteristics of the risk and uncertainty involved. There is no catalogue of precautionary measures that can be adopted, but the choice of the response to an uncertain risk depends on the issues raised in each case. In this sense, the precautionary principle is a principle under permanent construction and even a principle that is built in and through its application.[119]

The precautionary principle is also evolving. It obligates its recipients to carry out regular monitoring to check whether the conditions of the

European Commission, T-333/10, EU:T:2014:842; GC 17 Mars 2016, *Zoofachhandel züpke gmbh e.a. vs European Commission européenne*, T-817/14, EU:T:2016:157.

114 GC 16 September 2013, *Animal Trading Company e.a. vs European Commission*, *supra*, point 103.

115 Mathilde Hautereau-Boutonnet, Lara Khoury & Jean-Christophe Saint-Pau (eds.), L'influence du principe de précaution en droit de la responsabilité civile et pénale. Regards franco-québécois 214 (Les Éditions Revue de droit de l'Université de Sherbrooke 2015).

116 CJEU 4 July 2000, *Bergaderm et Groupil vs Commission of the European Communities*, C-352/98, EU:C:2000:361, points 41–42.

117 CJEU 12 July 1962, *Worms vs Haute Autorité*, C-18/60, EU:C:1962:26.

118 Chevallier, *supra* note 34, at 680.

119 Bonnet, *supra* note 38, at 1078–1083.

principle's application are still being met.[120] The European Commission thus considers that measures adopted based on the precautionary principle must be maintained "as long as scientific uncertainty persists and as long as the risk is deemed sufficiently high not to be accepted by society."[121] Precautionary measures are not of indefinite duration but rather must remain in place until the conditions of risk and uncertainty justifying the use of this principle remain. When these conditions change, the precautionary measures must be reviewed and, if necessary, modified.

While the adaptability and smoothness of the precautionary principle reflect its flexibility, *complexity* refers to its multidimensionality.

3.2 The Complexity of the Precautionary Principle

According to Edgar Morin, complexity is a fabric of heterogeneous constituents inseparably associated.[122] The adjective *complex* refers to the symbolic actions of embracing and wrapping.[123] Complexity is not the opposite of simplicity but of unidimensionality: complexity is what cannot be summarized in a single word, what cannot be reduced to a simple idea.[124] For Morin, understanding complexity requires a "change of perspective on the law" in the sense of opening it up, and that "complex thinking aspires to multidimensional knowledge."[125] Jacques Chevallier points out that two elements contribute significantly to the complexity of post-modern law: the "multiplicity of legal centres" that are entangled in the construction of law (it is a *plural* law) and the "fragmentation of the processes of drafting norms that now involve several actors" (the law is the product of *negotiation* among several actors).[126] In this perspective, the precautionary principle is complex since it is a plural principle, which is the result of negotiations between distinct subjects.

3.2.1 The Plurality of the Precautionary Principle

Plurality is generally understood as "the coexistence within the same political field of different legal spaces superimposed and combined in the spirit and

120 Émilie Gaillard, *L'œuvre créatrice des juges de l'Union européenne fondée sur le principe de précaution: quels enjeux pour la mise en œuvre d'un impératif juridique d'anticipation?*, *in* Principe de précaution et métamorphose de la responsabilité 87 (Luca D'Ambrosio, Geneviève Giudicelli-Delage & Stefano Manacorda (eds.), Collection de l'Institut des sciences juridiques et philosophiques de la Sorbonne 2018).

121 European Commission, *supra* note 105.

122 Morin, *supra* note 34, at 21.

123 Edgar Morin, *Les défis de la complexité*, *in* Le défi du XXIe siècle. Relier les connaissances, Paris, du 16 au 24 mars 1998, Journées thématiques conçues et animées par Edgard Morin 455 (Edgar Morin, Éditions Seuil 1999).

124 *Ibid.*

125 Morin, *supra* note 34, at 11.

126 Chevallier, *supra* note 34, at 675–677.

actions of each party."[127] Several concepts can be used to designate legal plurality. Reference can be made to ***plurijuralism*** (when targeting the plurality of legal systems),[128] ***polycentrism*** (when considering the plurality of centres for the creation of legal norms),[129] ***legal pluralism*** (to designate the plurality of legal orders),[130] or ***internormativity*** (in case where distinct disciplines contribute to the formation of the norm).[131] Although it is not always easy to decide between the different interpretations of plurality, one meaning seems particularly appropriate to explain the complexity of the precautionary principle under EU law: its internormativity. The concept of internormativity refers to a polycentric logic where different norms (legal and non-legal) and different actors concur on the definition of a rule of conduct.[132] From this perspective, the rule is no longer single-actor and legally focused but results from an interaction between several actors from several disciplines. From a theoretical point of view, three different conceptions of internormativity can be distinguished: pluri/multidisciplinarity, transdisciplinarity, and interdisciplinarity.[133] *Pluridisciplinarity*, or ***multidisciplinarity***, consists of juxtaposing a set of diverse disciplines developing their specific points of view. We are dealing with *coexistence* of different languages.[134] *Transdisciplinarity* implies that all disciplines abandon their particular point of view to produce autonomous knowledge, from which new objects and methods result; it is an ***integration*** of disciplines.[135] In the ***interdisciplinary*** model, research is carried out from the theoretical field of one discipline that develops common problems that also concern other disciplines. It is an ***articulation*** of knowledge that leads, through successive approaches, to partial reorganizations of the involved theoretical fields.[136]

The precautionary principle can be considered as an interdisciplinary principle that acts as a link between different disciplines.[137] The precautionary principle is a legal principle – that under EU law is applied in the field of

127 Jacques Commaille, *Normes juridiques et régulation sociale: retour à la sociologie générale*, *in* Normes juridiques et régulation sociale 13–22 (François Chazel & Jacques Commaille, LGDJ, coll. "Droit et Société" 1991).

128 Jean-Louis Bergel, Plurijuridisme, Actes du 8ème congrès de l'Association internationale de Méthodologie juridique (Presses Universitaires d'Aix-Marseille 2005).

129 Delmas-Marty, *supra* note 22, at 680.

130 Chevallier, *supra* note 34, at 673.

131 Jean Carbonnier, *Les phénomènes d'internormativité*, European Year Book in Law and Sociology 42–52 (1977).

132 Adélie Pomade, *Penser l'interdisciplinarité par l'internormativité. Illustration en droit de l'environnement*, 1 Revue interdisciplinaire d'études juridiques 85–106 (2012).

133 *Ibid.*

134 *Ibid.*

135 *Ibid.*

136 *Ibid.*

137 Luca D'Ambrosio, Geneviève Giudicelli-Delage & Stefano Manacorda, *Introduction*, *in* Principe de précaution et métamorphose de la responsabilité 27 (Luca D'Ambrosio, Geneviève Giudicelli-Delage & Stefano Manacorda (eds.), Collection de l'Institut des sciences juridiques et philosophiques de la Sorbonne 2018).

environment and public health – but the understanding of the precautionary principle is not limited to the legal domain. Analyzing the precautionary principle involves addressing the relationship between law and science and between law and political science. It also provides an understanding of how ethics, morality, philosophy, economics, and sociology influence decision-makers when making decisions about risk. This means that these disciplines (science, sociology, politics, philosophy, and economics) constitute the starting point for a different perspective on the legal dimension of the precautionary principle.[138] Consequently, through this principle, other disciplines enter the field of law, and because of the influence exercised by the precautionary principle, they evolve in step with legal regulation.[139]

Inter-normative, the precautionary principle is the product of negotiations conducted at different stages of its implementation.

3.2.2 The Negotiability of the Precautionary Principle

The crisis of reason that characterizes post-modern law has significant consequences for the process of developing the legal norm. In modern law, the rule was endowed with "a capital of authority that enabled it to obtain obedience and win the support of taxpayers."[140] In post-modern law, the norm has lost its binding character. If a norm is applied, it is because it is subject to the consent of its recipients. This presupposes that they are involved in its elaboration: prior to consultation, participation in the definition of the rule becomes the guarantee of its validity; the right thus becomes a negotiated right, which is the result of collective deliberation.[141] The negotiated nature of post-modern law is reflected in the transfer of competences from political decision-makers to professional bodies, expert committees, and administrative authorities, which, based on their technical knowledge, are better able to arbitrate between the various interests involved.

The precautionary principle can be considered as a negotiated principle. The application of this principle results from dialogue and exchange between policymakers and scientific experts.[142] Precaution is a risk management principle that is applied by policymakers. However, the scientific experts commissioned by decision-makers to assess the uncertain risk involved are the only ones who can evaluate the extent of this risk and thus provide policy guidance. On the one hand, without the input of scientific experts, decision-makers would not be able to adopt the precautionary principle since they would not have the

138 Véronique, Champeil-Desplats, Méthodologies du droit et des sciences du droit 343 (Dalloz 2014).

139 Jacques Chevallier, *L'internormativité. Les sources du droit revisitées*, 4 Théorie des sources du droit 689–715 (2013).

140 Chevallier, *supra* note 34, at 675.

141 *Ibid.*

142 De Sadeleer, *supra* note 35, at 174–183.

necessary skills to assess the reality of the risk and, consequently, the need to anticipate the threat. On the other hand, without policymakers, experts would be limited to a scientific risk assessment without the means to adopt a protection measure at the political level. As a result, the precautionary principle is negotiated: the content of this principle and its implementation methods derive directly from the relationship between experts and decision-makers.

4 Conclusion

The starting point of this chapter was the acknowledgement that we live in a post-truth society.[143] To understand the meaning and the implications of this definition, I recalled the process of the emergence of post-modernism, which constitutes the theoretical framework under which the notion of post-truth should be analyzed. In this regard, I argued that the precautionary principle is a paradigmatic principle of post-modern law. It is, indeed, flexible (in its double dimension of smooth and adaptable principle) and complex (as an interdisciplinary principle negotiated by scientific experts and political decision-makers). Though a question remains unsolved: Does post-modernism, *via* the precautionary principle, necessarily bring to post-truth? A twofold answer can be given to this question. First, one may consider that post-modernism and post-truth are *connected* phenomena whose roots lie in the questioning of the power of reason, science, and progress that characterized Western societies and legal systems beginning in the 1970s. Nonetheless, although post-truth is connected to post-modernism, it is *not a necessary consequence.* Indeed, if post-modernism *via* the precautionary principle opened the legal system to the notion of uncertainty and to the existence of diverging scientific data, it did not deprive the notion of truth of any significance as post-truth does.[144] Therefore, if post-truth indicates "a state in which the truth gets rid of its significance, a condition in which facts do not matter anymore,"[145] this cannot be the consequence of the precautionary principle. As indicated earlier, this principle is based on scientific facts, which shall be evaluated by scientific experts and appreciated by political decision-makers, but these facts are uncertain rather than certain. Secondly, it cannot be excluded that the precautionary principle *might contribute* to the progressive disconnection between facts and truth. On the one hand, the precautionary principle may legitimate the existence of many different "scientific truths," each of them corresponding to the diverging scientific opinions evaluating the risk distinctly at stake. In this scenario, the connection between facts and truth would be lost as a consequence of the plurality of the "scientific truths" available. On the other hand, the precautionary principle may play a part in allowing emotions and personal beliefs to

143 Mcintyre, *supra* note 5.
144 Han, *supra* note 25, at 3.
145 *Ibid.*

enter into the legal domain. Indeed, this principle grants the decision-makers with a broad margin of appreciation. The choice and the content of the measure to be adopted depend on the discretionary power of the authorities. If such authorities do not base their decision on the available scientific data, they might take a precautionary measure inspired more by personal beliefs and emotions than science. This may lead to the existence of diverging "political truths" and thus to the disconnection between facts and truth. To avoid both risks of having different "scientific" and "political" truths, the Court of Justice of the European Union has stressed the importance of defining the procedural obligations that the authorities should follow in implementing the precautionary principle and the conditions that the experts should comply with while evaluating the uncertain risk at stake. However, these are not absolute safeguards but relative guarantees that should be implemented and appreciated on a case-by-case basis as typical under the post-modern law.

6 The Precautionary Principle and the Burden of Proof in International Risk Regulation Trials

*Justo Corti Varela**

1 Introduction

Following a classic definition, we can say that the precautionary principle applies:

> "Where there are threats of serious or irreversible damage, lack of full scientific certainty shall not be used as a reason for postponing cost-effective measures to prevent environmental degradation."[1]

The precautionary principle is part of the decision-making process in the context of scientific uncertainty. Consequently, it was included in an important number of international treaties and agreements[2] regulating decision-making

* Justo Corti Varela, Associate Professor, National Distance Learning University (Spain), Deputy Dean on Quality and Innovation of the Law School. Former visiting professor at Paris Ouest La Defense Nanterre University (France) and visiting scholar at University College London. Chair of the Jean Monnet European Climate Law project. Corresponding Author: jcorti@der.uned.es

1 Principle 15 of the Rio Declaration on Environment and Development, 14 June 1992, United Nations Doc. A/CONF.151/26/Rev.1.

2 The first international instrument that included the principle was the Bremen Declaration of the International Conference on the Protection of the North Sea (1984) in item D3. Afterwards, it was incorporated into the Montreal Protocol on Substances that Deplete the Ozone Layer (1987), annexed to the Vienna Convention for the protection of the Ozone Layer (1985), in the Preamble; the Bamako Convention on the Ban on the Import into Africa and Control of Transboundary Movement and Management of Hazardous Wastes within Africa (1991), in Art. 4.3; in the United Nations Programme of Action from Rio – Agenda 21 Earth Summit (1992), in Arts. 17.1, 17.5, 17.21, 17.22, 17.97, 17.128, 18.40, 19.14, 19.48, 19.49, 19.60, 20.32, 22.5, 35.3, 35.5, 35.6; the United Nations Framework Convention on Climate Change (1992), Art. 3.3; The Agreement for the Implementation of the Provisions of the United Nations Convention on the Law of the Sea of 10 December 1982 relating to the Conservation and Management of Straddling Fish Stocks and Highly Migratory Fish Stocks – UN Fish Stocks Agreement- (1995), esp. Art. 6; the Cartagena Protocol on Biosafety to the Convention on Biological Diversity (2000), esp. Preamble and Arts. 10.6, 11.6 y 11.8; and the Stockholm Convention on Persistent Organic Pollutants (2001), esp. Arts. 4 y 8.7). For an in-depth study on these international instruments, see Nicolas De Sadeleer, Environmental Principles: From Political Slogans to Legal Rules 94 (Oxford University Press 2002); David Freestone & Ellen

DOI: 10.4324/9781003472421-6

in areas including the protection of life and health of people, animals, and plants, the protection of the environment, or the guarantee of food safety. Much more indirectly, the principle is also present throughout international trade law[3] and the law of the sea,[4] particularly when these systems of international law introduce exceptions to core principles such as free trade or freedom of fishing on high seas.

The precautionary principle, as it pertains to international literature, has been studied in depth.[5] It has not yet been recognized as a customary principle of international law;[6] however, this recognition would not be necessary for it

---

Hey, *Origins and Development of the Precautionary Principle, in* The Precautionary Principle and International Law: The Challenge of Implementation 3, 3 (David Freestone & Ellen Hey (eds.), Kluwer Law International 1996); Patricia Birnie, Alan Boyle & Catherine Redgwell, International Law and the Environment 154–164 (Oxford University Press 2009). For an analysis of the recognition in international treaties, see Arie Trouwbost, Evolution and Status of the Precautionary Principle 20 (Kluwer Law International 2002).

3 Because of the silence in WTO agreements, DSU case law does not recognize the precautionary principle as such, but it accepts that during the Agreement on the Application of Sanitary and Phytosanitary Measures, April 15, 1994, 1867 U.N.T.S. 493, (hereafter SPS Agreement) risk assessment, "a Member has decided to follow a precautionary approach could have a bearing on a panel's assessment of whether an SPS measure is "based on" a risk assessment as required by Article 5.1". See Panel Report, *European Communities – Measures Affecting the Approval and Marketing of Biotech Products*, WT/DS291/R; WT/DS292/R; WT/DS293/R (27 September 2006) hereafter *EC-Biotech Products*, para. 7.3065. There is no discussion that art. 5.7 of the SPS Agreement is founded on a precautionary philosophy. In this regard, see Joanne Scott, The WTO Agreement on Sanitary and Phytosanitary Measures 112 (Oxford University Press 2007).

4 For example, the Convention on the Protection of the Marine Environment of the Baltic Sea Area, Helsinki art. 3.2, March 22, 1974, 1507 U.N.T.S. 166

5 Arie Trouwhorst, *Prevention, Precaution, Logic and Law. The Relationship between the Precautionary Principle and the Preventative Principle in International Law and Associated Questions*, 2 Erasmus Law Review 105–127 (2009); Malgosia Fitzmaurice, Contemporary Issues in International Environmental Law 1–67 (Edward Elgar 2009); D. Grimeaud, *The Precautionary Principle in International Environmental and Trade Law, in* Juridische afbakening van het voorzorgsbeginsel: mogelijkheden en grenzen. Den Haag: Gezondheidsraad 24–26 (Michelle Faure & Ellen Vos (eds.), Maastricht University 2003); Simon Marr, The Precautionary Principle in the Law of the Sea: Modern Decision-Making in International Law (Martinus Nijhoff 2003); Arie Trouwborst, Evolution and Status of the Precautionary Principle in International Law (Springer 2002); Charles Leben (ed.), Le principe de précaution: Aspects de droit international et communautaire (Pantheon Droit International 2002); Tim O'Riordan, James Cameron & Andrew Jordan (eds.), Reinterpreting the Precautionary Principle (Cameron May 2001); Freestone & Hey, *supra* note 2.

6 Discussion has been particularly intense in WTO case law, where, due to the lack of official recognition in its treaties (as explained in footnote 3), it would be applicable only when it can be demonstrated that the precautionary principle was a general principle of customary international law, something that "appears less than clear." See Appellate Body Report, *European Communities – Measures Concerning Meat and Meat Products (Hormones)* WT/DS26/AB/R; WT/DS48/AB/R (16 January 1998) hereafter AB *EC-Hormones*, paras. 123 and 124; and, Panel report *EC-Biotech Products*, paras. 7.73 and 7.89. Beyond the WTO, only an award of the Permanent Court of Arbitration has recognized it clearly, in the *Iron Rhine Railway* case

to be considered in international judicial proceedings, especially where there is scientific uncertainty.[7] Judges apply the precautionary principle in a number of ways. On the one hand, regarding the material elements of the decision, it could be a justification and/or a mitigating circumstance for national decisions normally restricting international law principles, when there is lack of scientific proof, since it increases a government's room to manoeuvre in its decision-making. This is the judicial impact of the classical (administrative) use of the precautionary principle.

On the other hand, as an adjudicative rule, the precautionary principle can be understood as a decision-making tool for making procedural decisions in judicial trials, such as the burden or the assessment of proof.[8] The question is, in contexts where there is scientific uncertainty (a lack, or contradictory sources, of proof), whether the precautionary principle could reduce or even reverse the burden of proof, especially in situations when the subject pleading for the principle's application is using it as a way to be exempt from a general rule of international law.

The "proceduralization" of the precautionary principle demands some homogenization of the case law object of study. The precautionary principle is closely linked to risk management decisions, which are often manifestations of state sovereignty. In this sense, it is not advisable to compare disputes between states, where the principle of sovereignty is balanced upon disagreements between states and individuals. Similar arguments lead us to exclude

---

(*Reports of International Arbitral Awards*, vol. XXVII, pp. 35–125, para. 59). In EU law, it has been recognized as "EU" general principle (see case C-180/96, ECLI:EU:C:1998:192, para. 99–101; and case C-157/96, ECLI:EU:C:1998:191 para. 62–64). International literature agrees that it is an "emerging" principle: David Freestone, *Caution or Precaution: A Rose By Any Other Name . . .?*, 10(1) Yearbook of International Environmental Law 25–32 (2000); James Cameron, *The Precautionary Principle: Core Meaning, Constitutional Framework & Procedures for Implementation, in* Perspectives on the Precautionary Principle 30 (Ronnie Harding & Elizabeth Fisher (dirs.), The Federation Press 1999); or, at least, that it starts to be an international custom: Phillippe Sands & Jaqueline Peel, Principles of International Environmental Law 279 (Cambridge University Press 2012); James Cameron & Juli Abouchar, *The Status of the Precautionary Principle in International Law, in* Freestone & Hey, *supra* note 2, 29–52, 30. This idea of a principle in progress has been incorporated in the Seabed Dispute Chamber of ITLOS (see Advisory Opinion of 1 February 2011, para. 135).

7 Elizabeth Fisher, Risk Regulation and Administrative Constitutionalism 44–46 (Bloomsbury Publishing 2007).

8 Caroline Foster, Science and the Precautionary Principle in International Courts and Tribunals 245 (Cambridge University Press 2013). For the distinction between "administrative" and "adjudicative" burdens of proof in the application of the precautionary principle, see Panel Report *Japan – Measures Affecting Agricultural Products*, WT/DS76/R (27 October 1998) hereafter PR *Japan – Agricultural Products*, para. 8.13 and Panel Report *Japan – Measures Affecting the Importation of Apples*, WT/DS245/R, (15 July 2003), para. 8.41. For other "archetypical versions" of the precautionary principle ("uncertainty does not justify inaction," "uncertainty justifies action," and "shifting the burden of proof"), see Jonathan B. Wiener, *Precaution, in* The Oxford Handbook of International Environmental Law 597, 599 (Daniel Bodansky, Jutta Brunnée & Ellen Hey (eds.), Oxford University Press 2007).

courts of regional organizations that allow the transfer of sovereignty, like the EU, since in such disputes other principles (primacy) ultimately prevail. Consequently, we will only analyze international case law involving states where the precautionary principle has been invoked: the International Court of Justice ("ICJ"),[9] the Dispute Settlement Understanding ("DSU") of the World Trade Organization ("WTO"),[10] and the International Tribunal for the Law of the Sea ("ITLOS").[11] It is true that there are *ad hoc* arbitral awards *where* the precautionary principle has been taken into consideration.[12] However, the lack of clear case law doctrine, as well only as the small number of judicial decisions, makes it advisable to focus our attention on only the three judicial bodies previously mentioned.

2 *Actori Incumbit Probatio* in Cases of Scientific Uncertainty and the Obligation of Collaboration in Evidence Production

Both in common law and Roman law, if the party bearing the burden of proof fails to meet it, the case could be ruled upon without going into substantive arguments (commonly known as "*no evidence, no case*"). Although it is not

9 Request for an Examination of the Situation in Accordance with Paragraph 63 of the Court's Judgment of the 20th of December 1974 in the *Nuclear Tests* (New Zealand *v.* France) Case, 22 September 1995, *ICJ Reports* 1995, 288. Gabčíkovo-Nagymaros Project (Hungary v. Slovakia), 25 September 1997, *ICJ Reports* 1997, 7. Pulp Mills on the River Uruguay (Argentina *v.* Uruguay), 20 April 2010, *ICJ Reports* 1997, 14. Whaling in the Antarctic (Australia *v.* Japan: New Zealand intervening), 31 March 2014, *ICJ Reports* 2014, 226.

10 Panel Report, *European Communities – Measures Concerning Meat and Meat Products (Hormones)*, WT/DS26/R/USA (18 August 1997), and AB *EC-Hormones*; Panel Report *United States – Import Prohibition of Certain Shrimp and Shrimp Product*, WT/DS58/R/Corr.1 (15 May 1998), and *Appellate Body Report*, WT/DS58/AB/R (12 October 1998); PR *Japan – Agricultural Products*, and Appellate Body report, WT/DS76/AB/R (22 February 1999); Panel Report, *European Communities – Measures Affecting Asbestos and Asbestos-Containing Products*, WT/DS135/R (18 September 2000), and Appellate Body Report WT/DS135/AB/R (12 March 2001); PR *EC-Biotech Products*; Panel Report *United States – Continued Suspension of Obligations in the EC – Hormones Dispute* (Hormones II), WT/DS320/R (31 March 2008), and Appellate Body Report WT/DS320/AB/R (16 October 2008).

11 ITLOS, *Southern Bluefin Tuna Case* (New Zealand v. Japan; Australia v. Japan), provisional measures, cases 3 and 4, 3 and 16 August 1999; ITLOS *MOX Plant* case (Ireland v. United Kingdom), provisional measures, case 10, 3 December 2001; ITLOS *Land Reclamation by Singapore in and Around the Straits of Johor Case* (Malaysia v. Singapore), provisional measures, case 12, 8 October 2003.

12 For example, in the Permanent Court of Arbitration award *Iron Rhine Railway*, Reports of International Arbitral Awards, vol. XXVII, pp. 35–125, para. 59; or in the ICSID award Marion Unglaube *et.al.* vs. Costa Rica, cases ARB/08/1 and ARB/09/20, para. 130.

mentioned in the rules of proceedings,[13] international courts[14] follow this procedural principle, known as *actori incumbit probatio*.[15]

The lack of explicit wording in the procedural rules permits international courts to modulate the precautionary principle according to a number of circumstances. First, the status of the party as an applicant or a defendant is not necessarily determinative of the action, since the party alleging a claim generally bears the burden both when it is a claimant or a defendant in a case. This means that if the claim is a defence or exception, the burden of proof, of course, lies with that defendant. Second, international courts do not strictly follow assigning of the burden of proof to one party but rather promote "collaboration" in its production.[16] This rule is particularly important

13 It is neither in the ICJ, DSU, nor ITLOS proceeding rules. Its incorporation was discussed in the 2nd session of the International Law Commission on Arbitral Procedure: "La preuve, disions-nous, constitue une charge dont le non accomplissement peut se trouver automatiquement sanctionné par la perte du procès. L'adage *actori incumbit probatio* veut dire que la preuve incombe non pas au seul demandeur, mais à celui des plaideurs qui allègue un fait quelconque. La charge est répartie entre les deux plaideurs." Proposed text: "Toute partie qui allègue un fait susceptible d'avoir une pertinence sur la solution du litige doit en apporter tout au moins un commencement de prevue" See Report of the Special Rapporteur, Mr. Georges Scelle, A/CN.4/18, 2nd session of the ILC, *Yearbook of the International Law Commission* (1950), Vol. II, para. 69 and 72. It was not finally included in the Model Rules on Arbitral Procedure of 1958. However, it was incorporated in the Permanent Court of Arbitration optional rules: "Each party shall have the burden of proving the facts relied on to support its claim or defence" (Art. 24.1). Unfortunately, there is no clarification or amendment in Optional Rules for Arbitration of Disputes Relating to Natural Resources and the Environment, a sector where the precautionary principle could modify the allocation of proof. On the other hand, the principle is included in the UNIDROIT Principles of Transnational Civil Procedure (principle 21.1).

14 For example, in the *Whaling* case, the Precautionary Principle was not analyzed in the main judgement since Japan failed to prove that its program was based on scientific grounds.

15 Shabtai Rosenne, The Law and Practice of the International Court 1920–2015 1040 (Brill 2015); Mojtaba Kazazi, Burden of Proof and Related Issues: A Study on Evidence before International Tribunals 54 (Kluwer Law International 1996); Joost Pauwelyn, *Evidence, Proof and Persuasion in WTO Dispute Settlement. Who Bears the Burden?*, 1 Journal of International Economic Law 227–258, 235–237 (1998). For its recognition in the case law see, for example, the *Nicaragua Case* (ICJ Rep. 1984 p. 169), para 101: "it is the litigant seeking to establish a fact who bears the burden of proving it." Similarly, *Avena* case (ICJ Rep 2004, p. 128), para 55; *Burkina Faso and Mali* case (ICJ Rep 1986, p. 554), para. 65; *Cameroon v Nigeria* (Preliminary Objections) (ICJ Rep. 1998, p. 275), para. 319; *Bosnia and Herzegovina v Serbia and Montenegro* (*ICJ Reports* 2007, p. 43), para. 204; and *Pulp Mill* case, para. 162. Quoting ICJ case law, the principle has been used also by WTO. For example, Appellate Body Report *United States – Measures Affecting Imports of Woven Wool Shirts and Blouses from India*, WT/DS33/AB/R (23 May 1997) para. 323; Panel Report Turkey – Restrictions on Imports of Textile and Clothing Products, WT/DS34/R (19 November 1999), para 9.57; and Panel Report *Argentina – Safeguard Measures on Imports of Footwear*, WT/DS121/R (25 June 1999), hereafter PR *Argentina-Footwear*, paras. 6.34–6.40.

16 Report of the Special Rapporteur, Mr. Georges Scelle, A/CN.4/18, 2nd session of the ILC, *Yearbook of the International Law Commission* (1950), Vol. II, para 71: "les Etats en litige ont

both in WTO case law[17] and when cases are brought before the ICJ through mutual agreement of the parties.[18] This rule is necessary due to the view that it is important to bring as much evidence as possible before the Court, where, contrary to domestic law, there would be no explicit power which would enable the Court to compel the production of that evidence.[19] This particularity, as it pertains to international adjudication, is linked to the principles of good faith and fair resolution of conflicting claims.[20]

The scientific uncertainty that surrounds the application of the precautionary principle, as it pertains to taking evidence into account, is that much more difficult both when there is no scientific data and when parties have imbalanced access to that data. When the party bearing the burden is unable to establish a claim because data is only available to its counterpart, the need to protect judicial function could lead to a rebalancing of that obligation.[21]

This problem is tackled by case law from a variety of different perspectives. The ICJ and the ITLOS[22] follow a traditional view (*actori incumbit probatio*)[23] but add a duty of collaboration. In this regard, the ICJ said in the *Pulp Mills* case:

> It is . . . to be expected that the Applicant should, in the first instance, submit the relevant evidence to substantiate its claims. This does not,

l'obligation de collaborer de bonne foi à l'administration de la preuve. La partie qui allègue est tenue d'apporter, tout au moins un commencement de preuve. C'est un engagement implicite que prévoyait déjà l'article 23 de la Convention de La Haye de 1907 en matière de commission d'enquête et qu'a répété l'article 75 d'une façon abstraite: 'Les parties s'engagent à fournir au tribunal, dans la plus large mesure qu'elles jugeront possible, tous les moyens nécessaires pour la décision du litige'."

17 PR *Argentina-Footwear*, para 6.40; similarly, in Appellate Body Report *India – Pharmaceutical and Agricultural Chemical Products*, WT/DS50/AB/R (19 December 1997), hereafter AB India- Pharmaceutical Products, para 94.

18 See James Gerard Devaney, Fact-Finding before the International Court of Justice 192 (Cambridge University Press 2016). Devaney quotes some examples in this regard: Case Concerning Ahmadou Sadio Diallo (Republic of Guinea v, Democratic Republic of the Congo), Judgment, 30 November 2010, para 56: "[i] n short, when it comes to establishing facts such as those which are at issue in the present case, neither party is alone in bearing the burden of proof." Also, the case concerning rights of nations of the United States of America in Morocco, Judgment of August 27th, 1952, ICJ Reports 1952 176. Similarly, V.S. Mani, International Adjudication: Procedural Aspects, vol. 4, 198 (Kluwer Law International 1980).

19 Durward V. Sandifer, Evidence before International Tribunals, vol. 13, 112 (University Press of Virginia 1975).

20 Mani, *supra* note 18, at 198.

21 Some authors, like Caroline Foster, have connected this approach to Bentham's view that "he should have the burden on whom it would sit lightest." See Caroline Foster, *Burden of Proof in International Courts and Tribunals*, 27 Yearbook of International Law 27–86, 48 (2010) quoting James Bradley Thayer, *The Burden of Proof*, 2 Harvard Law Review 45, 56 (1890–1891).

22 *Southern Bluefin Tuna*, provisional measures order, para. 90

23 For example, in ICJ *Nuclear Tests* interim measures (Australia v. France and New Zealand vs. France).

> however, mean that the Respondent should not co-operate in the provision of such evidence as may be in its possession that could assist the Court in resolving the dispute submitted to it."[24]

The duty of collaboration is particularly important in the ICJ due to the specific characteristics of its proceedings, where analyzed facts "are often unique, often spread over a long period of time, and . . . frequently difficult and uncertain of access,"[25] further complicating the acceptance of proof.[26]

The WTO's case law follows a different approach which results in similar consequences. The production of evidence at the WTO is law- and economics-based. This means that the complainant may be exempt from bearing the burden of proof when either the assessment of the cost of proof or cost of error is exorbitant or the estimated likelihood that there will not be a balance between those costs.[27] This approach means that the burden of proof is often determined on a case-by-case basis, and the case law shows that, when there is scientific uncertainty, claims for collaboration are often granted.[28]

It is worth saying that collaboration in the production of evidence does not necessarily mean a shifting of the burden will be ordered. For example, in the *Avena* case, the ICJ did not discharge the United States ("US") from the burden of showing that Mexican nationals were also US nationals because the state did not demonstrate that it made real efforts to obtain the necessary information (the nationals' dates of birth and their parents' marital status at that time) from the Mexican authorities.[29] Even though Mexico had better access to such information, it was not obliged to provide the proof. Similarly, the WTO has said:

> There is nothing in the WTO dispute settlement system to support the notion that the allocation of the burden of proof should be decided on the basis of a comparison between the respective difficulties that may

24 *Pulp Mills* case paras 162, 163, 168. The wording recalls the famous statement of the Mexican Claims Commission in the Parker case: "Whilst ordinarily it is incumbent upon the party who alleges a fact to introduce evidence to establish it, yet before this Commission this rule does not relieve the respondent from its obligation to lay before the commission all evidence within its possession to establish the truth, whatever it may be." General Claims Commission (Agreement of 8 September 1923) United Mexican States, United States of America. Reports of International Arbitral Awards, Vol. IV, p, 39 para 6.

25 Robert Kolb, The International Court of Justice 943 (Hart Publishing 2014).

26 Devaney, *supra* note 18, at 240.

27 Michelle T. Grando, *Allocating the Burden of Proof in WTO Disputes: A Critical Analysis*, 9(3) Journal of International Economic Law 615–656 (2006).

28 PR *Argentina – Footwear*, para 6.40; similarly in AB *India – Pharmaceutical Products*, para 94, the AB stated that parties should be "fully forthcoming from the very beginning both as to the claims involved in the dispute and as to the facts relating to those claims . . . Claims must be stated clearly. Facts must be disclosed freely".

29 *Avena* case, para. 41, 55–57. For a comment see Shabtai Rosenne, The Law and Practice of the International Court, 1920–2005 1042 (4th ed., Brill 2006).

> possibly be encountered by the complainant and the respondent in collecting information to prove a case.[30]

The main problem arises when collaboration does not work or is not directly promoted by the court. In such cases, the conjunction of the principle *actori incumbit probatio* with scientific uncertainty could lead to a *probatio diabolica*[31] for the applicant, particularly for those that aim to protect the environment.[32] The incorporation of the precautionary principle into proceedings could help in obtaining solutions to this problem, particularly if the court allows for a shift in the burden (which will be addressed and discussed in Section 3) or, at least, in cases where the court reduces the necessary standard of proof (hereafter discussed in detail in Section 4).

3 The Precautionary Principle and the Burden of Proof in Interim Orders: Is It Possible to Shift the Burden?

Interim orders are precautionary as they, in essence, aim to preserve the *status quo* and prevent irreparable prejudice. As Judge Treves said in the *Southern Bluefin Tuna* case (provisional measures):

> The precautionary principle can be seen as a logical consequence of the need to ensure that, when the arbitral tribunal decides on the merits. . . . In other words, a precautionary approach seems to me inherent in the very notion of provisional measures.[33]

International courts require both of the following classical requisites: *fumus bonis iuris* and *periculum in mora*.[34] In cases dealing with scientific uncertainty, the difficulty in producing evidence focuses on the latter (i.e. on the level of risk and the timing of actions with which to avoid it). Following general rules, the burden lies with the applicant of the interim measures, but if they did not have access to the required information, the question is whether the precautionary principle would allow for a shift in that burden of proof. In other words, given the "reasonable scientific plausibility"[35] of the risk by the

30 Appellate Body Report, *European Communities – Trade Description of Sardines*, WT/DS231/AB/R (26 September 2002), para 281.

31 *Probatio diabolica* (Latin: "devil's proof") is a legal requirement to achieve an impossible proof.

32 Foster, *supra* note 8, at 230. Analyzing *Probatio Diabolica* in other international law contexts see Kazazi, *supra* note 15, at 332–340.

33 *Southern Bluefin Tuna*, provisional measures, separate opinion of Judge Treves, 9.

34 For a classical comment, see Peter J. Goldsworthy, *Interim Measures of Protection in the International Court of Justice*, 68(2) American Journal of International Law 258–277 (1974), which concerns, among others, the interim measures in nuclear weapons tests.

35 De Sadeleer, *supra* note 2, at 160.

applicant (i.e. the minimum scientific proof threshold that the precautionary principle requires), would the respondent be obligated to prove the safety of the *status quo* for rejecting the interim order?

The full shift of the burden of proof was analyzed in three interim orders, one by the ICJ ("*Nuclear Tests*") and two by the ITLOS ("*Mox Plant*" and "*Southern Bluefin Tuna*"). In regard to the first case, the ICJ, in 1973, provided provisional measures in proceedings against France by Australia and New Zealand due to atmospheric nuclear testing in the South Pacific because:

> Whereas for the purpose of the present proceedings it suffices to observe that the information submitted to the Court . . . does not exclude the possibility that damage to New Zealand might be shown to be caused by the deposit on New Zealand/Australia territory of radioactive fall-out resulting from such tests and to be irreparable.[36]

In this first case (*Nuclear Tests*), following a soft a*ctori incumbit probatio* approach, the court accepted the evidence provided by applicants in order to prove the "possibility" of damage. However, when New Zealand asked the court to re-examine the situation in 1995, because of France's underground testing, Judge Weeramantry did discuss the burden of proof of the environmental damage:

> There are two ways of approaching this question. The first is to place the burden of proof fairly and squarely upon New Zealand, and then ask whether a prima facie case has been made out of the presence of such dangers as New Zealand complains of.
>
> The second approach is to apply the principle of environmental law under which, where environmental damage of any sort is threatened. The burden of proving that it will not produce the damaging consequences complained of is placed upon the author of that damage. In this view of the matter, the Court would hold that the environmental damage New Zealand complains of is prima facie established in the absence of proof by France that the proposed nuclear tests are environmentally safe.[37]

Although it was a separate and dissenting opinion (the main decision did not discuss the burden of proof), it is interesting to see arguments where the threat of environmental damage is enough to warrant reallocating the burden

36 *Nuclear test* case (interim measures) para. 30 (New Zealand v. France), and para 29 (Australia v. France).

37 Request for an Examination of the situation. Dissenting Opinion of Judge Weeramantry. See Elihu Lauterpacht, C. J. Greenwood & A. G. Oppenheimer, International Law Reports, vol. 106, para. 348 (Cambridge University Press 1997), italics are ours.

of proof. To reinforce this approach, Judge Weeramantry used the argument of the access/availability of scientific information in a precautionary principle context in two methods. First, he states that "New Zealand has placed materials before the Court to the best of its ability, but France is in possession of the actual information." Second, regarding the lack of information, he puts forth affirmations that the precautionary principle

> springs into operation to give the Court the basic rationale for considering New Zealand's request and not postponing the application of such means that environmental degradation, until such time as the full scientific evidence becomes available in refutation of the New Zealand contention.[38]

The case of *Mox Plant* concerned a British project where a mixed oxide ("MOX") of plutonium dioxide and uranium dioxide fuel production occurred at the nuclear plant at Sellafiel in Cumbria, on the coast of the Irish Sea, just 112 miles from the Irish border. Ireland was concerned about the management of such radioactive materials so close to its borders, but it was not able to demonstrate the risk, scientifically. Nevertheless, it requested provisional measures grounded in the precautionary principle. The court (ITLOS) refused the request based on the lack of urgency, but it required the parties to cooperate in exchanging information about the risks or effects of operating the plant and to devise ways to deal with them as appropriate, grounding its decision on "prudence and caution."[39]

In a dissenting opinion, Arbitrator Griffith analyzed the question of the burden of proof:

> In my opinion the majority also is in error to assume, and to apply, the burden of proof as falling on Ireland. In this regard, I maintain that the obvious application of the precautionary principle (not considered by the majority) must shift the burden to the United Kingdom.[40]
>
> I regard the precautionary principle so engaged by Article 2(2)(a) as requiring that any finding adverse to Ireland be made in terms inverse to those found by the majority, namely that such a result was and is only open to be made on a finding that in fact there was no such potentially adverse effect. Clearly this was not a matter of fact established on the

38 *Id.* at para. 343.

39 *Mox Plant* (provisional measures), para. 82. Similar wording was used in Land Reclamation (*Malaysia vs. Singapore*), para. 92.

40 *Mox Plant* (dissenting opinion of Judge Gavan Griffith), para. 72

material before the Tribunal. Nor as I understand its position, was that contended for by the United Kingdom.[41]

In the *Southern Bluefin Tuna* case, the ITLOS studied whether Japan could develop a "pilot program" of experimental fishing that produced catches clearly beyond its allocation of 6,065 tons, as specified by the 1993 Convention for the Conservation of Southern Bluefin Tuna.[42] A dispute ensued over the scientific data regarding the impact of these captures on the tuna population. The tribunal resolved the provisional measures by requesting that parties maintain their quotas and avoid additional catching, as well as calling for collaboration in order to resolve scientific differences. Here, there was no assessment of the scientific arguments and, hence, no use for the burden of proof. In his separate opinion, Judge Laing underlined that although the ITLOS had not explicitly mentioned the precautionary principle, "it becomes evident that the Tribunal has adopted the precautionary approach for the purpose of provisional measures in such a case as the present." This does not mean, however, according to the opinion, that the Tribunal had "per se, engaged in an explicit reversal of the burden of proof," since such matters are "best reserved for the stage of the merits."[43]

Similarly, Judge Wolfrum, in the *Mox Plant* case, accepted the possibility of a reversal of the burden because of the application of the precautionary principle,[44] but not at the stage of provisional measures proceedings, since this would have required the tribunal to assess matters related to their merits.[45] In other cases where provisional measures were demanded, such as *Pulp Mills*,[46]

41 *Id.* at para 75. Art. 2(2)(a) quoted concerned the Convention for the Protection of the Marine Environment of the North-East Atlantic, Paris, 22 September 1992, in force 25 March 1998, 32 ILM 1069: "The Contracting Parties shall apply: (a) the precautionary principle, by virtue of which preventive measures are to be taken when there are reasonable grounds for concern that substances or energy introduced, directly or indirectly, into the marine environment may bring about hazards to human health, harm living resources and marine ecosystems, damage amenities or interfere with other legitimate uses of the sea, even when there is no conclusive evidence of a causal relationship between the inputs and the effects."

42 Convention for the Conservation of Southern Bluefin Tuna, Canberra, 10 May 1993, in force 20 May 1994, 1819 UNTS 360.

43 *Southern Bluefin Tuna* case, provisional measures, separate opinion by Judge Laing at para 19–21.

44 "There is no general agreement as to the consequences which flow from the implementation of this principle other than the burden of proof concerning the possible impact of a given activity is reversed. A state interested in undertaking or continuing a particular activity has to prove that it would result in no harm rather than the other side having to prove that it will result in harm," *Mox Plant*, provisional measures order, separate opinion Judge Wolfrum, para 5.

45 *Id.* at para. 8.

46 "Whereas Argentina has not provided evidence at present that suggests that any pollution resulting from the commissioning of the mills would be of a character to cause irreparable damage to the River Uruguay." Case concerning *Pulp Mills* (provisional measures), para 75.

the precautionary principle had no impact, and the measures were rejected because of the applicant's lack of sufficient evidence following a classical application of the principle of *actori incumbit probatio*.

The case law shows that, despite the precautionary nature of provisional measures, a full reversal of the burden of proof is hard to obtain. As the United Kingdom remarked in the *Mox Plant* case, provisional measures are an exception to the general rules since they allow for a remedy to be granted in the absence of an applicant fully proving its case. This creates a presumption against granting such measures, and consequently, the standard of proof applying to a provisional measure request should be high.[47] It is clear that the mere invocation of the precautionary principle is not enough to produce a reversal of the burden of proof. Authors like Caroline Foster support the idea that applicants should be required to provide, at least, *prima facie* proof of the risk before the burden is reversed and handed to the defendant.[48] This is difficult in interim order proceedings since, as Judge Wolfrum said,[49] it requires an assessment of the merits in advance. Only in cases where the importance of the risk is not under discussion (nuclear pollution, for example) have separate opinions demonstrated an openness to a direct shift in the burden.

4 The Precautionary Principle and the Burden of Proof in Main Proceedings: The Reduction of the Standard of Proof and *Prima Facie* Case

Contrary to interim orders, substantive hearings permit a deeper assessment of evidence and allow applicants more opportunities to prove (*prima facie*) the risk, and thus reverse the burden onto the defendant. The question is, What standard of proof would be required for the claimant to prove such a risk? Unfortunately, even those cases where the burden of proof was alleged in interim orders (*Southern Bluefin Tuna* and *Mox Plant*) did not continue to substantive hearings.

As mentioned in Section 1, international courts are flexible in regard to the amount of proof necessary to support judgements.[50] The standard of proof is decided on a case-by-case basis, depending on the nature of the issues and other circumstances.[51] The more serious the demands are against the sued

47 *Mox Plant* Case, written response of the United Kingdom, Request for provisional measures, paras. 128–129.

48 Foster, *supra* note 8, at 275.

49 See footnotes 43 and 44.

50 Georg Schwarzenberger, International Law as Applied by International Courts and Tribunals 192 (Stevens and Sons 1986).

51 Chittharanjan Felix Amerasinghe, *Presumptions and Inferences in Evidence in International Litigation*, 3(3) Law and Practice of International Courts and Tribunals 395–410, 245 (2004).

state, the higher the standard of proof that will be imposed on the applicant.[52] The fact that decisions are made this way could produce, however, a certain lack of predictability for litigants, as Judge Higgins said.[53]

As it specifically concerns the standard of (scientific) evidence necessary to apply the precautionary principle,[54] the ICJ has said in *Whaling in the Antarctic* that the standard is an "objective one," and that the court would also assess the "reasonableness" of such standards to their stated objectives.[55] This wording helps, to be sure, but it does not clearly articulate the standard which should be applied in similar situations.[56]

The application of the standard in the *Pulp Mills* case is probably more useful for these purposes. Argentina argued that the construction of pulp mills over the Uruguay River could produce harm to the environment. Both parties submitted a good amount of scientific evidence to support their own claims.[57] The applicant (Argentina) argued that the precautionary principle should lead to a reversal or at least an equal sharing of the burden of proof.[58] However, the court considered that the evidence produced by Argentina was insufficient, unclear, and unsubstantial, particularly as it pertained to demonstrating the scientific uncertainty essential for the application of the precautionary principle and, in the end, for producing the reversal of the burden.[59] This was not a *prima facie* case.

Prima facie evidence of scientific uncertainty as a pre-requisite for both the application of the precautionary principle and as a trigger for the shift of the

52 See, for example, *Corfu Channel* case, ICJ Reports 1949, p. 17. Similarly, *Military and Paramilitary Activities* case, ICJ Reports, p. 168; and Application of the Convention on the Prevention and Punishment of the Crime of Genocide (*Bosnia and Herzegovina v. Serbia and Montenegro*) ICJ Rep. 2007, para 208–209 and (*Croatia v. Serbia*) ICJ Rep 2015, para. 177. For a recent comment on this jurisprudence, Rosalyn Higgins et al., Oppenheim's International Law: United Nations paras. 29.369–29.373 (Oxford University Press 2018).

53 "The principal judicial organ of the United Nations should likewise make clear what standard of proof it requires to establish what sorts of facts." *Oil Platforms* case, separate opinion of Judge Higgins, para. 33.

54 The precautionary principle was part of the core of the allegations and surrounds the case in its entirety. It was not mentioned, however, in the main decision. Only the separate opinion of Judge Trindade includes a deep analysis of it. See *Whaling in the Antarctic*, separate opinion of judge C. Trindade, paras. 60–71.

55 *Whaling in the Antarctic*, para 67. For a comment, see Makane Moïse Mbengue, *Scientific Fact-Finding at the International Court of Justice: An Appraisal in the Aftermath of the Whaling Case*, 29(2) Leiden Journal of International Law 529–550 (2016).

56 Conf. Guillaume Gros, *The ICJ's Handling of Science in the Whaling in the Antarctic Case: A Whale of a Case?*, 6 Journal of International Dispute Settlement 578, 592–593 (2015).

57 *Pulp Mills*, paras. 229–264.

58 This idea of equal distribution of the burden was accepted in the separate opinions. See *Pulp Mills*, separate opinion of Judge Vinuesa, paras. 41–43.

59 *Pulp Mills*, para. 164.

burden could be a solution to this issue. This approach is normal in the WTO's case law. For example, in *EC-Hormones*, the Appellate Body said:

> [A] prima facie case is one which, in the absence of effective refutation by the defending party, requires a panel, as a matter of law, to rule in favor of the complaining party presenting the prima facie case.[60]

Accepting the use of *prima facie* evidence, at least for proving scientific uncertainty and risk in cases where evidence is difficult to obtain, is a way to reduce the overall standard of proof.[61] It could be a good solution for permitting applicants that advocate the court to use the precautionary principle to fulfil the a*ctori incumbit probatio* principle without having to support the entire weight of producing evidence.

5 Conclusions

The precautionary principle has slowly been accepted as a general principle of international law, at least in cases related to the environment. However, this acceptance does not go beyond administrative risk management. Understanding it as a risk management choice, courts and tribunals accept that it could justify manoeuvring room for those policymakers that have chosen a higher level of protection[62] (i.e. as a defence strategy). Unfortunately, little or hardly anything has been said in favour of its use as an applicant's argument against those countries that do not aim to take such protective measures in cases of scientific uncertainty. It is important to note that in understanding the precautionary principle, not only as a risk management choice but also as an adjudication principle useful for better allocation of the burden of proof, it is ultimately still an unresolved issue. However, some dissident opinions are opening space for hope, and probably, in the near future, international law judgements will start to accept the principle.

However, the precautionary approach to the burden of proof could clash with the classical *actori incumbit probatio*. Two possible solutions have been developed to address this situation. The first one, already used in case law because of its compatibility with the classical vision, calls for collaboration between parties in the production of scientific proof. A lack of collaboration by

60 It is true that in this case the precautionary principle was used as a defence. However, general rules of *prima facie* evidence are still useful. See EC-Hormones, Appellate Body decision, para. 104. For a comment on this, see Monika Ambrus, *The Precautionary Principle and a Fair Allocation of the Burden of Proof in International Environmental Law*, 21(3) Review of European Community & International Environmental Law 259–270, 267 (2012).

61 Pauwelyn, *supra* note 15, at 257.

62 In environmental law, a level of protection higher than the standard is permitted and normally encouraged since it fosters a progressive improvement in the prevention of ecological damage.

one of the parties could lead to the imposition to him/her of the burden of proof without using, directly, the precautionary principle as an adjudication principle. A second solution, only accepted in separate opinions, would be to produce a shift in the burden of proof based on the precautionary principle. Interim orders, because of their nature, could be thought of as being the better context for such a reversal. However, in practice, requiring some proof (*prima facie* evidence), at least of the level of risk and scientific uncertainty, is difficult to obtain before a substantial analysis of the case occurs. Moreover, as we have demonstrated, even in main proceedings, it is very difficult to prove that a reversal is necessary based on the application of the precautionary principle. The fact that *prima facie* evidence is required as a pre-requisite is such a high standard to obtain that it is difficult to say that the precautionary principle is neutralizing *actori incumbit probatio*. What we can say, however, is that the precautionary principle is, in fact, reducing the standard of proof without changing general evidence rules, generating a rapid rebuttal towards the respondent.

To sum up, while we wait for the case law to evolve towards a full reversal of the burden of proof, as some dissenting opinions have proposed, we can say that in the current state of jurisprudence, according to classical rules, the standard of proof that the applicant should produce in order to obtain protection from the court will be lower when the precautionary principle is applied.

7 Conscientious Objection

Rule of Law, Sexual and Reproductive Rights, and Scientific Reasonable Doubts

*Antonio Quirós Fons**

1 Introduction

The legal recognition of the right to conscientious objection and its exercise was initially confined to the military service. But over the last several decades, many European countries have professionalized this duty to the point that it is no longer compulsory. At the same time, the exercise of conscientious objection has become increasingly relevant in this region, due to another change in the international and European rule of law. Specifically, certain practices have now legally become fundamentally part of sexual and reproductive rights. Thus, international and European human rights laws have made individual states responsible for ensuring access to these sexual and reproductive healthcare goods and services.

Certainly, different healthcare professionals (medical practitioners, nurses, midwives, pharmacists, etc.) are allowed by international, European, and a wide range of national legal frames to opt out of providing certain goods and services pertaining to sexual and reproductive health care. This rule of law makes conscientious objection possible because it is considered as part of the fundamental right to ideological and religious freedom. Nevertheless, that same rule of law is, at the same time, responsible for excluding, or significantly reducing, the possibility of exercising the right to conscientious objection.

This chapter is based on a review of the literature covering relevant international legislation and guidelines, European human rights law, and case law, as well as different legal models regulating the concept of conscientious objection within European countries.

The scope of this review is to analyze whether these models allow an effective and respectful exercise of the right to conscientious objection when compared against the provision of certain goods and services related to sexual and reproductive rights.

To this end, the possibility of accepting the existence of any scientific evidence, or at least reasonable doubts in sound science issues that could endorse

* Antonio Quirós Fons is Associate Professor at Universidad Europea de Valencia (Spain). Corresponding Author: antonio.quiros@universidadeuropea.es

DOI: 10.4324/9781003472421-7

the moral conflicts in healthcare providers, will be explored in detail. The issues that will be discussed within the scope of this chapter are the treatments related to the morally alleged right to life: abortion, emergency contraception with effects associated with abortion, and the techniques involving in vitro fertilization that imply wasted or stored embryos.

Finally, some suggestions for change will be provided as a result of the analysis. An innovative result will be the convenience of regulating the conscientious objection, but not in such a way that makes its exercise impossible or legally ill-founded. Thus, the acceptance of scientific reasonable doubts, in addition to the moral grounds of the sexual and reproductive rights, will be a key factor for the creation of a mandatory rule of law that both respects and protects the diversity of founded opinions and beliefs while, at the same time, granting safe access to goods and services related to sexual and reproductive rights.

2 International and European Legal Framework for Conscientious Objection and Sexual and Reproductive Rights

The conscientious objection is still explicitly regulated as a right against the military service in some national legal frameworks.[1] But nowadays, it is globally considered as a part of another fundamental right. The right to freedom of thought, conscience, and religion is one that is protected by international human rights law. Article 18 of the International Covenant on Civil and Political Rights (ICCPR) recognizes this right, which also stipulates that freedom to manifest one's religion or beliefs might be subject to limitations necessary to protect the fundamental human rights of others.[2]

On the other hand, the main grounds for sexual and reproductive rights are found in international norms, including the Convention on the Elimination of All Forms of Discrimination against Women (CEFDW), adopted by the United Nations (UN) General Assembly in 1979, which guarantees women and men equal rights "to decide freely and responsibly on the number and spacing of their children and to have access to the information, education and means to enable them to exercise these rights."[3] The CEFDW also specifies that:

> States Parties shall take all appropriate measures to eliminate discrimination against women in the field of health care in order to ensure, on a basis of equality of men and women, access to health care services, including those related to family planning.[4]

1 Vid. i.e., Spanish Constitution, Art 30.2.

2 United Nations, International Covenant on Civil and Political Rights, entry into force 23 March 1976, Art. 18.

3 CEFDW, Art. 16, 1e.

4 CEFDW, Art. 12.

The combination of those two sets of rights (access to healthcare services and conscientious objection) can be found in international recommendations, such as the World Health Organization's (WHO) technical and policy guidance for health systems, specifically regarding abortion.[5] A last recommendation in the WHO guidance clearly treats one right, the conscientious objection, as a direct limit to the other right, access to health services:

> Health services should be organized in such a way as to ensure that an effective exercise of the freedom of conscience of health professionals in the professional context does not prevent patients from obtaining access to services to which they are entitled under the applicable legislation.[6]

This recommendation is substantially the same one made by the UN Committee on Economic, Social, and Cultural Rights, specifically within Article 12 of the International Covenant on Economic, Social, and Cultural Rights,[7] whose first paragraph recognizes the right of everyone to have the enjoyment of the highest attainable standard of physical and mental health.

The European Court of Human Rights (ECHR) case law appears in that WHO guidance, cited as a basic ground for the international human rights rule of law.[8] This treatment illustrates the legitimacy of the human rights law within the European Council as a referent, also at a global range. Therefore, in Europe, the right to conscientious objection is also seen as one dimension of the right to freedom of thought, conscience, and religion, which is recognized under Article 9 of the European Convention on Human Rights (hereafter "the Convention"). This Article has two paragraphs:[9]

> 1 Everyone has the right to freedom of thought, conscience and religion; this right includes freedom to change his religion or belief and freedom, either alone or in community with others and in public or private, to manifest his religion or belief, in worship, teaching, practice and observance.

5 World Health Organization, Safe Abortion (2nd ed., World Health Organization 2012).

6 *Id.* at 96.

7 Committee on Economic, Social and Cultural Rights, General comment No. 22 (2016) on the right to sexual and reproductive health (Article 12 of the International Covenant on Economic, Social and Cultural Rights), paras14 and 43.

8 European Court of Human Rights (ECHR), *Kontaktinformation-Therapie and Hagen v. Austria*, 57 (1988). The judgment is cited for illustrating the WHO recommendation about not entitling providers and institutions to impede women's access to lawful health services in laws and regulations.

9 Also, within the European Union, Art. 10 of the EU Charter of Fundamental Rights shares the same title and the first paragraph with Art. 9 of the Convention, but the second one is explicit about the right: "The right to conscientious objection is recognized, in accordance with the national laws governing the exercise of this right." It is also used by the EU Court of Justice, but with a more limited impact due to a more conditioned competence.

2 Freedom to manifest one's religion or beliefs shall be subject only to such limitations as are prescribed by law and are necessary in a democratic society in the interests of public safety, for the protection of public order, health or morals, or for the protection of the rights and freedoms of others.

As it pertains to conscientious objection in health care, the guarantee of freedom in this Article offers a protection to the external manifestations "in practice," as it translates into words or acts.[10] The European Court of Human Rights (ECHR) case law would address the limits expressed in the second paragraph of Article 9 by clarifying the following, as it relates to sexual and reproductive rights (included by the Court under Article 8):[11] an individual's belief cannot lead to the restriction of the rights of another person;[12] the right to conscientious objection may be restricted on the grounds of public interest in ensuring equal treatment for all users;[13] states must fulfil a range of procedural requirements to ensure that the right to abortion (where it is legal) is upheld in a practical and effective manner.[14]

3 Legal Framework for Conscientious Objection Related to Sexual and Reproductive Rights in European Countries

The exercise of the fundamental human right to conscientious objection in health care is facilitated at a national level in European countries.[15] Most countries have explicitly recognized this right in their case law as a part of the constitutional freedom of conscience.[16] As alluded to earlier, in Spain, the Constitution only refers to conscientious objection in the context of compulsory

10 For the protection of these outer manifestations, vid. ECHR, *Otto-Preminger-Institut v. Austria*, 20 September 1994, 295-A, 47; ECHR, *Kokkinakis v. Greece*, 25 May 1993, 260-A, 31.

11 Art. 8 of the Convention recognizes the right to respect for one's "private and family life, his home and his correspondence," subject to certain restrictions that are "in accordance with law" and "necessary in a democratic society."

12 ECHR, *Pichon and Sajous v. France*, n. 49853/99, 4 October 2001, 2001-X.

13 ECHR, *Eweida and Others v. United Kingdom*, n. 48420/10, 59842/10, 51671/10 and 36516/10 (2013), 27 May 2013, 105. This case is not related to conscientious objection in health care, but the grounds are the same. A stewardess was not allowed to show a necklace with a little cross because it was not accepted in the company dress code. During the trial, that corporative instructions were modified to no longer require the removal of the religious symbol, due to its tiny dimensions.

14 ECHR, *Tysiąc v. Poland*, 20 March 2007.

15 The Council of Europe has constated that there is a comprehensive and clear legal and policy framework governing the practice of conscientious objection by healthcare providers ensuring that the interests and rights of individuals seeking legal medical services are respected, protected, and fulfilled. Council of Europe's Parliamentary Assembly, Resolution 1763 (2010). The right to conscientious objection in lawful medical care. <https://assembly.coe.int/nw/xml/XRef/Xref-XML2HTML-en.asp?fileid=17909&lang=en>.

16 Vid, i.e., Hungarian Constitutional Court, judgment 64/1991 (XII.17) AB határozat. It considered that only non-therapeutic abortions (i.e. not medically prescribed) could be excluded from the normal activities of a gynaecologist.

military service,[17] but it also may be derived from the also constitutional protection of freedom of religion,[18] in the same way as other countries.[19]

At under constitutional level, almost all European countries recognize the right to conscientious objection in relation to abortion[20] and also, in some cases, for assisted reproduction.[21] Italy is an example of a country with a high percentage of registered objectors.[22] When, and where, this exception becomes statistically majoritarian, then the non-objectors are presented as victims of the legal system.[23] In Belgium, after euthanasia was decriminalized, the same conscientious objection clause was legally regulated.[24]

Regardless, a lower normative rank allows and regulates a conscientious objection. Generally, each statute of a professional order frequently contains a professional deontological code and sectorial regulation approved by the competent government.[25]

4 Collective Dimension of the Freedom of Conscience for Religious-Oriented Institutions

In the case of conscientious objection as related to private institutions, the challenge is not located in the employer–worker relationship but in the relationship between the institution and the government: the provided service can be publicly funded, not only allowed, as a demanded social service. The dilemma comes, however, when a whole community is well inhabited by an ideologically oriented healthcare institution and the authorities (local, regional, or national) try to impose some public policies in contrast or opposition to the beliefs on which the given institution is rooted.

17 Spanish Constitution, Art. 30.2., not used in decades, after the end of mandatory service in this state.

18 Spanish Constitution, Art. 16.

19 The German Constitution guarantees the unconditional freedom of conscience. Grundgesetz, Art. 4.1.

20 Some examples of national legislation in European states recognizing the right to conscientious objection in relation to the provision of abortion can be found in the following mandatory rule of law. Austria: General Social Security Act (Allgemeines Sozialversicherungsgesetz, Art. 97.2. It states that no physician, nurse, or paramedic is obliged to perform or to assist in a voluntary abortion; Belgium: Law of 3 April 1990, decriminalizing certain aspects of the voluntary interruption of pregnancy (Moniteur belge, 5 April 1990). It provides explicitly that no medical doctor, or any nurse or aide to the doctor, will be obliged to take part in the abortion; France: Code of Public Health (Code de la santé publique), Art. L.2212–8. Medical physicians can invoke a "conscience clause" and thus refuse to perform an abortion; Italy: Law 194, 22 May 1978, Art. 9.

21 Vid. i.e. Italy: Law 40, 19 February 2004, Art. 16.

22 Information<www.theguardian.com/world/2016/mar/11/italian-gynaecologists-refuse-abortions-miscarriages>.

23 One Recent Interview with a Non-Objector Can Illustrate This Fact <www.buzzfeednews.com/article/nishitajha/italy-abortion-rights-silvana-agatone>.

24 Law of 28 May 2002, decriminalizing euthanasia (Moniteur belge, 22 June 2002).

25 In Spain, this competence for approval depends on every autonomous community.

There is no international or national rule of law that directly recognizes this collective dimension of the right. Only a non-binding international recommendation at the European level can be located. The Council of Europe Parliamentary Assembly, in its Resolution 1763 (2010) on the right to conscientious objection in lawful medical care, declared that:

> [N]o person, hospital or institution shall be coerced, held liable or discriminated against in any manner because of a refusal to perform, accommodate, assist or submit to an abortion, the performance of a human miscarriage, or euthanasia or any act which could cause the death of a human foetus or embryo, for any reason.[26]

The ECHR case law does not focus on the particular issue of collective conscientious objection related to medical care, but it recognizes the collective dimension of the freedom of religion in the means used to express those religious beliefs.[27]

As for court judgements on the issue, probably the globally most famous case is the United States (US) Supreme Court case law related to "Obamacare" requirements imposed upon confessional institutions.[28] There was a long list of almost 50 cases, including institutions such as a Baptist university or a hospice run by Catholic nuns. These nuns were the first who succeeded in obtaining an exception from payment of employee's insurance, as it pertained to covering contraceptives, on religious grounds. The Supreme Court subsequently imposed the requirement of ensuring that women covered by those institutions' health plans could obtain, without cost, the full range of approved contraceptives from the US government.[29]

5 Referral as a Key Legal Requirement: Whose Duty?

In the aforementioned WHO guidance, there is a statement that imposes a double burden on the objector:

> Health-care professionals who claim conscientious objection must refer the woman to another willing and trained provider in the same, or

26 <https://assembly.coe.int/nw/xml/XRef/Xref-XML2HTML-en.asp?fileid=17909&lang=en>.

27 The state, due to the duty of neutrality and impartiality, cannot determine the legitimacy of the means used to express religious beliefs. ECHR, *Manoussakis and Others v. Greece*, 47; *Bayatyan v. Armenia* [GC], 120.

28 US Supreme Court, Per Curiam Opinion, Zubik v. Burwell (16 May 2016) <www.supremecourt.gov/opinions/15pdf/14-1418_8758.pdf>.

29 *Id.* This case illustrates the collective dimension of the recognition of freedom of conscience based on religious grounds. But it also goes beyond the perspective of abortion as challenging the right to life. In this case, it is admitted that a given healthcare institution does not agree with other means different from natural ones to avoid pregnancies, that is, abstinence, which is, at the same time, scientifically the most effective method, with a 100% success rate in front of other contraceptive methods.

another easily accessible health-care facility, in accordance with national law. Where referral is not possible, the health-care professional who objects must provide abortion to save the woman's life or to prevent damage to her health.[30]

It is important to clarify a common misconception as it relates to medical care: nobody is entitled to object when a patient's life is at risk. Further, a medical practitioner does not even consider the option of objection. Rather, he or she must save a life, and in doing so, the other involved human life (potential or not) always has a lesser chance of surviving surgical intervention. In this case, abortion is not provided; it only "happens" as an eventual or necessary consequence of the surgery, depending on every diagnosis, treatment, and outcome.

The measures recommended by the competent specialized international organization differ from the specific ones suggested by probably the most aptly named UN treaty body for sex and reproductive rights issues. The UN Committee on the Elimination of Discrimination against Women recommended that, if health service providers refused to perform certain reproductive health services based on conscientious objection, measures should be introduced to ensure that women are referred to alternative health providers.[31] However, as a result of this recommendation, the objector is not forced to perform the referral. The concerned state, therefore, must ensure that an appeal or review process should already be established to handle any refused abortion.[32] Any implicated process should also comprehend the obligation to refer the woman seeking abortion to another qualified healthcare practitioner who will agree to perform that abortion.

In some states, certain legal frames have imposed that duty of referral on the healthcare practitioner who has exercised his or her right to conscientious objection.[33] But in other jurisdictions, such frameworks have either been[34] or considered unconstitutional,[35] because the state, not the objecting indi-

30 World Health Organization, *supra* note 5, at 96.

31 General Recommendation No. 24 (20th session, 1999), Art. 12: Women and health, UN doc. A/54/38/Rev.1.

32 Most countries in Europe include this legal possibility. In the case of Sweden and Norway, the process is automatic, so the woman does not need to appeal the refusal. WHO, Global Abortion Policies Database <https://abortion-policies.srhr.org/countries/>.

33 For instance, Croatia: Law on Doctors' Activities (Zakon o liječništvu, OG 121/03,117/08); Czech Republic: Health Services Act (Zákon o zdravotních službách, 372/2011 Sb., 205/2015 Sb.); France: Public Health Code, 2013 (Code de la santé publique); Ireland: Health (Regulation of Termination of Pregnancy) Act 2018. WHO, Global Abortion Policies Database <https://abortion-policies.srhr.org/countries/>.

34 For instance, Italy and Portugal.

35 In Poland, it is not a requirement for an objecting doctor to make a referral since 2015, when the Polish Constitutional Court held this requirement unconstitutional, by arguing that it should be the state's duty, not the doctor's, to provide information to the patient about the possibility to have the service carried out.

vidual, is responsible for assuring access to the service. Thus, that same public authority is the one who must guarantee the availability of another qualified healthcare practitioner, which is especially important in geographically remote areas.

Midwife assistants or pharmacist extenders are more limited. The most extended rule states that nurses, midwives, and nursing associates who have a conscientious objection must tell colleagues, their manager, and the person receiving care that they have a conscientious objection to a particular procedure.[36] They must also arrange for a suitably qualified colleague to take over responsibility for that person's care.[37] Three cases involving midwives have been empirically studied in different member states within the European Union. These examples of conscientious objection are based on religious grounds.[38] What these cases have in common, as noted in local or national news, is that, because the public employer interprets the objection as an omission of deontological duties (helping the patient), a dismissal from the job occurred. In another professional situation, a pharmacist could not object to selling a concrete product when the pharmacy is the only one in the immediate large area.[39] The criteria used to make these determinations should be the result of an agreement between local authorities and professional colleges.

6 ECHR Case Law Trend

When a conscientious objection is authorized, and exercised, the act of objection is carried out by a civil servant and thus directly attributable to the respondent state. Thus, the ECHR considers the issues in terms of the positive obligation on the state authorities to secure the rights under Article 8 of the Convention (sexual and reproductive rights) to those citizens within their jurisdiction.

On the other hand, when the healthcare providers are not authorized to exercise the conscientious objection within the scope of their work, then the

36 Vid., i.e., Professional Standards of Practice and Behaviour for Nurses, Midwives and Nursing Associates (2nd ed., The Nursing and Midwifery Regulator for England, Wales, Scotland and Northern Ireland 2018), statement n. 4.4.

37 *Id.*

38 V. Fleming, B. Ramsayer & T. Š. Zakšek, *Freedom of Conscience in Europe? An Analysis of Three Cases of Midwives with Conscientious Objection to Abortion*, 44 Journal of Medical Ethics 104 (2017).

39 Vid., i.e., case law settled by Spanish Constitutional Court. Judgement 145/2015, 25 June (BOE n. 182, 31 July 2015). It recognizes the injury of the right to conscientious objection to a pharmacist who had been sanctioned because he neither had in his own pharmacy nor wanted to dispense preservatives and drugs containing the active principle levonorgestrel (also known as day after pill). Paradoxically, his freedom of conscience was recognized only for the case of the pill, not for the preservatives, which are available almost at every corner in a given populated place, not exclusively in pharmacies.

complaint is related to administrative and court decisions. As these acts are carried out by public institutions, the state authorities also have the positive obligation of securing such rights under Article 9 of the Convention.

For both sets of rights, national interferences are admitted in Articles 8 and 9. The ECHR, interpreting this possibility, leaves to the states a certain margin of appreciation in deciding whether and to what extent an interference is necessary. Therefore, in its decisions, the court determines whether the measures taken at the national level are primarily justified and proportionate.[40]

However, examining the ECHR case law, as far as healthcare conscientious objectors are concerned, a clear trend emerges. This trend tends to consider all the objectors' demands under Article 9 as ill-founded, when any national legislation makes the exercise of the conscientious objection explicitly incompatible with a profession's ultimate role.[41] Such national measures fall under the state's margin of appreciation, which, according to the last court judgements, is always welcome, justified, and proportionate.[42] According to case law recently enforced, a woman objecting to abortions cannot become a midwife in Sweden because, in that country, the exercise of objection is legally identified as an incomplete performance of all the duties inherent to the post. The very same woman, however, was able to become a midwife in Norway, while still objecting to abortion when applying for a position. There, a midwife's objection to abortion is allowed, because according to the international definition of the role of the midwife, assisting in abortion cases is not an essential duty (*conditio sine qua non*) inherent to that position.[43] Swedish rule of law ignores this international definition, and the ECHR has tolerated this national limitation.

40 ECHR, *Leyla Şahin v. Turkey* [GC], n. 44774/98, 110, 2005-XI, and *Eweida and others v. United Kingdom*, n. 48420/10 (2013), 27 May 2013, 84.

41 ECHR, *Grimmark v. Sweden*, 12 February 2020; *Steen v. Sweden*, 12 February 2020.

42 *Id.* Both cases are very similar, as it relates to midwives. In *Grimmark*, n. 26 and in *Steen*, n. 21, the Court observes "that Sweden provides nationwide abortion services and therefore has a positive obligation to organise its health system in a way as to ensure that the effective exercise of freedom of conscience of health professionals in the professional context does not prevent the provision of such services. The requirement that all midwives should be able to perform all duties inherent to the vacant posts was not disproportionate or unjustified. Employers have, under Swedish law, great flexibility in deciding how work is to be organised and the right to request that employees perform all duties inherent to the post. When concluding an employment contract, employees inherently accept these duties. In the present case, the applicant had voluntarily chosen to become a midwife and apply for vacant posts while knowing that this would mean assisting also in abortion cases."

43 "The midwife is recognised as a responsible and accountable professional who works in partnership with women to give the necessary support, care and advice during pregnancy, labour and the postpartum period, to conduct births on the midwife's own responsibility and to provide care for the newborn and the infant." International Confederation of Midwives (ICM), 2017 <https://web.archive.org/web/20170922213449/http://internationalmidwives.org/who-we-are/policy-and-practice/icm-international-definition-of-the-midwife/>.

That unbalanced position, a prejudice for any conscientious objector, should not be considered as a solution for those national authorities that are, or should be, condemned under Article 8 of the Convention, due to a failure in securing sexual and reproductive rights. In those cases, the objector has properly exercised his or her lawfully recognized right, but the applicant has not been properly provided their related goods and services by the health authority.[44] Here, the national interference is not a lawful recognition of the right to conscientious objection and its exercise but an institutional failure in timely and properly providing goods and services to applicants.

As a first set of concluding proposals, it has been constated that the right to conscientious objection is derived from the guarantee of freedom of religion stipulated in international and European human rights instruments, in national constitutions, or in specific legislation, where it is also explicitly recognized in cases of abortion and other services. This right should be regulated in order to ensure that, in circumstances where abortion and other services related to sexual and reproductive rights are legal, no woman shall be deprived from having effective access to those medical services.

However, the legal measures that are developed for that purpose at a national level should not impede the effective exercise of a profession or the access to a job that does not consist primarily of providing abortions or assisting in them. Moreover, imposing the burden of referral on the objector's shoulders may appear more practical and effective than depending on the employer's management, but it requires the informative cooperation in a procedure that the objector still considers as a legalized crime.

Another argument that advocates for eliminating conscientious objection is the increased amount of work that is subsequently put upon non-objecting colleagues. The same great flexibility, provided to the employer by the ECHR, in deciding how work is to be organized and the right to request that employees perform all duties inherent to the position may include also the possibility of alternative assignments to be fulfilled by the objector. These assigned alternative services would legitimately avoid any imbalance in the health provider objector's workplace.

7 Ethically Controversial Issues and Scientific Reasonable Doubts as a Ground for Conscientious Objection

Eugenics and quality of life. Due to the extremely high percentage of unborn children diagnosed with Down syndrome worldwide, it is necessary to talk about this kind of abortion and this concrete population as an object of discrimination, together with other persons with disabilities, who are automatically eligible either for abortion (before birth) or for euthanasia (once born, some years after). Nevertheless, the Down paradigm is very useful and

44 ECHR, *Tysiąc v. Poland*, 20 March 2007.

illustrative because Down syndrome is very easy to detect without any intrusive prenatal testing. The ethical dilemma, ignored in most legal frames, is related to a direct discrimination on genetic grounds. The main difference between this eugenic abortion and other categories is that, in general terms, the discussion about termination of pregnancy is focused on women's reproductive rights, considering the unwanted unborn child an expendable limit to the exercise of the right, whereas children with Down syndrome are being aborted on grounds of parental valuation of the quality of life of the child, once born, grown, and adult.[45]

That theoretical label does not change the facts, but it can illustrate the necessity of informing the parents properly. This is, again, a duty for the healthcare professionals involved in the matter. When trying to inform parents about the evidence-based experience of love and joy in persons with Down syndrome and their families,[46] some professionals could be discouraged by the threats of being sued, removed, or discredited. The first step in this process consists of providing complete medical counselling, based on sound science. The second step, the decision of whether to abort or not, must be taken by the parents following the principle of autonomy. The third step, the invocation of the conscientious objection, only occurs if the parents ask for an abortion.

Wasted or stored embryos and women's health. Some sectorial sound science still declares fecundation as the beginning of human life.[47] But the scientific beginning of human life should not be confused with the beginning of human personhood within a given rule of law, that is, the legal recognition of a person. This means that, depending on each rule of law, different early stages of human life are taken into consideration for a concrete protection.

Under a global understanding, a human being is legally recognized as a person when he or she is born. Nevertheless, regarding unborn human beings, in the field of extrauterine or *in vitro* fecundation (IVF), some legal definitions have reached the point of limiting the production and storage of embryos while protecting the already-implanted ones.[48] Thus, it is possible to

45 C. M. Reilly, *Medical Professionals as Agents of Eugenics*, 18 The National Catholic Bioethics Quarterly 237 (2018).

46 Between a lot of studies about particular fields of quality of life, it is interesting to note the evidence that youth with Down syndrome have not a lower quality of life compared with youth without Down syndrome, with the exception of emotional functioning, nowadays commonly associated, almost identified, with the sense of happiness. Cfr. M. Xanthopoulos et al., *Caregiver-Reported Quality of Life in Youth with Down Syndrome*, 189 The Journal of Pediatrics (2017).

47 Mainly, Biology and Genetics. At fertilization, all the genetic characteristics are already determined, and the resulting zygote is genetically distinct from either of its parents, what is considered a new individual of the species.

48 Judgements 53/1985, 212/1996, 116/1999, Spanish Constitutional Court. Embryos already well settled in the endometrium (implanted in the internal surface of the uterus) enjoy the status of nasciturus human beings, but pre-implanted embryos are not taken into legal consideration.

use IVF without strict controls and to develop technological advances in genetic research.[49] In fact, genetic modification is less contested when performed on human embryos than when done on vegetables and animals.[50] This is due to the visibility of the harm caused to nature and, consequently, the serious and immediate threat to health and the environment. Therefore, in the cases of genetically modified food or germ-line genetic intervention,[51] the use of the precautionary principle is already widely accepted for the best interest of future generations.

Human embryos involved in assisted procreation[52] have to meet more requirements in order to be covered by the precautionary principle, because a major degree of proof is still required, before acting, to prevent damage to the future generation, which is partially embodied by the produced and/or discarded embryos. They are individuals of these future generations, but any proof of irreversible damage is sombre. Subsidiarily, if embryo is not accountable, then it is only possible to refer some risks related to women's health. There are also some reasonable doubts in the context of reproductive health rights that also constitute a threat to health. Specifically, the question arises of what happens and what will happen to women applying for concrete treatments or taking concrete drugs without having been properly informed? Some scientific results are summarized next.

Some effects of the assisted reproductive technologies (ART) are adverse. Sound science demonstrates that in the race of obtaining genetically perfect or at least genetically reliable children, couples applying for ART should be informed beforehand about adverse obstetric and perinatal outcomes, an increased risk of birth defects, cancers, growth and development disorders, and individual predisposition to an increased risk of chronic ageing-related diseases, such as

49 As a matter of fact, mitochondrial replacement techniques (also called mitochondrial donation) are studied without any legal difference in the use of an egg or an already fertilized egg, that is, zygote (an egg, or ovum, being a female reproductive cell). Mitochondrial replacement techniques (MRT) entail modification of human oocytes and zygotes (earliest stage of an embryo) to prevent the transmission of mitochondrial DNA diseases from mother to child. UK Regulation uses a unified term ("permitted eggs and embryos") to include those "where unhealthy mitochondrial DNA is replaced by healthy mitochondrial DNA from a donor." *The Human Fertilisation and Embriology Regulations*, 572 (2015) <www.legislation.gov.uk/ukdsi/2015/9780111125816/contents>.

50 J. Corti, *What's Beyond Energy? How to Integrate Environmental and Health Challenges in Climate Change Agreements: The Case of Livestock Production and the Feedstuffs Trade*, 10 MPIL Research Paper Series (2019).

51 vid. several contributions in this same publication.

52 Regarding this particular right, the European Court of Human Rights has ruled that the right to family life proclaimed in Article 8 of the Convention does not guarantee either the right to found a family or the right to adopt (*Paradiso and Campanelli v. Italy* [GC], 2018, 141), but the right of a couple to conceive a child and to make use of medically assisted procreation for that purpose is protected by Article 8, as such a choice is a form of expression of private and family life (*S. H. and Others v. Austria* [GC], 2018, 82; *Knecht v. Romania*, 2018, 54).

obesity, type 2 diabetes, and cardiovascular disease.[53] This is, in short, the same fear that consumers face at the moment of purchasing genetically modified organisms (GMO) or fast food, because they have already accepted the evidences years ago reported by the Food and Agriculture Association of the United Nations (FAO), which are exactly the same effects for those persons seeking ART.[54] In this point, an objector to embryo experimentation and preimplantation diagnoses has more grounds than the sole beliefs based on statements about natural human reproduction and the worth of every embryo's life.

Contraception: reasonable doubts on abortive effects and women's health. Some contraception methods may also have abortive effects. If fertilization does occur, certain pills may prevent a fertilized egg from attaching to the womb (implantation).[55] Considering pregnancy only from the moment of implantation directly contests the scientific evidence that some contraception methods can have such effects before that time. If a physician or a pharmacist tries to exercise his or her right to conscientious objection, it is because he or she is convinced about the scientific possibility of that anti-implantation effect. Such use of emergency contraception may prevent a potential human life from properly developing. For that conscientious objector, the fertilized egg is not any more a plain egg, that is, a mere reproductive cell or gamete. If this side effect is legally reduced to emergency contraception, then the objector claiming to be spared of administrating certain pills or installing certain devices must also prove the scientific facts and results supporting that claim in court. If the official label on a concrete product only mentions that it is a contraceptive, then the pharmacist couldn't object at all to issuing the pill, an issue which has support in the consolidated case law[56] in the wider range of countries belonging to the Rome Convention.[57]

53 M. Chen & L. K. Heilbronn, *The Health Outcomes of Human Offspring Conceived by Assisted Reproductive Technologies (ART)*, 8 Journal of Developmental Origins of Health and Disease 388 (2017).

54 In its 2017 Report, the Food and Agriculture Organization of the United Nations (FAO) stated that the availability, affordability, and marketing of highly processed foods that are high in sugar and fats, often combined with more sedentary lifestyles, constitute obesogenic environments where many children are growing up. Obesity is a major risk factor for non-communicable diseases (the leading causes of death and illness worldwide), including cardiovascular disease, diabetes, and some cancers. Cfr. *The State of Food Security and Nutrition in the World 2017. Building Resilience for Peace and Food Security*, 18 (FAO 2017).

55 For instance, Plan B. US FDA's Decision Regarding Plan B: Questions and Answers <www.fda.gov/drugs/postmarket-drug-safety-information-patients-and-providers/fdas-decision-regarding-plan-b-questions-and-answers>.

56 ECHR, *Pichon and Sajous v. France*, n. 49853/99, 4 October 2001, 2001-X.

57 Short name for the Convention for the Protection of Human Rights and Fundamental Freedoms, also known as the European Convention on Human Rights (1950). Its parties are at the same time the 47 Council of Europe member states. The ECHR rules on applications alleging violations of the rights set out in the Rome Convention. Basic information available at <www.echr.coe.int/Documents/Court_in_brief_ENG.pdf>.

The aforementioned statement (some contraception methods may have abortive effects) is what makes conscientious objection possible and was the argument used by the Spanish Constitutional Court when ruling in favour of a pharmacist who did not want to sell emergency contraceptive pills.[58] As the actual product has, apart from contraceptive effects, anti-implantation effects, it is possible that an embryo won't be able to implant in an altered endometrium (uterus internal surface). It means that products such as levonorgestrel or ulipristal acetate (commonly known as ellaOne) may also prevent unwanted pregnancies also by an abortive, anti-implantation mechanism.[59] In the reports of the authorities responsible for allowing these products to market, it is interesting that nothing regarding this anti-implantation mechanism is listed.[60] Furthermore, the information, certified by labs, regarding the certainly unwanted side effects caused by hormonal contraceptives are silenced by some health authorities. The most dangerous of these effects is the risk of breast cancer,[61] not only related to miscarriage and abortion, but also recently linked to this kind of contraceptives.

Contraception implant. It is also scientifically recognized that the IUD (intrauterine device) has the same anti-implant effects as some other forms of contraception. Nevertheless, it was necessary for a doctor in Norway to claim her right to conscientious objection first at work, then in the courts.[62] This doctor did not want to implant the device, based on the grounds about the abortive effects of the IUD. Thus, the doctor was fired from her position by the municipality in 2015 (even though the employer knew of her objections when they hired her in 2011). In bringing suit, a lower court supported her claims, but healthcare authorities appealed to the Supreme Court of Norway. In 2018, Norwegian Supreme Court decided in her favour and cited in its judgement[63] a ruling by the European Court of Human Rights (ECHR) that refers specifically to Article 9 of the Convention, on freedom of thought, conscience, and religion, as one of the foundations of a "democratic society" within the meaning of the Rome Convention. The ECHR states in the cited case (Eweida) that:

> [I]n its religious dimension it is one of the most vital elements that go to make up the identity of believers and their conception of life, but it is

58 Judgement 145/2015 Spanish Constitutional Court (2015) BOE n. 182, cit.

59 J. Aznar, *Ulipristal Acetate. A New Emergency Contraceptive. Ethical Aspects of Its Use*, 59 Medicina e Morale (2010).

60 European Agency Report <www.ema.europa.eu/en/documents/product-information/ellaone-epar-product-information_en.pdf>.

61 C. L. Westhoff & M. C. Pike, *Hormonal Contraception and Breast Cancer*, 98 Contraception 171 (2018).

62 Sak 2018/199 Norges Hoyesterett (Norway's Supreme Court) <www.sauherad.kommune.no/_f/p2/i4aa2a8dc-87bf-4928-a447-9a05ce981131/dom-hr357603.pdf>.

63 *Ibid.*

also a precious asset for atheists, agnostics, sceptics and the unconcerned. The pluralism indissociable from a democratic society, which has been dearly won over the centuries, depends on it.[64]

Digital contraception. Natural Cycles describes itself as the first smartphone application ("app") to be certified as a contraceptive by European Union health authorities and by the Food and Drug Administration (FDA) in the United States.[65] This constitutes already an alternative to the hormonal contraception, based not on freedom of conscience grounds but on the need for unmet planning methods due to the side effects caused by the pill, such as migraine or depression. Furthermore, recent studies about such apps that use dates of menstruation and basal body temperature or simply estimate the menstrual cycle fertile window confirm very similar results. One shows that fertility awareness–based methods of contraception (contraceptive mobile application) increase short-term pregnancy rates relative to hormonal contraception but have no effect on long-term pregnancy rates.[66] The other has revealed that a given app's effectiveness is within the range of other user-initiated contraceptive methods.[67] This turn to natural methods such as fertility apps, based on health reasons, is now favoured by sound science. It gives also a chance to those aforementioned objectors. However, there are two types of professionals who could appeal to these alternatives: those who are reluctant to issue the hormonal methods due to the aggressive side effects, and those who exalt intercourse to the level of a sacred and consequently religious issue. The first ones will have to defend themselves from being labelled as just another equivalent of an anti-vaccinationists.[68] The other ones must be prepared to be derided for believing that human beings behave as the monogamous lovebirds Agapornis,[69] living in an abiding couple.

64 ECHR, *Eweida and Others v. United Kingdom*, n. 48420/10, 59842/10, 51671/10 and 36516/10 (2013), 27 May 2013, 79.

65 *Natural Cycles*, as it is declared in its webpage (<www.naturalcycles.com/>), is the first and still only one to be cleared by both institutions for the use of birth control. They also back a 93% effectiveness with typical use and 98% with perfect use with research. E. Berglund Scherwitzl et al., *Perfect-Use and Typical-Use Pearl Index of a Contraceptive Mobile App*, 96 Contraception (2017).

66 E. Berglund Scherwitzl et al., *Short- and Long-Term Effect of Contraceptive Methods on Fecundity*, 24 The European Journal of Contraception & Reproductive Health Care (2019).

67 V. Jennings et al., *Perfect- And Typical-Use Effectiveness of the Dot Fertility App Over 13 Cycles: Results from a Prospective Contraceptive Effectiveness Trial*, 24 The European Journal of Contraception & Reproductive Health Care (2019).

68 In fact, the largest survey about attitudes to immunization around the world (child vaccination scepticism) reveals that the number of people who say they have little confidence or trust in vaccination has increased. Wellcome Global Monitor 2018, June 2019 <https://wellcome.ac.uk/reports/wellcome-global-monitor/2018>.

69 Lovebirds, or Agapornis, are small parrots. The name combines the Ancient Greek αγάπη agape, meaning "love," and όρνις ornis, meaning "bird." It describes their strong, monogamous pair

8 Conclusion and Proposals

Conscientious objection is generally admitted as essential part of the freedom of conscience. Its exercise is reduced to highly controversial ethical issues, such as abortion, where the objector considers that it goes against the human right to life in one of its stages. He or she respects the right to life as a fundamental human right with its universal, inalienable, inviolable, and indivisible traits. But he or she also takes note of certain scientific foundations behind the consideration of what human life is, challenged by the rule of law in many international organizations and countries, but still recognized in some national jurisprudence, as it is the Spanish Constitutional Court case law.[70]

The objections should refer to specific services in which the objectors are directly involved, so they should have also previously informed their employers about their convictions. However, personal opinions may change. Therefore, a reversion or a just adopted objection should also be allowed. Such a delicate personal position must be seen as legitimate, both by a coherent professional life (wherein he or she denies the service also in private practice) and by consistent principles upheld by well-known institutions. The mainly invoked principle is the firm conviction of not being able to take part in any directly pursued termination of human life at any stage of its development by artificial means. When another human life is at risk, that termination is one possible effect of the treatment, but it is not directly pursued.

Protecting the benefit of the doubt on a given topic, based precisely on sound scientific evidence, will relativize the force of the law and permit a personal and autonomous opt-out decision. For this purpose, it shouldn't be necessary to make the objector walk all the way through the calvary of three- or four-staged trials in order to have a final recognition of the personal freedom of conscience. Furthermore, authorities shouldn't doubt on the goodwill of objectors, who are also firmly convinced of contributing to the health of others by refraining from doing things that harm people, such as contaminating the environment.

The public institutions must guarantee the provision of health services at any time. It should not mean that a compulsory referral to another concrete practitioner must necessarily be done by the objector. It is the employer who is entitled to provide such a qualified service. In this sense, good examples of resource optimization are the legal procedures establishing an automatic revision process. Specifically, the objector notifies his or her objection to the patient and informs it to their employer, and the patient does not need to activate any appeal process because the employer immediately looks for another qualified professional who is willing to provide the service.

---

bonding. J. A. Jobling, The Helm Dictionary of Scientific Bird Names 36 (Christopher Helm 2010).

70 Judgement 145/2015 Spanish Constitutional Court (2015) BOE n. 182, cit.

It should also be reasonable to establish an alternative service or task to be done by the objector. This assigned alternative service would have the legitimate scope of avoiding any imbalance in the health provider objector's workplace.

Finally, the beauty of the natural ways may be also considered. A more environmentally concerned approach to human life could be helpful in order to interpret the international law of human rights in a universal way, not only following globalized trends. The international standards developed for environmental protection constitute an enriched soil on which it is now possible to cultivate human life protection or, at least, to allow a minimum of individual freedom to cultivate it as an exception to the general rule. Thus, a more ecological mind towards human nature and body would help to accept, in some countries with one-way-of-thinking rule of law, the possibility of biodiversity within the public health and civil law policies, taking into consideration that maybe the conscientious objectors belong to a species in danger that all of us, authorities also, must protect.

8 Assessing the Soundness of Science to Determine Reactive and Proactive Regulatory Change

Human Fertilisation and Embryology Authority, Mitochondrial Donation, Treatment Add-Ons, and Future Challenges for Regulation

*Gemma Hobcraft**

1 Introduction[1]

This chapter will consider how the regulator of assisted reproduction in the United Kingdom, the Human Fertilisation and Embryology Authority (HFEA), has attempted to ensure that regulation enacted autonomously by the HFEA or recommended to be enacted through legislative change are based on sound science, as well as ethically and legally sound propositions. It will consider an example of proactive regulation in relation to treatment add-ons and an example of reactive regulation in relation to mitochondrial donation. It concludes by considering an emerging issue for assisted reproduction – particularly in relation to direct-to-consumer genetic testing – and what the challenges are for regulation in this cross-border issue, where donor-conceived people can intentionally or inadvertently find out about genetic relatives through the linkages that can be made on the DNA databases to which people have provided DNA samples.

* Please note that this chapter was written in 2019 with minor amends made in 2021. Gemma Hobcraft was previously an Authority member of the Human Fertilisation and Embryology Authority (HFEA). The views expressed in this article are hers and not (nor intended to be) those of the HFEA/Department of Health.

1 Mitochondria create the energy in cells needed to power our bodies, and when they are faulty, it can result in severe difficulties. In mitochondrial donation, eggs or embryos are created using the intended parent(s)' genetic material and healthy donated mitochondria. Two techniques have been approved for mitochondrial donation in the UK – maternal spindle transfer (MST) and pronuclear transfer (PNT). In MST, the intended mother's nuclear genetic material is taken from their egg and put into donated eggs (which have already had their nuclear genetic material removed). For PNT, egg and sperm of intended parent(s) are fertilised to create an embryo, and then the nuclear genetic material within each embryo is transferred into embryos created using donated eggs and sperm.

DOI: 10.4324/9781003472421-8

International consensus and standard-setting documents can take considerable time and effort to create, particularly when they relate to matters concerning reproduction and the human genome. The United Nations Educational, Scientific, and Cultural Organization (UNESCO) Universal Declaration on the Human Genome and Human Rights was adopted in November 1997, but work on it started in 1993. Such declarations, given the effort and compromise often required to reach consensus agreement on wording, are not easy to amend, nor is it straightforward to ensure that they are interpreted as a living instrument (in contrast to the living instrument approach to the interpretation of the European Convention on Human Rights and Fundamental Freedoms). International documents, whilst of considerable significance and import, are often limited to standard-setting or drawing bright lines on key issues. This can often mean that despite well-intentioned international agreements, national regulation often is expected to step up to fill the space in regulation and be the bedrock of either permissiveness, permission, or protection in areas where scientific development outpaces legislative or regulatory change.

The HFEA was established as a result of the Human Fertilisation and Embryology Act 1990[2] following the first "test tube" baby being born in London in July 1978, which led to the need for regulation and a detailed report which led to the regulatory framework put in place through the HFEA 1990. In many ways, this was trailblazing in terms of independent regulation of assisted reproductive issues and provided the impetus for other countries to establish their own rules/authorities.

In the European context, the European Cell and Tissue Directive[3] requires member states to have a "competent authority" for the purposes of cells and tissues (which includes gametes [eggs and sperm] and embryos).[4] The HFEA (until Brexit) was the national competent authority for the purposes of gametes, and the Human Tissue Authority was (until Brexit) the national competent authority in relation to other tissues.

Two separate topics relating to the HFEA are considered: firstly, the HFEA's horizon scanning function and its role in relation to advice on treatment add-ons, and secondly, developments in mitochondrial donation. These two topics arguably contrast areas where the HFEA can act autonomously to introduce and impact regulatory change and those where legislative changes via parliament are required, which can result in slower progress (although perhaps less slow when compared to international progress in legislating on mitochondrial donation).

2 Human Fertilisation and Embryology Authority, *The Human Fertilisation and Embryology Act 1990* (1990).

3 Council Directive (EC) Directive 23/2004 on setting standards of quality and safety for the donation, procurement, testing, processing, preservation, storage, and distribution of human tissues and cells (EC Tissue Directive) (2004).

4 A list of the national competent authorities can be found here: <https://ec.europa.eu/health/sites/health/files/blood_tissues_organs/docs/competentauthorities_tissues_cells_en.pdf>.

The horizon scanning function of the HFEA monitors emerging techniques in the field of assisted reproduction and scrutinizes the studies and science behind them. To assist with the horizon scanning function, the Scientific and Clinical Advances Advisory Committee (of the HFEA) at the time of writing has a published approach to the examination of emerging science to consider what, if any, sound science-based changes should be recommended to the HFEA on issues that they do or do not already regulate.

The mitochondrial donation topic considers the process of assessing science in this field that required legislative change to enact. The process demonstrated the importance of demystifying science and enabling it to be communicated through public consultation to try to ensure that sound science could be understood and therefore could inform understanding and recommendations for legislative-based changes.

2 The Human Fertilisation and Embryology Authority (HFEA)

The HFEA is the national regulator in the United Kingdom for assisted reproduction. Assisted reproduction relies on scientific developments, and decisions must be made about the ways in which these can or should be used in human reproduction research or treatment. There are often legal and ethical considerations at play when such decisions are being made. The Nuffield Council on Bioethics, in their consideration of emerging biotechnologies, highlighted that tension can exist for regulators in this field: "On the one hand, regulation is expected to manage and mitigate the risks associated with emerging biotechnologies; on the other, it is expected to do this while enabling, or even facilitating, the delivery of substantial, possibly transformative benefits."[5] It is not always an easy path for a national regulator to walk particularly when issues emerge from activities that are not within the regulatory remit of an organization, such as with the HFEA and the challenges of direct-to-consumer DNA testing.

The UK has a prominent position in relation to the regulation of assisted reproduction and human embryo research, in large part because the first baby born via *in vitro fertilization* (IVF) – in 1978 – was born in London. This precipitated a Voluntary Licensing Authority and Interim Licensing Authority and led to the 1982 Committee of Inquiry into Human Fertilisation and Embryology. In 1990, the Human Fertilisation and Embryology Act came into force, establishing the independent statutory regulator of the Human Fertilisation and Embryology Authority.[6] The approach taken to regulation was one of statutory prohibition of certain activities (e.g. use only of legally permitted

5 Nuffield Council on Bioethics, *What Is an "Emerging Biotechnology"?* 136 (2019) <http://nuffieldbioethics.org/report/chapter-downloads/chapter-downloads>.

6 Human Fertilisation and Embryology Authority, *Celebrating 40 Years of IVF* (2018) <www.hfea.gov.uk/celebrating-40-years-of-ivf/>.

gametes or embryos) with permission for other activities regulated through a licensing system. The regulatory oversight put in place a range of compliance measures, including a code of practice, to set out best practice and provide more information to clinics on how to comply with key regulatory requirements and licensing conditions with inspections to check compliance with the regulatory requirements. The Human Fertilisation and Embryology Authority is independent as an "arm's length body" of the Department of Health "working independently from Government providing free, clear and impartial information about fertility treatment, clinics and egg, sperm and embryo donation."[7] It is funded by licence fees, IVF treatment fees, and a grant from the UK central government.

3 Horizon Scanning

The Scientific and Clinical Advances Advisory Committee (SCAAC) is a subcommittee of the Authority. SCAAC meets three times a year to consider advances in science and clinical practice which are relevant to the Authority's work. SCAAC members are appointed from the pool of members of the Authority (including a proportion of lay members) and some non-Authority co-opted members to ensure a range of knowledge and expertise. SCAAC is tasked with an annual horizon scanning function which aims to "identify issues that could have an impact on the field of assisted reproduction or embryo research" in order that "the Authority can be aware of potential licence applications and prepare, if necessary, a policy of position or relevant patient information."[8] The "issues are identified from journal articles, conferences and contact with experts such as members of the Authority's Horizon Scanning Panel."[9] This information is analyzed by SCAAC and "feeds into the business planning of the Executive, the Scientific and Clinical Advances Advisory Committee (SCAAC) and the Authority's consideration of ethical issues and standards"[10]

A method for classifying and prioritizing issues has been established.[11] New issues are classified with the following criteria: within HFEA's remit, high patient demand/clinical use if introduced, technically feasible, ethical issues raised, or public interest. New issues are classified as either high priority (if at least three criteria are met), medium priority (if at least two criteria

7 Human Fertilisation and Embryology Authority, *Science and Clinical Advances Advisory Committee* (2019) <www.hfea.gov.uk/about-us/our-authority-committees-and-panels/scientific-and-clinical-advances-advisory-committee-scaac/>.

8 Human Fertilisation and Embryology Authority, *Prioritisation of Issues Identified Through the Horizon Scanning Process* (2018) <www.hfea.gov.uk/media/2598/scaac-prioritisation-of-issues-identified-february-2018.pdf>.

9 *Ibid.*

10 *Ibid.*

11 *Ibid.*

are met), and low priority (where unlikely to impact on research or treatment in the near future, but published studies on the issue will continue to be collected to monitor the issue).[12] By way of example, as a result of being identified as high-priority topics at the time of writing,[13] SCAAC received briefings on the following:[14]

> [Mitochondrial donation; synthetic human entities with embryo-like features, or] SHEEFS; impact of stress on fertility outcomes; impact of microbiome on fertility and fertility treatment outcomes; genome editing; embryo culture media; health outcomes in children conceived by Assisted Reproductive Technology (ART); alternative methods to derive embryonic and embryonic-like stem cells; new technologies in embryo testing (including embryo biopsy and non-invasive methods for Pre-Implantation Genetic Diagnosis (PGD)); and treatment add ons.[15]

4 Treatment Add-Ons

The focus of this section is on the approach taken by SCAAC to treatment add-ons. Add-ons are additional treatments/tests that can be provided to those undergoing clinical fertility treatment. This is not only an issue in the UK but also a global issue for IVF patients, who can be routinely offered and charged for a selection of adjunct treatments and tests or add-ons (as recognized by Harper et al.).[16] Patients may understand that the treatment add-on may improve chances of a live birth, but the clinical evidence may not always be sufficiently robust or present to support such an understanding. Add-ons can include embryo glue, pre-implantation genetic screening, assisted hatching, etc., often at an additional cost to the patient(s). As Nardo has noted, there are concerns in relation to long-term safety testing and the need for follow-up of those who use these add-ons to monitor resulting live births and the well-being of any children born.[17]

SCAAC's focus on add-ons was to reflect on sound science (particularly randomized control trials [RCT]) to help inform patient and to ensure that new technology actually provides an opportunity for clinical benefit to patients.[18]

12 *Ibid.*

13 *Ibid.*

14 Please consult the HFEA website for more recent issues that SCAAC has been considering since this article was written.

15 *Ibid.*

16 Joyce Harper et al., *Adjuncts in the IVF Laboratory: Where Is the Evidence for 'Add-on' Interventions?* 32(3) Human Reproduction 485 (2017).

17 Luciano Giovanni Nardo et al., *British Fertility Society Policy and Practice Committee: Adjuvants in IVF: Evidence for Good Clinical Practice*, 18(1) Human Fertility 2 (2015).

18 Human Fertilisation and Embryology Authority, *Treatment Add Ons* (2018) <www.hfea.gov.uk/treatments/explore-all-treatments/treatment-add-ons/>.

In September 2017, a working group was established to develop a "consensus statement on responsible use of treatment add ons."[19] It found that the nine most common add-ons are offered in around 70 per cent of clinics and that

> [m]ost add-ons did not have a strong evidence base to show effectiveness and many clinics were not making it clear to patients that this evidence was weak. Patients were confused about the merits of add-ons and were not sure who to trust for information.[20]

As a result, the HFEA introduced a "traffic lights" system for add-ons developed with SCAAC with the aim of providing patient-focused information. The initial ratings given looked at evidence published in the last ten years (only RCTs) and assessed the quality of the evidence using GRADE methodology.[21] The evidence and rating are to be annually reviewed, and the traffic light method rates – in a way hopefully accessible to patients/consumers – the effectiveness of the most commonly offered add-ons, as follows:

***Green** – more than one good-quality study which shows the procedure is safe and effective.*
***Amber** – growing body of evidence which is showing promising results but where further research is required.*
***Red** – no evidence to show add-on safe and effective.*

Whilst the full benefit of the traffic light system is yet to be analyzed, this relatively quick and reactive approach to treatment add-ons is an example of patient-focused responsive regulation: finding a way to communicate science in a digestible and clear way (at a time when it can be confusing for individuals undergoing treatment).

5 HFEA and Mitochondrial Donation

This "case study" focuses on a proactive approach to developing regulation in the field of assisted reproduction through the legalization of mitochondrial donation, demonstrating how research can become treatment, or at least the possibility of treatment. Mitochondria are in every bodily cell, and they are required for cells to function properly. Under the 1990 Act, a permitted gamete or embryo did not include one where the DNA had been altered; therefore, if mitochondrial donation were to be permitted, the definition of "permitted"

19 *Ibid.*
20 *Ibid.*
21 Human Fertilisation and Embryology Authority, *Treatment Add Ons Update* (2018) <www.hfea.gov.uk/treatments/explore-all-treatments/treatment-add-ons/>.

gamete or embryo would have to be amended.[22] This occurred when the Human Fertilisation and Embryology Act 1990 was amended in 2008 and a route was built in to potentially permit future regulations "to prevent the transmission of serious mitochondrial disease."[23]

There was an elongated timeline from initial idea to the legal reality of mitochondrial donation. The difference between treatment add-ons and mitochondrial donation is that treatment add-ons were already happening and there were concerns surrounding the lack of regulation around these methods in an already often-costly treatment sector, whereas mitochondrial donation was the realm of research and a decision had to then be made as to whether the point had been reached where research should be permitted to become treatment. Such a change is controversial and arguably requires scrutiny, given that mitochondrial donation does involve a change to the DNA of the gamete/embryo.[24] In many ways, the UK was a trailblazer as it was with initial IVF regulation also, there was no similar approach to draw from to inform regulation.

The seemingly slow creep to permitting mitochondrial donation in treatment began with permission being granted for research into mitochondrial donation. In 2001, the Human Fertilisation and Embryology (Research Purposes) Regulations 2001 – extended the purposes of research permissible on early human embryos. In 2004, Newcastle University made an application for a research licence from the HFEA to research the use of pronuclear transfer to avoid mitochondrial disease. In 2005, that research licence was granted. In 2008, the Human Fertilisation and Embryology Act 2008 was passed – with specific provision to allow for regulations to permit clinical application of "techniques that alter the DNA of an egg or an embryo to prevent the transmission of serious mitochondrial disease."[25]

In 2010, the HFEA's SCAAC considered the use of mitochondrial donation to avoid mitochondrial disease, and in November 2010, the government was invited to consider using the HFEA 2008 regulation, making power to permit mitochondrial donation as a clinical treatment, in principle. In 2011, the Secretary of State for Health asked the HFEA to scope "expert views on the effectiveness of and safety of mitochondrial transfer."[26] In 2011, 2013, and

22 Human Fertilisation and Embryology Authority, *supra* note 2, at s.3ZA.

23 *Id.* at s.3ZA(5); Department of Health, *Mitochondrial Donation: A Consultation on Draft Regulations to Permit the Use of New Treatment Techniques to Prevent the Transmission of a Serious Mitochondrial Disease from Mother to Child*, 8 (February 2014) <https://assets.publishing.service.gov.uk/government/uploads/system/uploads/attachment_data/file/285251/mitochondrial_donation_consultation_document_24_02_14_Accessible_V0.4.pdf>.

24 *Id.* at 10.

25 *Id.* at s.3ZA (5); Lyndsey Craven et al., *Research into Policy: A Brief History of Mitochondrial Donation*, 34(2) Stem Cells 265 (2016).

26 Human Fertilisation and Embryology Authority, *Mitochondrial Replacement Consultation Advice to Government* (2013) <www.hfea.gov.uk/media/2618/mitochondria_replacement_consultation_-_advice_for_government.pdf>.

2014, reports were published by an independent panel of the HFEA, which included undertaking a public consultation on the issue of whether there was public support for mitochondrial donation as a treatment method. In 2012, the Nuffield Council on Bioethics[27] carried out a public consultation and provided a report. It is interesting to note that this is an example of where

> public engagement is bi-directional: it can serve as a means for researchers to inform the public as well as for researchers to receive input and perspective from the public . . . engaging the public in deliberating about policy decision may help to legitimize approaches to a morally challenging decision.[28]

In 2013, the HFEA published advice to the government that there was general support for permitting mitochondrial donation in the UK.

In February 2014, draft regulations were published, and a further consultation document was launched. In December 2014, the regulations were laid before Parliament. In February 2015, there was a debate on the regulations and a vote on whether to approve the regulations. The regulations were approved with 382 in support and 128 against. Later that month, the House of Lords debated the draft regulations and voted by 280 to 48 for the regulations to become law. In March 2015, the regulations were signed into law.[29] In 2015, therefore, mitochondrial donation became technically legal in the UK; however, it was for the HFEA to regulate how this change in law would be translated into regulated clinical treatment. It took 17 years of debate for this legislative change to occur. The regulations came into force in October 2015 alongside the HFEA's system for licensing clinics to use mitochondrial donation and for approving individual applications.[30]

The HFEA determined that it would only accept applications once an independent panel of experts was satisfied that the methods used for mitochondrial donation were sufficiently safe.[31] In 2016, progress was made and an expert panel considered that it was now appropriate to offer mitochondrial donations technique as clinical risk reduction treatment in carefully selected patients.[32]

27 Nuffield Council on Bioethics, *Novel Techniques for the Prevention of Mitochondrial DNA Disorders, an Ethical Review* (2012) <http://nuffieldbioethics.org/wp-content/uploads/2014/06/Novel_techniques_for_the_prevention_of_mitochondrial_DNA_disorders_compressed.pdf>.

28 National Academies of Sciences, Engineering, and Medicine, *Framework for Addressing Ethical Dimensions of Emerging and Innovative Biomedical Technologies: A Synthesis of Relevant National Academies Reports*, 9 (2019).

29 Human Fertilisation and Embryology Authority, *The Human Fertilisation and Embryology (Mitochondrial Donation) Regulations 2015 No. 572* (2015).

30 *Ibid.*

31 Human Fertilisation and Embryology Authority, *supra* note 8, at 4.

32 *Ibid.*

In December 2016, the HFEA made the decision to approve the use of mitochondrial donation in certain specific cases where pre-implantation genetic diagnosis was inappropriate and unlikely to be successful. Clinics, therefore, were able to apply to vary their licences to permit the use of MST and PNT in clinical treatment, and once the variation is granted, the clinic can then apply on a patient-by-patient basis for permission to treat individual patients using these techniques.

In 2017, the HFEA received its first application from a clinic to vary its licence to permit the use of PNT in treatment.[33] The HFEA Licence Committee granted Newcastle Fertility Centre permission to vary their licence.[34] In the summer of 2017, the HFEA Statutory Approvals Committee considered the first patient-specific application for PNT use in treatment. This application was approved and signalled the first time that mitochondrial donation could be used as treatment in the UK. However, at the time of writing, there is no reported live birth following mitochondrial donation treatment in the UK, but there are three reported live births globally. One live birth was a birth resulting from a trial between a Spanish company and the Institute of Life IVF Centre in Athens, Greece,[35] using the maternal spindle transfer method (MST) for a woman who had poor egg quality, not an individual who had mitochondrial disease.[36] Following this birth, the European Society of Human Reproduction and Embryology (ESHRE) published a statement which made clear the concern for any form of spindle transfer method being used in such cases:

> ESHRE recommends extreme caution on the use of spindle transfer in human oocytes as a clinical application to address fertility problems. This treatment, also known as mitochondrial donation, involves the replacement of chromosomes of donor oocytes with the chromosomes of the patients, with the aim of correcting cytoplasmic disorders. This technique was originally developed for the treatment of women carrying life-threatening mitochondrial diseases to prevent the birth of affected children. After expert evaluation, it was made legal in 2015 in the UK, where each application, available only from licensed centres, is considered on a case by case basis and authorized only for those cases with a clear medical need and having no alternative.
>
> Recently, researchers from a Greek Institute reported the birth of a healthy boy following the use of spindle transfer in a 32-year-old woman without an inherited mitochondrial disease, who had failed four previous

33 University of Newcastle, *Newcastle Awarded World's First Mitochondrial Licence* (2017) <www.ncl.ac.uk/press/articles/archive/2017/03/mitochondrialicence/>.

34 Human Fertilisation and Embryology Authority, *supra* note 8, at 4.

35 MST is not legal in Spain which is why there was the partnership with a Greek clinic.

36 Catherine Heffner, *First Baby Born in Mitochondrial Donation for Infertility Trial* (Bionews, 15 April 2019) <www.bionews.org.uk/page_142476#:~:text=A%20baby%20conceived%20via%20IVF,not%20affected%20by%20mitochondrial%20disease>.

cycles of IVF. Whether there was an identifiable "cytoplasmic disorder" is unclear.

At the present stage, and until this technology has been proven to be effective and safe, ESHRE strongly discourages the use of mitochondrial donation to alleviate an infertility condition. In line with the document issued by HFEA, the UK fertility regulator, and co-signed by ESHRE and other scientific societies on new introduction in IVF, we support the need for a responsible use of evidence-based treatments in fertility practice.[37]

6 Reactive vs. Proactive Regulation in a Globalized World

The protracted path to legalization and regulation of mitochondrial donation as a method of treatment makes plain that scientific progress most often has its utility in application. Establishing that something works through research is of limited use if it can then not (once it has progressed through safety requirements) be used in treatment. Regulation does not end with legalization – it often begins with legalization. There is an obligation (just as with the treatment add-ons issue) to keep literature under review, to monitor children born through this technique, and to keep the soundness of science under review. This raises the issue of whether the speed of regulation is ever a relevant consideration, or must such issues be driven predominantly by safety considerations?

Developments that are not prevented by regulation, because they have not been foreseen, often necessitate reactive regulation – because it is often not clear that a development has become an issue until it becomes one. Take, for example, direct-to-consumer genetic testing (DTC-GT), whereby individuals can purchase an online kit – they provide a sample of DNA. This is sent for analysis, and information is returned about their genetic health risks/ancestry/ matching with others who may be related to them, etc., depending on their selected purposes for undertaking the test and what they opt for. There have been concerns raised by some members of the medical profession about how accurate these online testing results might be.[38]

It is estimated that "[o]ver 3 million people have already used direct-to-consumer genetic testing to find information about their ancestry, and many are participating in international genetic genealogy databases that will

37 ESHRE, *Spindle Transfer in the Treatment of Infertility: An ESHRE Position Statement ESHRE* (2019) <www.eshre.eu/Press-Room/ESHRE-News/2019>; Human Fertilisation and Embryology Authority, *The Responsible Use of Treatment Add-Ons in Fertility Services – A Consensus Statement* (2018) <www.hfea.gov.uk/media/2792/treatment-add-ons-consensus-statement-final.pdf>.

38 Hannah Devlin, *Senior Doctors Call for Crackdown on Home Genetic Testing Kits*, The Guardian (21 July 2019) <www.theguardian.com/science/2019/jul/21/senior-doctors-call-for-crackdown-on-home-genetic-testing-kits>.

match them with relatives."[39] It is recognized that this has the potential (if it has not done so already) to ride roughshod through the carefully constructed provisions of the HFEA in relation to the disclosure of data held about individuals who are donor-conceived. The regulatory regime within the UK allows donor-conceived persons to access identifying information about their donors once they reach the age of 16.[40] Donors are also able to access information about any children born through use of the donor's gamete.[41]

There is evidence that DTC-GT is being used to circumvent anonymity with parents of donor-conceived individuals or the offspring themselves who use the internet and genetic testing to find donor-siblings or donor.[42] Even if a sperm donor has not undertaken DNA testing and joined a database, a relative of a sperm donor who has can be enough to identify the donor through genetic matching. This highlights that "[t]he development of DTC genetic testing companies manifests an increasing desire to frame our identity in genetic terms, whether it is in relation to health or in relation to kinship."[43] As Braverman states, "[s]imply put, direct-to-consumer testing shifts the control from the clinician into the hands of the consumer."[44]

This is symptomatic of the way that the world and data within it, including our most personal data, our DNA, is so interconnected. Even if we make choices about our privacy, others related to us or providing information about us may make different choices, with or without fully understanding the potential implications for the privacy of others by doing so, which impacts concepts of informed consent and personal autonomy. The HFEA has, responded to this issue, recognizing that their current strategy "puts patients (including donors and donor-conceived people and the quality of care and support they received at the centre of" their work[45] by seeking to "ask DNA genetic testing and matching companies to provide more prominent, detailed information in relation to donor conception," despite recognizing that as an organization they "have no regulatory levers with companies to require this."[46] However, this highlights the lack of regulatory teeth that the HFEA has to

39 Joyce C. Harper, Debbie Kennett & Dan Reisel, *The End of Donor Anonymity: How Genetic Testing Is Likely to Drive Anonymous Gamete Donation out of Business*, 31(6) Human Reproduction 1135–1140 (2016).

40 Human Fertilisation and Embryology Authority, *The Human Fertilisation and Embryology Act 2008*. S.31ZA (1)-(4) (2008).

41 *Ibid.* at s.31ZD.

42 Harper, Kennett & Reisel, *supra* note 38, at 1137.

43 Pascal Borry et al., *Anonymity 2.0: Direct-to-Consumer Genetic Testing and Donor Conception*, 101(3) Fertility and Sterility 630 (2014).

44 Andrea Braverman, *How the Internet Is Reshaping Assisted Reproduction: From Donor Offspring Registries to Direct-to-Consumer Genetic Testing*, 11 Minnesota Journal of Law, Science & Technology 493 (2010).

45 Human Fertilisation and Embryology Authority, *Authority Papers* (2018) <www.hfea.gov.uk/media/2655/2018-09-12-authority-papers-final.pdf>.

46 *Ibid.*

address organizations that they do not regulate but that impact those who they do seek to protect through regulation.

As with many issues relating to assisted reproduction, fertility journeys can straddle borders and nations when regulatory regimes generally do not. For example, even if an original donation of gametes occurs in a country where donation is anonymous, that "anonymity is not guaranteed, as they may be traced if their DNA, or that of a relative, is added to a database."[47] It is also noted that "globally there is much variability, both regarding local regulations and the cultural values and expectations in which these legal frameworks are embedded."[48] In an increasingly globalized and connected world, reproductive tourism – where patients attend countries for treatments that are not permitted in their home country or to access a particular treatment – and surrogacy raise particular issues that call for an international response. The importance of cross-border co-operation is recognized in recent American National Academies of Sciences (NAS) reports which "have emphasized international collaboration and engagement in an era of growing connectedness" in this field of emerging technologies.[49] However, it is difficult to frame how this would be achieved and to unpick which, if any, organizations would be able to create such international regulatory consensus, and even if that were possible, it would be even harder to see how that would have regulatory teeth. The World Health Organization (WHO) is attempting to do this in relation to human genome editing through its Expert Advisory Committee on Developing Global Standards for Governance and Oversight of Human Genome Editing. However, this is one very specific (albeit important) issue which does not address the range of issues that could benefit from international consensus/regulation within the field of assisted reproduction. The more time that passes with these issues going unregulated, the more any regulation will have to be reactive to events that have already unfolded – putting the genie back in the bottle is arguably much harder than controlling how and when the genie can leave the bottle in the first place.

There are new challenges for privacy rights, and the question is whether to accept that we now exist in a "post-privacy" era or whether privacy protection needs to be strengthened because of advances in assisted reproduction.[50] It is important to understand the connected, data-driven world and how this is to be regulated and what the rationale is for such regulation. Is it easier to just assume that tighter regulation is what is required or is "the answer . . . not to erect even more authoritative regimes of managing genetic knowledge, but . . . to re-think

47 Harper, Kennett & Reisel, supra note 38 at 1138.

48 Ibid. at 1136.

49 National Academies of Sciences, Engineering, and Medicine, *supra* note 27.

50 Maren Klotz, *Wayward Relations: Novel Searches of the Donor-Conceived for Genetic Kinship*, 35(1) Medical Anthropology 45 (2016).

what normative concepts these regimes were established to uphold."[51] It may be that there are different arguments to be made about how to facilitate the connection of existing genetically related individuals (if at all) versus how to regulate new technologies that seek to edit not-yet-existing individuals.

Perhaps the recent publication by the National Academies for Sciences in America provides a helpful steer for how to address "ethical dimensions of innovative biomedical technologies."[52] The NAS-proposed framework contains eight core considerations to act not as a checklist but as a way of balancing competing considerations when considering regulatory or policy responses to innovate biomedical technologies. The core considerations are not in a hierarchy or order of importance, save for the first consideration: "promotes societal value." This is given primacy and prominence for the following reasons:

> Biomedical innovation is principally justified by its potential to benefit society and individuals through improving health and well-being. While scientific knowledge production alone may have intrinsic value, it is ultimately the ability of biomedical research that justifies its pursuit, especially in the face of potential risks or harms (Emanuel et al., 2000).[53]

Sound science is perhaps easier to assess and understand when starting with a new issue and looking to make "[r]recommendations to the government are pragmatic when they fit within its regulatory rules and limits,"[54] as seen with the albeit-long but careful path to the regulation of mitochondrial donation as a possible treatment option in the UK. Where it can get harder is when something is introduced to the market with specific assisted reproduction–related regulatory oversight (as seen in relation to treatment options) and then action has to be taken to assess once something is already in place. Two areas in this chapter (treatment add-ons and mitochondrial donation) relate to treatment and prospective children. The third, DTC-GT, relates to more often already-existing donor-conceived individuals, donors, and families.

The HFEA arguably has a clearer regulatory role and nexus in relation to treatment add-ons because they occur in clinics that the HFEA license, inspect, and regulate. As to DTC-GT, the HFEA simply has to appeal to the goodwill of these companies, which the HFEA does not regulate to seek their co-operation in terms of provision of information to those who may be accessing their services. This increases awareness that such services may actively be used by those seeking out those who are related to them or may inadvertently result in such an outcome so that individuals are fully informed when it comes to making their decision as to whether to test or not.

51 *Id.* at 54.
52 National Academies of Sciences, Engineering, and Medicine, *supra* note 27.
53 *Id.* at 5.
54 *Id.* at 10.

Unless or until there is further regulation of such commercial entities and the issues relating to human rights and non-state actors and how international law and regulation should operate in relation to corporations and companies who hold considerable data that crosses borders and lives, collaboration, appealing to the goodwill of the relevant companies, and public information may be the only methods available to address these unforeseen issues. The question remains as to how, such unforeseen issues (as the use of DTC-GT for donor-conceived kinship matching) can be better anticipated and proactively, rather than reactively, historically addressed. It is perhaps clear that whilst the key issue with the internet and assisted reproduction was that "the role of the intended parents" had "evolved from passive customers to informed consumers," the challenge for 2020 and beyond is to recognize that the expansion of DTC-GT has led to donor-conceived individuals to be able to also be "informed consumers," where they attempt to find out more about their genetic heritage. As recently noted by Kennett (2019), perhaps the more appropriate definition of DNA in the context of assisted reproduction should be "DNA = donor not anonymous," in recognition of the fact that the way DTC-GT has been used means that anonymity is no more[55] and that the focus should be on "support, counselling and privacy" and its availability to all parties.[56] It is a discernible challenge for regulation to address these issues and to consider how to ensure access to such support services around internet testing and perhaps not one that an assessment of the soundness of science can assist with.

7 Conclusion

In conclusion, in the absence of clear international guidelines in the field of assisted reproduction in a world which is now highly data-connected and where, as was seen, with one mitochondria live birth can involve efforts in organizations between countries to use new technology (see the Spain/Greece example earlier), national regulation is very important. However, national regulation can vary considerably in scope, reach, methods, and tools for regulation and degrees of independence. In an era where ensuring sound science is behind policy decisions, it is arguably important that national regulators of assisted reproduction, where they exist, are empowered to make impartial, independent, and sound science-based decisions, but decisions that also recognize the context and realities of what the shape of assisted reproduction looks like in the twenty-first century.

55 Harper, Kennett & Reisel, *supra* note 38, at 1135.

56 Yvonne Collins, Donor Conception and Direct to Consumer DNA Testing (*BioNews*, 24 June 2019) <www.bionews.org.uk/page_143527>.

9 Use of Smartphone Applications in the Democratic Decision-Making Process[†]

Mihail Stojanoski and Lilla Vukovich***

1 Introduction

One of the first people to be wary about new technology was none other than Socrates, who warned about the negative consequences that would be brought by writing things down. In his opinion, this action ultimately resulted in forgetfulness and loss of memory.[1] Later, in 1492, at the dawn of the printing press, a prominent German monk named Johannes Trithemius said, "He, who ceases from zeal for writing because of printing, is no true lover of the Scriptures."[2] He vehemently opposed printed books, only later to begin printing his own work, conceding that it had not been such a bad idea after all. It seems that no matter how far we go back in history, the fear of new technology was and is always present, and more or less similar arguments are put forward each time someone comes up with a new idea. Smartphone applications ("apps") are no exception. Whether by a show of hands or a secret ballot, the process of democratic decision-making has accompanied humanity for centuries. New technologies seem to reshape everything in our lives, and the process of democratic decision-making is no exception.

Although the majority of elections throughout the world today are organized by means of paper ballot, e-voting is gaining popularity. One of the simplest definitions of e-voting is an election, or a referendum, which involves the

† The opinions expressed in this publication are those of the authors. They do not reflect the opinions or views of the organizations where the authors are or have been employed.

* Mihail Stojanoski is Assistant Manager of the European Roma Rights Centre in Brussels and PhD candidate in the field of human rights at the University of Strasbourg, former case-processing lawyer at the European Court of Human Rights. Corresponding Author: mihail.stojanoski@mail.com

** Lilla Vukovich is Legal officer at the Department for the Execution of Judgments of the European Court of Human Rights and former case-processing lawyer at the European Court of Human Rights. Corresponding Author: lilla.vukovich@gmail.com

1 As he refused to write down his thoughts, it was his student Plato who provides us with this information. See, Plato, ***Phaedrus**, in* The Dialogues of Plato translated into English with Analyses and Introductions 1110 (Benjamin Jowett (ed.), Oxford University Press 2009).

2 Cited in Brann L. N., The Abbot Trithemius (1462–1516): The Renaissance of Monastic Humanism 158 (Brill 1997).

DOI: 10.4324/9781003472421-9

use of electronic means to cast and/or count the vote.[3] This means that the use of any electronic equipment, including smartphone apps, would fall under e-voting.

Having said this, we observe that in the past decade, there has been increased interest for internet voting worldwide (in Switzerland, Estonia, Moscow City, and several relatively low-impact votes in the United States, for example), with varying levels of success.[4] This conversation has gained traction in large part due to the recent advancements made in the field of blockchain and the ever-increasing proliferation of smartphone devices. In addition, we observe that due to the recent outbreak of the COVID-19 virus and the strict confinement measures that followed it, some countries have had to postpone elections.[5] Internet voting, and, by extension, smartphone voting, could provide an elegant solution to this problem.

On the other hand, the use of smartphone applications in the democratic decision-making process carries novel risks and threats which have to be addressed before the technology is deployed for wider use. This includes risks such as the disruption of the flow of information brought on by fake news depicted on electronic and (in particular) social media, the possibility of cyberattacks, the need to involve private parties in the voting process, and many others.

The chapter aims to analyze the impact that smartphone apps have in three segments of the democratic decision-making process, presented in a chronological order of occurrence in the context of a vote. First, we examine their impact on how voters receive information, which forms the basis for their decisions on election day. Then we explore the impact that apps have (or could have) on voting. Lastly, their impact on the possibility to share one's vote with others as a manifestation of freedom of expression. We will provide a brief, non-exhaustive review of practical examples from Europe and the United States and explore some benefits and challenges present in the three phases of the democratic decision-making process described earlier, in the hope that this work might serve as a useful discussion point for policymakers and a basis for future research.

2 Receiving Information

Several scientific papers and many journalistic reviews have recently examined the feasibility of voting through a smartphone app and, more generally,

3 The terminology is borrowed from Recommendation CM/Rec(2017)5 of the Committee of Ministers to member States on standards for e-voting [2017]. This follows an earlier Recommendation CM/Rec(2004)11 [2004]. On this issue, also see Jörgen S. Svensson & Ronald Leenes, *E-Voting in Europe: Divergent Democratic Practice*, 8(1,2) Information Polity 3–15 (2003).

4 For details on these examples, see Section 3.3, which follows.

5 For example, elections had to be postponed in France, Poland, and North Macedonia.

through the internet.[6] Although the casting of the ballot lies at the heart of the democratic decision-making process, we put forward that the internet and smartphone apps already have a significant impact at a much earlier stage.

2.1 *Phone Apps as a Source of News*

Before delving into the issue further, we first need to acknowledge that the primary decision-making with regard to any vote takes place on a personal level. Optimally, each voter should make their decision on the basis of carefully gathered information and research (although this is not always the case).[7] Information today is made available in a variety of ways and is received through watching, reading, or listening to information outlets, whether through television, radio, printed media, or the internet.

Smartphones play an ever-increasing role in accessing daily news. According to a survey made by the Pew Research Centre in July 2019, mobile devices have become one of the most common ways to obtain news in the United States. The survey reveals that 57 per cent of US adults get news on a mobile device. This percentage is 72 per cent among people aged 18–29.[8] Knowing that many news outlets now own and operate their respective smartphone apps, thereby dispensing with the need for conventional internet browsers, it follows that smartphone apps as a source of news serve a big part of the adult population. In this vein, it should also be mentioned that news aggregators, which often use their own apps, make up a significant part of the market.[9]

Social media platforms, which are increasingly relied on as news sources, have a tendency to be accessed through smartphone apps as well.[10]

Although the benefits of receiving news through a smartphone app, such as easy access, speed, and access to a variety of providers, are undeniable, smartphone apps fall victim to the broader problems that emerge in the internet era

6 David Jefferson et al., *What We Don't Know About the Voatz "Blockchain" Internet Voting System* (2019) <https://cse.sc.edu/~buell/blockchain-papers/documents/WhatWeDontKnowAbouttheVoatz_Blockchain_.pdf>.

7 Voting behaviour is an interesting field of study which goes beyond the scope of this chapter. For further discussion on the issue, see, for example, Rui Jorge da Silva Antunes, *Theoretical Models of Voting Behaviour* (2010) <www.researchgate.net/publication/242653736_Theoretical_models_of_voting_behaviour>.

8 Mason Walker, *Americans Favor Mobile Devices Over Desktops and Laptops for Getting News*, Pew Research Centre (2019) <www.pewresearch.org/fact-tank/2019/11/19/americans-favor-mobile-devices-over-desktops-and-laptops-for-getting-news/>.

9 For data on the use of news aggregators and their popularity, see *Weekly Usage of News Aggregators Worldwide in 2017, by Region* (Statista 2017) <www.statista.com/statistics/718132/news-aggregators-worldwide/>.

10 Around 20% of adults in the United States stated that they '*get news often*' through social media: Sarah Perez, *Pew: Social Media for the First Time Tops Newspapers as a News Source for US Adults* (2018) <https://techcrunch.com/2018/12/10/pew-social-media-for-the-first-time-tops-newspapers-as-a-news-source-for-u-s-adults/?guccounter=1&guce_referrer_us=aHR0cHM6Ly93d3cuZ29vZ2xlLmNvbS8&guce_referrer_cs=J9T5rENr_GnM4lBtJjnqRQ>.

of news. For example, the dissemination of fake news, especially taking into consideration its massive proliferation on social media, poses a significant risk to news reliability.[11] Therefore, ease of access to news is a double-edged sword, and the risks of biased information have been recognized by many legislators.[12]

2.2 *Voting Advice Applications*

In the context of the democratic decision-making process, another use of smartphone apps for receiving information are the voting advice applications (VAAs).[13] These are special types of computer-based opt-in web surveys which assist voters in the electoral decision-making process by analyzing and comparing their policy preferences with the programs of running candidates or parties. VAA users fill out a questionnaire indicating their position on a wide range of policy issues (for example, "Should the government abolish university tuition fees?" or "Should people be given the right to choose assisted death?"). After comparing the answers with the programs of each running party or candidate, the application produces a rank-ordered list indicating the parties or candidates that stand closest to the user's policy preferences.[14]

VAAs started in the Netherlands in 1989 with a booklet called the Stem-Wijzer, which contained 60 statements abstracted from political party programs and was primarily aimed to educate junior high school students. This later snowballed into an internet-based product built on the same concept. Nowadays, VAAs are used widely, and in some countries (the Netherlands or Germany, for example), certain VAAs (for example, StemWijzer[15] or Wahl-O-Mat)[16] have evolved into extremely popular political phone apps used by millions of voters.[17] It should also be mentioned that the European Union (EU) launched a VAA called EU-Vox during their 2014 elections.

11 This is a hotly debated issue which extends beyond the scope of the chapter. A very good read which has also been relied on in further research on the topic is Hunt Allcott & Matthew Gentzkow, *Social Media and Fake News in the 2016 Election*, 31(2) Journal of Economic Perspectives 211–236 (2017) <https://pubs.aeaweb.org/doi/pdfplus/10.1257/jep.31.2.211?source=post_page---------------------------&>.

12 Among others, the new pieces of legislation enacted in France and Germany have stirred a lot of debate. One recent discussion on this topic was published by Forbes: S. Chandler, *French Social Media Law Is Another Coronavirus Blow to Freedom of Speech* (2020) <www.forbes.com/sites/simonchandler/2020/05/14/french-social-media-law-is-another-coronavirus-blow-to-freedom-of-speech/>.

13 For more information and comprehensive research materials, see the Research Network on Voting Advice Applications of the University of Dusseldorf at <http://vaa-research.net/>.

14 Diego Garzia & Stefan Marschall (eds.), Matching Voters with Parties and Candidates. Voting Advice Applications in Comparative Perspective (European University Institute Press 2014) <http://hdl.handle.net/1814/34156>.

15 For more information, see the VAA's website: <https://stemwijzer.nl/>.

16 Similarly, for more information, visit the VAA's website: <www.bpb.de/politik/wahlen/wahl-o-mat/>.

17 Garzia & Marschall S., *supra* note 14.

The VAAs reflect a movement towards the massive use of smartphone apps for a variety of issues and offer a simple digest of policies as opposed to an otherwise thorough examination of the policies of all candidates/parties. Although they carry the risk of influence by the app vendor on the individual's decision, they nonetheless provide an easy substitute for otherwise extensive research that may prove too cumbersome for some in the modern world. It has also been suggested that using a VAA may have a positive impact on voter turnout, especially among the younger population.[18]

3 Voting by Means of a Smartphone App

Now that we have discussed the "pre-vote" stage, the chapter will analyze the potential of smartphone apps to be used for casting the actual vote in elections or referenda. We consider it necessary to examine the legal and technical aspects of using a phone app for voting, and to present some examples of voting where apps have been used. Lastly, we examine some advantages and challenges that follow the paradigm shift towards internet/app voting.

3.1 Legal Aspects

The Council of Europe adopted a comprehensive set of standards in 2004 specifically addressing e-voting, which, at that time, had been at its early stages of development.[19] This intergovernmental organization whose rationale is to monitor, protect, and promote democracy, rule of law, and human rights in its 46 member states[20] is the only international organization to have issued recommendations on the regulation of e-voting.[21] Following the first recommendation in 2004, two guidelines were approved in 2010 which were intended as practical tools to facilitate implementation of the 2004 recommendation.[22]

18 Javier Ramos, Javier Padilla & Enrique Chueca, *Voting Advise Applications (VAAs) and Young Voting Behavior in European Election*, European Consortium for Political Research Joint Sessions of Workshops (2018) <https://ecpr.eu/Filestore/PaperProposal/d105a1af-9077-47d0-8c4a-560afdbf3a0b.pdf>.

19 Council of Europe Recommendation Rec (2004)11, *supra* note 3.

20 The Council of Europe is an international organization established in 1949; today it includes 46 member States covering all European Union members as well as Albania, Andorra, Armenia, Azerbaijan, Bosnia and Herzegovina, Georgia, Iceland, Liechtenstein, Republic of Moldova, Monaco, Montenegro, North Macedonia, Norway, San Marino, Serbia, Switzerland, Turkey and Ukraine.

21 As established in: Ardita Driza Maurer, *Updated European Standards for E-voting, The Council of Europe Recommendation Rec(2017)5 on Standards for E-voting* (2017) <www.researchgate.net/publication/321952003_Updated_European_standards_for_e-voting_The_Council_of_Europe_recommendation_Rec20175_on_standards_for_e-voting>. At the moment of writing, no other international document or recommendation in this regard could be found to exist.

22 *Guidelines on Transparency of E-Enabled Elections of the Council of Europe Directorate General of Democracy and Political Affairs*, Directorate of Democratic Institutions, Council of Europe (2011) <https://rm.coe.int/CoERMPublicCommonSearchServices/DisplayDCTM

The two guidelines and the recommendation were recently revised and replaced by Recommendation (2017)5 on standards for e-voting.[23]

The new recommendation lays down 49 standards which include numerous principles and procedural safeguards. These standards are intended as objectives for national governments to meet when implementing e-voting in order to ensure compliance with democratic requirements. Moreover, the document includes a "glossary of terms" providing definitions of, *inter alia*, e-voting and remote e-voting, the latter being relevant for phone app–based voting.[24]

According to Recommendation (2017)5, "e-voting" means "the use of electronic means to cast and/or count the vote." Compared to the definition provided by the 2004 recommendation, the novelty is to extend e-voting to the process of tallying votes by electronic means.[25] Given that the recommendation defines "remote e-voting" as "the use of electronic means to cast the vote outside the premises where voting takes place in general," smartphone app voting would fall under this category.

The 49 standards are grouped into eight chapters, each of which addresses different general principles or procedural safeguards alluded to earlier. The recommendation thus puts forward that universal, equal, free, and secret suffrage must be ensured at all times in the course of e-voting. In other words, the election process shall be accessible, understandable, and easy to use for all voters and, in particular, for persons with disabilities. Voter authentication should ensure that each voter can unmistakeably identify himself/herself and cast one single vote. The process shall secure the free formation and expression of the voter's opinion, meaning, that the voter's choice shall not be affected by the voting system or by any undue influence. Lastly, the voter should be able to verify that his/her vote was cast as intended. The voting process shall be organized in a way which would exclude anything that would endanger the secrecy of the vote. In this respect, special attention should be paid to privacy and data protection concerns and making sure that the system stores and processes personal data and authentication information only to the extent strictly necessary.

Although Recommendation (2017)5 aims at setting standards for e-voting in general, certain standards are particularly relevant in the context of phone app–based voting. For example, standard no. 3 provides that "[u]nless channels of remote e-voting are universally accessible, they shall be only an

---

Content?documentId=090000168059bdf6> and *Guidelines for Developing Processes that Confirm Compliance with Prescribed Requirements and Standards in the Region (Certification of E-Voting Systems)*, Directorate General of Democracy and Political Affairs, Directorate of Democratic Institutions (2011) <https://rm.coe.int/CoERMPublicCommonSearchServices/DisplayDCTMContent?documentId=090000168059bdf8>.

23 The integral text is available at <https://search.coe.int/cm/Pages/result_details.aspx?ObjectID=0900001680726f6f>.

24 Brann, *supra* note 3.

25 This definition is now in line with the one used by OSCE; see *Handbook for the Observation of New Voting Technologies*, OSCE/ODIHR (2013) <www.osce.org/odihr/elections/104939>.

additional and optional means of voting." The recommendation thereby acknowledges the optional nature of any phone app–based voting, considering that the necessary channel for remote e-voting, namely, access to the internet, is not universally accessible for the time being.[26] Standard no. 4 states that "[b]efore casting a vote using a remote e-voting system, voters' attention shall be explicitly drawn to the fact that the e-election in which they are submitting their decision by electronic means is a real election or referendum."[27] This standard addresses the issue of disseminating clear information to the public about the role of the vote. This is increasingly important in a scenario where there is no personal contact between the voter and an elections official, unlike in traditional ballot casting.

The preceding standards should be met in order to ensure that remote e-voting, and, in particular, phone app–based voting, would not fall short of the requirements of the democratic process. Further to this point, standard no. 28 prescribes that "[b]efore introducing e-voting, member States shall introduce the required changes to the relevant legislation," thereby making sure that the relevant issues surrounding e-voting are regulated as a matter of public policy instead of allowing technology companies to set the rules.[28]

3.2 Technical Aspects

A smartphone app is a piece of software designed to run on a smartphone or tablet. Smartphone apps usually provide a specific function to assist the user, such as a game, a dictionary, access to a news portal or bank account, tracking of sport activities, or managing flight tickets.

For a smartphone app to be used in the voting process, certain technical steps are necessary. In a nutshell, the voter should first download a government-approved voting app. He/she should then undergo authentication[29] and cast the vote by selecting one of the offered options. The app then plays a role in the tallying of the votes, and the results are made public.

The app should probably be developed by a private company ("vendor"). Many questions arise as to the role of the vendor both after the initial phase of development and the relationship between the vendor and the government. We put forward that the vendor can be retained to either operate the app in partnership and under supervision of the government, or control over the app can be handed over to the government, with the vendor only being retained

26 *Explanatory Memorandum to Recommendation CM/Rec(2017)5 Committee of Ministers of the Council of Europe to Member States on Standards for E-Voting* (2017) <https://rm.coe.int/168071bc84>.

27 *Ibid.*

28 See in this respect, Maurer, *supra* note 21.

29 See Emad Abu-Shanab, Rawan Khasawneh & Izzat Alsmadi, *Authentication Mechanisms for E-Voting*, *in* Human-Centered System Design for Electronic Governance 75 (Saqib Saeed & Christopher Reddick (eds.), IGI Global 2013).

as an external participant to the process. The staff involved in the process will need to undergo training, and instructions will need to be issued to the general public on how to use and operate the app.

Verification/authentication of identity, which is crucial for the reliability of the results, can easily become the bottleneck of the whole operation. In e-voting, three categories of authentication methods have emerged so far: knowledge-based, token-based, and biometric.[30] The knowledge-based method is built on the voter's knowledge of a password or a PIN. The token-based method reinforces the password or PIN by the use of a tool (for example, a smartcard) physically in the voter's possession. The biometric method relies on biometric data about the voter which is collected and then authenticated on the day of the vote. The preceding methods can also be combined, resulting in the existence of many different models in practice.[31]

The casting of a vote needs to be completely secure. To accomplish this, much faith has been put in blockchain technology, which, some argue, can be used to achieve all the legal requirements of a smartphone app vote.[32] Blockchain should further allow for the preservation of voter anonymity, make vote tampering a mere theoretical probability, and allow for the possibility of a recount or audit.[33] To borrow an analogy from Kshetri and Voas, blockchain-enabled voting would entail issuing each voter a "wallet" containing the user's credentials. Each voter would hold a single "coin" representing one opportunity to vote. Casting a vote would transfer the voter's coin to a candidate's wallet. A voter can spend his or her coin only once.[34]

The proponents of blockchain would argue that that technology is designed to be resistant to any alteration of the data, because once verified, the data cannot be modified retroactively without the modification of data on the entire network of computers participating in the verification process.[35] However, a lot of concerns are raised about the reliability and safety of internet voting, particularly emphasizing the shortcomings of blockchain.[36] These concerns are discussed in more detail in Section 3.4.

30 *Id.* at 76.

31 For the biometric method, see the example from West Virginia, United States, in Section 3.3.

32 Among others, see Kyree Leary, *Blockchain Might Be About to Change the Way We Vote*, World Economic Forum (2017) <www.weforum.org/agenda/2017/09/blockchain-could-be-about-to-change-how-you-vote>.

33 *Ibid.*

34 Nir Kshetri & Jeffrey Voas, *Blockchain-Enabled E-voting*, 35(4) IEEE Software (2018) <https://libres.uncg.edu/ir/uncg/f/N_Kshetri_Blockchain_Enabled_2018.pdf>.

35 See more at Arvind Narayanan et al., Bitcoin and Cryptocurrency Technologies: A Comprehensive Introduction (Princeton University Press 2016) <www.lopp.net/pdf/princeton_bitcoin_book.pdf>; see also Raval Siraj, What Is a Decentralized Application? Decentralized Applications: Harnessing Bitcoin's Blockchain Technology (O'Reilly Media, Inc. 2016) <www.oreilly.com/library/view/decentralized-applications/9781491924532/>.

36 For a technical discussion regarding one example of internet voting (the Scytl-SwissPost voting system), see Sarah Jamie Lewis, Olivier Pereira & Vanessa Teague, *How Not to Prove*

3.3 *Practical Examples*

In this chapter, we will present three practical examples from Europe and the United States where phone apps played a significant role in the voting process. These examples include Estonia, where the use of a phone app serves only a secondary function, as part of the verification of the electronically cast ballot; the Swiss Canton Zug, where a phone app–based voting process is in the trial period; and West Virginia (United States), where the Voatz app has already made it possible for a small group of participants to vote in an actual election.

3.3.1 *Estonia*

Although the Estonian system is computer-based and mobile devices play only a secondary role in the verification process, it is worth discussing, given that Estonia has been a pioneer in electronic state governance.

One of the numerous electronic services provided by the Estonian government is voting through the internet (I-voting).[37] When the country introduced its online voting system in 2005, it became the first to offer internet voting nationwide. Since then, it has used the system in local, national, and EU elections several times. In the parliamentary elections in 2019, over 44 per cent of participating voters cast their ballots online.[38]

Following the recommendations of the Organization for Security and Co-operation in Europe (OSCE) upon the 2011 elections, Estonia's online voting legal framework has improved. As the most important development, the Parliament established a specialized Electronic Voting Committee in order to address the recommendations of OSCE to increase accountability and transparency.[39] Moreover, in order to address the issue of verification, the National Electoral Committee introduced a specific process for voters to verify that their internet-based vote had been cast as intended. The verification is done by using a separate smart device (mobile phone or tablet). This device reads a code shown on the voter's computer screen upon completion of the voting. The mobile device then temporarily displays the voter's choice, enabling the voter to verify that his/her vote was recorded as cast.[40] The smart

---

Your Election Outcome: The Use of Non-Adaptive zero Knowledge Proofs in the Scytl-SwissPost Internet Voting System, and Its Implications for Decryption Proof Soundness (2019) <www.semanticscholar.org/paper/How-not-to-prove-your-election-outcome-The-use-of-%2C-Lewis-Pereira/c2290262dfb69edea989a06486b799a68f36435e>.

37 For further details, see the official government website <https://e-estonia.com/solutions/e-governance/i-voting/>.

38 And participation has been constantly on the rise. The data is available on the website of the Estonian election board <www.valimised.ee/en/archive/statistics-about-internet-voting-estonia>.

39 See OSCE/ODIHR, *Election Expert Team Final Report on Parliamentary Elections of Estonia of 1 March 2015* (2015) <www.osce.org/odihr/elections/estonia/160131?download=true>.

40 *Ibid.*

device–based verification system was implemented and used in the 2019 national elections as well.[41]

3.3.2 Zug, Switzerland

The Swiss canton of Zug created a global hub for crypto and blockchain development (i.e. the “Crypto Valley”) and became one of the world’s leading ecosystems for crypto, blockchain, and distributed ledger technologies.[42] Zug conducted a blockchain-based test vote in 2018. The trial vote was aimed at implementing Zug’s digital ID system that was launched in November 2017. As a country with regular referendum votes, Switzerland – in particular its constituencies – proved to be an optimal place to test blockchain voting solutions.

For the test run, citizens were requested to vote on a fictitious issue using their smartphones, combining the use of a blockchain to record the results with the city’s existing electronic ID system, which provides each citizen with a unique digital identity.[43] Seventy-two citizens participated in the vote.[44]

Following the project, a detailed report focusing on the technical aspects was published by the City of Zug in cooperation with the Lucerne University of Applied Sciences and Luxoft.[45] The report found that the project provided solid proof that blockchain-based e-voting could work in reality. The report emphasized that the blockchain-based phone app voting had clear advantages compared to traditional voting procedures. For example, the blockchain system increased both the security and the transparency of voting without endangering the anonymity of the voters.[46]

Following the test vote, the city of Zug conducted an online survey amongst the approximately 220 digital ID holders. Ninety-five people took part. The evaluation of the survey revealed a generally high level of acceptance for the internet-based voting process, considering that more than three-quarters of the participants welcomed the introduction of e-voting. Despite this generally high level of approval, scepticism regarding the security of e-voting was still present. Moreover, many were of the opinion that the population of Zug

41 See OSCE/ODIHR, *Election Expert Team Final Report on Parliamentary Elections of Estonia of 3 March 2019* (2019) <www.osce.org/odihr/elections/estonia/424229?download=true>.

42 Helen Partz, *Crypto Valley’s Zug to Run Switzerland’s First Blockchain-Based Municipal Vote*, Cointelegraph (2018) <https://cointelegraph.com/news/crypto-valley-s-zug-to-run-switzerland-s-first-blockchain-based-municipal-vote>.

43 Malek Murison, *Swiss Town Votes Via Blockchain, While Blockchain Bank Tools Up*, Internet of Business (2018) <https://internetofbusiness.com/swiss-blockchain-voting-trial/>.

44 *Switzerland’s First Municipal Blockchain Vote Hailed a Success*, Swissinfo (2018) <www.swissinfo.ch/eng/business/crypto-valley-_-switzerland-s-first-municipal-blockchain-vote-hailed-a-success/44230928>.

45 *Evaluation of the Blockchain Vote in the City of Zug*, Zug Stadt, Lucerne University of Applied Sciences and Luxoft (2018) <www.stadtzug.ch/_docn/1938568/eVoting_Final_Report_ENG.pdf>.

46 *Ibid.*

should still be able to vote by letter in addition to e-voting. Although the participants found the voting process simple and reliable, some struggled with technical problems with their digital ID.[47]

3.3.3 *West Virginia, United States*

Voter participation through a blockchain-secured smartphone app developed by the company Voatz was introduced in 2018 for absentee voters in West Virginia in the United States. While paper ballots could still be cast, the system offered a new possibility for participation for members of the military which were deployed abroad.[48] The platform used biometric identification methods in addition to government-issued ID. The voters first needed to take a photo of their ID, passport, or driving licence with the smartphone camera. They then recorded a video of their face in real time, which was used by face recognition software to ensure a match. After making their choice, the voters used the smartphone's fingerprint scanner to cast the ballot.[49]

Among the 183 people who requested the app, 160 downloaded it, and 144 cast their votes through it.[50] Voter turnout research on the West Virginia vote concluded that among people living overseas, having a mobile voting option had increased requests for ballots by 6–9 per cent, and it had increased voter turnout by 3–5 per cent. One study estimates that half the people casting a ballot with the mobile app would not have voted if mobile voting was not available.[51]

Although the West Virginia voting received some positive feedback,[52] there have been many sceptical voices as well. Critics are mainly targeting Voatz, the vendor, for failing to disclose detailed technical data about the app in spite of it being used in public elections.[53] While Voatz is relying on an intellectual property argument to avoid such disclosures, the authors argue that, given the public interest at stake, relevant data should be disclosed nonetheless. Field experts claim that the Voatz system has not gone through any federal or public certification, and the company has not disclosed its source code or allowed its system to be examined openly by third-party experts. It has not been subject

47 *Ibid.*

48 Aaron Mak, *West Virginia Introduces Blockchain Voting App for Midterm Election*, Slate (2018) <https://slate.com/technology/2018/09/west-virginia-blockchain-voting-app-midterm-elections.html>.

49 Irene Solaiman, *Defending Vote Casting: Using Blockchain-based Mobile Voting Applications in Government Elections*, Harvard Kennedy School, Belfer Center (2018) <www.belfercenter.org/publication/defending-vote-casting-using-blockchain-based-mobile-voting-applications-government>.

50 Anthony Fowler, *Promises and Perils of Mobile Voting*, 00(0) Election Law Journal (2020).

51 *Ibid.*

52 For example, Alex Tapscott, *It's Time for Online Voting*, New York Times opinion (2018) <www.nytimes.com/2018/11/05/opinion/online-blockchain-voting.html>.

53 Jefferson et al., *supra* note 6.

to open testing in mock elections either.[54] In the same study, concerns were raised about the voter identification and authentication process and, in particular, about the privacy of sensitive information collected during authentication. Voatz had contracted Jumio, a third-party company, for its face recognition software, used to match the ID photo taken by the voter with the other biometrical data provided by him or her. As a consequence, Jumio collected an extraordinary amount of sensitive personal information about voters, such as their name, address, birth date, facsimile of their signature, and other data. Researchers imply that the handling of this considerable amount of data is not regulated properly, thereby risking a privacy breach.[55]

More recently, researchers at MIT published a paper about the security analysis of the Voatz app, voicing serious concerns about the system's vulnerabilities.[56] The paper concludes that the Voatz app is not secure and can easily be exposed to attacks. There are flaws in the app that might enable attackers to monitor the casting of votes, but also to change ballots or block them without the users' knowledge.[57] The researchers suggest that any near-future plans to use the app for high-level elections should be abandoned. They argue that "[i]t is the burden of the developer of any system to prove that their system is as secure, to both the public and the security community, before it can be trusted as a crucial component in the democratic process."[58]

Voatz, of course, reacted promptly to the accusations and declared them unfounded. They argued that MIT's research method was flawed as the researchers were analyzing an outdated Android version of the app. Moreover, the examined app was never connected to Voatz's servers, thereby meaning that the interactions between the system components had been hypothetical and thus simply false.[59]

Following the West Virginia elections, the Voatz app has continued to be used in federal, state, and municipal elections in Denver, Oregon, and Utah.[60]

3.4 Advantages and Challenges

The possibility to cast a vote through a smartphone app may have a positive impact on voter turnout and accessibility. As turnout is an increasing concern,

54 *Ibid.*

55 *Ibid.*

56 Michael A. Specter, James Koppel & Daniel Weitzner, *The Ballot Is Busted Before the Blockchain: A Security Analysis of Voatz, the First Internet Voting Application Used in U.S. Federal Elections* (2020) <https://internetpolicy.mit.edu/wp-content/uploads/2020/02/SecurityAnalysisOfVoatz_Public.pdf>.

57 Matthew Rosenberg, *Voting on Your Phone: New Elections App Ignites Security Debate* (2020) <www.nytimes.com/2020/02/13/us/politics/voting-smartphone-app.html>.

58 Specter, Koppel & Weitzner, *supra* note 56.

59 *Voatz Response to Researchers' Flawed Report* (2020) <https://blog.voatz.com/?p=1209>.

60 Specter, Koppel & Weitzner, *supra* note 56.

app voting would provide a convenient alternative for people who, for any reason, could not physically attend the polling station or rely on ordinary mail services to cast their vote. One example in this regard occurred with West Virginia voters living overseas, where a 3–5 per cent increase in turnout was estimated. In addition, the same study found that half of the people who used the app would not have voted without it.[61]

Smartphone app voting may also make the voting process more accessible for persons with disabilities, who until now were on the sidelines on this issue.[62]

Some proponents argue that the novelty factor provided by smartphone app voting should lead to voters paying increased attention to elections, which would otherwise elicit lower interest.[63] However, research has shown that internet voting is most popular among middle-aged voters and least popular among youth,[64] which appears somewhat counterintuitive, given that young people generally have a higher rate of adaptability to new technology. Other studies have found that introducing internet voting did not have any, or had little to no, impact on turnout.[65] Therefore, in spite of the optimistic expectations, it is not a given that smartphone app voting will have a positive impact on turnout.

Another claim on behalf of smartphone app voting is that it would bring improved accuracy, security, and transparency. Although paper ballot voting itself can hardly be the subject of a cyberattack, the results can still be tampered with. Furthermore, paper ballot voting can easily be compromised due to human error, either when filling out the ballot[66] or when tallying the votes. Smartphone app voting, especially if we consider the promises of blockchain technology, might address all these concerns successfully.

However, blockchain technology has come under heavy criticism lately. Several authors have raised concerns over blockchain voting lacking sufficient

61 See the example from West Virginia U.S. in section 3.3 above.

62 According to information from the Fundamental Rights Agency of the European Union, the number of polling stations accessible for people with disabilities varies between 2% and 50% in member states. This information only takes into account people with physical disabilities. See *Information Sheet of the EU Fundamental Rights Agency* on voting rights for people with disabilities <https://fra.europa.eu/sites/default/files/voting_rights_for_people_with_disabilities.pdf>.

63 Fowler, *supra* note 50.

64 This is true for voters in Canada. See Keith Archer et al., *Recommendations Report to the Legislative Assembly of British Columbia*, Independent Panel on Internet Voting (2014) <https://elections.bc.ca/docs/recommendations-report.pdf>.

65 See, for example, Micha Germann & Uwe Serdült, *Internet Voting and Turnout: Evidence from Switzerland*, 47 Electoral Studies (2017) <https://doi.org/10.1016/j.electstud.2017.03.001>; Nicole Goodman & Leah Stokes, *Reducing the Cost of Voting: An Evaluation of Internet Voting's Effect on Turnout* (2018) <https://papers.ssrn.com/sol3/papers.cfm?abstract_id=2849167>; and Archer et al., *supra* note 64 at 13.

66 See the 2002 Help America Vote Act (HAVA), a piece of United States legislation reflecting on this issue. More information is available on the website of the US Election Assistance Commission <www.eac.gov/about_the_eac/help_america_vote_act.aspx>.

reliability and being open to attack.[67] Vulnerability of the system to foreign (and domestic) attacks remains a key concern. If an attack on the voting system happens, evidence suggests that trust in the system itself will be diminished regardless of whether the attack was successful.[68]

Research has shown different conclusions in respect of trust of voters in the context of blockchain technology. On one hand, in the Swiss canton of Zug, the online survey following the blockchain test vote revealed that more than 20 per cent of the participants believed that blockchain technology could make electronic voting more secure.[69] On the other hand, another survey of US public opinion about voting technology showed that telling respondents that online voting will be secured by blockchain had little effect on their confidence, and it even reduced their willingness to vote online.[70]

A proposed system of app voting may have many more technical concerns (such as energy consumption and speed) which fall beyond the scope of this chapter (and the expertise of its authors). From a legal standpoint, however, data protection and privacy issues remain an open question, one which does not seem to be sufficiently addressed by the developers of Voatz in their recent response to an academic paper which raised, among others, these questions as well.[71] Sharing of such data with third parties remains an additional concern, especially given its appeal and value for marketing purposes.

4 Sharing (Imparting) of Information

We put forward that sharing, or (to borrow from the European Court of Human Rights – "the ECHR") imparting of information, plays a very important role in the democratic process, notably in the exchange of ideas and freedom of expression. Sharing information by means of a phone app in the context of a vote is a relatively new possibility, and it recently stirred some debate before the ECHR. Given that the chapter already examined the impact of apps on the information flow before a vote and on the voting process itself, this information sharing aspect, which follows the vote, will be analyzed last.

In several states in the United States, it is illegal to share a photo of your own ballot paper. The state of New Hampshire implemented a law in 2014 that introduced fines up to $1,000 for violation. Similar laws prohibit recording

67 For example, Specter, Koppel & Weitzner, *supra* note 56.

68 Solaiman, *supra* note 49; About concerns raised following the 2016 presidential elections in the U.S., see Sharon Bernstein & Grant Smith, *Ahead of November Election, Old Voting Machines Stir Concerns Among U.S. Officials*(2018)<www.reuters.com/article/us-usa-election-votingmachines/ahead-of-november-election-old-voting-machines-stir-concerns-among-us-officials-idUSKCN1IW16Z>.

69 Zug Stadt, Lucerne University of Applied Sciences and Luxoft, *supra* note 45.

70 Fowler, *supra* note 50.

71 Voatz Response to Researchers' Flawed Report, *supra* note 59, posted in response to criticism raised in Specter, Koppel & Weitzner, *supra* note 56.

inside the polling place in the states of Texas, Florida, Kentucky, Nevada, and North Carolina.[72] Further, several European states adopted regulations about the publishing of information on media channels by voters regarding their choices. Albania and Iceland have explicitly imposed a ban on revealing of voting choices by publishing a photograph.[73] Portugal, Armenia, and Estonia impose general restrictions on the disclosure on how voters cast their ballots. Lastly, the National Electoral Commission in Portugal has adopted a practice of prohibiting voters from taking photographs of their ballot papers and publishing it on internet platforms.[74]

As imparting information is protected under Article 10 of the European Convention on Human Rights ("the Convention"), a similar issue recently ended up before the ECHR. The case was about a smartphone application developed by a frivolous political party called the Hungarian Two-Tailed Dog Party (in Hungarian, the "*Magyar Kétfarkú Kutya Párt*," or "MKKP" for short), which was created in 2006 for the purpose of political satire and entertainment. Initially, it made political promises such as eternal life, world peace, one workday per week, smaller gravity, free beer, and low taxes, but later on, it started to get involved in actual social and political issues, while still maintaining their trademark satirical and humorous style.

The MKKP became highly involved during the campaign preceding the October 2016 migrant quota referendum in Hungary, by mocking the government's anti-immigrant messages, which were at the centre of the ruling party's campaign. In the course of the campaign, several opposition parties called on voters to cast invalid ballots that would not count in the final tally but could still be interpreted as rejecting the government's proposals. In this vein, shortly before the vote, the MKKP made available the "the cast-an-invalid-vote app" in order to encourage voters to share photos of their invalid ballots. The aim was to motivate voters to express their disapproval of the government's campaign in a creative way. The app provided for anonymous participation and allowed users to comment on information that was posted. On the day of the referendum, altogether, 3,894 photos were shared, many of which were humorous or satirical (e.g. funny or even vulgar drawings or comments were added, without actually casting a valid vote).

Shortly after the launch of the application, the MKKP was fined for having infringed on the principles of fairness and secrecy of elections. It challenged the decision domestically to no avail. The MKKP then took the case to the ECHR, claiming a violation of the right to freedom of expression protected under Article 10 of the Convention.

72 Information by state is collected and made available by the Digital Media Law Project <www.dmlp.org/state-law-documenting-vote-2012>.

73 *Magyar Kétfarkú Kutya Párt v. Hungary* no. 201/17 [GC] (ECHR 20 January 2020) §41

74 *Ibid.*

The Court's Fourth Section delivered its unanimous judgement in January 2018, finding a violation of MKKP's right to freedom of expression. On 20 January 2020, those findings were confirmed by the Grand Chamber of the ECHR, thereby explicitly connecting phone applications with the fundamental right to freedom of expression. The ECHR emphasized that Article 10 of the Convention guarantees the right to impart information and the right of the public to receive it. Furthermore, Article 10 of the Convention applied not only to the content of the information but also to the means of transmission or reception, since any restriction imposed on those means necessarily interfered with the right to receive and impart information.[75] The Court thus accepted that "the mobile application was a means put in place by the MKKP for voters to impart their political opinions, allowing them to exercise their right to freedom of expression."[76]

The conclusion is that for the ECHR, the smartphone app possessed a communicative value and therefore could be used to express an opinion on a matter of public interest. Consequently, the sanctioning of the MKKP for making the application available had interfered with its right to freedom of expression.

Accordingly, following the interpretation of the ECHR's judgement, an app in itself can be considered a medium on equal footing with newspapers, television, and other media. It is questionable, however, whether the Court arrived at this conclusion only in the context of a phone app developed by a political party or if these conclusions equally apply to any phone app that is capable of serving as a channel to express opinions. The judgement emphasized the importance of the fact that the app was made available by a political party and that it intended to convey a political message. One could wonder, had the context been different, namely, in the absence of a clear element of political speech, if that would have led the Court to a different conclusion, at the expense of the app developer.[77]

We note that imparting information about one's voting choice in the example earlier was done voluntarily and in the spirit of a political debate. In any event, given the diverse approaches to this question between countries, further legislative developments should be expected in this field in the direction of regulating the aforementioned communicative value of apps.

5 Conclusion

It is beyond contention that smartphone apps have penetrated virtually all fields of our lives. For this chapter, we chose to examine some examples of

75 *Ibid.*
76 *Ibid.*
77 Petra Gyöngyi, *Magyar Kétfarkú Kutya Párt (MKKP) v. Hungary: Technology Meets Freedom of Expression and the Rule of Law in an Electoral Context* (2020) <https://strasbourgobservers.com/category/magyar-ketfarku-kutya-part-mkkp-v-hungary/>.

smartphone app influence on the democratic decision-making process in the pre-vote, vote, and post-vote stages. We do not argue that this list is exhaustive. There are many other aspects of a vote that can be connected – directly or indirectly – to a smartphone app, such as geolocation services, reminders to vote, candidate campaigning via social media (which are also accessed through apps), etc.

As to the pre- and post-vote stages impact of apps, we put forward that there is little controversy. The issue of fake news is a generic problem of the information era, and one which may be amplified by the growing use of apps, but it is a problem which requires solutions of a wider and systemic nature. Given that any solutions that may be applied to that problem will be simply transposed to smartphone apps, we see no rationale to address it in this chapter, which has a much narrower focus. The aspect of post-vote impact of apps, as examined in this chapter, is a field that will further develop as it seems that a number of different approaches exist that speak directly on this issue.[78] We put forward that apps have a significant impact on freedom of expression and on human rights in general, and the extent of that impact merits further research.

As to the direct influence on the voting process, we can see that such apps have seen very limited practical application so far, and it is, therefore, early to pass judgement on their future. The results so far have been encouraging, but many concerns have been raised, including, but not limited to, cybersecurity, data, and privacy protection. Cyberattacks are a serious concern for the future of app and internet voting in general, especially given that such attacks are scalable. Namely, a single attack can have a much greater impact on the voting system as a whole, compared to traditional in-person paper voting. Further to this point, it is hard to reach any definite conclusion as to the utility of blockchain technology, which, despite some promise, has come under heavy criticism. We put forward that this is in part because blockchain was designed as a decentralized system, free of supervision from a central authority, which seems to be in contrast with the requirements of an official election or referendum, which would require oversight.

However, we note that no large-scale official elections or referenda so far have been held via app voting. In Estonia, an app was used only as a supplementary tool in the voting process, and the vote itself was not cast through an app. In this regard, we propose that phone apps should gradually and cautiously be introduced as an additional means of voting. By doing this, states could make voting available to categories of people which would have otherwise had their ability to vote impeded.[79] Furthermore, the perceived risks

78 We make reference here to the "banning" approach, versus the ECHR approach of granting apps the quality of media (albeit in a very narrow context), as discussed in Section 4 earlier.

79 We make reference here to the example of West Virginia, United States, which, although limited, and the app used potentially riddled with flaws, still shows promise when it comes to voter turnout, as discussed in Section 3.3 earlier.

could be tested in a real-life environment only by gradually extending the use of apps, which would also generate more data that would lead to better research and conclusions. We put forward that the advantages from the use of voting apps, such as convenience, increased turnout, faster tallying, and even the potential for broadcasting results live, can come to light only by cautiously extending their use.

Lastly, we observe a lack of more developed legislative input in the field of online voting, let alone smartphone voting. In this respect, we consider that the Council of Europe Recommendations offer a good basis for necessary legislative development. Otherwise, we run the risk that technology companies (and thereby private interests) will decide on the rules effectively governing the field of e-voting, and that is something that, on the basis of public interest, cannot be allowed.

10 Procedural versus Substantive Approaches to Scientific Evidence in the Opinions of Advocates General

*Alexandra Molitorisová** *and Ciarán Burke***

1 Introduction: Questions of Law Versus Questions of Fact Before the Court of Justice

In disputes before judicial and quasi-judicial bodies, questions of law and questions of fact[1] are often differentiated.[2] This bifurcation is important, for example, in case of an appeal. Before superior and supranational judicial instances, questions of fact generally recede into the background, whereas questions of

* Alexandra Molitorisová is Faculty member at Faculty of Law, University of Bayreuth, Bayreuth, Germany. Corresponding Author: alex.molitorisova@gmail.com

** Ciarán Burke is Professor and Senior Research Fellow at the Jena Center for Reconciliation Studies at the Friedrich Schiller University, Jena, Germany. Corresponding Author: ciaran.burke@eui.eu

1 For example, the WTO Appellate Body clarified the distinction between questions of law versus questions of fact in Appellate Body Report, *EC Measures Concerning Meat and Meat Products (Hormones)*, WT/DS26/AB/R, WT/DS48/AB/R, adopted 13 February 1998, DSR 1998: I, 135: "Appellate review is limited to appeals on questions of law covered in a panel report and legal interpretations developed by the panel. Findings of fact, as distinguished from legal interpretations or legal conclusions, by a panel are, in principle not subject to review by the Appellate Body. The determination of whether or not a certain event did occur in time and space is typically a question of fact. . . . Determination of the credibility and weight properly to be ascribed to . . . a given piece of evidence is part and parcel of the fact finding process and is, in principle, left to the discretion of a panel as the trier of facts. The consistency or inconsistency of a given fact or set of facts with the requirements of a given treaty provision is, however, a legal characterisation issue. It is a legal question." However, it is not always easy to distinguish the two types of questions, and in some cases, even the Appellate Body challenged some of the panel's factual findings. See, for example, *European Communities – Measures Affecting Asbestos and Asbestos-Containing Products*, WT/DS135/AB/R, Appellate Body Report, DSR 2001: VII, 3243. If questions of fact are to be brought into the scope of appellate review, it is required that they are challenged under Article 11 of the Dispute Settlement Understanding relating to the function of Panels. See Michelle T. Grando, Evidence, Proof and Fact-Finding in WTO Dispute Settlement 59, 65 (Oxford University Press 2009).

2 Arguably, such divide can be characterized as porous, "slippery," or "elusive," as the US Supreme Court pronounced, and some scholars would say that any attempt to distinguish the two questions is doomed to fail from the start. See Ronald J. Allen & Michael S. Pardo, *The Myth of the Law-Fact Distinction*, 97 Northwestern University Law Review 1769, 1770 (2003). The authors of this chapter agree that there are line-drawing problems with the distinction between law and fact. However, attempting to classify issues in a case as either fact or law may help fine-tune the standard of review.

DOI: 10.4324/9781003472421-10

law dictate judicial decisions, since the scope of review of factual findings of lower courts may be limited.[3] As such, differentiation between questions of law and questions of fact often entails an effective division of competences between courts of fact and law (usually lower courts) and courts of law alone (usually superior – appellate or cassation courts).[4] Such a differentiation appears logical, as the lower courts are closer to the fact-finding process in terms of time and physical distance.[5] The dividing lines between questions of law and questions of fact are, of course, not uniform and may depend to a large degree on the context of a case.[6] In particular, the boundaries are often fluid in the adjudication of matters involving scientific evidence.[7] Such matters muddle questions of law and questions of fact, especially before international instances, in deciding "what happened," "what is likely to happen," "what was foreseeable," and "what would have happened had things gone differently."[8]

Perhaps no other international judiciary is entangled in the differentiation of various questions of law and fact more deeply than the European Court of Justice (ECJ), given its unique brand of reasoning in terms of method and legitimacy.[9] Before the ECJ, questions of law and fact arise in a variety of

3 See James G. Devaney, *The Law and Practice of Fact-Finding before the International Court of Justice,* 20 (PhD thesis, European University Institute 2014). Of course, such description is not without a reservation. For example, before the European Court of Human Rights, both questions of law and questions of fact are relevant, albeit subject to restraint, when the court approaches political dimensions of a case. See Giacinto della Cananea, *Judicial Review of Administrative Action in Italy: Beyond Deference? in* Deference to the Administration in Judicial Review: Comparative Perspectives 290 (Guobin Zhu (ed.), Springer 2019). Before the Court of Justice of the European Union, the division depends on the nature of the proceedings. For example, in the preliminary ruling proceedings, national courts have a monopoly over questions of fact. See Damien Chalmers, Gareth Davis & Giorgio Monti, European Union Law 159 (CUP 2019).

4 See for example, Thomas W. Merrill, *Article III, Agency Adjudication, and the Origins of the Appellate Review Model of Administrative Law*, 111(5) Columbia Law Review 940 (2011).

5 cf Devaney, *supra* note 3, at 44.

6 See for example, Warner H. Randall, *All Mixed Up About Mixed Questions*, 7 The Journal of Appellate Practice and Process 101, 102 (2005) and Twinning William, *Narrative and Generalizations in Argumentation about Questions of Fact*, 40 South Texas Law Review 351 (1999).

7 See Caroline Foster, Science and the Precautionary Principle in International Courts and Tribunals: Expert Evidence, Burden of Proof and Finality 78 (Cambridge University Press 2011). In this chapter, scientific evidence is a reference to scientific literature, studies, raw scientific data, official statistics, as well as various reports of national and international institutions and bodies touching upon different scientific fields. This definition is one suggested by the authors of this chapter.

8 Chief Justice Robert French, Judging Science, *The 13th Greek-Australian International Legal and Medical Conference* (May 2011) <https://www.hcourt.gov.au/assets/publications/speeches/current-justices/frenchcj/frenchcj30may11.pdf>.

9 See Michal Bobek, *Legal Reasoning of the Court of Justice of the EU*, 39 European Law Review 579–581 (2014); ACTIONES, *Handbook on the Techniques of Judicial Interactions in the Application of the EU Charter*, Module 6 – Judicial Dialogue Furthering the Application of the EU Charter in Criminal Law, <www.eui.eu/Projects/CentreForJudicialCooperation/Documents/Module-7.pdf>.

contexts: in the review of legality of European Union (EU) acts (annulment), in the preliminary ruling procedure, during the infringement procedure, or in appeal against a decision of the General Court.[10] Moreover, they arise in the context of various subject matters: public health, environment, product liability, transport operator liability, food law, or more generally, risk regulation,[11] and further in the context of competition law,[12] discrimination,[13] or human rights under the EU Charter.[14] In addition, the ECJ, as the authoritative interpreter of EU law, utilizes a variety of specific legal tests, analytical tools, principles, and rules.[15] Such mixing of questions of fact and law is palpable, for example, in the case of the proportionality analysis, the assessment of reasonableness or appropriateness of a contested measure, in risk assessment, or in the application of the precautionary principle.[16] In this *sui generis* setting, there is an entire matrix of possibilities where scientific evidence may play a part.

Adducing and admitting scientific evidence create a special tension between questions of law and questions of fact for courts such as the ECJ, which may, depending on the type of proceedings, exercise only a limited review of the evidence.[17] This limitation, however, does not affect the Court's ability to subject a contested act of rigorous scrutiny and consider any evidence adduced.[18] For example, on the basis of scientific evidence, the Court may draw inferences from that evidence, which is considered a question of law.[19] However, it must

10 Articles 263–269 TFEU. In this chapter, we are not concerned with disputes between the EU and its servants pursuant to Article 270 TFEU.

11 See, for example, Case C-393/01 *France v Commission* [2003] ECR I-05405, Opinion of AG Mischo, concerning emergency measures to combat bovine spongiform encephalopathy.

12 Koen Lenaerts, *Some Thoughts on Evidence and Procedure in European Community Competition Law*, 30 Fordham International Law Journal 1463 (2006).

13 Consider direct and factual discrimination. See Case C-170/84 *Bilka – Kaufhaus GmbH v Karin Weber von Hartz* [1986] ECR 01607.

14 This is just an illustrative list. As for a case concerning the EU Charter of Fundamental Rights, see, for example, Case C-473/16 *F v Bevándorlási és Állampolgársági Hivatal* [2018] ECR I-36.

15 Benedikt Pirker, Proportionality Analysis and Models of Judicial Review: A Theoretical and Comparative Study 235–278 (Europa Law Publishing 2013).

16 See Hans-Peter Nehl, *Judicial Review of Complex Socio-Economic, Technical and Scientific Assessments in the European Union, in* EU Executive Discretion and the Limits of Law 177 (Joana Mendes (ed.), Oxford University Press 2019).

17 See, for example, Joined Cases C-211/03 *HLH Warenvertriebs GmbH and* C-299/03 and C-316/03 to C-318/03 *Orthica BV v Bundesrepublik Deutschland* [2005] ECR I-05141. See also Koen Lenaerts, Ignace Maselis & Kathleen Gutman, EU Procedural Law 392–393 (Oxford University Press 2014).

18 Case C-101/12 *Herbert Schaible v Land Baden-Württemberg* ECLI:EU:C:2013:334, Opinion of AG Wahl, para 38, referring to Case C-59/11 *Association Kokopelli v Graines Baumaux SAS* ECLI:EU:C:2012:28, Opinion of AG Kokott.

19 See Case C-128/15 *Spain v Council* ECLI:EU:C:2016:585, Opinion of AG Saugmandsgaard Øe, paras 86–87, where he states that interpretation of data is a matter of the exercise of the decision-maker's discretion. The decision-maker may not completely ignore the relevant data but may disregard those which he suspects to be erroneous and fraudulent.

also decide whether that evidence ought to be sufficient to establish a particular fact, which is inherently a question of fact.[20] Similarly, the Court must be able to establish whether a particular factor was taken into consideration by a decision-maker, which constitutes a question of fact, and must be able to decide how much discretion the decision-maker should be afforded, that is, a question of law. The understanding as to how the Court deals with scientific evidence, that is, how it adduces it, analyzes it, admits it to the procedure, and uses it to answer some questions of law or fact, may in turn help one to appreciate the Court's legal production and reasoning as well as improve overall understanding of EU law.

To maintain its mission, the Court is supported by independent advisors – advocates general (AGs) – who often assist in complex cases[21] and propose a possible legal solution.[22] Only where it considers that the case raises no new point of law, for example, where the Court may easily draw on its previous case law,[23] may the Court decide, after hearing from the AGs, that the case should be determined without a submission from the AGs.[24] A good deal of scholarship has been devoted to the added value of AGs in particular fields, such as comparativism[25] or human rights adjudication.[26] It notes that AGs' opinions resemble the Court's judgements, and that they are cited as persuasive authority by litigants.[27] Leading scholars further observe that AGs' opinions set out facts in greater detail than corresponding judgements, cite sources not cited in those judgements, and raise issues beyond the pleadings of parties.[28] They note that even though AGs' opinions may not be ultimately followed by the Court, they have nonetheless helped greatly in the creation of a distinct and

20 See, for example, the Hon Justice Margaret Joan Beazley AO, The Distinction between Questions of Fact and Law: A Question Without Answer? *The Land and Environment Court Conference* (May2013),<https://supremecourt.nsw.gov.au/documents/Publications/Speeches/Pre-2015-Speeches/Bergin/Beazley_20130524.pdf>.

21 AG's advice is used in less than half of the cases before the Court. See Message de M. Wahl, 6 February 2019 <curia.europa.eu/jcms/jcms/p1_1630353/en>.

22 There are eight of them, each appointed for six years. See Article 252 TFEU.

23 Koen Lenaerts, *EU Citizenship and the European Court of Justice's 'Stone-by-Stone' Approach*, 1 International Comparative Jurisprudence 7 (2015), citing Case C-87/12 *Kreshnik Ymeraga and Others v Ministre du Travail, de l'Emploi et de l'Immigration*, ECLI:EU:C:2013:291.

24 Article 20 of the Statute of the Court of Justice of the European Union.

25 L. Faircloth Peoples, *The Use of Foreign Law by the Advocates General of the Court of Justice of the European Communities*, 35 Syracuse Journal of International Law and Commerce 2 (2008).

26 Gráinne de Búrca, *After the EU Charter of Fundamental Rights: The Court of Justice as a Human Rights Adjudicator*? 20(2) *Maastricht Journal of European and Comparative Law* 168–184 (2013).

27 Cyril Ritter, *A New Look at the Role and Impact of Advocates-General – Collectively and Individually*, 12 Columbia Journal of European Law 758 (2005–2006).

28 *Id.* at 758–759.

identifiable body of EU law.[29] In this manner, AGs' influence on ideas generated within the Court is undeniable.[30]

However, no scholarly contribution has yet attempted to treat AGs' work with evidence, proof, and fact-finding. It may be asked: What is the value of AGs to the Court when dealing with borderline and mixed questions of law and fact, if they are employed only if cases raise new points of law? And how do AGs work with evidentiary matters that implicate both questions of law and fact? Since AGs are summoned to offer opinions concerning complex questions of law that often require advice or preliminary assessment,[31] it is possible to hypothesize that AGs will advance new approaches to the fact/law frontier in EU law. Even if not followed, AGs' reasoning pertaining to scientific evidence may reveal the advantages and disadvantages of a particular approach to evidentiary scrutiny. It is thus possible to inquire whether AGs may enjoy special influence on the creation of rules governing the examination of scientific evidence.[32]

In this area, we are interested in understanding of this added value of AGs in scrutinizing complex evidentiary issues that occur at the intersection of (new) questions of law and fact. We are interested in providing critical reflections concerning the analytical apparatus AGs utilize to examine scientific evidence, while taking into account the nature of cases presented to the Court and the AGs' role within the Court. ECJ cases provide abundant possibilities for analyzing the preceding lines of inquiry and create enormous space for empirical research.[33] Focusing on cases in which AGs delivered an opinion creates a subset of ECJ cases of a certain legal importance that is practicable in size, if time-bound, allowing for a detailed qualitative examination of the process of fact-finding and treatment of proof and evidence. The body of cases mentioned further in this chapter was selected on the basis of textual research of the Court's database, which identified opinions that made references

29 Laura Clément-Wilz, *The Advocate General: A Key Actor of the Court of Justice of the European Union*, *in* Cambridge Yearbook of European Legal Studies, vol. 14, 2011–2012 588 (Catherine Barnard, Markus Gehring & Iuiola Solanke (eds.), Hart Publishing 2012).

30 *Ibid*. Clément-Wilz recalls Case C-6/54, *Netherlands v High Authority of the European Coal and Steel Community* [1954–1956] ECR 00103, Opinion of AG Roeme, and Case C-8/55 *Fédération Charbonnière de Belgique v High Authority of the European Coal and Steel Community* [1954–1956] ECR 00245, Opinion of AG Lagrange.

31 As Bobek noted: "Everybody values extra help in complex and novel cases." See Michal Bobek, *A Fourth in the Court: Why Are There Advocates General in the Court of Justice?*, *in* Cambridge Yearbook of European Legal Studies Vol. 14, 2011–2012 535 (Catherine Barnard, Markus Gehring & Iuiola Solanke (eds.), Hart Publishing 2012).

32 See Mel Marquis, *Rules That Govern Rules: Evidence, Proof and Judicial Control in Competition Cases*, *in* European Competition Law Annual 2009: The Evaluation of Evidence and Its Judicial Review in Competition Cases 15–92 (Claus-Dieter Ehlermann & Mel Marquis Mel (eds.), Hart Publishing 2009).

33 See Urška Šadl & Suvi Sankari, *The Elusive Influence of the Advocate General on the Court of Justice: The Case of European Citizenship*, 36(1) Yearbook of European Law 421–441 (2017).

to scientific evidence.[34] In that manner, we analyzed opinions of AGs Bobek (CZ), Bot (FR), Cruz Villalon (SP), Fennelly (IE), Jääskinen (FIN), Geelhoed (NL), Kokott (DE), Maduro (PT), Mengozzi (IT), Mischo (LUX), Saugmandsgaard Øe (DN), Sharpston (UK), Wahl (SWE), and Wathelet (BE).

In order to undertake a workable case law analysis, we proceed with a formulation of an analytical framework. We present the framework in Section 2 of this chapter. On the basis of this framework, we continue with the relevant case law analysis in Section 3. The purpose of creating an analytical framework is not only to assess individual cases in isolation but also to observe common trends and features between the cases examined. The case law analysis enables us to assess the implications of a broader context of fact-finding and evidentiary reasoning before the Court. This is discussed in Section 3. This analytical framework could also be understood as a novel manner of determining the scope of review. Its novelty reposes in the determination of the scope of review as an interchange between questions of law and questions of fact, which depend on the evidentiary material presented to or found by the Court.

2 Creating a Framework for Evidentiary Case Law Analysis

Our analytical framework for the assessment of AGs' opinions reposes upon four reflections. Although the first two reflections may not seem specifically related to evidence, but rather to broader institutional and individual considerations, it is important to include them, because in systems without clearly delimited evidentiary rules, evidentiary work should be studied in conjunction with the institutional setting, procedural rules, as well as personal commitment of the fact-finder.[35] This is often the case of the international judiciary.[36]

The first consideration relates to the general role of AGs in the ECJ as advisors of special utility.[37] This utility does not lie in influence measurable by

34 See Foster, *supra* note 7. We searched through the curia.europa.eu search engine. We limited our analysis to the opinions issued between 1/1/2000 and 5/5/2019. We searched the expressions "scientific literature," which rendered 12 results; "scientific data," which rendered 64 results; "scientific study," which rendered 14 results; and "scientific evidence," which rendered 81 results. References to legal academic literature were not considered. We then focused on the analysis of opinions of those AGs whose opinions appeared in the search results at least five times. If two AGs from the same member state were to be included in the analysis, we gave preference to those who work with scientific evidence more frequently and those who were more recently working at the Court. We then look more deeply in the work of the selected AGs and search through their opinions, particularly focusing on references in their opinions that could reveal specific independent work with scientific evidence.

35 See Hock Lai Ho, A Philosophy of Evidence Law: Justice in the Search for Truth 248–262 (Oxford University Press 2008) on fact-finders asserting epistemic autonomy and critical judgement.

36 cf Devaney, *supra* note 3, at 27–67.

37 About the historical background to the creation of the position of AGs at the Court, see Ami Barav, *Le commissaire du gouvernement près le Conseil d'État français et l'avocat général près la Cour de justice des Communautés européennes*, 26 Revue internationale de droit comparé 809

a single indicator (such as the number of cases in which AGs' opinions were followed) but in the fact that AGs deliver a profound analysis on the basis of the applicable legal sources (regulations, national laws, case law, international treaties and law) – an individual reasoned submission in open court[38] that has a potential qualitative impact on the Court's case law.[39] This may be reflected in the number of references to AGs' opinions in the Court's judgements or their reception in academic circles.[40] However, further "measures" of influence are possible. For example, AG Wahl reasoned that even where the Court did not accept the AG's proposal, hopefully, the opinion prompted reflection and criticism and, in that sense, was useful.[41] Per AG Wahl, the opinions' added value is to provide a context to the solution to a legal problem, that is, to connect the factual circumstances of the case to previous case law.[42] AGs, however, not only apply the law to facts but also provide information concerning the "advantages and disadvantages of a proposed [or alternative] solution," of a legal and possibly economic nature.[43] As such, in evidentiary matters, the Court may contemplate points related to evidence raised by AGs.

The second reflection involves the understanding of AGs as unique deliberators whose education, personal experiences, legal traditions, and reasoning affect their individual analyses, not as a "collective" or "collegial" adjudicator or as a group of advisors classed according to their "generation."[44] AGs are chosen "from persons whose independence is beyond doubt and who possess the qualifications required for appointment to the highest judicial offices in their respective countries or who are juriconsults of recognised competence."[45] Therefore, emphasis must be afforded to the individualized manner in which AGs approach evidentiary matters. The selected AGs represent a variety of professional backgrounds spreading from public service to private practice, to education, and to the judiciary. Three AGs served prior to their appointments as judges of the ECJ (AG Mengozzi, AG Wathelet, and AG Wahl). One was

(1974). About the clarification of their role vis-à-vis the historical origins see Case C-17/98 *Emesa Sugar (Free Zone) NV v Aruba* [2000] ECR I-00675.

38 Article 252 TFEU.

39 See Carlos Arrebola, Ana Júlia Maurício & Héctor Jiménez Portilla, *An Econometric Analysis of the Influence of the Advocate General on the Court of Justice of the European Union*, 5(1) Cambridge Journal of International and Comparative Law 82–112 (2016). See also Adam Lazowski, *Advocates General and Grand Chamber Cases: Assistance with the Touch of Substitution*, 14 Cambridge Yearbook of European Legal Studies 635 (2012).

40 See Wahl, *supra* note 21. See also Ritter, *supra* note 27.

41 See Wahl, *supra* note 21.

42 See Wahl, *supra* note 21. See also Ritter, *supra* note 27, at 764.

43 See Wahl, *supra* note 21. See also Šadl & Sankari, *supra* note 33, at 426 suggesting that "AG influence is most often implicit, and manifested in the Court's reasoning, interpretation, outcome, and the choice of law and legal sources (precedent) in the same case, as well as in subsequent related cases."

44 Sionaidh Douglas-Scott, Constitutional Law of the European Union 203 (Pearson Education Limited 2002).

45 Article 253 TFEU.

appointed AG twice (AG Mischo). Three occupied the highest posts in national judiciary (AG Fennelly, AG Jääskinen, and AG Cruz Villalon). One held other posts in national judiciary (AG Bot). Some had a purely academic background (AG Kokott and AG Maduro). Some occupied high political functions (AG Wathelet, AG Saugmandsgaard Øe, and AG Geelhoed). AG Bobek and AG Sharpston have backgrounds in research, education, and legal practice that one may characterize as mixed. Although career background has been cited as a strong factor affecting the influence rate of AGs on the Court, we are rather wary of research that correlates measurements of certain criteria of influence with the AG's background.[46] What is perhaps more interesting from the perspective of evidentiary work is that 8 out of 14 AGs examined have some kind of educational background in common-law jurisdictions.[47] This may have proven beneficial, since common-law jurisdictions are known for developing specialism in law of evidence as a discrete body of law and practice.[48] Three of the remaining six likely had direct extensive experience with fact-finding at the level of lower judiciary or the General Court.[49] The second reflection may be understood as contextual information to the research that evidentiary reasoning at the EU level is not unique to juriconsults of a certain professional background, nationality, gender, or age.

The third line of reflection relates to the procedural rules of the Court devoted to evidentiary matters and to the role that AGs play in these matters. Evidence may be presented in written format (applications, statements of case, defences and observations, replies, and all supporting papers and documents) as well as in the oral part of the procedure before the Court (via witnesses and experts). Moreover, the Court may require the parties, the member states (MS), and the institutions, bodies, offices, and agencies to produce all documents and to supply all information that the Court considers desirable or necessary for the proceedings.[50] The Court may also, after hearing the AG, prescribe the measures of inquiry that it considers appropriate, setting out the facts to be proved.[51] AGs take part in the measures of inquiry,[52] and they may take the lead in the examination of experts who have submitted reports to the Court. AGs may, however, not object that an individual is not competent

46 Šadl & Sankari, *supra* note 33, at 433.

47 AGs Bobek, Fennelly, Sharston, Mischo, Kokott, Mengozzi and Wathelet.

48 See John Jackson & Paul Robert, *Beyond Common Law Evidence: Reimagining, and Reinvigorating, Evidence Law as Forensic Science*, *in* The Oxford Handbook of Criminal Processes (Darryl K. Brown, Jenia Iontcheva Turner & Bettina Weisse (eds.), Oxford University Press 2019).

49 AGs Bot, Jäaskinen and Wahl.

50 Article 61–62 of the Rules of Procedure.

51 *Id.* at Article 63. The following measures of inquiry may be adopted: a request for information and production of documents, the commissioning of an expert's report, an inspection of the place or thing in question.

52 *Id.* at Article 65(2).

to act as an expert.[53] No official statistics on the use of measures of inquiry, by the Court itself or AGs, are available, though some authors note that the Court's annual reports mention that the General Court make "avid use" of them.[54] Some other authors are, however, more pessimistic about the number of experts' reports commissioned.[55]

In the context of the preliminary ruling procedure, AGs may also request the parties or other persons to submit all such information relating to the facts, and all such documents or other particular, as they may consider relevant, and send them questions to be answered at the hearing.[56] This competence mirrors that of the judge-rapporteur. After hearing only the AGs, in the procedure concerning references for a preliminary ruling, clarifications from the referring court or tribunal are also sought.[57] After hearing the AGs, the Court may also re-open the oral part of the procedure, in particular if it considers that it lacks sufficient information or where a party presents a new fact that could be potentially decisive.[58] In the re-opened procedure, parties can make additional written submissions, additional measures of inquiry may be ordered, and AGs may deliver a supplementary opinion.[59] From a procedural perspective, given their wide range of competencies under the Rule of Procedures, the importance of the AGs' role in matters of evidence is undisputable.

The fourth reflection generally relates to considerations that must be taken into account by the Court when dealing with evidence. First, it is important to note that the Court's scope of review varies depending on the type of proceedings in question: it defers matters of fact to a national court in cases involving the preliminary ruling procedure; however, in cases of the infringement procedure or the review of legality, the Court must establish the factual accuracy, reliability, and consistency of any evidence and must verify whether the evidence contains all information necessary for the assessment of a complex situation.[60]

53 *Id.* at Article 72.

54 Niamh Nic Nic Shuibhne & Marsela Maci, *Proving Public Interest: The Growing Impact of Evidence in Free Movement Case Law*, 50(4) Common Market Law Review 975 (2013).

55 See Eric Barbier de la Serra & Anne-Lise Sibony, *Expert Evidence before the EC Courts*, 45 Common Market Law Review 943 (2008).

56 Rules of Procedure, *supra* note 50, at Article 62. For example, the Court, after hearing AG Reischl, requested the parties to reply to certain questions and gave each of them the opportunity of putting forward observations on those replies. See Case C-85/76, *Hoffmann-La Roche & Co. AG v Commission* [1979] ECR 00461.

57 Rules of Procedure, *supra* note 50, at Article 101.

58 There are numerous cases that can be cited as examples in which the Court ordered to re-open the procedure, such as in C-262/10 *Döhler Neuenkrichen*, ECLI:EU:C:2012:559. In contrast, in *Wouters*, the Court refused to re-open the oral procedure as it considered to be in possession of all the relevant facts (Case C-309/99 *Wouters and Others* [2002] ECR I-01577). As cited in Lenaerts, Maselis & Gutman, *supra* note 17, at 777.

59 Lenaerts, Maselis & Gutman, *supra* note 17, at 777. See, for example, Case C-2/90 *Commission v Belgium* [1992] ECR I-04431.

60 See, for example, Case C-12/03 P *Commission v Tetra Laval BV* [2005] ECR I-00987, para 39.

Also, in appeals from the General Court, the Court may exercise review of evidentiary matters, though this is limited to the cases where it determines that there have been substantive inaccuracies in the General Court's findings.[61] The breadth of the Court's review also depends upon whether it affords wide discretion to a decision-maker under scrutiny. It can be that the Court scrutinizes a measure in a substantive fashion, meaning, the Court evaluates the content of the measure on the basis of technical and scientific merits.[62] Or it may be that the Court merely verifies the decision-maker's compliance with special duties to apply the principles of excellence, independence, and transparency to complex assessments.[63]

The Court has also developed some evidentiary standards in its case law,[64] one of which states that mere generalization does not constitute evidence[65] or that a causal link may be established by "serious, specific and consistent" evidence.[66] Furthermore, certain evidentiary requirements may be formulated directly by EU acts and therefore shape analytical approaches to evidence.[67] Evidentiary requirements contained in EU acts may be further refined in the Court's case law.[68] Moreover, it is possible that a description of certain factual

61 See, for example, Case C-433/10 P, *Volker Mauerhofer v Commission* [2011] ECR I-00048. Also, in 2019, the Court also adopted new rules on whether or not to allow appeals from the General Court (Chapter 1a of Title V of the Rules of Procedure).

62 cf Eric A. Posner & Jacob Gesner, *Timing Rules and Legal Institutions*, 121(2) Harvard Law Review 573 (2007).

63 See Paul Craig, EU Administrative Law 648 (Oxford University Press 2012).

64 *Evidentiary standards* refer to different standards of proof, that is, how much and what quality of evidence is required to prove a fact. See, for example, Matthias Oesch, Standards of Review in WTO Dispute Resolution 167–168 (Oxford University Press 2003).

65 Case C-388/07 *The Incorporated Trustees of the National Council for Ageing (Age Concern England) v Secretary of State for Business, Enterprise and Regulatory Reform*, [2009] I-01569.

66 Case C-621/15 *N. W and Others v Sanofi Pasteur MSD SNC and Others* ECLI:EU:C:2017:484, para 37.

67 *Evidentiary requirements* refer to rules that govern the type of evidence (such as expert evidence, documentary evidence) or types of facts (such as considering economic requirements or specific scientific evidence, such as ornithological criteria) that need to be proved in a case. See, for example, Case C-635/17, *E. v Staatssecretaris van Veiligheid en Justitieon* ECLI:EU:C:2018:973, Opinion of AG Wahl, paras 57–67, the duty to provide a plausible explanation for the lack of official evidence or the family relationship. Other evidentiary requirements follow from the discretionary powers afforded to a decision-maker who is called upon to establish the existence of certain conditions (e.g. abnormally low). See Herwig H. C. Hofmann, *The Interdependencies between Delegation, Discretion and Duty of Care*, *in* EU Executive Discretion and the Limits of Law 220–238 (Joana Mendes (ed.), Oxford University Press 2019).

68 For example, as regards requirements to be taken into account by assessments under the Habitats Directive. Such assessments must contain "complete, precise and definitive findings capable of removing all reasonable scientific doubt as to the effects of the works proposes on the protected site." See Case C-461/17, *Brian Holohan and Others v An Bord Pleanála* ECLI:EU:C:2018:649, Opinion of AG Kokott, para 29.

situations may be contained in the recitals of EU acts[69] and would need to be accounted for in the interpretation of those acts.[70] It is also possible that factors that may be taken into consideration are expressly listed in EU acts or may be inferred from the acts' objectives.[71] In certain instances, EU measures do not precisely specify the admissibility of, or the weight to be given to, evidence; however, national rules specifying these issues must not reverse the burden of proof.[72] Last but not the least, the Court, confronted with evidence, will often consider certain EU legal principles which may, in their respective field of application, alter the Court's scope of review and reasoning. These legal principles are the principle of procedural autonomy of EU law[73] and the precautionary principle in cases that involve scientific uncertainty.[74]

3 Case Law Analysis

Taking evidence into account implies a certain method of thought. Building upon previous literature,[75] the chapter distinguishes two main approaches to examining scientific evidence adopted by AGs that are here designated as "substantive" and "procedural" and a possible mixed approach. This is a proposed general theoretical division that can be applied to ECJ's judgements as well as decisions of other judicial bodies (the International Court of Justice, the World Trade Organisation Dispute Settlement Body, *etc.*).

In terms of the procedural approach, we searched for instances involving treating the quality of production of evidence, observing rules governing evidence generation, such as the requirements of expertise, democratic participation, peer review, consultations, the relationship with international research, but also compliance with the principles of scientific independence and transparency. The procedural approach can also involve inspecting the robustness of underlying data and the verification of methods used to produce evidence (such as

69 Recital 3 of Decision 2015/774 of the European Central Bank of 4 March 2015 on a secondary markets public sector asset purchase programme.

70 For example, Council Regulation (EC) No 21/2004 of 17 December 2003 establishing a system for the identification and registration of ovine and caprine animals was passed in the aftermath of the foot-and-mouth disease crisis of 2001, as is stated in its preamble, which explains its value in controlling the spread of infectious diseases among animals in cross-border trade.

71 Hofmann, *supra* note 67, at 220–238.

72 Case C-310/14 *Nike European Operations Netherlands* ECLI:EU:C:2015:690, para 43.

73 Lorna Woods, Philippa Watson & Marios Costa, Steiner & Woods EU Law 194–195 (13th ed., Oxford University Press 2017).

74 See Case C-331/88 *The Queen v Minister of Agriculture, Fisheries and Food and Secretary of State for Health* [1990] ECR I-04023. See also Case T-392/02 *Solvay Pharmaceuticals BV v Council* [2003] ECR II-04555.

75 Alberto Alemanno, *The Emergence of the Evidence-Based Judicial Reflex: A Response to Bar-Siman Tov's Semiprocedural Review*, 1(2) The Theory and Practice of Legislation 327–340 (2013). See also Patricia Popelier, *Preliminary Comments of the Role of Courts as Regulatory Watchdogs*, 6(3) Legisprudence 257–270 (2012).

economic tests).[76] The procedural approach is a method of analyzing scientific evidence by focusing on how it is produced.[77] It is based on ruling on deliberative values that are intrinsic to the proceduralization of the decision-making process.[78] In principle, the procedural approach is characterized by acceptance (not opposition) of findings and inferences that result from submitted evidence that followed from a certain system of "epistemic governance."[79] The procedural approach accepts the decision-making superiority of an executive/legislative body under scrutiny.[80] For procedural approaches, it is often characteristic that AGs espouse the facts put forward by parties in observations, either submitted in writing or by alternative means, noting only the manner in which certain conclusions were reached. In terms of the mixed approach, we considered AGs' work with *travaux préparatoires*, such as impact assessments, for the purposes of observing compliance with principles of good administration, as well as the examination of these assessments' conclusions. In terms of the substantive approach, we searched for examples of AGs substantially reviewing and drawing their own inferences from scientific evidence. We also searched for examples of how AGs engage with evidence adduced by parties to a dispute and included examples of opinions in which AGs undertook independent factual research or compared the opinions and conclusions of different experts and researchers, for example, by interpreting available scientific studies or statistics. We were also interested in opinions in which AGs recognized situations of scientific uncertainty. We also noted opinions in which scientific evidence aided interpretation of legislative notions. Finally, we included a selection of opinions that represented signature-like approaches to evidence.

The case law analysis that follows is divided into three parts corresponding to the approaches identified earlier.

3.1 A Procedural Approach

Procedural approaches may manifest themselves in several ways. Let us consider a couple of examples.

Procedural approaches place review of evidence in the context of good administration.[81] In *Nickel Institute*, AG Bot dealt with a question concerning

76 Bernard van de Walle de Ghelcke, *Economic Reasoning before the European Union Courts in Competition Law*, 44 Bruges European Economic Policy Briefings 1–30 (2018).

77 In a sense, this broadly corresponds to the so-called *Remia* formula. See Case C-42/84 *Remia BV and others v Commission* [1985] ECR 02545, para 34.

78 The procedural approach was first used in the review of legality of EU acts against the subsidiary principle. See also Popelier, *supra* note 75, at 266.

79 cf Marija Bartl, *Contesting Austerity: On the Limits of EU Knowledge Governance*, 44(1) Journal of Law and Society 164–165 (2017).

80 Popelier, *supra* note 75, at 266.

81 The right to good administration is embedded in Article 41 of the EU Charter. Per Hofmann, good administration entails several procedural rights, such as the right to a fair hearing, the right to a reasoned act, the right to defence, the right to effective judicial remedy, and

the classification of a dangerous substance (nickel) according to EU rules, where this classification depended on a chosen method. It was alleged that an incorrect method had been used, resulting in the substance being improperly classified as dangerous.[82] AG Bot was asked to consider whether the Commission had committed a manifest error of assessment or whether it had stepped outside the bounds of its discretion when deciding about the method. In his reasoning, AG Bot took notice of the process of legislating for the Directive on Dangerous Substances and specific studies describing in detail the discussions which led to the adoption of the contested method.[83] He noted that the Commission produced a study on the chosen method, the Organization for Economic Co-Operation and Development (OECD) made references to the method, and that the method was mentioned in further studies of legal commentators.[84] He further noted that "a broad range of scientific experts, meeting in working parties and committees, as well as representatives from the nickel sector . . . were brought together and assessed the issue."[85] According to AG Bot, this evidence suggested that the method had been scrutinized by experts.[86] In essence, AG Bot's approach compared the conclusion reached by the Commission to that of experts and paid close attention to the complex regulatory processes of adoption of the contested measure.

This can be considered a typified procedural approach to evidence. In addition, the case also provides a good example of how procedural approaches may help the Court arrive at a satisfactory answer, as far as the duty to state reasons as enshrined in Article 296(2) TFEU is concerned. As follows from the Court's case law, whether the duty was fulfilled must be assessed by referencing not only to the wording of the measure but also to its context, as well as the whole body of legal rules governing the matter in question.[87] Although

---

information rights (access to information, access to documents, access to the file). See Herwig Hofmann, *General Principles of EU law and Administrative Law*, *in* European Union Law 196–225 (C. Barnard & Steven Peers (eds.), Oxford University Press 2014). In another work, Hofmann and Mihaescu argue that the concept is still evolving and that "it is best understood as a framework concept on the basis of the rule of law and principles of procedural justice which draws together a range of rights, rules and principles guiding administrative procedures with the aim of ensuring procedural justice, public administrative adherence to the rule of law, and sound outcomes for administrative procedures." Herwig Hofmann & Bucura C. Mihaescu, *The Relation between the Charter's Fundamental Rights and the Unwritten General Principles of EU Law: Good Administration as the Test Case*, 9(1) European Constitutional Law Review 86 (2013).

82 Case C-14/10 *Nickel Institute v Secretary of State for Work and Pensions* [2011] ECR I-06609, Opinion of AG Bot. See also a similar Case C-15/10 *Étimine SA v Secretary of State for Work and Pensions* [2011] ECR I-06681, Opinion of AG Bot, paras 158–169.

83 *Id.* at *Nickel Institute*, Opinion of AG Bot, paras 59–77.

84 *Id.* at para 59. Some of these legal commentators were influential as they were also cited in the Commission's documents; see footnote 29 of the Opinion.

85 *Id.* at para 73.

86 *Id.* at para 71.

87 Case C-63/12 *Commission* v *Council* ECLI:EU:C:2013:752, para 99, and Case C-62/14 *Gauweiler and Others* ECLI:EU:C:2015:400, para 70.

the Court did not recognize a general right to participate in complex regulatory processes, AG Bot's observations revealed the importance of the participatory context in which the duty to state reasons had been fulfilled. This was employed in the Court's conclusions: "[A]s the Advocate General has observed . . . where the persons concerned are involved in the process by which a measure comes about, the requirement to state reasons may be circumscribed, since they acquire information through their involvement."[88]

Procedural approaches are used in contexts in which the Court has difficulties in monitoring highly technical and information-intensive activities.[89] In *Weiss and Others*,[90] AG Wathelet considered that the minutes of the European Central Bank (ECB) Governing Council's monetary policy meetings provided sufficient evidence of required standards of diligence (the duty of care).[91] On this point, AG Wathelet followed the Court's previous case, which stated that "in view of [European System of Central Banks (ESCB)]'s broad discretion, nothing more can be required of the ESCB apart from that it use its economic expertise and the necessary technical means at its disposal, to carry out [an] analysis with all care and accuracy."[92] Also in this case, AG Wathelet's observations and procedural approach were particularly important to the Court in order to answer the question as to whether the duty to state reasons had been satisfied by the decision-maker. AG Wathelet, like AG Bot, extensively observed the context in which the duty to state reasons materialized and pointed out that the successive ECB decisions had consistently been clarified by the publication of press releases, introductory statements by the president of the ECB at press conferences, accompanied by answers to the questions raised by the press, and by the accounts of the ECB Governing Council's monetary policy meetings, which outline the discussions within that body.[93] The Court reiterated these findings in its judgement[94] and concluded that all those various documents established that the ECB duly stated the reasons behind the contested measure.[95] To some authors, such reasoning signified difficulties with recognizing the politicization of the ECB mandate.[96]

88 Case C-14/10 *Nickel Institute v Secretary of State for Work and Pensions* [2011] ECR I-06609, para 100.
89 Hofmann, *supra* note 67.
90 Case C-493/17 *Heinrich Weiss and Others* ECLI:EU:C:2018:815, Opinion of AG Wathelet.
91 The duty of care was first explicitly identified as a principle of EU law in the opinion of AG van Gerven in 1991. Case C-16/90 *Detlef Nölle v Hauptzollamt Bremen-Freihafen* [1991] ECR I-05163, Opinion of AG van Gerven.
92 *Heinrich Weiss and Others*, Opinion of AG Wathelet, *supra* note 90, at para 152.
93 *Id.* at paras 133 to 138 and 144 to 148.
94 Case C-493/17 *Heinrich Weiss and Others* ECLI:EU:C:2018:1000, judgment of the Court (Grand Chamber) of 11 December 2018, paras 37–41.
95 *Id.* at paras 42–43.
96 See Pier Domenico Tortola, *The Politicization of the European Central Bank: What Is It, and How to Study It?*, 58(3) Journal of Common Law Market Studies 501–513 (2020).

Procedural approaches are importantly used in the proportionality analysis,[97] particularly in situations entailing broad deference.[98] In an annulment proceeding, AG Geelhoed dismissed the contention about the breach of the principle of proportionality by the EU legislature by observing that "the prohibition of animal testing for cosmetic products and ingredients represents a policy decision of considerable sensitivity which necessitate a delicate global analysis of the advantages and disadvantages" of the proposed system.[99] AG Geelhoed noted in particular that such analysis took place in lengthy and complex procedures that involved many meetings, consultations, and conciliation.[100]

Procedural approaches also play a pivotal role in reviewing risk assessments, since risk assessments are, by definition, the process-based multiple-step activities of a decision-maker, usually preceding a measure under review.[101] According to AG Bobek, a risk assessment is based on generally accepted scientific data.[102] However, the assessment is not about the details of bibliographies (citations) – it is about solid science demonstrating real risk.[103] It is about quality of data.[104] Procedural approaches often emphasize the latest scientific research. To AG Bobek, a full scientific risk assessment clearly implies up-to-date science.[105] International standards are valuable elements for assessments, as they are based on extensive professional debate and expertise.[106] However, the possibility of completely

97 As per AG Jääskinen, "the general principle of proportionality requires that measures adopted by [EU] institutions do not exceed the limits of what is appropriate and necessary in order to attain the legitimate objectives pursued by the legislation in question; when there is a choice between several appropriate measures, recourse must be had to the least onerous, and the disadvantages caused must not be disproportionate to the aims pursued." See Case C-77/09 *Gowan Comércio Internacional e Serviços Lda v Ministero della Salute* [2010] ECR I-13533, Opinion of AG Jääskinen, para 78.

98 Popelier, *supra* note 75, at 257.

99 Case C-244/03 *France v Parliament and Council* [2005] ECR I-04021, Opinion of AG Geelhoed, para 93.

100 *Id.* at paras 93 and 100.

101 To AG Jääskinen, risk assessments are pretty straightforward and objective exercises provided there is "an established and undisputed methodology" – if there is none, risk assessments entail discretion and choices. See *Gowan*, Opinion of AG Jääskinen, *supra* note 97, at para 71. AG Mischo cited numerous sources on risk analysis and its sub-parts – risk assessments and risk management in Case C-192/01 *Commission v Denmark* [2003] ECR I-09693, paras 89–97.

102 Case C-672/15 *Procureur de la République v Noria Distribution SARL* ECLI:EU:C:2016:961, Opinion of AG Bobek, para 85, as far as the application of Article 5 of Directive 2002/46/EC is concerned.

103 *Id.* at para 88.

104 This also follows from previous Court's case-law: Joint Cases C-387/15 and C-388/15 *Hilde Orleans and Others v Vlaams Gewest* ECLI:EU:C:2016:583, para 51 and the case-law cited.

105 *Noria Distribution*, Opinion of AG Bobek, *supra* note 102, at para 26.

106 Case C-190/16 *Werner Fries V Lufthansa CityLine GmbH* ECLI:EU:C:2017:225, Opinion of AG Bobek, para 56. Here, he relied on a previous of Case C-447/09 *Reinhard Prigge, Michael Fromm, Volker Lambach v Deutsche Lufthansa AG* ECLI:EU:C:2011:321, Opinion

national up-to-date research cannot be excluded, and even an international standard may be called into question by submitting strong evidence to the contrary.[107] In other words, public authorities cannot ignore relevant international opinions, but when they disagree, they must justify why they take a different approach.[108] Similar thoughts are echoed by other AGs. For AG Kokott, relying on previous case law,[109] risk must be plausible, assessed in line with the most reliable scientific data and the most recent results of international research.[110]

Procedural approaches do not review international scientific research substantively; they only ensure that it formed part of the basis for the decision-making under review. In so doing, they often emphasize a multiplicity of sources from which evidence may be drawn. In *Nickel Institute*, AG Bot admitted that the data required for nickel classification may be obtained from a variety of sources, including not only the results of previous tests, information taken from reference works, and the literature and information derived from practical experience but also the results of validated structure–activity relationships and expert judgements.[111]

Procedural approaches pay respect to the position of the decision-maker vis-à-vis the evidence production and its assessment. In *Commission v. Bulgaria*, AG Kokott submitted a recommendation in the case concerning avian protection areas, that decisions expressing the scientific opinion of national bodies "have great evidential value . . . since the authorities that adopt them are more familiar with the situation on the ground than the Commission or the Court."[112] Similarly, AG Wahl, in *Schaible*, was convinced that "when [the Commission] decided to adopt Regulation No 21/2004, the EU legislature was in a position to base its decision on a vast and detailed body of technical and scientific data."[113] In this case, with the help of AG Wahl's work, the Court was able to point to various studies carried out in the aftermath of the 2001 epizootic disease crisis.[114] All those studies supported a deeper revision of the regulatory framework on the identification and registration of ovine and caprine animals and the adoption of Regulation (EC) No 21/2004.[115] In

---

of AG Cruz Villalon, para 66: "The fact that international regulations such as JAR-FCL 1.060a lay down that age-limit as an absolute and general rule is of itself sufficient evidence that the requirements of this provision of the directive will be satisfied."

107 *Werner Fries*, Opinion of AG Bobek, *supra* note 106, at para 58.

108 *Id.* at para 83.

109 Already in Case C-304/84 *Criminal Proceedings against Claude Muller and Others* [1986] ECR 01511, para 24, the Court held that MS must provide some account of the results of international research when adopting food safety measures.

110 Case C-358/14 *Poland v Parliament and Council* ECLI:EU:C:2015:848, Opinion of AG Kokott, para 97.

111 *Nickel Institute*, Opinion of AG Bot, *supra* note 82, at para 55.

112 Case C-141/14 *Commission v Bulgaria* ECLI:EU:C:2015:528, Opinion of AG Kokott, para 29.

113 *Schaible*, Opinion of AG Wahl, *supra* note 18, at para 61.

114 Case C-101/12 *Herbert Schaible v Land Baden-Württemberg* ECLI:EU:C:2016:8, para 57.

115 *Ibid.*

this context, the Court established that the regulation contained obligations necessary to achieve its aims.[116]

Procedural approaches also pay respect to the requirements attached to the position of the decision-maker, such as the stated duty of care or the duty to give reasons. For AG Bobek, in complex scientific hazard assessments, it is expected that a diligent administrator first assembles all the available data and, on the basis of that data, opts for an appropriate method.[117] Hence, procedural approaches also help the Court ascertain whether the decision-makers followed the rules that they established for themselves, that is, whether they acted in non-arbitrary manner.[118] Finally, procedural approaches pay respect to the discretion of the decision-maker that deflects from the substantive examination of reasons behind decisions. This is usually the case where complex economic or socio-economic considerations must be taken into account.[119] This can mean that the standard of judicial review is reduced, and that the proportionality test is restricted. Arguably, the nature of this kind of judicial review is necessary for the Court to obey separation of powers and institutional equilibrium.[120] On the other hand, procedural engagement with evidence may lead to the overreliance of the evidence presented by parties and overlooking the problems with epistemic governance of the decision-maker.[121]

3.2 *Mixed Approaches – Impact Assessments*

In their evidentiary work, AGs often consider *travaux préparatoires*, including explanatory memoranda of measures under review,[122] or other preparatory

116 *Id.* at 57–58.

117 Case C-691/15 P *Commission v Bilbaína de Alquitranes, SA and others* ECLI:EU:C:2017:646, Opinion of AG Bobek, para 68.

118 Alberto Alemanno, *The Better Regulation Initiative at the Judicial Gate: A Trojan Horse within the Commission's Walls or the Way Forward?* European Law Journal 382–400 (2009).

119 Case C-380/03 *Germany v Parliament and Council* [2006] ECR I-11573, para 145. See also Hofmann, *supra* note 67. Several scholars, especially in competition law cases, hope for more economics- and econometric-based evidence. On this point, AG Kokott noted that "[t]here are mounting calls for European competition law to adopt a more economic approach. It is my view that, in its replies, the signal effect of which is likely to extend well beyond the present case, the Court should not allow itself to be influenced so much by current thinking ('Zeitgeist') or ephemeral trends" in Case C-23/14 *Post Danmark A/S v Konkurrencerådet* ECLI:EU:C:2015:343, Opinion of AG Kokott, para 4, See also Pavlina Hubková, *Economic Reasoning in the Court of Justice of the EU: A Study on the Use of Economics in Competition Case-Law* (LL.M. thesis, European University Institute 2014).

120 See Case C-244/03 *France v Parliament and Council* [2005] I-04021, Opinion of AG Geelhoed, para 91.

121 Bartl, *supra* note 79. See also Eva Thomann, Philipp Trein & Martino Maggetti, *What's the Problem? Multilevel Governance and Problem-Solving*, 5(1) European Policy Analysis 37–57 (2019).

122 Case C-528/13 *Geoffrey Léger v Ministre des Affaires sociales, de la Santé et des Droits des femmes and Etablissement français du sang*, Opinion of AG Mengozzi, para 31. See also

works of the EU legislature.[123] Impact assessments (IA) are one such tool, integrating transparency and rational decision-making and amounting to an "essential procedural requirement" within the meaning of Article 263(2) TFEU.[124] References to IA may be used in both substantive and procedural approaches to evidence, and AGs (as well as the Court) refer to IAs in a variety of contexts: to support interpretation of legislative intent, to document that the decision-maker stated reasons for its intervention, to interpret a legislative notion, or to provide context.[125]

For example, AG Wathelet in *T-Mobile Austria* supported his conclusions as to whether the Directive on Payment Services applied to credit transfers, that is, whether credit transfer was a recognized payment instrument by reference to the impact assessment.[126] He referred to the IA in support of particular propositions: that the practice of surcharging has often led to abusive pricing by certain merchants, and that surcharging was also used to generate higher income.[127] This served as a proof of what was happening on the market.

As it pertains to the duty to state reasons, AG Sharpston observed in *Spain v. Council* that, in the absence of an IA, certain choices by the Commission and the Council, such as setting a specific 65–35 per cent split between decoupled and coupled aid to the cotton sector, appeared arbitrary and were not convincingly justified.[128] In other words, in the absence of an IA, there was a lack of basis for the Court's conclusions and for the appropriate level of review. The Court built upon AG Sharpston's opinion and set out a shift towards a greater (substantive) scrutiny of basic facts behind reviewed measures.[129] The Court decided that the Council did not prove to the Court that it actually exercised its discretion when it fixed the new cotton support scheme, "involving the taking into consideration of all relevant factors and circumstances of the case."[130] The Court, therefore, could not ascertain whether the legislature exceeded the bounds of its broad discretion when reaching the specific aid split for

---

Lenaerts Koen & Gutiérrez-Fons José A, *To Say What the Law of the EU Is: Methods of Interpretation and the European Court of Justice*, EUI Working Papers AEL 2013/9 (2013).

123 See, for example, Case C-482/17 *Czech Republic v Parliament and Council of the European Union* ECLI:EU:C:2019:321, Opinion of AG Sharpston, para 100 concerning urgency to adopt a measure on control of the acquisition and possession of weapons. See also Case C-477/14 *Pillbox 38 (UK) Limited v The Secretary of State for Health* ECLI:EU:C:2015:854, Opinion of AG Kokott, para 174–177.

124 Alemanno, *supra* note 118, at 394.

125 See also Popelier, *supra* note 75, at 261, according to whom fact-finding through *travaux préparatoires* such as IAs may help assess the rationality behind the weighting of subsidiarity and economic efficiency.

126 Case C-616/11 *T-Mobile Austria GmbH v Verein für Konsumenteninformation* ECLI:EU:C:2013:691, Opinion of AG Wathelet, para 55.

127 *Id.* at paras 76 and 83.

128 Case C-310/04 *Spain v Council* [2006] ECR I-07285, Opinion of AG Sharpston, para 94.

129 Case C-310/04 *Spain v Council* [2006] ECR I-07285, paras 84 and 103. See below chapter III.C b).

130 *Id.* at para 122.

cotton.[131] On the other hand, in a case concerning scientific uncertainty, AG Kokott noted that although the IA contained useful evidence for potentially less strict alternatives than the measure considered, the IA was not binding upon the EU legislator.[132] The Court ultimately followed the AG's opinion.[133]

In *Luxembourg v. Parliament and Council*, AG Mengozzi, in assessing the proportionality of the measure to be annulled, merely considered that the applicant failed to maintain the burden of proof and did not furnish a proof that the legislative choice of the EU legislature involved was manifestly incorrect or inappropriate.[134] AG Mengozzi referred to earlier case law, which established that in the case of a proportionality analysis in a complex context, the Court cannot substitute its own assessment for that of the Community legislature.[135] For the Court, the IA was a proof of procedural character that the Commission studied various options, eliminated the most restrictive options, and adopted the option with a smaller financial impact.[136] Acting in accordance with the IA guidelines convinced the Court that the measure was proportional.[137] Rather than examining whether Luxembourg had adduced evidence of "manifest inappropriateness," the Court noted that Luxembourg did not propose any less-restrictive but equally effective measures, contradicting the IA, that would illustrate that the principle of proportionality had not been satisfied.[138]

131 *Id.* at paras 98, 117, 121–122, 124, 126, 128 and 131–135.

132 Case C-343/09 *Afton Chemical Limited v Secretary of State for Transport* [2010] ECR I-07027, Opinion of AG Kokott, paras 83–84.

133 Case C-343/09 *Afton Chemical Limited v Secretary of State for Transport* [2010] ECR I-07027, para 57.

134 Case C-176/09 *Luxembourg v Parliament and Council* [2011] ECR I-03727, Opinion of AG Mengozzi, paras 102–103. Compare this to a preliminary ruling procedure such as Case C-473/98 *Kemikalieinspektionen V Toolex Alpha AB* [2000] ECR I-05681, Opinion of AG Mischo, paras 85–88, where AG Mischo noted that the Commission was unable to produce any scientific evidence to contradict Swedish studies regarding the toxicity of trichlorethylene. Sweden asserted that toxicity limits were unknown, and the Commission did not provide evidence that Sweden could impose limit values on exposure to trichlorethylene. Therefore, that would not have been a satisfactory alternative to the prohibition on the use of the substance. Also, in an infringement procedure brought against Italy on the grounds of violating free movement of goods, AG Mischo pointed out that the only evidence that Italy adduced in the case as regards the public health justification of prohibition of drinks with a high level of caffeine was a decision of the national Board of Health, a decision with little relevance. See Case C-420/01 *Commission v Italy* [2003] ECR I-06445, Opinion of AG Mischo, paras 39–41.

135 *Id.* at *Luxembourg v Parliament and Council*, Opinion of AG Mengozzi, para 98.

136 Case C-176/09 *Luxembourg v Parliament and Council* [2011] ECR I-03727, para 65.

137 *Id.* at paras 69–71.

138 *Id.* at para 67. This can be contrasted with Case C-491/01 *The Queen v. Secretary of State for Health* [2002] ECR I-11453, Opinion of AG Geelhoed, concerning tobacco advertisements, para 249, where a broad measure of discretion by the Community legislature meant that the AG did not require a proof of the anticipated effect of Directive 2001/37/EC within the proportionality analysis, namely, a change in smoking habits.

IAs may also be used as proof of legislative intent, such as of the objective to be achieved by an adopted measure and certain factual circumstances surrounding the adoption of the measure.[139] AG Maduro referred to an IA for these purposes in *Vodafone*, and he cited that IA to support his conclusion regarding the existence of a market failure and appropriateness of the contested regulatory responses.[140] This case represented the first occasion on which the Court expressly relied on the IA.[141] The reference to the IA supported the conclusion as to the proportionality and to the necessity of the Roaming Regulation.[142] In *Swedish Match*, AG Saugmandsgaard Øe noted that the IA accompanying the adoption of Directive 2014/40 acknowledged that tobacco for oral use is less harmful than tobacco for smoking – a fact that was thus established as undisputed among parties.[143] The same IA also served as a proof of the fact that other possible measures would not achieve the health protection objective of the legislator.[144] In *Phillip Morris*, AG Kokott noted that the explanatory memorandum for the measure under review and "the comprehensive preparatory work by the Commission staff in connection with the impact assessment" documented the need for regulation/harmonization.[145]

3.3 *Substantive Approaches*

3.3.1 *Substantive Judicial Review*

Substantive approaches to evidence underpin a recent trend towards a more rationality-oriented substantive judicial review that is a response to

139 Nehl, *supra* note 16, at 160.

140 In Case C-58/08 *Vodafone Ltd and Others v Secretary of State for Business, Enterprise and Regulatory Reform* [2010] ECR I-04999, Opinion of AG Poiares Maduro, paras 30 et seq, the validity of Regulation (EC) No 717/2007 of the European Parliament and of the Council of 27 June 2007 on roaming on public mobile telephone networks within the Community and amending Directive 2002/21/EC was put into question as regards its proportionality, subsidiarity, and contribution to the improvement of conditions for the functioning of the internal market.

141 Case C-58/08 *The Queen, on the Application of Vodafone Ltd and Others v Secretary of State for Business, Enterprise and Regulatory Reform* [2010] ECR I-04999.

142 *Id.* at paras 55, 58 and 65.

143 Case C-151/17 *Swedish Match AB v Secretary of State for Health* ECLI:EU:C:2018:241, Opinion of AG Saugmandsgaard Øe, para 45.

144 *Id.* at para 83.

145 Case C-547/14 *Philip Morris Brands SARL and Others* ECLI:EU:C:2015:853, Opinion of AG Kokott, para 239 and 295. The case concerned the interpretation and validity of a number of provisions of Directive 2014/40/EU of the European Parliament and of the Council of 3 April 2014 on the approximation of the laws, regulations, and administrative provisions of the member states concerning the manufacture, presentation, and sale of tobacco and related products and repealing Directive 2001/37/EC as regards an adequate legal basis for the adoption of the Directive concerned and respecting of the principles of subsidiarity and proportionality.

evidence-based requirements imposed (or self-imposed) on decision-makers.[146] Substantive approaches presuppose that there is a clear basis for dissecting the decision-maker's assessments (measures).[147] In order to do so, it must be possible to identify whether the decision-maker assembled all available data, decided about its sufficiency, and opted for the chosen measure on the basis of that data.[148] This corresponds to the duty of care or good administration, that is, to take into consideration "all relevant factors and circumstances of the situation which the act intends to regulate."[149] Therefore, substantive approaches are particularly good in reviewing bound decisions that are limited to establishing whether certain facts or circumstances were present.[150]

Assessing the duty of care is a conceptual tool that we already described under procedural approaches to evidence earlier. It follows, however, that assessing the duty of care also represents the first parameter to be taken into consideration in order to assess any evidence substantively. Assessing the duty of care is a gateway to both approaches, since any legitimate standard of judicial review requires the establishment of facts that played a role in the decision-making process and in the exercise of discretion.[151] Broadly speaking, the duty of care assessment usually takes part under the heading "proportionality," or its sub-category, "necessity," but may also be conducted under other EU standards, such as "the principle of precaution" or "non-discrimination."[152] The intensity with which the courts review the compliance with the duty of care determines whether the decision-maker is afforded wide or narrow discretion.[153] The duty of care must therefore be assessed against factual questions, such as whether a specific piece of data, a report, or a finding is a relevant fact and gives rise to the obligation to take it into account, and whether that relevant fact has been taken into account. To Hofmann, "declaring most factors relevant as input to decision making to be included in the notion of fact and subject to review" represents an elegant way around the distinction between questions of law and questions of fact.[154]

In this regard, AGs provide the first signpost for the Court to recognize complex assessments of a scientific, including medical and technical, nature. They may help the Court in addressing the comprehensiveness of evidence,

146 Alemanno, *supra* note 75.
147 *Bilbaína*, Opinion of AG Bobek, *supra* note 117, at para 69.
148 This follows from the Court's judgment in *Tetra Laval*, *supra* note 60.
149 Case T-122/15 *Landeskreditbank Baden-Württemberg – Förderbank v European Central Bank* ECLI:EU:T:2017:337, paras 139 and 147.
150 Hofmann, *supra* note 67. See Joined Cases C-78/16 and C-79/16 *Giovanni Pesce and Others* ECLI:EU:C:2016:340, Opinion of AG Bot, paras 120–122.
151 Nehl, *supra* note 16, at 158.
152 See, for example, Case C-244/03, *France v Parliament and Council* [2005] ECR I-04021, Opinion of AG Geelhoed, paras 110–188.
153 Hofmann, *supra* note 67.
154 *Ibid.*

including situations in which certain factors or information are omitted from the analysis and in identifying specific evidentiary material necessary for the assessment.[155] In other words, the AGs' work may help the Court determine whether the EU legislature based its choice on objective criteria, taking into account all relevant facts and the technical and scientific data available at the time of adoption of the measure under review.[156] This type of assessment is now mandated by an established case.[157] Substantive approaches must, however, respect the EU's constitutional framework, which determines the scope of review of EU judiciary and the separation of powers: it is not accepted that the Court substitutes its assessment for the assessment of the decision-maker and undertakes a fresh iteration of the decision-making process.[158]

3.3.2 Scientific Uncertainty

Substantive approaches are used to identify scientific controversy or uncertainty. This often arises in the context of risk assessment and risk management and leads to the application of the precautionary principle and the principle of proportionality.[159] The importance of AGs' work in this area is illustrated by the fact that the first reference to the precautionary principle in the Court's case law was made by AG Cosmas in his opinion in *Diego Cali*.[160] In subsequent cases, AGs further contributed to the understanding of the principle.[161]

155 Such as calculating direct labour costs. See *Spain v. Council*, Opinion of AG Sharpston, *supra* note 128.

156 *Afton Chemical*, *supra* note 133, at para 34.

157 *Spain v Council*, *supra* note 129, at para 122.

158 Nehl, *supra* note 16, at 158.

159 According to Flückiger, the principle of proportionality has the final word on precautionary measures. Flückiger Alexander, *Case-Law Sources for Evaluating the Impact of Legislation: An Application of the Precautionary Principle to Fundamental Rights*, 2 The Theory and Practice of Legislation 1–15 (2016).

160 Case C-343/95 *Cali & Figli v SEPG* [1997] ECR I-01547, Opinion of AG Cosmas. The mention of the precautionary principle was based on the then Article 130r of the EC Treaty (Maastricht), which prescribed the Community policy on the environment be based on the precautionary principle and on principles that preventive action be taken. In the context of the case, AG Cosmas recognised prevention of pollution as a public authority activity. See José Luís Da Cruz Vilaça, EU Law and Integration: Twenty Years of Judicial Application of EU Law 328 (Hart Publishing 2014). This has been preceded by some more modest and timid pronouncements of the ECJ in *Mondiet* case concerning the validity of Council Regulation (EEC) 345/92 concerning the conservation of fishery resources. See Case C-405/92 *Etablissements Armand Mondiet SA v Armement Islais SARL* [1993] ECR I-06133.

161 Alberto Alemanno, *The Shaping of the Precautionary Principle by European Court. From Scientific Uncertainty to Legal Certainty*, *in* Valori Costituzionali e Nuove Politiche del Diritto: Scritti Raccolti del Decennale della Rivisat (Cuocolo Lorenzo & Lupária Luca (eds.), Halley Editrice 2007). See also Cruz Vilaça, *supra* note 160 citing Case C-184/97, *Commission v Germany* [1999] ECR I-07837, Opinion of AG Mischo; Case C-94/98, *Rhône-Poulenc Rore et al v Licensing Authority* [1999] ECR I-08789, Opinion of AG La Pergola, and Case C-318/98, *Criminal Proceedings against Giancarlo Fornasar et al.* [2000] ECR I-04785, Opinion of AG Cosmas. See also Case C-111/16, *Giorgio Fidenato and others*, Opinion of AG Bobek, para 31.

Uncertainty is identified on the basis of available scientific evidence. AG Geelhoed, in *W. Han*, noted that "the scientific reports make it abundantly clear that there is a lack of adequate and reliable data" and, hence, a lack of clarity regarding the acceptable limits for contamination with *Listeria monocytogenes*.[162] For AG Jäaskinen, the current state of scientific knowledge made it impossible to take a firm stance as to establishing certain facts.[163] For AG Bot, scientific uncertainty, that is, silence of science or its failure to provide proof, also constitutes objective information, which can form the basis of legal analysis.[164]

From the perspective of assessing the lawfulness of a measure which involves or has been preceded by a risk assessment, it is immaterial whether risks can be proven with sufficient accuracy, according to the current state of scientific research, because of "the insufficiency inconclusiveness or imprecision of the results of studies conducted."[165] For AG Fennelly, the fact that reputable scientific studies reached a contrary conclusion, and the legislator acted upon one set of such studies, does not mean that the legislator did not have reasonable grounds for acting.[166] Nor does the absence of "hard" scientific studies prevent the legislature from adopting a measure.[167] Moreover, AG Kokott regarded scientific uncertainty as a temporary state and reasoned that the appearance of new scientific evidence would oblige the decision-maker to rethink the rules.[168] This may, indeed, be mandated by the contested measure itself.[169]

162 Case C-121/00, *Criminal proceedings against W. Hahn* [2002] ECR I-09193, Opinion of AG Geelhoed, para 50.

163 In particular, regarding high blood pressure, whether or not a high consumption of sodium in either sodium bicarbonate or sodium chloride is more harmful. See Case C-157/14 *Neptune Distribution v Minister for Economic Affairs and Finance*, Opinion of AG Jäaskinen, para 49.

164 Case C-34/10 *Oliver Brüstle v Greenpeace eV*, Opinion of AG Bot, para 79.

165 See Case C-269/13 P. *Acino v Commissio* ECLI:EU:C:2014:255, para 58; Case C-157/14 *Neptune Distribution* ECLI:EU:C:2015:823, para 82; or Case C-477/14 *Pillbox 38 (UK) Limited v The Secretary of State for Health* ECLI:EU:C:2016:324, para 55. See also *Swedish Match*, Opinion of AGSaugmandsgaard Øe, *supra* note 143, at paras 52–53.

166 Cases C-376/98 *Germany v Parliament and Council* [2000] ECR I-08419 and C-74/99 *Imperial Tobacco and Others* [2000] ECR I-08599, Opinion of AG Fennelly, para 160 following the Court in Case C-180/96 *United Kingdom v Commission* [1998] ECR I-02265, para 99, where there is uncertainty as to the existence of risks to human health, the institutions may take protective measures without having to wait until the reality and seriousness of those risks become fully apparent.

167 *Id.* at para 160.

168 *Afton Chemical*, Opinion of AG Kokott, *supra* note 132, at para 97. One may compare it to the opinion of AG Tizzano, according to which "scientific progress is a continuous process and . . . the newness of [new scientific] evidence can therefore not be assessed on the basis of, so to speak, legalistic criteria as to the moment at which it was officially placed in the public domain or at which the evidence acquires a different relevance." Case C-512/99 *Germany v Commission* [2003] ECR I-00845, Opinion of AG Tizzano, para 78.

169 For example, the Directive containing rules on MMT (metallic additives in fuel) authorized the Commission to conduct an assessment of the risk, to develop a methodology, and

The evidence required to justify a particular measure depends on the claim.[170] It is the persuasiveness of the evidence that justifies protective measures without waiting for the scientific debate to be resolved to the satisfaction of all interested parties.[171] Such persuasive evidence could, for example, result from extensive research, conducted over a much longer period, or from decisive scientific advice directed to the decision-maker.[172] It is, however, possible to suggest that the legislature does not need to be completely consistent with the scientific advice.[173] In general, it is only important that the decision-maker show that the risk addressed by the measure is not purely hypothetical but can materialize,[174] and that the purpose is subject to a heavy burden of proof.[175] This means that for the Court, it is sufficient to identify studies pointing out in some (unqualified) way to the existence of risk. In this line, AG Saugmandsgaard Øe opined that it is for the legislature to evaluate the reliability and relevance of the available studies, to interpret the results, and to determine the relative weight to be assigned to each relevant study.[176] On the other hand, for AG Bot, it was sufficient that the relevant opinions of the European Food Safety Authority taken into account by the EU legislature showed "a significant correlation," thereby sufficiently substantiating potential risk in accordance with current scientific knowledge.[177]

Situations of scientific uncertainty, therefore, in their turn, prompt AGs to consider procedural approaches to evidence – that is, to treat the quality of evidence production (as opposed to the quality of evidence itself) and to verify

---

to report the conclusions to the Parliament and the Council. In harmonization, one of the most dynamic legislative area of the EU, Article 100a(3) of the Treaty establishing the European Community (Amsterdam) already in 1997 required the institutions to take account of any scientific developments ("new development based on scientific facts") in adopting rules which have as their object the establishment and functioning of the internal market and concern health, safety, environmental protection, and consumer protection. This chapter was subject to a number of cases and AG opinions. See, for example, Case C-491/01 *The Queen v Secretary of State for Health* [2002] ECR I-11453, Opinion of AG Geelhoed and Case C-467/98 *Denmark v Commission* [2002] ECR I-09519, Opinion of AG Tizzano.

170 *Germany v Parliament*, Opinion of AG Fennelly, *supra* note 166.

171 This is paraphrased statement taken from Case C-352/98 P *Laboratoires pharmaceutiques Bergaderm SA and Jean-Jacques Goupil v Commission* [2000] ECR I-05291, Opinion of AG Fennelly, para 35, likely inspired by the common-law tradition where the preponderance of evidence standard is satisfied when an alleged fact is more likely than not, considering the "weight, quality and persuasiveness" of the evidence. See Claudia Di Marzo, *Italy*, *in* Medical Malpractice and Compensation in Global Perspective 230 (Ken Oliphant & Richard W. Wright (eds.), De Gruyter 2013).

172 *Laboratoires pharmaceutiques Bergaderm v Commission*, Opinion of AG Fennelly, *supra* note 171, at para 35.

173 See *Spain v Council*, Opinion of AG Saugmandsgaard Øe, *supra* note 19, at para 55.

174 See *Swedish Match*, Opinion of AG Saugmandsgaard Øe, *supra* note 143, at para 39.

175 Case C-434/02 *Arnold André GmbH & Co. KG v Landrat des Kreises Herford* [2004] ECR I-11825 and *Swedish Match*, Opinion of AG Geelhoed, *supra* note 143, at para 98.

176 See *Swedish Match*, Opinion of AG Saugmandsgaard Øe, *supra* note 143, at para 48.

177 *Giovanni Pesce*, Opinion of AG Bot, *supra* note 150, at para 116.

whether the process of scientific evaluation is "as complete as possible"[178] to support the validity of precautionary measures.[179] AG Geelhoed opined that for the adoption of an EU measure in situations concerning scientific uncertainty, scientific consensus is not needed and proper and recent scientific studies will suffice.[180] The Court concurred only to the extent that the scientific controversy concerning new tobacco products that prevailed at the time of the adoption of the contested Council Directive 89/622/EC allowed the EU legislature to rule out that such products posed no danger to human health.[181] The EU legislator was able to prove that it took account of the development of scientific information as well as based the measure on a high level of protection in health matters.[182]

3.3.3 Evidence Adduced by Parties

For parties to the proceedings, it is not enough to merely disagree on the inferences drawn from scientific evidence obtained by the Court.[183] Parties need to produce contradictory evidence to seriously question facts or the interpretation thereof (such as whether the duties of the decision-maker were fulfilled or to show a manifest error or appraisal).[184] This is more so in areas where foresight of the decision-maker is curtailed by uncertainty.[185] Only in this way may AGs use substantive approaches to weigh evidence submitted by parties to the proceedings. For example, in *Spain v. Council*, an action for annulment, AG Sharpston was confronted with the assessment of the legality of a regulation concerned with state aid for the production of cotton. Although she did not want to play the role of an economic adjudicator concerning the positions and figures submitted by parties to the proceedings, she eventually concluded that neither the Council nor the Commission had produced evidence before the Court that contradicted Spain's estimates (for direct labour costs, essential for the calculation of production aid) or proved that they should have been

178 See Case C-528/16 *Confédération paysanne and Others* ECLI:EU:C:2018:20, Opinion of AG Bobek, referring to Joined Cases C-58/10 to C-68/10 *Monsanto and Others* [2011] ECR I-07763, para 77.

179 *Swedish Match*, Opinion of AG Saugmandsgaard Øe, *supra* note 143, at para 39.

180 *Arnold André*, Opinion of AG Geelhoed, *supra* note 175, at para 94.

181 *Arnold André*, *supra* note 175, at para 49.

182 *Id.* at paras 50–54.

183 As to the difference between scientific evidence and inference, it is interesting to note that AG Sharpston admitted, on the basis of different language version of Article 95(5) EC, that new conclusions drawn from existing data may constitute new scientific evidence. See of Joined cases C-439/05 and C-454/05 P, *Land Oberösterreich and Austria v Commission* [2007] ECR I-07141, Opinion of AG Sharpston, para 124.

184 *Philip Morris Brands SARL and Others*, Opinion of AG Kokott, *supra* note 145, at para 97.

185 In *Philip Morris Brands SARL and Others*, this was, for example, the area of future market activity in which forecasts may have been reviewed as to their plausibility at most. *Philip Morris*, Opinion of AG Kokott, *supra* note 145, at para 88.

disregarded.[186] Under those circumstances, the decision-maker committed a manifest error of assessment when adopting the contested regulation and violated the principle of proportionality.

In a similar fashion, in *Poland v. Commission*, a case concerning forest management measures, AG Bot examined whether the facts justifying the action were sufficiently substantiated and whether the claims of parties were sufficiently supported by evidence.[187] He compared the evidence on file to the written observations and arguments of Poland at the hearing, and some of his findings were used by the Court (for example, in regards to the volume of timber extracted compared to the set volume of harvestable timber).[188] AG Bot discovered many discrepancies between Poland's arguments and other evidence, including deficiencies in the data used, that the relevant decisions were adopted before all relevant data had been collected, that the decisions were adopted on old data, and made some related observations that outrightly dismissed Poland's claims.[189] AG Bot dismissed also other arguments put forward by Poland because only assessments carried out in the light of best scientific knowledge could have supported the adoption of the relevant decisions by the Polish authorities.[190] However, there was also a lot of scientific uncertainty as to how to halt the spread of the spruce bark beetle, whether to combat the spread is actually desirable, or whether the spread was a part of a natural cycle.[191] In that case, due regard must have been paid to the precautionary principle integrated into Article 6(3) of the Habitats Directive.[192] To AG Bot's mind, the evidence in the case showed that the potential risks in the case "had not been fully identified, assessed and, where appropriate ruled out"; therefore, the Polish authorities were not in the position to lawfully adopt the contested measures or to rely on any derogation from the Habitats Directive.[193]

AG Mischo, in a case concerning the lawfulness of measure by which Denmark granted marketing authorization to an ordinary foodstuff enriched with

186 *Spain v Council*, Opinion of AG Sharpston, *supra* note 128, at para 95. Who should provide the decisive evidence is a matter of the burden of proof that varies depending on the particular case. It can also flip rapidly. cf *Land Oberösterreich*, Opinion AG Sharpston, *supra* note 183, at para 115.

187 Case C-441/17, *Commission v Poland* ECLI:EU:C:2018:80, Opinion of AG Bot, para 156.

188 Case C-441/17, *Commission v Poland* ECLI:EU:C:2018:255, para 176 and further para 136.

189 *Commission v Poland*, Opinion of AG Bot, *supra* note 187, at paras 159–164.

190 *Id.* at para 165. Similarly, AG Geelhoed also demanded that the German government provide concrete scientific evidence to support its claim that the *Düngeverordung*, a national regulation on good manuring and fertilizing practice implementing the Nitrates Directive, assumes nitrogen losses at flat-rate values based on scientific data and not a specific calculation method. See Case C-161/00 *Commission v Germany* [2002] ECR I-02753, Opinion of AG Geelhoed, para 47.

191 *Commission v Poland*, Opinion of AG Bot, *supra* note 187.

192 *Id.* at para 167.

193 *Id.* at para 168–172.

vitamins only if the Codex Alimentarius provided for such enrichment and only if the level of enrichment was justified by the nutritional needs of Denmark's population, thoroughly engaged with every argument made by the parties to the case.[194] A number of alternative measures were considered, including mentioning vitamin content on the packaging or a warning.[195] AG Mischo then even suggested a possible wording of a warning about the vitamin content, though he then became critical of his own suggestion in light of the predicted consumer behaviour.[196] AG Mischo concluded that Denmark satisfactorily proved persisting scientific uncertainty as to the risk posed to health by the addition of vitamins to foodstuffs and considered Denmark's measure proportionate.[197] He observed that the risk assessment should involve a case-by-case examination of products to be placed on the market, and that none of the documents presented before the Court gave reason to believe that Denmark did not proceed on such basis.[198] The Court completely disagreed with this assessment and ruled that the Danish practice was disproportionate due to its systematic character and because it did not involve a detailed assessment on a case-by-case basis.[199] AG Mischo and the Court directly clashed on the assessment of factual circumstances in the case.

In *Colin Wolf*, a case examining national legislation responsible for laying down an age limit of 30 for recruitment to an intermediate career post in the fire service, AG Bot substantively examined the detailed replies of the German government and noted that it was apparent from the studies submitted that increased age brings reduced capacity in the cardiovascular system, lungs, musculature, and strength of the human body.[200] On the basis of the submissions made by the German government, which referred to established medical and biological data, he went on to understand the phenomenon of premature aging in difficult working conditions and concluded that the age limit was justified.[201] The Court agreed with AG Bot's opinion and, in a sweeping fashion

194 Case C-192/01 *Commission v Denmark* [2003] ECR I-09693, Opinion of AG Mischo, paras 116–142.

195 *Id.* at paras 133–134.

196 *Id.* at paras 133–136.

197 *Id.* at para 144. In a similar way, in Case C-24/00 *Commission v France* [2004] ECR I-01277, AG Mischo observed, in relation to the prohibition of energy drinks, that France satisfactorily proved that such drinks present health problems, by pointing to studies of the *Conseil supérieur d'hygiène publique de France* as a scientific authority, para 108. On the other hand, the Commission failed to put forward any scientific or other evidence capable of undermining the risk analysis in relation to the dangers posed by the drinks to the public, para 110. The Commission, in AG Mischo's as well as the Court's opinion, did not prove that France did not fulfil its obligations under Article 30 EC Treaty.

198 *Id.* at paras 116–117.

199 Case C-192/01 *Commission v Denmark* [2003] ECR I-09693, paras 56–57.

200 Case C-229/08 *Colin Wolf v Stadt Frankfurt am Main* [2010] ECR I-00001, Opinion of AG Bot, paras 33–34.

201 *Ibid.*

essentially repeating the arguments of the German government and lacking AG Bot's interest in detail, concluded that the contested measure was proportionate and necessary to the objective sought.[202]

A similar example may be found in AG Mengozzi's opinion in *Commission v. United Kingdom*, in which he substantively examined the findings of studies commissioned by the UK government and took them as proving certain facts, such as that the final cost–benefit ratio of solutions adopted for water treatment did not justify the UK government taking any further measures.[203] A very similar task presented itself before the Court, because in circumstances in which the Commission adduced sufficient evidence relating to the failure of a member state to fulfil obligations, it was up to the member state to challenge in substance and in detail the evidence of the Commission and "the consequences flowing therefrom."[204] The Court, therefore, had to examine various agglomerations one after another for the conditions for the application of the Urban Waste Water Treatment Directive, and in particular the concept of "best technical knowledge not entailing excessive costs" (BTKNEEC), or the exception thereto.[205] The Court arrived to the same conclusion as AG Mengozzi, except for with regard to one agglomeration, namely, Sunderland (Whitburn). AG Mengozzi included a very detailed substantive analysis of the situation,[206] whereas the Court satisfied itself with a shorter analysis, ultimately concluding that it missed information on the costs to work out the assessment under the BTKNEEC concept.[207] The cost related to a technological solution requiring the enlargement of an existing interceptor tunnel in order to improve the quality of waters received.[208] To AG Mengozzi, that information did not seem important, because the benefit obtained by the tunnel would be so marginal (0.3 per cent) that "the cost/benefit ratio did not justify taking any further measures."[209]

In *Vodafone*, a case concerning the validity of the Roaming Regulation, AG Maduro considered evidence submitted by Vodafone and inferences drawn on the basis of said evidence. He observed that the evidence submitted must not necessarily support the inference, and that other inferences could be possible:

> [T]he clustering of prices in this manner could equally be regarded as evidence of the absence of price competition in relation to roaming,

202 Case C-229/08 *Colin Wolf v Stadt Frankfurt am Main* [2010] ECR I-00001, paras 41–44.
203 Case C-301/10 *Commission v United Kingdom* ECLI:EU:C:2012:36, Opinion of AG Mengozzi, paras 84 and 85.
204 Case C-301/10 *Commission v United Kingdom* ECLI:EU:C:2012:633, paras 72–73.
205 *Id.* at paras 74–94.
206 *Commission v United Kingdom*, Opinion of AG Mengozzi, *supra* note 203, at paras 69–86.
207 *Commission v United Kingdom*, *supra* note 204, at paras 74–83.
208 *Commission v United Kingdom*, Opinion of AG Mengozzi, *supra* note 203, at para 83.
209 *Id.* at para 84.

> supporting the conclusion that the previous higher prices would have remained in place were it not for the legislator intervention.[210]

He concluded that the EU legislature's choice did not show signs of being manifestly in error.[211] The Court arrived at the same conclusion. It seemed rather unequivocal about the inferences that it drew from the observations submitted by the Council and other EU institutions as to effects of the Roaming Regulation on wholesale and retail charges.[212] What makes it a landmark case is that the Court principally relied upon the IA that examined various options, "assessed the economic impact of various types of regulations and effects of different charging structures."[213] AG Maduro also did a fine and critical job when engaging with evidence provided by the Dutch government in *Commission v. the Netherlands*, a case concerning the conflict between the principle of free movement and the requirement of health protection.[214] He pointed out that Netherlands failed to substantiate some of its claims via scientific studies, examined adduced scientific assessments in detail, and was critical about the proof they conveyed.[215] Specifically, he questioned the reference to nutritional needs assessment as a general and automatic criterion for the potential danger of nutrients and evidential value of the studies adduced possess. The Court agreed with AG Maduro and, in its judgement, pinpointed precisely this part of the Opinion.[216]

Dealing with evidence substantively often involves considering statistical evidence and drawing inferences on this basis. AG Jäaskinen, for example, considered statistics as to the risk to road safety associated with certain vehicles submitted by Poland and Lithuania in *Commission v. Poland*, a case concerning the registration of vehicles which have their steering equipment on the right side.[217] AG Jäaskinen found the statistics inconclusive and inadequate:[218]

> [I]n so far as they may be the result of other road safety factors, it is not possible to establish from those statistics that the rate of accidents caused in their national territory by vehicles which have their steering equipment on the right is significantly higher than the rate of accidents

210 *Vodafone*, Opinion of AG Maduro, *supra* note 140, at para 43.
211 *Ibid.*
212 *Vodafone, supra* note 141, at paras 55–66.
213 *Id.* at para 55.
214 Case C-41/02 *Commission v Netherlands* [2004] ECR I-11375, Opinion of AG Maduro.
215 *Id.* at paras 41–49.
216 Case C-41/02 *Commission v Netherlands* [2004] ECR I-11375, para 57.
217 Case C-639/11 *Commission v Poland* ECLI:EU:C:2013:728, Opinion of AG Jäaskinen.
218 Compare this to the irrelevancy of statistics noted in Case C-246/99 *Commission v Denmark* [2002] ECR I-06943, AG Ruiz-Jarabo Colomer, paras 43–44.

of the same type occurring in the territory of Member States in which the legislation is less demanding.[219]

The Court made the same observation and dismissed the statistics as not satisfying "the requisite standard of the relationship."[220] Both AG Jäaskinen and the Court arrived at the same conclusion as Poland's failure to fulfil their obligations under the relevant EU acts.

In *The Scotch Whisky*, AG Bot used statistical evidence to assess the objective of the imposition of minimum unit pricing (MUP) of alcohol.[221] AG Bot observed on the basis of the data provided by the referring court that alcohol consumption increases with income, and the quantity of the cheapest alcoholic beverages purchased per week falls as the incomes of hazardous or harmful drinkers rise.[222] In this way, he analyzed the impact of the imposition of MUP on prevention of consumption of cheap alcoholic beverages by hazardous and harmful drinkers.[223] The Court found this observation persuasive and relied on it in its judgement.[224]

The findings of AGs using substantive approaches to evidence have been, to some extent, accepted by the Court. There is no exact pattern; the acceptance depends on the quality of reasoning with which facts are connected to law and on the relevance of that connection. Relevance is indeed a grey zone, in which factual and legal appraisal are overlapping.[225] For example, in *Commission v. Bulgaria*, AG Kokott's fact-finding was generally well-received and used in the subsequent Court's decision. The Court referred to her opinion when she (1) drew inferences from the underlying data as to the loss of attractiveness of bird sites,[226] (2) accepted the evidence on concentrations of birds and its implications,[227] (3) accepted the suggestions of recent observations,[228] and (4) pointed to the lack of evidence adduced by Poland that would entail a detailed assessment regarding the ornithological situation.[229]

3.3.4 Interpretation of Notions

To interpret a notion, AGs also use statistics and cite other relevant publications. For example, in *Pešková and Peška*, AG Bot used statistics compiled by

219 *Commission v Poland*, Opinion of AG Jäaskinen, *supra* note 217, at para 100.
220 Case C-639/11, *Commission v Poland* ECLI:EU:C:2014:173, para 62.
221 Case C-333/14, *The Scotch Whisky Association and Others v The Lord Advocate and the Advocate General for Scotland* ECLI:EU:C:2015:527, Opinion of AG Bot, paras 66 and 129.
222 *Id.* at 129–130
223 *Ibid.*
224 Case C-333/14, *Scotch Whisky Association and Others v The Lord Advocate and the Advocate General for Scotland* ECLI:EU:C:2015:845, para 36.
225 Nehl, *supra* note 16, at 177.
226 Case C-141/14 *Commission v Bulgaria* ECLI:EU:C:2016:8, para 77.
227 *Id.* at para 34.
228 *Id.* at para 37.
229 *Id.* at para 96

the Federal Aviation Authority and the French *Service technique de l'aviation civile* to interpret the notion of "extraordinary circumstances" under the Flight Compensation Regulation concerning collisions of birds and aeroplanes.[230] In *Léger*, AG Mengozzi investigated the meaning of "sexual behaviour" with the help of *travaux préparatoires* for Directive 2004/33, though without finding a satisfactory explanation.[231] The AG's conclusion, therefore, was to refer to the common meaning of the term.[232]

Determining the common or ordinary meaning of a notion amounts to a process of fact-finding and therefore raises questions of fact.[233] In that sense, in interpreting a notion, an AG may give regard to general literature or to documents produced by international organizations, or to general (undisputed) observations. In *Finnair Oyj*, AG Sharpston sought to determine the ordinary meaning of "writing," particularly in the context of businesses that routinely perform services for their customers.[234] In *Spain v. Council*, she cited the *Shorter Oxford English Dictionary* to define the notion of "production" in economic terms.[235] In *Commission v. Malta*, she cited the *Oxford Dictionary* and the *Langencheidt* to define "judicious."[236]

As opposed to finding an ordinary meaning, finding a legal technical meaning of words is a question of law.[237] In *Neptune Distribution*, AG Jäaskinen was asked to interpret the concept of "the equivalent value for salt" in respect of certain nutritional claims and considered evidence adduced by the Parliament, which referred to relevant World Health Organization (WHO) documents and the Council, which in turn referred to the Codex Alimentarius.[238] This is not surprising, because the Court itself attached a great degree of importance to the Codex, as well as to the Agriculture Organisation of the United Nations (FAO) in its seminal judgement of *Commission v. Germany* concerning purity

230 Case C-315/15 *Marcela Pešková and Jiří Peška v Travel Service A.S.* ECLI:EU:C:2016:623, Opinion of AG Bot, paras 29–31.

231 *Léger*, Opinion of AG Mengozzi, *supra* note 122, at para 31.

232 *Ibid.*

233 See The Hon Justice M J Beazley AO, *The Distinction Between Questions of Fact and Law: A Question Without Answer?*, 25 The Land and Environment Court Conference (May 2013).

234 Case C-258/16 *Finnair Oyj v Keskinäinen Vakuutusyhtiö Fennia* ECLI:EU:C:2017:1016, Opinion of AG Sharpston, paras 40–50.

235 *Spain v Council*, Opinion of AG Sharpston, *supra* note 128, at para 39.

236 Case C-557/15 *Commission v Malta* ECLI:EU:C:2017:613, Opinion of AG Sharpston, para 86.

237 Case C-558/07 *S.P.C.M. SA, C.H. Erbslöh KG, Lake Chemicals and Minerals Ltd Hercules Inc. v Secretary of State for the Environment, Food and Rural Affairs* [2009] ECR I-05783, Opinion of AG Kokott, para 90. Similarly, AG Jääskinen draws attention to the book *Food and Chemical Toxicology* as regards the unique issues of risk assessment of vitamins and minerals, not, however, of its own motion, but because the book was referred to by one of the parties in its written observation. The book is cited extensively. See Case C-446/08 *Solgar Vitamin's France and Others v Ministre de l'Économie, des Finances et de l'Emploi and Others* [2010] ECR I-03973, Opinion of AG Jäaskinen, para 139.

238 *Neptune Distribution*, Opinion of AG Jäaskinen, *supra* note 163, at para 33.

requirement for beer as early as 1987.[239] In *Étimine*, AG Bot extended the reading of the expression "normal handling or use" of a substance relying on the precautionary principle, so to cover everyday acts.[240]

3.3.5 *Judicial Notice*

The substantive approach may help the Court take notice of certain facts. Judicial notice is an act of a court by which it acknowledges undisputed or well-known facts.[241] For example, it could include the fact that Brussels is the capital of Belgium. Judicial notice no longer requires a proof. Contrary to their American counterparts, EU courts operate without guidance as to what kind of facts may be judicially noticed and how to take judicial notice.[242] Despite a lack of guidance, many examples of what can be broadly described as judicial notice may be found in AGs' opinions. In some jurisdictions, a classification of judicial notices is possible, such as that distinguishing between judicial notice without inquiry, judicial notice after inquiry, or judicial notice within a judge's own personal notice.[243] However, to the authors, there was no obvious classification after reviewing AGs' opinions.

AG Bot, for example, considered scientific facts regarding embryonic development in *Brüstle v. Greenpeace*.[244] AG Sharpston noted the role of environmental organizations, citing *The Logic of Collective Action: Public Goods and the Theory of Groups* and citing statistics of court involvement.[245] AG Cruz Villalon considered risk theory at considerable length, observing how individuals experience their lives and citing *Accelération: Une critique sociale du temps*.[246] AG Geelhoed commented on the attractiveness of snus.[247] AG Wahl observed

239 Case C-178/84 *Commission v Germany* [1987] ECR 01227, para 44.

240 Case C-15/10 *Étimine SA v Secretary of State for Work and Pensions* ECLI:EU:C:2011:179, Opinion of AG Bot, paras 84–85.

241 See James B. Thayer, *Judicial Notice and the Law of Evidence*, 3(7) Harvard Law Review 285–312 (1890).

242 Rule 201 of the US Federal Rules of Evidence. Judicial Notice of Adjudicative Facts of the Federal Rules of Evidence.

243 See Romilly Edge et al. (ed.), Evidence 13–14 (17th ed., Oxford University Press 2014).

244 *Brüstle*, Opinion of AG Bot, *supra* note 164, at paras 84–95. The Court, on the other hand, relied exclusively on the observations presented to the Court. See Case C-34/10, *Oliver Brüstle v Greenpeace e.V.* [2011] ECR I-09821, para 48. See also AG Bot noting facts about the olive oil production in the EU and about the symbolism of olive trees in the Mediterranean, giving a piece of poem of Gabriele D'Annunzio to illustrate this. *Giovanni Pesce*, Opinion of AG Bot, *supra* note 150, at paras 1–4.

245 Case C-263/08 *Djurgården-Lilla Värtans Miljöskyddsförening v Stockholms kommun genom dess marknämnd* [2009] ECR I-09967, Opinion of AG Sharpston.

246 Case C-293/12 *Digital Rights Ireland Ltd v Minister for Communications, Marine and Natural Resources and others* ECLI:EU:C:2013:845, Opinion of AG Cruz Villalon, para 146.

247 *Arnold André*, Opinion of AG Geelhoed, para 175. Also, one may compare this to AG Wathelet accepting a presumption on the part of the average consumer regarding the beneficial effects of milk for health, presented by the referring court and confirmed by the scientific

the conditions in which goats and sheep are traded.[248] AG Kokott noted the coolness or fun factor that may be associated with unusual or particularly striking packaging of cigarettes.[249] For AG Kokott, in *Commission v. Bulgaria*, it was common ground "that almost the entire world population . . . of the red-breasted goose, which is universally considered to be endangered, spends the winter on the west coast of the Black Sea."[250] AG Sharpston took it as a matter of fact that cotton must be ginned close to its place of production and cannot be transported long distances, and that within an agricultural community heavily dependent on the production of cotton, local cotton-related employment will comprise both farm labour and ginning labour.[251] AG Mengozzi, in *Léger*, took notice of the maximum period of storage of blood.[252] AG Léger observed in *Ministero della Salute* that "the contamination of the environment by GMOs is a well-known phenomenon and is regularly reported in the media."[253]

For the purposes of judicial notice, AGs may also refer to general scientific literature. AG Kokott had recourse to the *Principles of Chemical Nomenclature* when explaining certain facts concerning monomer properties.[254] Similarly, AG Jääskinen drew attention to the book *Food and Chemical Toxicology* as regards the unique issues of risk assessment of vitamins and minerals, not, however, of his own motion, but because the book was referred to by one of the parties in its written observation.[255]

3.4 Individual Approaches

Apart from the two main approaches to scientific evidence in AGs' opinions, a veritable patchwork of individual approaches is evident from our analysis. This may be shown by the very nature of facts in each particular case, but also by each AGs' different style of reasoning, specialization, and preparedness in examining underlying evidence. In what follows, the examples include opinions

---

community, citing Court of Auditors' evaluation of EU School Milk scheme, the French *Académie nationale de médecine*, and the World Health Organization's Guiding Principles for Feeding Non-Breastfed Children 6–24 Months of Age. Case C-609/12 *Ehrmann AG v Zentrale zur Bekämpfung unlauteren Wettbewerbs eV* ECLI:EU:C:2013:746, Opinion of AG Geelhoed, para 48.

248 *Schaible*, Opinion of AG Wahl, *supra* note 18, at para 75.

249 *Philip Morris Brands SARL and Others*, Opinion of AG Kokott, *supra* note 145, at para 191.

250 *Commission v Bulgaria*, Opinion of AG Kokott, *supra* note 112, at para 53.

251 *Spain v Council*, Opinion of AG Sharpston, *supra* note 128, at para 87.

252 *Léger*, Opinion of AG Mengozzi, *supra* note 122, at para 56.

253 Case C-132/03 *Ministero della Salute v Coordinamento delle associazioni per la difesa dell'ambiente e dei diritti degli utenti e consumatori, Federconsumatori* [2005] I-04167, Opinion of AG Léger, para 81.

254 *S.P.C.M.*, Opinion of AG Kokott, *supra* note 237, at para 90.

255 The book is cited extensively. See *Solgar Vitamin's*, Opinion of AG Jäaskinen, *supra* note 237, at para 139.

that stood up in the case law analysis because of personal commitment of AGs towards evidence evaluation, running the proverbial extra mile.

For example, AG Mengozzi, in *Léger*, not only considered the specific epidemiological situation in France in order to corroborate the necessity of the measure at issue but also went on to verify factors relating to health technology, such as the economic viability and scientific feasibility, and factors relating to technological possibility and proportionality of costs (cost/benefit ratio) involved in alternatives.[256] AG Mengozzi was prepared to consider epidemiological data, provided that it was reliable, recent, and representative.[257] In his reasoning, he consulted statistical data on the MSM[258] population and HIV infection rates.[259]

AG Kokott, in an infringement procedure, considered the evidence submitted by both parties, assessed their persuasiveness, and compared them to international references, technical studies, and more recent observations. For AG Kokott, international criteria used for the classification of bird protection sites were not binding; however, they provided a point of reference for the Court when assessing whether the MS had fulfilled its obligations under EU law.[260] In *SPCM*, she criticized that the relation between proportionality review and bounds of discretion is not always clear in the case law and pointed out that in order to give the principle of proportionality a practical effect, the Court must examine whether there are obviously less intrusive measures or even whether the burdens are proportionate to the aim pursued, not only whether a measure is manifestly inappropriate.[261]

AG Jäaskinen did not consider the statistics presented by the parties to be conclusive; he questioned the causation and considered the evidence adduced inadequate.[262] He referred to evidence of international practice and standards from numerous sources, giving regard to the position of international studies.[263] AG Geelhoed, in his opinions, often considered the nature of health risks, including fatal consequences, contamination, or techniques of production.[264] In matters concerning adequacy/suitability, AG Wahl was accustomed to employing studies on the feasibility and reliability of systems, citing the positive results of the measure at issue, referencing an implementation study conducted by the Commission, a publication of the World Organization of Animal Health, a final report of a large-scale project coordinated by the Joint Research Centre, and other reports, or citing studies on costs.[265] AG Bot often

256 *Léger*, Opinion of AG Mengozzi, *supra* note 122, at para 57.
257 *Id.* at para 54.
258 Men who have sex with men.
259 *Léger*, Opinion of AG Mengozzi, *supra* note 122, at para 60.
260 *Commission v Bulgaria*, Opinion of AG Kokott, *supra* note 112, at para 36.
261 *S.P.C.M.*, Opinion of AG Kokott, *supra* note 237, at paras 72–76.
262 *Commission v Poland*, Opinion of AG Jäaskinen, *supra* note 217, at para 100.
263 *Neptune Distribution*, Opinion of AG Jäaskinen, *supra* note 163, at para 33.
264 *W. Hahn*, Opinion of AG Geelhoed, *supra* note 162.
265 *Schaible*, Opinion of AG Wahl, *supra* note 18.

mastered both procedural and substantive approaches. Within a single opinion, in *Wolfgang Glatzel*, he cited the latest statistics concerning road safety in Europe and took judicial notice of an "indisputable" fact that "driving in general, and driving vehicles . . . requires a strong visual function, which in turn presupposes good visual acuity an and unimpaired field of vision."[266] He also quoted a report produced by the Eyesight Working Group and WHO classification and concluded that the EU followed the advice of the experts and that the measure at issue did not appear to go beyond what is necessary to achieve the objective of improving road safety.[267]

AG Bobek stands out in comparison with other AGs. His approach is pragmatic, and he often inquires what is practically achievable by national decision-makers as far as evidentiary matters are concerned. He instructs referring courts on evidentiary issues, for example, what evidence to adduce, to demonstrate that a measure is manifestly inappropriate (such as statistical data), or what factual assessment of the quality and comprehensiveness of individual research to perform.[268] This is apparent in cases in which he does not stop short by stating that evidentiary matters, such as whether a full scientific assessment was conducted, are for a national court to resolve. He advises national courts on what may or may not constitute irrefutable proof that a full assessment was carried out.[269] The approach is similar to AG Mengozzi's in *Léger*, in which he directed the referring court to a specific question of fact and advised it on what evidentiary material could aid the court in determining the economic viability and the scientific feasibility of a particular method of blood transfusion.[270] AG Mengozzi went as far as to suggest how a questionnaire directed at the MSM population should be refined so that it would provide an improved evidence base for the risk assessment, so that the national court could determine whether the discretion exercised by the respondent government was proportionate.[271] This was reiterated in the Court's subsequent judgement.[272] A similar example comes from AG Wahl. He suggested using psychological examination in the asylum procedure before national authorities that would be "based on methods, principles and notions generally accepted by the scientific community . . . capable of producing sufficiently

266 Case C-356/12 *Wolfgang Glatzel v Freistaat Bayern* ECLI:EU:C:2013:505, Opinion of AG Bot, para 46.

267 *Id.* at paras 54–56.

268 See for example, *Noria Distribution*, Opinion of AG Bobek, *supra* note 102.

269 This may be contrasted with AG Jääskinen setting out principles on the basis of which a national court should evaluate the specific nature of the scientific data provided by the national scientific bodies concerning, *Solgar Vitamin's*, Opinion of AG Jääskinen, *supra* note 237, at paras 95–122.

270 *Léger*, Opinion of AG Mengozzi, *supra* note 122.

271 *Id.* at paras 61–62.

272 Case C-528/13 *Geoffrey Léger v Ministre des Affaires sociales, de la Santé et des Droits des femmes and Etablissement français du sang* ECLI:EU:C:2015:288, para 67.

reliable results."[273] AG Wahl, of course, knew that it is not for the Court to rule on the reliability or pertinence of specific types of psychological examination; he nevertheless guided the national court to possibly disregard expert pieces of evidence that would be "biased, unsubstantiated or based on controversial methods and theories" as a matter of factual review.[274]

For AG Bobek, evidentiary matters appear to conflict with certain underlying principles that govern procedures before the Court, as well as national courts. This is the principle of procedural autonomy of MS – a principle that is curbed by the principles of equivalence and effectiveness of EU law.[275] According to AG Bobek, it is not the Court's role "to deduce detailed rules of evidence and proof"; however, in his opinions, he aims to assist national courts and authorities in finding limits to those rules.[276] In some of his opinions, he also took the opportunity to elucidate certain concepts pertaining to evidentiary matters, such as the difference between direct and indirect evidence, the use of circumstantial evidence in the absence of direct evidence,[277] specific evidentiary requirements,[278] irrelevance of evidence,[279] or the notion of representativeness of sample proving emission values.[280] Although such opinions may be regarded as sector- or case-specific, their applicability may be tested in other cases and contexts.

4 Conclusion: Trends and Common Features

The examples provided in Section 3 of this chapter illustrated that the opinions of AGs that engage with evidentiary matters have indeed a special utility, not only to the Court, but also to national courts and administrations. They inform on who bears the burden of proof, suggest the required proof of evidence, help answer whether the duty to state reasons was fulfilled or whether a manifest error of assessment was committed, balance the evidence supplied by the parties, or cite data from studies that were referenced in each party's

273 Case C-473/16 *F v Bevándorlási és Menekültügyi Hivatal* ECLI:EU:C:2017:739, Opinion of AG Wahl, para 47.

274 *Id.* at paras 49 and 52.

275 Case C-621/15 *W X Y v Sanofi Pasteur MSD SNC* ECLI:EU:C:2017:176, Opinion of AG Bobek, para 16.

276 *Id.* at 16–17.

277 *Id.* at 55.

278 *Id.* Specific evidentiary requirements (such as exclusion of presumptions) may make it practically impossible to establish causation or certain facts. Compare this to much more ambiguous "evidentiary requirements may be less strict where public health is at stake" by AG Fennelly in *Germany v Parliament and Council, supra* note 161.

279 In Bobek's view, *irrelevancy* means "there is no rational or logical link between the evidence presented and the inference drawn." *Sanofi Pasteur*, Opinion of AG Bobek, *supra* note 275, at para 64.

280 Case C-320/15 *Commission v Hellenic Republic* ECLI:EU:C:2017:246, Opinion of AG Bobek.

submissions. In their opinions, AGs identify situations of scientific uncertainty, consider complex assessments, and note the breadth of discretion of given decision-makers. At the same time, in their capacity as independent and innovative legal advisers to the Court, AGs hardly resist the temptation to conduct independent factual research[281] and to discuss the scientific validity and merits of scientific arguments raised by parties.[282] This may, however, provably facilitate the Court's assessments and evidentiary reasoning. In theory and in practice, the opinions of AGs are requested where they are needed the most. Our analysis could not confirm whether opinions of AGs are consistently requested in cases involving complex evidentiary matters at the borderline of questions of fact and questions of law. However, it confirmed that AGs' opinions carry important impact as it pertains to evidentiary matters in the judicial review that involves proportionality analysis in combination with risk assessment. Calling AGs to a case has the potential to lead to an effective allocation of evidentiary work between the Court, the AG, the parties to the proceedings, and the referring court, and therefore to enhance the epistemic capacity of the Court.[283] Evidentiary issues are becoming more complex, and legal and factual aspects of cases are becoming more intertwined. Therefore, in order to increase the decisive impact of AGs in evidentiary matters, a certain specialization of AGs is warranted.[284] Currently, it is the responsibility of the First Advocate General, appointed for a year term, to assign cases to the remaining AGs.[285] AGs are equipped with an analytical apparatus that highlights the context of the case and that links the facts (evidence) to the previous case law, even in cases involving complex, scientific, and technical assessments. For the moment, such analytical apparatus is mostly located in the duty-of-care concept which crystallizes the relationship between facts and law and between scientific input and legal analysis, including the proportionality analysis.[286]

Substantive approaches must be executed with caution: they may show signs of epistemic difficulties,[287] methodological limitations,[288] inaccurate determination of facts, or alternative interpretations of statistical evidence. There

281 As a very clear demonstrative example of this, consider AG Wahl debating the use of expert advice from psychologists in asylum proceedings in Case C-473/16 *F v Bevándorlási és Állampolgársági Hivata*, Opinion of AG Wahl, para 36.

282 cf Alemanno, *supra* note 161.

283 cf Alemanno, *supra* note 75.

284 For example, AG Mischo first delivered an opinion concerning measures to combat bovine spongiform encephalopathy in Case C-1/00, *Commission v. France*, and set out to the Court the factual and scientific background that was later used in his second opinion in Case C-393/01, *France v. Commission*, para 1, proving a certain continuity in the subject matter.

285 See Ritter, *supra* note 27, at 3.

286 cf Hofmann, *supra* note 67.

287 Question of information overload and the fact that the internet brought the world's library to the courthouse. See Elizabeth Thornborg, *The Curious Appellate Judge: Ethical Limits on Independent Research*, 28 Review of Litigation 132–201 (2008).

288 Popelier, *supra* note 75, at 267.

is also a sense of awkwardness in carrying out interdisciplinary research[289] and concerns with legitimacy, not only in terms of the executive/judiciary divide, but also with respect to the legal/scientific divide.[290] On the other hand, the procedural engagement with evidence may lead to an overreliance on experts and science and to narrowing the standard of review to the assessment of production of scientific evidence.[291] AGs are further constrained by the following procedural uncertainties: the standard of proof at the Court of Justice was shaped very slowly (most importantly in competition law cases), and there are no admissibility standards, no standards on judicial notice, and few standards on the relevance of evidence. Despite these caveats and difficulties, the opinions of AGs may reveal to the Court where such problems exist. They may bring viable perspective to the intersection of questions of law and questions of fact and new angles in evidentiary matters. AGs and the Court may enhance each other's understanding of factors behind evaluations of scientific evidence and share a gate-keeping role as regards the latter's admissibility and relevance. However, further research that would extensively trace the influence of the AGs' factual research on the Court's output remains warranted.

289 Roland Ismer & Christian von Hesler, *Ex Post Review of Legislatorial Prognoses by the European Court of Justice: The Temporal Dimension of Rational Law-Making*, 4(2) The Theory and Practice of Legislation 279–301 (2016).

290 Popelier, *supra* note 75, at 267–269.

291 According to Bar-Siman-Tov, judges make value judgements about which procedural rules merit protection themselves, thus fuelling uncertainty as to the role and weight of the procedural aspect in the overall judicial decision. See Bar-Siman-Tov Ittai, *Semiprocedural Judicial Review*, 6(2) Legisprudence 271–300 (2012).

11 Climate Justice in the Anthropocene and Its Relationship With Science and Technology

The Importance of an Ethics of Responsibility†

Paolo Davide Farah and Alessio Lo Giudice***

The possibility of there being responsibility in the world, which is bound to the existence of men, is of all objects of responsibility the first.

(Hans Jonas, *The Imperative of Responsibility*, 1979)§

1 Climate Change as a Global Phenomenon

In September 2019, a meeting of the Intergovernmental Panel on Climate Change (IPCC) was held. The IPCC is the United Nations (UN) body that evaluates climate science, the state of knowledge on climate change, and its implications and potential future risks, as well as puts forward adaptation and mitigation options to counter the effects of climate change.[1] The IPCC reports provide scientific information that can assist and support governments and national authorities at all levels, including regions and cities, for

† An extended version of this chapter was first published as Paolo Davide Farah, Alessio Lo Giudice, 55 Connecticut Law Review 819 (2023).

* Paolo Davide Farah, Full Professor, West Virginia University, Eberly College of Arts and Sciences, John D. Rockefeller IV School of Policy and Politics; Founder and Director of the West Virginia University, Energy Justice and Just Transition Lab; Founder, President, Director, Principal Investigator and Senior Research Fellow, at gLAWcal—Global Law Initiatives for Sustainable Development (United Kingdom). Email Addresses: paolofarah@yahoo.com; paolo.farah@glawcal.org.uk

** Alessio Lo Giudice, Full Professor of Philosophy of Law and Legal Theory, University of Messina Law Department (Italy). Dean of the Faculty of Law, University of Messina. Member, Board of Directors of the scientific journal Teoria e Critica della Regolazione Sociale; Member, Board of Directors of the University Centre for Studies in Bioethics (CESB).

§ The authors will focus on the ethics of responsibility as a way to promote climate justice and the future generations highlighting the importance of the work of Hans Jonas.

1 The IPCC was created in 1988 by the World Meteorological Organization (WMO) and the United Nations Environment Programme (UNEP). The IPCC is formed by the countries which are members of the UN and the WMO.

DOI: 10.4324/9781003472421-11

addressing current relevant domestic climate and sustainability issues and for the best well-informed science-based policy and law decisions.[2] The IPCC reports are also extremely productive in that they nourish conversations among countries and governments who are parties to the international climate change negotiations[3] in the context of the United Nations Framework Convention on Climate Change (UNFCC).[4] Based on research conducted by 107 scientists, the most recent report on glaciers and the ocean (known as the "Special Report on the Ocean and Cryosphere in a Changing Climate") was published.[5] The report focuses on how pollution will affect both the climate and human life by the end of the century. A concerning issue, documented in the report, indicates that glacial melting and the increasing global temperatures could lead to a much faster rise in sea levels in comparison with previous estimates. Further, the report indicates that, from 2005 to 2015, the North and South Poles lost roughly 4 trillion metric tons of mass.[6] Mountain glaciers are set to lose 280 million tons of mass a year, which in turn is likely to cause avalanches and water pollution. For example, the Mont Blanc glacier complex is currently losing more than 60 cm a year and is polluting its surroundings with severe geomorphological effects.[7] Glaciers also contain toxic substances accumulated over the years of mostly anthropogenic origin, such as DDT, coal dust, and heavy metals that, if released into river water, will cause serious damage to the environment.[8]

2 On the role of IPCC and international environmental policy-making, see Kal Raustiala, *Non-state Actors in the Global Climate Regime*, International Relations and Global Climate Change 95 (2001); Bernd Siebenhüner, *The Changing Role of Nation States in International Environmental Assessments – The Case of the IPCC*, 13 Global Environmental Change 113 (2003); Silke Beck et al., *Towards a Reflexive Turn in the Governance of Global Environmental Expertise. The Cases of the IPCC and the IPBES*, 23 GAIA-Ecological Perspectives for Science and Society 80 (2014).

3 Paolo Davide Farah & Marek Prityi, *The Anthropocene and Climate Change in the Post-Paris Agreement Debate*, *in* Ethics and Politics of Space for the Anthropocene (Anu Valtonen, Outi Rantala & Paolo Davide Farah (eds.), Edward Elgar Publishing 2020) <www.elgaronline.com/view/edcoll/9781839108693/9781839108693.00005.xml>.

4 Regarding the importance of UNFCCC in the evolution of international environmental law see: E. Lisa F. Schipper, *Conceptual History of Adaptation in the UNFCCC Process*, 15 Review of European Community & International Environmental Law 82 (2006); Jutta Brunnée & Charlotte Streck, *The UNFCCC as a Negotiation Forum: Towards Common But More Differentiated Responsibilities*, 13 Climate Policy 589 (2013); Lukas Hermwille et al., *UNFCCC Before and After Paris – What's Necessary for an Effective Climate Regime?*, 17 Climate Policy 150 (2017).

5 IPCC, *Special Report on the Ocean and Cryosphere in a Changing Climate* (September 2019) <www.ipcc.ch/srocc/>.

6 Andrew Shepherd et al., *A Reconciled Estimate of Ice-Sheet Mass Balance*, 338 Science 1183 (2012).

7 *Mont Blanc Glacier at Risk of Collapse, PM Calls for Climate Action* (Reuters, 25 September 2019) <www.reuters.com/article/us-italy-glacier-idUSKBN1WA1AF>.

8 Christian Bogdal et al., *Blast from the Past: Melting Glaciers as a Relevant Source for Persistent Organic Pollutants*, 43 Environmental Science & Technology 8173 (2009).

The literature covered in the Special Report also highlights the consequences of climate change. Even in the event that global low-emission target as set forth under the Paris Agreement will be reached by 2100, glaciers are still forecasted to lose at least 18 per cent of their mass compared to their 2015 level. For glaciers located in Central Europe and Asia, the estimate could be as high as 80 per cent.[9] Further, if the objectives of the Paris Agreement will not be met in 2100, then the global temperature will rise by 4°C. With a joint effort of the international community to reduce emissions, the increase could be limited to 2°C. Along with the melting of glaciers and increasing global temperature, sea levels could rise roughly 84 cm, forcing 280 million people to leave their homes due to the effects of floods and other extreme weather events.

The report underlines the global nature of human-induced climate change. Not only does this phenomenon affect individual countries, but the interconnections and interlinkages are also not limited to a single state but spreads across the globe with a wide array of interdependent factors. At an empirical level, climate change is closely interconnected with the globalization phenomenon. If we look at the relationship between global production processes, supply chains, and the business decisions regarding manufacturing sites, the pervasiveness of climate change becomes clear. The rising awareness in the global community over the negative effects of climate change and the approaching sustainability crisis[10] open up reflection on the need to set up political structures capable of governing phenomena that have a global scope and that cannot, consequently, be simply governed at national level.[11] Thus, globalization is the central theoretical and interpretative background of this chapter and will be used as a starting point to reflect on the shifting processes at the political, social, and economic level due to climate change and the ever-evolving related consensus. Next, the relationship between the Anthropocene Epoch and the concept of climate justice, intended here as a framework for the political interpretation of the effects of climate change,[12] will be analyzed. Drawing on the concept of ethics of responsibility introduced by Hans Jonas, the final section integrates rationality into the current climate justice framework.

9 IPCC, *supra* note 5, at 17.

10 Paolo Davide Farah, *Sustainable Development Goals in Europe and Their Intersection with the Business & Human Rights Framework*, *in* Business and Human Rights in Europe: International Law Challenges (Angelica Bonfanti (ed.), Routledge Publishing 2018); Paolo Davide Farah, *Los Objetivos de Desarrollo Sostenible En Europa y Su Intersección Con El Marco de Los Negocios y Los Derechos Humanos*, 15 Revista de Direito Internacional 189 (2018).

11 Paolo Davide Farah & Piercarlo Rossi, *National Energy Policies and Energy Security in the Context of Climate Change and Global Environmental Risks: A Theoretical Framework for Reconciling Domestic and International Law through a Multiscalar and Multilevel Approach*, 20 European Energy and Environmental Law Review 232 (2011).

12 Farah & Prityi, *supra* note 3.

2 Globalization and Multilateralism and Role of Science and Technology

In the midst of the COVID-19 pandemic, the title of the cover page of the *Economist* of 16 May 2020 could not be more emblematic: "Goodbye globalization. The dangerous lure of self-sufficiency."[13] One of the editorials, titled "Has COVID-19 killed globalization?" highlights how there is "a new propensity for self-sufficiency and the closure of borders around the world, to the point that about 90% of the world's population lives in states with closed borders."[14] According to that same editorial, the consequence of the pandemic on globalization "is that the movement of people, goods and capital has suffered a vertical decline, probably unprecedented." On a similar note, a few weeks earlier, the French president Emmanuel Macron, in the *Financial Times*, declared that he considered the COVID-19 pandemic "as an event that will change the nature of globalization and the structure of international capitalism."[15] In addition, during the same period, former president Trump, during an interview with *Fox Business*, reiterated the severe impact of COVID-19 on international economic policy: "This pandemic shows that the era of globalization is over." In short, the impression is that these considerations on the systemic effects of the COVID-19 pandemic, somehow apocalyptic, should be reviewed from a standpoint reflecting, in a more analytical way, at least on two fundamental types of globalization (and multilateralism): economic and political. A brief analysis of these two manifestations of globalization, connected but, at the same time, distinct, allows, more generally, to begin a reflection on the relationships between individuals and an environment profoundly changed as a result to climate change.

Regarding the economic aspect, globalization is, first and foremost, a way to strengthen up to the point of exasperating interdependence at the economic level. This exasperation is made possible by science, technological developments, and advancements. It would not be possible to understand the expansion of the globalization phenomenon and of global capital if we fail to consider the importance of science and the technological revolution, in particular in the transport sector and in the information and communication technologies (ICT). Within ICT, it is important to consider with the most recent technologies, such as artificial intelligence, big data, and blockchain,[16]

13 The Economist, *Goodbye Globalisation: The Dangerous Lure of Self-Sufficiency* (16 May 2020) <www.economist.com/weeklyedition/2020-05-16>.

14 The Economist, *Has Covid-19 Killed Globalisation?* (16 May 2021) <www.economist.com/leaders/2020/05/14/has-covid-19-killed-globalisation>.

15 Victor Mallet & Roula Khalaf, *FT Interview: Emmanuel Macron Says It Is Time to Think the Unthinkable* (Financial Times, 16 April 2020) <www.ft.com/content/3ea8d790-7fd1-11ea-8fdb-7ec06edeef84>.

16 Paolo Davide Farah & Marek Prityi, *Public Administration in the Age of Globalization and Emerging Technologies from Theories to Practice Symposium Issue: Blockchain Technology and the Law*, 88 UMKC Law Review 397 (2019).

and the consequent reduction of trade costs (mostly logistics and transportation). Globalization is, therefore, a product of science and technology, supported in its development by political choices favourable to the liberalization of international trade. Political choices, in turn, have found impetus and fulfilment in the favourable geopolitical context that was determined with the fall of the Berlin Wall and with the predominance of the Washington Consensus in international relations. As a product of science and technology, the process of economic globalization is often described as irreversible.[17] This might be true, but when we refer to its economic or political projections, such as free trade on one side and multilateralism on the other, it is arguable that globalization is actually not set in stone and it can be eventually reversed, because these concepts, along with freedom and liberties, can be very important liberalism principles. The epistemological purpose of science and technology is, in fact, its own enhancement. Living in the era of advanced science and technology, we all understand how the latter is not driven by predetermined goals but rather by the internal logic of a self-powering discourse increasingly accelerated by the results achieved. It is reasonable to assume that this dynamic, once triggered, cannot be effectively hampered by the momentary political reactions of closure resulting from the impact of the pandemic.[18] Nonetheless, in reality, if we carefully examine the directions and policies of some of the most important economies in the world, such as the United States (US), China, or the European Union (EU), closure and divide might be considered the better method for re-establishing the power balance and dynamic in a globalized post–Cold War era.

The logic of science and technology is deemed to prevail, because it has generated a process rooted in the organizational structure of global value chains. Certainly, the interconnection between the different world economies, at the technological and infrastructural level, is the product of 50 years of investments and organizational choices of transnational elites that cannot be so easily undermined by a simple and temporary legislative act or by any political decisions. However, this does not mean that a reverse process to globalization and multilateralism is not possible, or a new political reality where all countries contemporarily behave in the same way and have a major focus on domestic issues as opposed to global issues. From the other side, the globalization that refers specifically to science and technology has such a profound impact on the social sphere that determines the very self-representation of humans. Political choices that, in theory, are able to put on hold globalization

17 The literature on globalization is, of course, endless. Here it is, at the very least, necessary to refer to two "classics," such as Ulrich Beck, What Is Globalization? (John Wiley & Sons 2018); Zygmunt Bauman, Globalization: The Human Consequences (Columbia University Press 1998).

18 Among others see: Martin Heidegger, The Question Concerning Technology, and Other Essays (Garland Publisher 1977); Emanuele Severino, Il Destino della Tecnica (Bur 2011); Umberto Galimberti, Psiche e Techne (Feltrinelli Editore 2010).

are highly unlikely but still possible when they affect multilateralism and international collaboration and support towards unilateralism, independence, and self-reliance. Humans who have been, since the very start of civilization, *homo technologicus*[19] today are even more or less consciously embedded with advanced technology and frame their understanding of reality via that technology. Humans rely on science and technology, not only in the actions which determine the speculative processes of financial capitalism, but also in daily activities which assume that technological interconnection at a global level as unavoidable. This is certainly not a new phenomenon but is a key tenet of civilization. Science and technology, in fact, are always present in shaping our way of being humans.[20] On the economic side (which is the original one), when connected to science and technology, it is fair to say that the *requiem* of globalization appears difficult to justify. On the political side, in its connotations related to multilateralism, science and technology still have to be assessed through additional stress tests and monitoring of the domestic policies, which will be adopted in the years to come.

What can be said about the political side? This side of the coin of the globalization process must be associated, above all, with the range of experiences related to multilateralism and the so-called *global governance*.[21] Regardless of the historical genesis and legal frameworks, several global governance institutions are aimed at coordinating political choices at a multilateral level. For this reason, global governance institutions,[22] such as the World Trade Organization (WTO), World Health Organization (WHO), International Labour Organization (ILO), International Monetary Fund, World Bank, and the Internet Corporation for Assigned Names and Numbers (ICANN), are the political expressions of globalization. Yet by looking at the most recent cases, namely, the economic crisis of 2008 and, of course, the health crisis of 2020, the inability of global governance institutions to govern global challenges

19 For an overview of the concept, see Michel Puech, Homo Sapiens Technologicus (Le Pommier 2015).

20 For masterful descriptions of the role of technology from an anthropological and philosophical point of view, see Arnold Gehlen, Man in the Age of Technology (Columbia University Press 1980); Carlo Sini, L'uomo, la Macchina, l'Automa. Lavoro e Conoscenza tra Futuro Prossimo e Passato Remoto (Bollati Boringhieri 2009).

21 The literature on this concept is now vast. For their precious reconstructive character and for the depth of the analysis, refer to James N. Rosenau, Ernst-Otto Czempiel & Steve Smith, Governance Without Government: Order and Change in World Politics (Cambridge University Press 1992); Jan Kooiman, Modern Governance: New Government-Society Interactions (SAGE Publications 1993); Antonino Palumbo & Salvo Vaccaro, Governance. Teorie, Principi, Modelli, Pratiche nell'era Globale (Mimesis 2007); Maria Rosaria Ferrarese, La Governance tra Politica e Diritto (Il Mulino 2010); Alberto Andronico, Viaggio al Termine del Diritto (Giappichelli 2012).

22 For an analysis of what has been labelled as institutions of the globalization, see Maria Rosaria Ferrarese, Le Istituzioni della Globalizzazione. Diritto e Diritti Nella Società Transnazionale (Il Mulino 2000).

appears stark clear. The case of climate change is even more emblematic, as demonstrated by the inability of the United Nations (UN) system to effectively deal with environmental degradation. All this leads us to maintain that economic globalization does not correspond, today, to an adequate level of political multilateralism capable of governing phenomena of social importance that are increasingly taking place at the global level. Attempts to strengthen the political dimension of economic globalization, so far, have failed. There are many factors and reasons at the institutional and structural levels which are able to explain this failure. The prevalence of an economic approach over social and cultural advancements under the globalization discourse has inspired the activity of most of global governance institutions to date. As a matter of fact, this approach has reduced the possibility to affirm, at a global level, the primacy of non-trade concerns (NTCs) over economic profits.[23] On the contrary, the impression has often been given that we are faced with the lack of political control, particularly democratic control, accountability in the global decision-making processes that affect our lives.[24] This is precisely because the only effective political institutions able to cope with global challenges have remained anachronistically anchored at the national level. According to some commentators,[25] the COVID-19 pandemic and the consequent inability to govern it at a global level, as shown, for example, by the evanescent actions of the WHO, have done nothing but confirm the delay on the political level of the globalization processes. At this level, there is no trace of a truly global policy, of what Jürgen Habermas has repeatedly described as a world domestic policy.[26]

When we use the word "globalization," we actually often refer to the political consequences of globalization, which is multilateralism as opposed to unilateralism. Globalization and multilateralism sometimes overlap, and their use is interchangeable. But other times they are not referring to the same theoretical concepts, or to the same causes and effects. Multilateralism, as a system to address global challenges, relies on a wide array of state and non-state

23 For more information on the role of NTCs in international economic law, see Paolo Davide Farah, *Trade and Progress: The Case of China*, 30 Columbia Journal of Asian Law 51 (2016); Paolo Davide Farah & Elena Cima (eds.), China's Influence on Non-Trade Concerns in International Economic Law (Routledge 2016); see also Paolo Davide Farah, *Foreword to Global Values and International Trade Law*, *in* Global Values and International Trade Law (Csongor István Nagy (ed.), Routledge 2021).

24 Paolo Davide Farah, *Foreword to Technocracy and the Law: Accountability, Governance and Expertise*, *in* Technocracy and the Law: Accountability, Governance and Expertise (Alessandra Sofia Arcuri & Florin Coman-Kund (ed.), Routledge 2021).

25 Lee Jones & Shahar Hameiri, *COVID-19 and the Failure of the Neoliberal Regulatory State*, Review of International Political Economy 1 (2021); Marin Larionova & John Kirton, *Global Governance after the COVID-19 Crisis*, 15 International Organisations Research Journal 7 (2020); see contra: Martin Wolf, Why Globalization Works (Yale University Press 2004).

26 This topic is addressed in a skilful manner in Jürgen Habermas, The Postnational Constellation: Political Essays (MIT Press 2001).

actors, often with conflicting priorities and interests. Power dynamics, as well as a particular ideology underlying the core theoretical assumptions, together played a role in shaping the core interests of a supposedly homogeneous international community. Reality is far from the unrealistic idea that global challenges, such as environmental degradation, could be meaningfully addressed by this community. The rise of emerging economies, coupled with the development of an intricate web of transnational corporations,[27] due to the global expansion of capital, is bringing new impetus and innovative ideas to reframe the conduct of multilateral actors way before the arrival of COVID-19 occurs. The COVID-19 pandemic, conceived here as a crisis in the coherence of international priorities, demonstrates how key tenants of multilateralism – trust, cooperation, and transparency – are drastically downplayed at the expense of a comeback of unilateralism (antagonism, secrecy, and distrust). Specifically, the closing of borders, national sovereignty, and the protection of national citizens rather than the underserved have been prioritized as responses to the pandemic across the globe.[28] The situation regarding vaccinations follows a similar path. Realistically, the end of the pandemic will be reached in a timely manner by those developed countries who managed to secure from pharmaceutical corporations a number of doses which outweigh their overall population.[29] For least developed countries, however, the situation is more dramatic. Internal dysfunctionalities of multilateralism characterize not only the vaccination phase but also the amount of financing and resources available to respond to the pandemic. A recent study points out that multilateral institutions such as the International Monetary Fund have been hesitant to provide the much-needed liquidity to developing countries and that the "world community is failing to deliver its own assessment of current gaps and is falling far short of doing 'whatever it takes.'"[30] The COVID-19 pandemic is also pushing for a reconfiguration of the traditional balance of power in multilateral institutions. China, India,[31] and Russia highlighted the failure of multilateral institutions to provide global public

27 Angelica Bonfanti (ed.), Business and Human Rights in Europe: International Law Challenges (Routledge 2019).

28 Florian Bieber, *Global Nationalism in Times of the COVID-19 Pandemic*, 50(1) Nationalities Papers (2020); Benjamin Opratko et al., *Cultures of Rejection in the Covid-19 Crisis*, 44 Ethnic and Racial Studies 893 (2021).

29 EU Commission, *3rd Contract with BioNTech-Pfizer for 1.8 Billion Doses* (20 May 2021) <https://ec.europa.eu/commission/presscorner/detail/en/ip_21_2548>. "European Commission signed a third contract with the pharmaceutical companies BioNTech and Pfizer. It reserves an additional 1.8 billion doses on behalf of all EU Member States, between end 2021 to 2023."

30 Thomas Stubbs et al., *Whatever It Takes? The Global Financial Safety Net, Covid-19, and Developing Countries*, 137 World Development 105171, 6 (2021).

31 Khan Sharun & Kuldeep Dhama, *COVID-19 Vaccine Diplomacy and Equitable Access to Vaccines Amid Ongoing Pandemic*, Archives of Medical Research (2021) <www.sciencedirect.com/science/article/pii/S0188440921001120>.

health protection and equitable access to medicine, not only as a consequence of COVID-19, but also in previous negotiations regarding access to medicine.[32] At the same time, rather than confronting the issue at a multilateral level, these countries moved in a sparse and unorganized way to promote national interests abroad in what has been termed as vaccine diplomacy. The EU and the United States are acting in a similar manner and are still internally reviewing vaccines (sourced from China and Russia) already deemed to be safe for emergency use by the World Health Organization (WHO). Further, in the case of the United States, the nation is also reviewing Vaxzevria, which comes from a company in the EU. Since the Congress of Vienna, multilateral institutions have been established precisely in order to address global challenges brought on by a global pandemic, which is a perfect testing ground. Yet without trust, cooperation, and transparency amongst its members, an alternative to multilateralism should at least be researched and considered.

Moreover, the year 2020 might be remembered as an additional step towards a continued loss of trust in the expertise of technocrats globally. If we look at the management of COVID-19 by the World Health Organization (WHO) and the slow and contradictory position of its director general, Tedros Adhanom, the problem of accountability appears to be the most prevalent issue.[33] Since February 2020, the emergence of COVID-19 and the entire controversy surrounding the World Health Organization (WHO) and its role in what has been defined as an international fiasco has been debated, while numerous casualties have continued to emerge, and the number of deaths has increased. This took place despite WHO experts telling the entire world that there was no reason to panic, and then those same experts changed their opinions months later once the pandemic had become truly global.[34] In addition, these same experts have constantly issued guidelines and opinions that are continually being criticized by other experts. Those critics and negative commentators should concede their understanding of the difficult position and work of the WHO at the intersection of expertise and geopolitics and their operating within a legal framework with its own limitations (which has slightly been approved by the most recent health regulation).[35] Other countries have

32 Jayashree Watal, *Public Health, Intellectual Property Rights, and Developing Countries' Access to Medicines*, *in* China's Influence on Non-Trade Concerns in International Economic Law (Routledge 2016).

33 The case of face masks is an example of the different positions taken by the WHO during the health crisis. The Editorial Board, *World Health Coronavirus Disinformation* (Wall Street Journal, 5 April 2020) <www.wsj.com/articles/world-health-coronavirus-disinformation-11586122093>.

34 Jacqueline Howard, *WHO Stands by Recommendation to Not Wear Masks If You Are Not Sick or Not Caring for Someone Who Is Sick*, CNN <www.cnn.com/2020/03/30/world/coronavirus-who-masks-recommendation-trnd/index.html>.

35 Christopher M. Weible et al., *COVID-19 and the Policy Sciences: Initial Reactions and Perspectives*, Policy Sciences 1, 10 (2020). For an overview of the problems faced by the WHO to counteract the pandemic, see: *COVID-19 and International Law: What Went*

expressed their dissatisfaction with the role played by the WHO, while still others have called for the resignation of the WHO director, but only the United States decided to withdraw its funding from the organization. Yet the position of the United States should also be assessed in light of the anti-multilateral tendency of the Trump presidency and its administration, further expressed by the withdrawal from the 2016 Paris Climate Agreement.[36] The Biden–Harris administration promised they would revise both of these decisions on the first day of their administration.[37] States did not do well in this pandemic either.[38] In fact, similarly, at a national level, virologists led the political conversation not only on COVID-19 but also, most alarmingly, on other aspects far from their expertise. An agreement, even on basic points, such as the need of wearing face masks, is still absent, resulting in generating visible confusion and apprehension among citizens. Aside from virologists, other experts, such as journalists and economists, are increasingly offering their expertise regarding COVID-19 and present themselves as the most appropriate actors to manage the long-term effects of the pandemic. Do we really need these unaccountable experts (of any discipline) changing their minds based on political opportunities?

Furthermore, while some countries adopted one opinion of experts and entire nations have been quarantined in the last few months as a result (like Italy, France, United Kingdom, and Spain), other nations, like Sweden, continued business as usual, with the objective of establishing herd immunity, also in accordance with other expert opinions.[39] No matter which expert was followed, each strategy resulted in the loss of life. It is not known which decision was the "correct" choice. Were there other suggestions that could have been adopted by the experts? Maybe. Would it lead to a better outcome? It is unclear. This is just one example of how experts and technocrats making decisions related to governance have either made bad decisions or simply did not know what the best decision was to take, despite their expertise. In fact, new issues emerged as a result of great disagreements between experts and technocrats. While experts such as doctors were pushing for the adoption of policies that save people's lives, technocrats at the government level were looking to

---

Wrong and What Can We Learn from It? <www.biicl.org/events/11373/covid-19-and-international-law-what-went-wrong-and-what-can-we-learn-from-it>.

36 Thomas G Weiss, *The UN and Multilateralism under Siege in the Age of Trump*, 4(1) Global Summitry (2018).

37 For an analysis of the first 100 days in office and the importance of environmental protection: Sonja Thielges, *Biden's Climate Agenda: Domestic Policy Scope and Potential Arenas for Transatlantic Cooperation*; and for the health sector Joanne Silberner, *How Joe Biden Has Changed US Healthcare in Just 100 Days*, 373 BMJ (2021).

38 Andrea Lavazza & Mirko Farina, *The Role of Experts in the Covid-19 Pandemic and the Limits of Their Epistemic Authority in Democracy*, 8 Frontiers in Public Health (2020) <www.ncbi.nlm.nih.gov/pmc/articles/PMC7372112/>.

39 Rachel Elisabeth Irwin, *Misinformation and De-Contextualization: International Media Reporting on Sweden and COVID-19*, 16(62) Globalization and Health 9–10 (2020).

avoid a great economic disaster and loss of jobs. This only further complicated the decision-making process at state and supranational levels, where the decision of closing entire airports and borders was made only after the disaster occurred. All these issues bring to light another fundamental question: How do we effectively deal with the limits of expert knowledge in a crisis situation created by a new pandemic?

The ongoing global pandemic has, more than ever before, made it clear among the non-experts and the general public opinion that the role of experts in the policy- and regulation-making process is the cornerstone of society in our contemporary world. Due to the effects of globalization, the decisions of governments and international organizations have an enormous impact on the life of communities and citizens of countries throughout the world. The global pandemic has just reminded us that barriers and walls might give the impression to part of the public opinion of being protected by what is unknown and "alien." As for fighting against climate change, the challenges of mitigation cannot be underestimated and cannot be solved by one country alone but rather require a global effort. Also, public health is a matter that needs a global coalition to promote scientific collaboration and exchange among experts and scientists around the world to protect each and every community and family for the common future we share on this Earth.

3 The Great Acceleration of the Anthropocene

As previously addressed, especially in the case of COVID-19, the analysis of globalization is connected with the relationship among humans, science, and technology and the ability of that science and technology to affect human action.[40] In this sense, the background of globalization is an inescapable interpretative reference for adequately questioning climate change as an agent of economic, social, and legal change. In order to improve the understanding about climate change, globalization, along with science and technology, should be taken as an interpretative reference to shed lights on the relationships between humans and non-humans in current society.[41] Humans have

40 Literature on Science, Technology, and Society is extensive; for some key references, see Sheila Jasanoff, States of Knowledge: The Co-Production of Science and the Social Order (Routledge 2004); Sheila Jasanoff, *Serviceable Truths: Science for Action in Law and Policy*, 93 Texas Law Review 1723 (2014); Philip L. Bereano, *Saving Us From Ourselves: The Interaction of Law and Science-Technology: Comment*, 47 Denver Law Review 671 (1970); Simon A. Cole & Alyse Bertenthal, *Science, Technology, Society, and Law*, 13 Annual Review of Law and Social Science 351 (2017).

41 Paolo Davide Farah, *The Role of Imagination, Marginalized Communities, Law and Technology in Building an Ethical Approach to the Anthropocene*, *in* Ethics and Politics of Space for the Anthropocene (Anu Valtonen, Outi Rantala & Paolo Davide Farah (eds.), Edward Elgar Publishing 2020); Anu Valtonen & Outi Rantala, *Introduction: Reimagining Ways of Talking about the Anthropocene*, *in* Ethics and Politics of Space for the Anthropocene (Anu Valtonen, Outi Rantala & Paolo Davide Farah (eds.), Edward Elgar Publishing 2020)

developed at such extent their relations with technology (and science) that they ended up becoming a product of their very own technology, like the most evident examples of artificial intelligence and big data can demonstrate. The pandemic shows how the rapid diffusion and spread of COVID-19 is mainly due to technological advancements in the field of transportation and in the creation of interdependencies of the global society. Technology is the main vehicle of the pandemic, because as a technological product, it gives life to economic and productive activities without borders and globally interconnects them from a technical point of view. This has led to increases with respect to mobility, transport, exposure to substances of any kind, and human interactions. The fertile soil of global interdependence cannot, in its general scope, be "governed" by any traditional state or regional subject. This, as previously anticipated, reveals the structural political delay of the globalization processes. But in the same way, science and technology were also the solutions to the problem in that less than one year after the appearance of COVID-19, scientific advances managed to provide a few responses through the use of vaccines.

The prevailing "techno-global" trait of the pandemic allows us to identify the areas to further explore for understanding how to interpret phenomenon such as climate change. It is precisely in the relationships between humans and non-humans that we should look at and, specifically, how these relationships have been consolidated by technological advancement. A relationship evidently distorted for the needs of the forces of production and for the lifestyle that, consequently, belongs to us. The relationship of human domination over the environment is increasingly counterproductive for the very survival of human life.[42] The environment on which the virus spread is not an abstract, untouched, and natural environment but has been created and formalized by humans. An environment historically produced by humans and for human purposes in the quest for modernization. This environment facilitates pollution and destruction of global commons, jumps of viruses amongst different species which, together with manipulation of fauna, generate infectious diseases transmitted by animals. Deforestation also enables widespread diffusion of viruses.[43]

<www.elgaronline.com/view/edcoll/9781839108693/9781839108693.00005.xml>; Giovanni Frigo, *Beyond the Capitalocene: An Ecocentric Perspective for the Energy Transition*, *in* Ethics and Politics of Space for the Anthropocene (Anu Valtonen, Outi Rantala & Paolo Davide Farah (eds.), Edward Elgar Publishing 2020) <www.elgaronline.com/view/edcoll/9781839108693/9781839108693.00005.xml>.

42 Paolo Davide Farah, *Foreword to Sustainability and Peaceful Coexistence for the Anthropocene*, *in* Sustainability and Peaceful Coexistence for the Anthropocene (Pasi Heikkurinen (ed.), Routledge 2016).

43 Rodrick Wallace et al., Clear-Cutting Disease Control: Capital-Led Deforestation, Public Health Austerity, and Vector-Borne Infection (Springer 2018).

Consequently, due to COVID-19,[44] the necessity to balance sustainable development and globalization[45] has become even more important as a result of the recent events which the world is currently witnessing and perfectly fits into the broader discussions related to the necessary changes and improvements of the international legal norms and systems of governance towards the protection of non-trade concerns.[46] At the core meaning of NTCs, there is the assertion that it is not really possible to have economic growth in the long term without a real geographical and geological balance between human activities and the Earth's habitat. In general, we need to have an effective paradigm shift in the idea of industrialization and, particularly, in the development of cities. Any further expansion of the human race must happen with much more consideration given to the protection and respect of the flora and fauna. Otherwise, nature might continue to show us more and more visible negative effects on our human society, with unpredictable spillover effects,[47] such as what has been occurring for COVID-19 thus far. Security, trade, investment, economic growth, and environmental protection are so far separated components of national policy that should now be balanced and reconciled with a holistic and more naturally oriented vision.

Even before the pandemic, Eugene Stoermer and Paul Crutzen suggested that this environment is part of a new geological epoch: the Anthropocene.[48] This is the present era in which human activities are the main cause of environmental changes, at the territorial, structural, and climatic level. The imprint of humans and the weight of anthropogenic activities on the global ecosystem are increasingly marked. Of course, climate change is the most obvious and sparkling effect of this epoch. The effects that global warming produces on the ecosystem, such as the melting of glaciers, or extreme weather events, such as tsunamis, hurricanes, and droughts, are dramatically increasing and becoming more the rule than the exception and more than isolated incidents.

44 Ruiyun Li et al., *Substantial Undocumented Infection Facilitates the Rapid Dissemination of Novel Coronavirus (SARS-CoV2)*, Science 1 (2020).

45 Paolo Davide Farah, *L'Unione Europea e i Valori Non Commerciali Nel Sistema Globale Degli Scambi*, *in* Cittadinanza europea e diritti umani (Louis Godart (ed.), Pubblicazioni del Sottosegrerio di Stato alla Presidenza del Consiglio dei Ministri del Governo Italiano 2018); Paolo Davide Farah, *EU and CARICOM: Dilemmas versus Opportunities on Development, Law and Economics (Foreword)*, *in* EU and CARICOM: Dilemmas Versus Opportunities on Development, Law and Economics (Alicia Roberts, Stephen Hardy & Winfried Huck (eds.), Routledge 2020).

46 Farah, *Trade and Progress*, *supra* note 23; Farah & Cima, *supra* note 23.

47 David Quammen, Spillover: Animal Infections and the Next Human Pandemic (W. W. Norton & Company 2013).

48 Paul J. Crutzen & Eugene F. Stoermer, *The Anthropocene*, 41 GBP Newsletter 17–18 (2000); Paul J. Crutzen, *Geology of Mankind*, 415 Nature 23 (2020); Paul J. Crutzen, Benvenuti nell'Antropocene. L'uomo ha Cambiato il Clima, la Terra Entra in una Nuova Era (Mondadori 2005). Anu Valtonen, Outi Rantala & Paolo Davide Farah (eds.), Ethics and Politics of Space for the Anthropocene (Edward Elgar Publishing 2020).

Climate change affects not only the environment but also the social dimension framed as the material living conditions of humans. For this reason, it would be essential to assess the relationships among science, technology, and society. Important analyses have already been examined in order to understand at which point science and technology are helping human beings and from which point they are harming nature (to include human beings, themselves, and non-humans).

The Anthropocene epoch differs from the Holocene based on a stratigraphic investigation at the level of the Earth's surface. The relationship between the Anthropocene epoch and climate change is very close, considering that the Anthropocene epoch is characterized precisely as an era in which there is a clear global climate change generated by a process that can be traced back to the advent of the steam engine, then passing through the dizzying late-modern industrial growth combined with the increase in transport, communications, the use of chemicals, and the general level of consumption.[49] The increase in CO_2 emission levels would be nothing more than one of the most evident and relevant indicators of the technical-economic process of the second modernity capable of directly affecting global climatic conditions. Not surprisingly, the "Great Acceleration," which consolidates the period of the Anthropocene, is placed in the period of time that elapses between 1945 and today.[50]

4 From Ecological Modernization to Climate Justice

Even though the concept of the Anthropocene epoch comes from natural sciences, the historical, political, cultural, and social connotations are of key importance. The "progressive" and expansive narrative of the Anthropocene epoch questions, rooted in modernity, are continuously reiterated in the context of economic globalization. At the same time, we can identify, through an oversimplification, two general approaches that derive from the contemporary awareness of the character conspicuously counterproductive of human action with respect to the environment.

The first approach can be associated with the umbrella concept of ecological modernization[51] or the neoliberal promoted idea of sustainable development.

49 Will Steffen et al., *The Trajectory of the Anthropocene: The Great Acceleration*, 2 The Anthropocene Review 81, 81–98 (2015).

50 John Robert McNeill & Peter Engelke, The Great Acceleration: An Environmental History of the Anthropocene Since 1945 (Harvard University Press 2014).

51 In China, this concept has been reframed by highlighting the need to connect modernization with the populace. Sam Geall & Adrian Ely, *Narratives and Pathways Towards an Ecological Civilization in Contemporary China*, 236 The China Quarterly 1175 (2018). On Ecological modernization see: J. Huber, New Technologies and Environmental Innovation (Edward Elgar 2004); Arthur P. J. Mol, David A. Sonnenfeld & Gert Spaargaren (eds.), The Ecological Modernisation Reader: Environmental Reform in Theory and Practice

This approach does not deny the techno-economic assumptions that generated the Anthropocene epoch but is only trying to reduce environmental degradation via a wide array of market-based mechanisms or political commitments on the green transition. Under this approach, science and technology are seen as tools to design a production process able to progressively reduce the harmful effects of human activities on the environment. This is the dominant approach and could also be seen in international climate summits,[52] which try to strike a balance between economic development and sustainable development and only recently acknowledged the need and the importance of intergenerational equity.[53] Still, the international climate change negotiations have involved representation from the civil society, including the business sector as well as multinational companies that committed to cut their emissions regardless of the eventual signature of the Paris Agreement. Ecological modernization remains anchored, despite several attempts to reverse the trend, to the foundations of techno-economic capitalism, and this could be one of the reasons for its failure as an effective strategy at a domestic and global level. In fact, such an approach does not involve a radical rethinking of lifestyles, production

(Routledge 2009). For a sectoral and emblematic reflection on the issues of the relationship between the model of sustainable development and the juridical-economic logic of the global scenario, see cf. P. D. Farah & T. Otvos, *Competition Law and Trade in Energy vs. Sustainable Development: A Clash of Individualism and Cooperative Partnerships*? 2 Arizona State Law Journal 497–513 (2018).

52 International Climate Conferences, also referred as Conferences of the Parties (COP) (Conferences of the Parties, understood as countries that have acceded to the United Nations Framework Convention on Climate Change – UNFCCC), were launched for the first time in 1992 in Rio de Janeiro. In fact, the UNFCCC was held in Rio in that year, informally known as the Earth Summit, and the resulting document from this convention is known as the Rio Declaration. This convention gave birth to the first international environmental treaty. The treaty was aimed at reducing greenhouse gas emissions based on the hypothesis of global warming and did not set mandatory limits for greenhouse gas emissions for individual nations. The treaty was, therefore, from this point of view, legally non-binding. Yet the established framework included the possibility for the signatory parties to adopt, at special conferences, additional acts (called "Protocols") which could set mandatory emission limits. The most important of such Protocols, adopted in 1997 and entered into force in 2005, is the Kyoto Protocol. During the COP 2007 in Bali and the COP 2009 in Copenhagen, however, no concrete results were obtained. To solve this impasse, the following two COPs, after 2009, placed emphasis on boosting dialogues between interested parties and established the Green Climate Fund. The fund was aimed at supporting developing countries in their efforts to reduce environmental degradation in their medium plan. A key milestone for international environmental law was reached during the 2015 Paris Climate Conference with the Paris Agreement. Within the Paris Agreement, 196 countries committed to limit the increase in the global average temperature well below 2°C. The Paris Agreement officially entered into force on 4 November 2016. On the contrary, the last four UNFCCC COPs did not obtain the expected results, and in 2020, the COP, to be held in Glasgow, had been postponed due to COVID-19.

53 Edith Brown Weiss, *Intergenerational Equity in a Kaleidoscopic World*, 49 Environmental Policy and Law 3 (2019).

models, and criteria for the distribution of wealth,[54] which is becoming more and more necessary to try to revert the irreparable damage which has already been caused against the Earth. Ultimately, when confronted with budget constraints and possible civil unrest or protests, policymakers might continue to shape their policies by giving higher priority to the economic consequences of their decisions, such as job losses or financial disruption, instead of the environmental consequences. For this reason, it is essential that both leaders and the common people understand the long-term economic and social consequences of putting the environment as the top priority for any governmental or political agenda.

The second, and alternative, approach is the one of climate justice and intergenerational equity.[55] It is a polysemic concept, able to evoke two different ideas. First, in a narrow sense, legal remedies, under the logic of multilevel systems,[56] could be proposed on the basis of the damage caused to individuals or communities due to climate change. This is clearly represented by the growing number of climate change litigation occurring around the world.[57] The second idea, attached to climate justice, which covers its theoretical underpinning in a much broader sense, is a conceptual strategy rooted in political activism, social movements, and world civic politics with respect to climate change and environmental protection, but without an immediate recourse to legal instruments of enforcement and implementation.[58] It seems that this second meaning is the most commonly attributed to climate justice due to

54 For an overview of alternatives to the current global governance system, see: Margaret Stout & Jeannine M. Love, A Radically Democratic Response to Global Governance: Dystopian Utopias (Routledge 2016); Margaret Stout & Jeannine M. Love, Integrative Governance: Generating Sustainable Responses to Global Crises (Routledge 2018).

55 M. Robinson, Climate Justice: Hope, Resilience, and the Fight for a Sustainable Future (Bloomsbury Publishing 2018); H. Shue, Climate Justice: Vulnerability and Protection (Oxford University Press 2016); James Goodman, *From Global Justice to Climate Justice? Justice Ecologist in an Era of Global Warming*, 31(4) New Political Science 499–514 (2009); Tim Hayward, *Human Rights vs Emission Rights: Climate Justice and the Equitable Distribution of Ecological Space*, XXI Ethics and International 431–450 (2007); V. Shiva, Earth Democracy. Justice, Sustainability, and Peace (Southend Press 2005).

56 Farah & Rossi, *supra* note 11.

57 Kars De Graaf & Jan H. Jans, *The Urgenda Decision: Netherlands Liable for Role in Causing Dangerous Global Climate Change*, 27 Journal of Environmental Law 517 (2015); Renee N. Salas, Wendy Jacobs & Frederica Perera, *The Case of Juliana v. US – Children and the Health Burdens of Climate Change*, 380 New England Journal of Medicine 2085 (2019); More recently, the judgment of the Hague District Court highlights a key breakthrough in climate change litigations: Steef M. Bartman & Cornelis De Groot, *The Shell Nigeria Judgments by the Court of Appeal of the Hague, a Breakthrough in the Field of International Environmental Damage? UK Law and Dutch Law on Parental Liability Compared*, 18 European Company Law (2021).

58 Neil Carter, The Politics of the Environment: Ideas, Activism, Policy (Cambridge University Press 2018).

the rise of political ecology[59] as a hotly debated and researched field, with an evident connection between the theories and the practice actioned particularly by environmental non-governmental organizations (NGOs) and civil society groups. The expression "climate justice" identifies global warming as the cause of an ethical and political concern. Against this background, the term "justice" is not directly related with the satisfaction of legal claims in a technical sense but rather involves an ethical reflection that includes the link between human rights, collective rights, and the historical contribution and responsibilities of political and economic subjects with regard to climate change. At the heart of this approach, there is the critique of the greater damage suffered by vulnerable populations and communities, particularly in the Global South, as a result of climate change due to the industrialization, economic development, growth, and wealth created in the Global North. Particular attention is therefore paid to the different historical contributors to global pollution and climate change. It requires a balanced approach which encompasses both the most affected by climate change and those who are more generally affected by the conditions that generate such changes and that involve lifestyles capable of producing high emissions and poor efficiency in the use of environmental resources.[60] In this sense, climate justice aims at the protection of the most vulnerable as they lack the adequate resources for dealing with the environmental and socio-economic effects of climate change. The most vulnerable in highly developed and industrialized societies (such as children, women, and migrants) often coincide and share similar needs with the same populations of the less developed and poorer regions around the globe.

Climate justice, intended here as ethical-political justice, has been elaborated and proposed chiefly by the most committed NGOs working on environmental issues.[61] The words "climate justice" only recently entered, with resistance, the lexicon used by the international economic institutions, the UN, and the international climate negotiations. The 2016 Paris Agreement marks a partial turning point with respect to the prevalence of the ecological approach to modernization. The Agreement emphasizes the concept of

59 Thomas Albert Perreault, Gavin Bridge & James McCarthy (eds.), The Routledge Handbook of Political Ecology (Routledge 2015).

60 Rajendra K. Pachauri et al., Facing Global Environmental Change: Environmental, Human, Energy, Food, Health and Water Security Concepts, vol 4 (Springer Science & Business Media 2009); Christian Schubert, *Green Nudges: Do They Work? Are They Ethical?*, 132 Ecological Economics 329 (2017).

61 For the contribution of NGOs to international climate change negotiations, see, in general: Katharina Rietig, *The Power of Strategy: Environmental NGO Influence in International Climate Negotiations*, 22 Global Governance 269 (2016); and for a specific analysis of Greenpeace: Edwin R. Stafford, Michael Jay Polonsky & Cathy L. Hartman, *Environmental NGO – Business Collaboration and Strategic Bridging: A Case Analysis of the Greenpeace – Foron Alliance*, 9 Business Strategy and the Environment 122 (2000).

climate justice[62] and its importance in the actions to be carried out to reach a just and equitable green transition. At a regional level, for example, the European Union Parliament resolution of 16 January 2018 on women, equal opportunities, and climate justice, often the most affected categories, includes reference to the concept of climate justice.[63] The resolution argues that the EU, in line with its capabilities, can contribute to improving legal and political structures in support of climate justice by promoting the construction of an international framework aimed at

> adopt[ing] a gender-responsive, human-rights-based approach . . . to avert, minimise (sic) and address displacement related to the adverse impacts of climate change, which acknowledges that women and girls belong to the most vulnerable groups displaced by climate change and are therefore particularly vulnerable to trafficking and gender-based violence.[64]

Through the concept of climate justice reconstructed here, the emphasis is therefore placed on the social and spatial inequalities that technical-economic evolution has entailed and on the unequal distribution of the costs of this approach. The concept is supported at the theoretical level by the literature on environmental history[65] and political ecology,[66] in which the origins and developments of the ecological crisis have been reconstructed for decades. These factors enabling the crisis should be analyzed at both the material level (as in the case of terrestrial environmental degradation) and the theoretical or symbolic level (as in the case of the perception of the world itself and in the conceptions of individual and collective life that have established themselves over time). Not surprisingly, environmental history highlights[67] the relationship

62 The preamble of the Paris Agreement posits noting the importance for some of the concept of "climate justice" when taking action to address climate change: "Paris Agreement" <http://ec.europa.eu/clima/policies/international/negotiations/paris/index_en.htm>.

63 European Parliament, *Women, Gender Equality and Climate Justice* 2018 [2017/2086(INI)] 9.

64 *Id.* at para 16; on a similar note, see Cillian Lohan, *Opinion of the European Economic and Social Committee on 'Climate Justice'* 2018 [2018/C 081/04] 9 "calls for the EU and its Member States to develop the principle of climate justice; insists that the greatest injustice of our failure to tackle climate change effectively would be the detrimental effects on poor countries and populations, and on women in particular"; European Parliament, On climate change: a European strategic long-term vision for a prosperous, modern, competitive and climate neutral economy in accordance with the Paris Agreement 2019 [2019/2582 (RSP)].

65 Ranjan Chakrabarti, Situating Environmental History (Manohar Publishers 2007); J. Donald Hughes, What Is Environmental History? (John Wiley & Sons 2016); Gilbert F. LaFreniere, The Decline of Nature: Environmental History and the Western Worldview (Oak Savanna Publishing 2012).

66 Perreault, Bridge & McCarthy, *supra* note 59.

67 Jason W. Moore, *Marx's Ecology and the Environmental History of World Capitalism*, 12 Capitalism Nature Socialism 134, 136 (2001): "Every phase of capitalist development entails a new, more expansive and more intensive, exploitative relation to the land."

between Western civilization processes and the progressive degradation of the biosphere. In addition, political ecology acknowledges the relationship between colonial power and environmental degradation.[68] For all these reasons, climate justice, in its more political connotation, leads to a radical rethinking of the trajectories of the Western process of civilization.[69] Other countries' experiences, if historically grounded, could also help in further strengthening environmental protection at the global level.[70] Pursuing the ideal of climate justice implies the need to question individual and collective lifestyles,[71] but also the very structure of production processes.

The most disruptive long-term effect of climate justice is the awareness of the inadequacy not only of our lifestyles but also of the institutions used to deal with climate change. It is an approach that leads us to understand how a global policy is urgently needed. This leads, again, to discovering how political categories still have a meaning today in order to overcome the friend/enemy distinction. In the Anthropocene epoch, there needs to be an understanding of how politics must increasingly come to terms with the following fundamental oppositions: the conflicts among humans and between humans and non-humans. Further, it is necessary to have a genuine and honest consideration of the negative effects that human activities caused, including a deliberately manipulated and endangered environment that puts the very deep essence of the Earth and the life of both humans and non-humans at stake.

Ecological crises also show a peculiar feature of social systems and organization in the age of globalization. Against the background of a structurally complex real world, social systems are faced with an environment (not in the biophysical sense but in the social and cultural one) in which the number of particular situations, given by the concrete and feasible possibilities, has increased exponentially due to the acceleration of technological and economic advancements. The selection of the possibilities offered by the environment, aimed at reducing the gap between the multiplicity of possible and feasible experiences aimed at reducing social complexity, is, consequently, increasingly unmanageable. As Niklas Luhmann has masterfully explained, the reduction of this complexity is the operation that constitutes, and in some way justifies, the systems and, in particular, the social sub-systems (law, politics, economics, science, morals, etc.)[72] as specific tools aimed at reducing the distance that ex-

68 Tim Forsyth, *Political Ecology and the Epistemology of Social Justice*, 39 Geoforum 756, 759 (2008).

69 Stout & Love, *supra* note 54.

70 Paolo Davide Farah, *Strategies to Balance Energy Security, Business, Trade and Sustainable Development: Selected Case Studies*, 13 The Journal of World Energy Law & Business 95 (2020).

71 For a critical analysis of the degrowth movement, see Giorgos Kallis et al., *Research on Degrowth*, 43 Annual Review of Environment and Resources 291 (2018).

72 Regarding the legal social sub-system and the concept of juridical order as a product of social context, see Santi Romano, The Legal Order (Routledge 2017); Paolo Davide Farah, *L'influenza Della Concezione Confuciana Sulla Costruzione Del Sistema Giuridico e Politico Cinese*, *in*

ists between expectations and concretely experientable possible futures.[73] The global environment is a complex context and requires categories which are not so easy to combine with the needs of social systems, which are, most of the time, evidently a representation of needs and instances developed at local level. In fact, social systems struggle to delimit their own scope with respect to the global environment. In this context, it is necessary to continue to proactively face the challenges to bring unity to the dichotomy between global and local through the concept of glocal and glocalism.[74] A sub-system such as the political one tasked via the exercise of the power of political forces and public administration,[75] to govern complexity, ends up submitting more and more to other sub-systems (although this does not correspond to a Luhmannian theoretical representation) whose communication codes respond to logics inevitably different from the political ones. There is a growing understanding among citizens, and common people around the world, that we live in the same Earth, experience similar needs, and all desire for a future for us and our children. The concept of "global village" can help us understand how science and technology have modified how humans perceive time and space: "the time has ceased and the space has vanished."[76] But nature and non-humans do not follow the same rules, and their needs might remain immutable for centuries. Global environmental movements, helped in their concerted actions by social media and technology, are able to transform this concept of a "global village" towards a more understandable concept of a community of shared (environmental) values towards a healthy environment for our children and future generations. This activism also has important implications in terms of environmental awareness at the local, national, and international political levels. Leaders are becoming more and more accountable for the choices on policies that have implications or ramifications in the environmental sphere. Public opinion now requires, more than ever, that their leaders' decisions are based in sound science and not simply economically driven.

Precisely for these reasons, climate justice can only be the vehicle of a political metamorphosis generated by climate change, but only if this is supported by a rationally acceptable ethical foundation. A foundation that

---

Identità europea e politiche migratorie (Giovanni Bombelli & Bruno Montanari (eds.), Vita e Pensiero 2008).

73 Niklas Luhmann, Social Systems (Stanford University Press 1995).

74 Joyeeta Gupta, Kim van der Leeuw & Hans de Moel, *Climate Change: A "Glocal" Problem Requiring "Glocal" Action*, 4 Environmental Sciences 139 (2007); Erik Swyngedouw & Maria Kaïka, *The Making of "Glocal" Urban Modernities*, 7 City 5 (2003).

75 Niklas Luhmann, Politische Planung: Aufsätze zur Soziologie von Politik und Verwaltung (Westdeutscher Verlag 1971); Niklas Luhmann, Trust and Power (Wiley 1979).

76 Marshall McLuhan coined the phrase "global village" in his book *The Gutenberg Galaxy* and it developed the concept in more detail in Marshall McLuhan & Bruce R. Powers, The Global Village: Transformations in World Life and Media in the 21st Century (Oxford University Press 1992).

is able to oppose, at least at the theoretical level, the prevalence of the codes of the economic sub-system over the political one. Without a solid foundation, climate justice risks being confused with a mere, albeit legitimate, anti-capitalist instance and therefore being reduced to a mere ideological option. Such a theoretical framework should place and precisely identify future generations as actual victims of the damages caused by the environmental crisis. This would allow, at the very least, supporting the conceptual core of the demands advanced in the name of climate justice through an ethically based political approach that places at the centre of the paradigm that we are all human beings, we are all brought together by the care and consideration for our children's and grandchildren's future and well-being, and the fact that we only have one Earth to preserve and use to keep in a healthy environment. The next section, drawing on Hans Jonas's ethics of responsibility, analyzes possible ways to move forward in the environmental crisis.

5 The Need for a Trans-Temporal Ethics

If the concept of climate justice seeks to chiefly address the protection of vulnerable people, future generations should represent an inescapable point of reference for any environmental strategy and policy.[77] It is precisely because future generations have no voice and safety net, that they are passive subjects with respect to the effects of choices made by others, and thus they embody the very category of vulnerability.[78] It is no coincidence that one of the most solid elaboration of environmental ethics[79] is the one proposed by Hans Jonas,[80] in which the reference to future generations plays a leading role.

77 For an in-depth analysis of the philosophical implications of an ethics of responsibility aimed at protecting future generations and the environment, see Iñigo Gonzalez-Ricoy & Axel Gosseries (eds.), Institutions for Future Generations (Oxford University Press 2016); Stephen M. Gardiner, A Perfect Moral Storm. The Ethical Tragedy of Climate Change (Oxford University Press 2011); Ferdinando Menga & Matthias Fritsch, *Phenomenology and Responsibility Towards Future Generations*, 5(2) Metodo. International Studies in Phenomenology and Philosophy 7–16 (2017); Ferdinando Menga, L'emergenza Del Futuro. I Destini Del Pianeta e La Responsabilità Del Presente (Donzelli Editore 2021); Ferdinando Menga, Etica Intergenerazionale (Morcelliana 2021); Fabio Ciaramelli & Ferdinando Menga (eds.), Responsabilità Verso le Generazioni Future: Una Sfida al Diritto all'etica e alla Politica (Editoriale scientifica 2017).

78 For a philosophical-juridical reflection on the category of vulnerability, see, among others, Gianfrancesco Zanetti, Filosofia della vulnerabilità. Percezione, discriminazione, diritto (Carocci Editore 2019); Orsetta Giolo & Baldassare Pastore, Vulnerabilità. Analisi multidisciplinare di un concetto (Carocci Editore 2018).

79 For a valuable reconstruction of the different approaches in this context, see: Stephen Mark Gardiner et al., Climate Ethics: Essential Readings (Oxford University Press 2010).

80 On the scholarship of Hans Jonas on environmental ethics: Theresa Morris, Hans Jonas's Ethic of Responsibility: From Ontology to Ecology (SUNY Press 2013); Lewis Coyne, Life, Technology and the Horizons of Responsibility (Bloomsbury Publishing 2020); Vittorio

On a closer look, the interests of future generations in environmental matters, which could be translated into positive or negative rights with duties and obligations attached, acquire a complete, philosophical, and juridical meaning. Yet these rights should be intended as reflections of human duties, and above all, those duties that are addressed via public and collective policies are able to guarantee these rights even if they are not yet in existence. This peculiar relationship between rights and duties rests, as in the case of Jonas, on a critical reading of modern technology and of how advancements in this field have a role in the social reality. The benefits from technology should be placed on a parallel track which contains a reflection on the threats that they have for the survival of humans and non-humans. Technological processes and advancements, especially emerging technologies, such as artificial intelligence, blockchain, and big data, cannot be easily compared to those of previous geological epoch. Indeed, the Anthropocene epoch teaches us that:

> Modern technology, informed by an ever-deeper penetration of nature and propelled by the forces of market and politics, has enhanced human power beyond anything known or even dreamed of before. It is a power over matter, over life on earth, and over man himself.[81]

The radically new character of emerging technologies which shape humans as technological bio-products, such as genetically engineered humans, makes both classical and modern ethics partially inadequate. The analysis of the rational-based foundation of moral behaviour clashes with the focus on future generations. In order to adapt ethics to the problems posed by technological advancements, it is necessary to change the perspective, especially with regards to time. The frame of reference cannot be the present but, necessarily, should be projected towards the future. This projection in the life and the world to come should be rooted in both the present and in the past with a genuine and informed memory of the mistakes and challenges that humans have faced when their actions were not carefully considering the hope for eternity of human beings and the infinity of the nature, the Earth, and the cosmos. The human should make decisions after careful reflection beyond the limits of time and space of his or her own physical existence and with contemplation of the invisible beyond the visible.

Hösle, Filosofia della Crisi Ecologica (Einaudi Editore 1992); Maria Loredana Furiosi, Uomo e Natura nel Pensiero di Hans Jonas (Vita e Pensiero 2003); Karl-Otto Apel, Paolo Becchi & Paul Ricoeur, Hans Jonas: il Filosofo e la Responsabilità (Albo Versorio 2004); Paolo Becchi, La Vulnerabilità della Vita. Contributi su Hans Jonas (La Scuola di Pitagora 2008).

81 Hans Jonas, The Imperative of Responsibility: In Search of an Ethics for the Technological Age IX (The University of Chicago Press 1984).

A perspective that opens through what Jonas defines as a heuristic of fear, which

> must tell us what is *possibly* at stake and what we must beware of. The magnitude of those stakes, taken together with the insufficiency of our predictive knowledge, leads to the pragmatic rule to give the prophecy of doom priority over the prophecy of bliss.[82]

Jonas's vision on duties and obligations and the consequent ethics of responsibility implies and requires an ethical reflection to make the best decisions now in light of a sustainable and positive future(s).[83] On the other hand, without an ethical conscience, the discourse on the rights of future generations[84] – and we would also argue the same as it pertains to climate justice – risks being reduced to a pure rhetorical exercise because it lacks adequate anthropological support. As can be seen from Jonas's reflections and from the techno-economic reading of the Anthropocene epoch, the contemporary context is unlike the past, not only of the pre-modern era, but also of the first centuries of modernity. In fact, the potential of contemporary technology, which allows to produce irreversible effects in the short, medium, long, and very long term, is able to question the very existence of humanity as a species and the image of the man himself as being endowed with freedom and autonomy. The "ontological" novelty is that humans, thanks to science and technology, have become more dangerous for nature than nature once was for them:

> Take, for instance, as the first major change in the inherited picture, the critical vulnerability of nature to man's technological intervention – unsuspected before it began to show itself in damage already done. This discovery, whose shock led to the concept and nascent science of ecology, alters the very concept of ourselves as a causal agency in the larger scheme of things. It brings to light, through the effects, that the nature of human action has *de facto* changed, and that an object of an entirely new order – no less than the whole biosphere of the planet – has been added to what we must be responsible for because of our power over it.[85]

82 *Id.* at X.

83 E. R. Rowland, Molly S. Cross & Holly Hartmann, Considering Multiple Futures: Scenario Planning to Address Uncertainty in Natural Resource Conservation (U.S. Fish and Wildlife Service, June 2014); Jonathan Star et al., *Supporting Adaptation Decisions through Scenario Planning: Enabling the Effective Use of Multiple Methods*, 13 Climate Risk Management 88–94 (2016).

84 For an overview of the relation between Jonas and Foucault's scholarship on the topic, see: Paul Alberts, *Responsibility Towards Life in the Early Anthropocene*, 16 Angelaki 5 (2011); Lars Botin, *The Technological Construction of the Self: Techno-Anthropological Readings and Reflections*, 19 Techné: Research in Philosophy and Technology 211 (2015).

85 Jonas, *supra* note 81, at 6–7.

But the transformation given by the awareness of the vulnerability of nature that comes from the human's own capability of studying and understanding more and more the effect of his or her own actions through sound science-based analysis is associated, inevitably, with the awareness of his or her vulnerability as human species, which is essentially part of the nature itself and also in a technically manipulated and, therefore, unpredictably dangerous environment. On one hand, these transformations call for overturning the ethical perspective itself. The problem is given by the fact that the modern ethical tradition of the West remains anchored to the moral quality of the concept of acting in the present and not in the future. On the other, it is not projected onto the unpredictable and indeterminate long-term consequences of our actions. Affirming, as Kant did, that "I ought never to act except in such a way that I can also will that my maxim should become a universal law"[86] means that humans must act now by respecting others' freedoms, because not doing so would mean accepting, for the sake of logical consistency, possible violations of their own freedom by others in the future. This entails a duty with respect to the mutual and present relationships of humans, but not with respect to the humanity that in itself takes place in history. The categorical imperative directly evokes the concept of humanity, as when Kant writes: "Act in such a way that you always treat humanity, whether in your own person or in the person of any other, never simply as a means, but always at the same time as an end."[87] However, it refers to an agent and another who live a common present, unless you understand the "otherness" discussed here in a trans-temporal category.

But this last meaning of the term "otherness," in relation to Kant's discussion, must be excluded according to Jonas's interpretation. The categorical imperative implies an agreement of reason with itself. It assumes the existence of a society of rational human agents, and given this assumption, the action must be able to be thought of without any self-convolution as an acceptable practice on the part of the existing community. The logical need to avoid self-conflict, in other words, has, as a reference area, also logical and not moral, the present humanity and not the future. As Jonas argues, from this point of view, "[t]here is no self-contradiction in the thought that humanity would once come to an end, therefore also none in the thought that the happiness of present and proximate generations would be bought with the unhappiness or even nonexistence of later ones."[88] From the Kantian point of view, the problem arises from the difficulty, if not impossibility, of qualifying as rational subjects, to whom we must keep in mind when we perform actions today, individuals who do not yet exist and who, in a logical-theoretical sense, may never

86 Immanuel Kant, Groundwork of the Metaphysic of Morals 70 (402) (Hutchinson's University Library 1947).

87 *Id.* at 96 (429).

88 Jonas, *supra* note 81, at 11.

exist. At the end of the day, the moral universe is substantiated, according to this conception, in the horizon of contemporaneity, limiting the concept of time to be considered in both our reflections and the decision-making process just to the present. These claims, with respect to our behaviours, come from those who live with us in the world, from those who currently feel influenced by our actions and omissions.[89]

For Jonas, the synchronic ethics just described is "content," as the basis of moral action, with a knowledge accessible to all people with goodwill. As Kant said, "human reason can, in matters of morality, be easily brought to a high degree of accuracy and precision even in the most ordinary intelligence,"[90] and "there is no need of science or philosophy for knowing what man has to do in order to be honest and good, and indeed to be wise and virtuous."[91] It would be precisely the limit given by the synchronic contextualization of such an ethical approach to devalue the scientific contribution, especially that of a predictive nature, as a cognitive support of moral action. Moreover, Jonas points out that even classical ethics, such as Aristotelian ethics, which are certainly more sensitive towards the cognitive contribution to the moral choice, do not appeal to a properly theoretical science of a predictive type. In the context of these ethical reflections, the knowledge of the situation depends on the experience and judgement that are formed here and now, which do not presuppose a strictly scientific knowledge capable of predicting the long-term effects of the actions of each one and, a fortiori, the effects of the involuntary aggregation of the conduct of humans. "Good" and "evil" are identified in the context of a short-term context: "This 'knowledge' proper to virtue (of the 'where, when, to whom, and how') stays with the immediate issue, in whose defined context the action as the agent's own takes its course and within which it terminates."[92]

Further, to the traits of traditional ethics, especially modern ethics, as a synchronic ethics and therefore devoid of the support of theoretical science, is also added, according to Jonas, the fundamentally anthropocentric character deriving from a strictly infrahuman conception. The impact on non-human objects is not relevant in the context of this ethical tradition precisely because the whole field of *techne*, such as manual knowledge, is not perceived, for objective historical reasons, as an activity capable of questioning the self-preservation of nature. In the period prior to the Anthropocene epoch, the very question of the possibility of permanent damage to the integrity of the natural environment was not seriously raised "because

89 One of the most significant recent contributions to a rational and argumentative foundation of the imperative of responsibility to future generations is represented by Ferdinando G. Menga, Lo Scandalo Del Futuro. Per una Giustizia Intergenerazionale (Storia e Letteratura 2017).

90 Kant, *supra* note 86, at 59 (Preface).

91 *Id.* at 72 (404).

92 Jonas, *supra* note 81, at 6.

techne as an activity conceived itself as a determinate tribute to necessity and not as an indefinite, self-validating advance to mankind's major goal, claiming in its pursuit man's ultimate effort and concern."[93] So this conceptualization for the modern ethics before the Anthropocene does not only exclude future generations from the paradigm but also automatically removes the role of nature and non-humans due to their equal lacking of being rational subjects from our own perspective, interpretation, and the analysis of reality. But these non-humans are actually living the present, without the possibility of expressing, in our human language, their disagreement about the human choices and actions that affect their habitat and their own existence. Numerous species are disappearing from the Earth due to global warming, deforestation, and pollution. These are the missing links which represent the extinct species, damaging the natural evolution, and ultimately our Earth biodiversity. Nature and non-humans, once again, do respond to other rules than humans, not rationally identifiable in an anthropogenic term, and they have an equally different dimension of time more based on geological era, namely, centuries or millennia. Removing the actual negative impacts and damaging effects on nature and non-humans from the considerations about the decisions of humans is irremediably endangering our Earth. It might also ultimately risk the extinction of the human race, thereby leaving the Earth to be inhabited by other species capable of surviving the new environmental and climate conditions caused by the damaging actions of humans.

6 Hans Jonas's Imperative of Responsibility as the Ethical Foundation of Climate Justice

In Jonas's reading, the Western ethical tradition, founded on a synchronic and anthropocentric conception, appears inadequate to face the moral dilemmas produced by the technological civilization of the second modernity. It is precisely the technological focus of contemporary human beings that requires a change of perspective. First of all, this reversal of paradigm passes from a conception of duty no longer limited in an anthropocentric sense. Following Jonas's lead, it is more than reasonable, in the context in which we live, to ask whether or not human beings have the duty to take care of the biosphere and protect biodiversity. The question of duty is one that is rationally based on the *de facto* domination, unprecedented compared to the past, of humans against the environment. But the recognition of the existence of a moral claim on the part of the biosphere does not presuppose a questionable representation of the anthropomorphization of the natural environment. In reality, it is equivalent to the adoption of a point of view placing, at the centre, rational subjects as integral parts of the environment to be preserved.

93 *Id.* at 4.

From a natural science and geographical perspective, nature and the environment are more rational than, or at least as rational as, human beings. Non-humans and humans have always had similar self-preservation instincts and a fundamental tendency to behave in a manner that avoids injury and maximizes chances of survival. As from the Anthropocene epoch, it seems that a fracture has happened. The majority of humans have gradually moved from the countryside and now live in modern and industrialized cities or locations far from nature. In most cases, they do not need to fight to provide food, water, and/or shelter to their families, and they do not have an immediate perception of how nature and biodiversity are more and more affected by industrialization, the related means of production, global commercialization, and their overgrowing needs connected to both consumerism and market demands. Consequently, due to their lack of awareness of the impending risk and their contemporary far distance from nature, human beings did not immediately realize the need to reverse their actions, which are endangering the environment, because their self-preservation instinct was not triggered by the external factors that are more visible in nature. Nature follows rules that are certainly rational and include rational subjects in the paradigm, but with very different categories and perspectives than human equivalents. Anthropocentrism is a structural trait of ethical reasoning, despite Jonas's claim to neutralize it. But it can take on a moderate connotation if the very concept of the environment is understood as the synthesis and coexistence of nature and culture, as a biosphere and biodiversity and human presence. On the other hand, the representation of the Anthropocene epoch surely leads to such a conception of the environment. If so, environmental rights lose any ideological characterization to assume a rational foundation from an ethical point of view. If this is the case, as Jonas maintains,

> [i]t would mean to seek not only the human good but also the good of things extrahuman, that is, to extend the recognition of 'ends in themselves' beyond the sphere of man and make the human good include the care for them.[94]

The synchronic foundation of traditional ethics should, therefore, be questioned. The rights of future generations should coincide and be positively combined with environmental law in a diachronic and therefore trans-temporal perspective. Thus, a new moral imperative, adapted to such a change of perspective, would be: "Act so that the effects of your action are compatible with the permanence of genuine human-life."[95]

It is an imperative based on the level of historical rationality, starting from the awareness of the potential of contemporary technology that is able to

94 *Id.* at 7.
95 *Id.* at 11.

produce structurally and incessantly long-term effects. Consequences that affect the complex environment given by humans for how it is integrated into the biosphere. A new imperative that, on a strictly ethical level, is justified considering that, before respecting the freedom of others to do anything that does not violate our freedom, we must allow those other people in a trans-temporal sense to exist as moral subjects. The principle of the responsibility of humans towards future generations, which bases the rights of each generation on the basis of the duties of the present generation, is philosophically justified by the first purpose of humanity, which is to continue to be and to be there. This principle feeds on fear, in the sense of apprehension for the vulnerability of those who do not yet exist (on the model of the ethics of parental responsibility). A fear that should lead to prudent public action, which intervenes as a precaution, as enshrined, for example, in Principle 15 of the Rio Declaration. The Rio Declaration States that

> [i]n order to protect the environment, the precautionary approach shall be widely applied by States according to their capabilities. Where there are threats of serious or irreversible damage, lack of full scientific certainty shall be not used as a reason for postponing cost-effective measures to prevent environmental degradation.[96]

It is a principle, one which can be deduced from Jonas's imperative, which is aimed mainly at public policy and not directly at the behaviour of private individuals. Again, Jonas's ethics of responsibility differs from Kant's view. The coherence invoked by Jonas's imperative and the principle of responsibility is, in fact, one that should be between the ultimate effects of our actions and the permanence of human activity in the future. For this reason, the causal order of reference is not given by private behaviour but by political choices of a collective nature. The universalization that this imperative implies is not hypothetical, as in the Kantian case of the logical projection of the subject with respect to the representation/imagination of all the others. Instead, it is a universalization that is measured on the basis of the practical success calculated over the time horizon of the future. Therefore, the ethics of responsibility feeds on the cognitive contribution given by predictive science. On the basis of this contribution, in fact, its success is measured.

All this brings us back to the background from which we started. It brings us to the framework of the global world and the awareness of the need to remedy the political failure of globalization. Jonas's ethics of responsibility acquires, in fact, full meaning only in a global perspective and call into question the establishment of effective political structures of governance of

96 Rio Declaration, Rio Declaration on Environment and Development, *Report of the United Nations Conference on Environment and Development, Rio de Janeiro* (1992). Available at UN doc. A/CONF.151/26 (Vol. I) (UN General Assembly, 12 August 1992). See also (51).

globalization capable of affecting an emblematically global phenomenon such as that of climate change.[97] But the ethics of responsibility also makes it possible to pull the threads of reflection on the relationship among science, technology, and the Anthropocene epoch. Responsibility towards future generations is justified because of the technical domination as the result of a self-perpetuating process and the evidence of the Anthropocene epoch as an environmental and anthropic result of this domain. In other words, the principle of responsibility is supported by the very fact of a technically manipulated environment which risks calling into question the conditions of possibility for the permanence of human life. At the same time, in light of the relationship between the technical and Anthropocene epoch, it is clear that the ethics of responsibility represents a rational foundation for the conception of climate justice. If taken seriously, the environmental ethics here, sketched and reworked starting from Jonas's reflections, stands in contrast with the techno-economic model that dominated the second modernity. Unlike the perspective given by ecological modernization, the ethics of responsibility makes it possible to theoretically institute collective choices that can lead to rethinking models of development, production processes, and lifestyles. The impression is that climate justice, as an aspiration not only for a fair distribution of the costs of climate change but also of political responsibilities, can bring about a reversal of the trend in public institutional choices. This reversal can occur only if it identifies, as the basis of its proposal, the protection of vulnerability understood in a radical sense by embodying within its theoretical framework future generations and their rights. From this perspective and focus, rationally based on the ethical and not ideological level, it is factually consequential and politically sustainable to derive an expansion of the protected subjects that include the most vulnerable groups in the present time. But to achieve this result, it is necessary that a global and universal projection of the aspirations of climate justice occurs. Further, this projection must coincide with the rights of the future generations and therefore of the preservation of a healthy environment in which they will live. There is no gap between present vulnerability and future vulnerability; they are two faces of the same coin. By protecting the latter, justice is done to the former in the name of the continuity of the species (and having in mind the hope of eternity and the wishes of infinity well above ourselves) that allows us to belong to humanity beyond our historical time:

> The object's self-owned futurity is the truest futural aspect of the responsibility, which thus makes itself the guardian of the very source of that irksome unpredictability in the fruits of its labors. Its highest fulfillment, which it must be able to dare, is its abdication before the right of the never-anticipated which emerges as the outcome of its care. Its highest

97 Farah & Prityi, *supra* note 3.

duty, therefore, is to see that responsibility itself is not stifled, whether from its source within or from constraints without. In the light of such self-transcending width, it becomes apparent that responsibility as such is nothing else but the moral complement to the ontological constitution of our *temporality*.[98]

98 Jonas, *supra* note 81, at 107.

12 The Science-Based Policy-Making Process as Established in the Paris Agreement (2015)

*Anthi Koskina**

1 Introduction

The last decades' developments in science and technology resulted in the strong "expansion of the knowledge base, accompanied by an unprecedented speed in transformation of frontier scientific inventions into practical use."[1] Following this trend, evidence-based law-making – defined as the use of rigorous research evidence by the lawmaker, instead of relying only on political and ideological reasoning – has been on the rise;[2] to be precise, this continuing upward trend has been observed since the 1970s in national law[3] and, a few years

* Anthi Koskina is a Postdoctoral researcher at the School of Law of the University of Athens, a scientific collaborator at the National Observatory of Athens (NOA) and teaches at the College IdEF / Université Paris XIII. Corresponding Author: akoskina@law.uoa.gr

1 Communication from the Commission to the European Parliament, the Council, the Economic and Social Committee, and the Committee of the Regions Life Sciences and Biotechnology COM (2002) *Life Sciences and Biotechnology – A Strategy for Europe* [2002] OJ C 55/03, para. 1.1.

2 Rob van Gestela & Jurgen de Poorte, *Putting Evidence-Based Law Making to the Test: Judicial Review of Legislative Rationality*, 4 The Theory and Practice of Legislation 155 (2016).

3 Science advisory bodies have been established in many countries to allow the use of scientific evidence in policy-making, such as, for example, in English Law: "The origin of evidence-based approaches can be traced back to the 1980s when the British government increasingly emphasized the need for informed policy and practices based on an accurate and challenging foundation of evidence", Vishwanath V. Baba & Farimah Hakem Zadeh, *Toward a Theory of Evidence Based Decision Making*, 50 Management Decision 832 (2012); also, "in the UK in the form of the Food Standard Agency (FSA), the Human Fertilisation and Embryology Authority (HFEA) and the National Institute for Health and Care Excellence (NICE)," P. Horton & G. W. Brown, *Integrating Evidence, Politics and Society: A Methodology for the Science – Policy Interface*, 4 Palgrave Commun (2018) <www.nature.com/articles/s41599-018-0099-3>. The same applies to American Law: "[I]n 1990, the United States Congress established in law the U.S. Global Change Research Program (USGCRP) and called for the provision of usable information on which to base policy decisions relating to global change" (US Congress, 1990). The law referred to usable information as knowledge that could be "readily usable by policy makers attempting to formulate effective strategies for preventing, mitigating and adapting to the effects of global change (*Id.*)," Lisa Dilling & Maria Carmen Lemos, *Creating Usable Science: Opportunities and Constraints for Climate Knowledge Use and Their Implications for Science Policy*, 21 Global Environmental Change 680 (2011); in the United States precisely, "the first

DOI: 10.4324/9781003472421-12

after, in international law[4] as well. In this sense, science appeared to be an appropriate tool to resolve not only everyday problems (*via* the production of equipment for home or commercial use) but also complex regulatory issues.[5]

In reality, the legitimacy of using science in policy-making is questioned. Thus, on the one hand, the broadest public view considers that it is difficult for policymakers to translate scientific data into legal frameworks and policy practice.[6] But on the other hand, the reliance on scientific data for policy-making was empirically proved to be more than appropriate.[7] On this basis, science has been increasingly used in specific areas of law, sometimes even resulting in the creation of a tangible *science-based policy-making process.*

A good example of this is provided by international environmental law, which aims at tackling, *inter alia*, the climate change issue (namely, a global phenomenon identified, measured, and reported *first* by scientists as the negative environmental consequences of industrial development). Hence, in this field of law, climate change knowledge, monitoring data, and science input acquired a leading role from the beginning, and an evidence-based approach was adopted as soon as in the 1992 Convention. In particular, the 1992 Convention was already clearly encouraging states to draw on scientific evidence[8] and to build further on the scientific consensus that the increasing concentration of CO_2 is amplifying the natural greenhouse effect.[9]

---

serious attempts to base environmental and public health policy on science began in the 1970s with a series of ambitious federal laws," Wendy E. Wagner, *The Science Charade in Toxic Risk Regulation*, 95 Columbia Law Review 1613 (1995).

4 The evidence-based approach was used to initiate and negotiate various treaties of international law since 1999, such as the WHO Framework Convention on Tobacco Control, Kenji Shibuya et al., *WHO Framework Convention on Tobacco Control: Development of an Evidence Based Global Public Health Treaty*, 327 BMJ Clinical Research 154 (2003). It was likewise used in bilateral treaties of environmental law, such as in the 1991 Canada – US Air Quality Agreement, J. W. Moore et al., *Towards Linking Environmental Law and Science*, 3 FACETS 375 (2018).

5 Horton & Brown, *supra* note 3. At the same time, one must bear in mind that there are also negative opinions on the increasing role of science in policy-making, for example, Head, Brian, *Evidence-Based Policy: Principles and Requirements.Strengthening Evidence-Based Policy in the Australian Federation* 13–26 (Productivity Commission, Melbourne, Australia 2010) ("This increased respect for research and evaluation was generally welcomed by policy researchers . . ., although some were troubled by the implicit preference for quantitative precision and for technical expertise over other forms of knowledge.").

6 Eric Biber, *Which Science? Whose Science? How Scientific Disciplines Can Shape Environmental Law*, 79 The University of Chicago Law Review 509 (2012).

7 In policy-making, the emphasis is now put in data rather than dogma, John Holmes & Rebecca Clark, *Enhancing the Use of Science in Environmental Policy-Making and Regulation*, 11 Environmental Science & Policy 702, 704 (2008).

8 1992 Convention, Preamble: "Recognizing that steps required to understand and address climate change *will be . . . most effective if they are based on relevant scientific . . . considerations* and continually re-evaluated in the light of new findings in these areas" (emphasis added).

9 In 1992, the IPCC had officially reported evidence for global warming that may be rated as "substantial and credible," Charles Weiss, *Scientific Uncertainty and Science-Based Precaution*, 3 International Environmental Agreements: Politics, Law and Economics 137, 150 (2003).

In this context, one may have expected that such a framework – encouraging states to rely on scientific input and adopt policies based on scientific considerations – would have been sufficient to convince policymakers of the need to implement drastic (and well adapted to the importance of the global phenomenon) measures. However, contrary to that, almost 20 years later, the climate change goals were not achieved. Accordingly, the international community was questioning the efficiency of the 1992 Convention, in relation to its policy-making process.

Hence, it would appear from a certain angle that the Paris Agreement, adopted in 2015, attempted, in response to these concerns, to build more solid and efficient linkages between science and law, in order to better take into account the climate change knowledge acquired thus far.

Starting from the premise that the policy-making (or decision-making) process consists of several different stages,[10] this book chapter attempts to examine whether one of the principal goals (first of the 1992 Convention, and then of the Paris Agreement) to address climate change "on the basis of the best available knowledge [Preamble]" takes shape through a literature review on evidence-based decision-making and international environmental law. In particular, this analysis focuses on examining in which manner reliable science input is promoted and taken into account at each stage of the decision-making process.

This chapter suggests that what may be referred to as a *science-based policy-making process in the Paris Agreement* eventually consists of facilitating and fostering the use of scientific information *at all stages* in the policy-making process, and precisely in reference to (a) designing or deciding measures, (b) implementation, and (c) evaluation or assessment of policies.[11] As evidence-based policy-making is increasingly discussed and used in numerous fields of law,[12] this chapter will examine in which precise form and articles the scientific input is associated to environmental decision-making.

10 "Sackett et al. (2000) define two separate stages for evidence-based practice: first, the stage of generating evidence, which relies on the academic body of a profession, and second, the stage of using that evidence in practice, and making informed decisions based on those practices," Baba & Zadeh, *supra* note 3. Also, on decision-making stages (precisely applied to environmental law), Terje Aven, *Risk Assessment and Risk Management: Review of Recent Advances on Their Foundation*, 253 European Journal of Operational Research 1, 2 (2016).

11 "Ideally, decisions and consequences are evaluated, and the results cycle back to redesign and improve the original formulation in what can be conceptualized as a simplified policy cycle," Moore et al., *supra* note 4.

12 "[F]ields such as early year education and crime prevention which were set up as experimental trials, as well as efforts to review evidence in order to draw lessons of 'what works' in these complex social policy realms" and "the health sector is routinely cited as a key inspiration for many current calls for EBP (*n.b.* Evidence Based Policy) today due to its development of the field of evidence-based medicine, which established how the choice of clinical interventions should be informed by rigorous research and a systematic review of effectiveness," Justin Parkhurst, The Politics of Evidence from Evidence-Based Policy to the Good Governance of Evidence 14–15 (Routledge Abingdon Oxon UK, 2017).

2 First, the Fostering of Scientific Input

The evidence-based policy-making process is defined as the use of rigorous scientific knowledge in policy-making.[13] Unfortunately, there does not yet appear to be any globally accepted definition of science, due to the various sensibilities and interests at stake[14] and despite the common view that scientific knowledge must, in any case, result from a scientific method[15] (see e.g., the use, for practical reasons, of technical jargon to address particular aspects of scientific knowledge).[16]

For this reason, the concepts of "science," "scientific information," "scientific knowledge," etc. are not being defined in the climate change treaties, and neither is a definition from any external authoritative source or glossary used.[17] These concepts, which in reality seem to be used interchangeably, appear to be explained by reference to their purpose: in this specific context, the proper analysis to decide whether climate information or knowledge – whatever its form of expression is – consists effectively in science only requires a finding that said scientific input has an effective linkage with climate change.

In particular, it was set out in Article 3.3 of the 1992 Convention – and then reaffirmed in key international agreements on climate change that followed it[18] – that

> [t]he Parties should take precautionary measures to anticipate, prevent or minimize the causes of climate change and mitigate its adverse effects.

13 There is a lot of debate on what may be regarded as the "use" of evidence in policy-making and what may be regarded as "rigorous knowledge" as well, Parkhurst, *supra* note 12, at 24.

14 "There is no single definition of 'science', and lobbyists frequently chose which definition suits their interests best in exploiting evidence", D. Fisk, *Environmental Science and Environmental Law*, 10 Journal of Environmental Law 3 (1998). More than that, there is no consensus even on the criteria "upon which to define science from non-science," Michael S. Carolan, *Scientific Knowledge and Environmental Policy: Why Science Needs Values*, 3 Environmental Sciences 229 (2006).

15 "[G]ood-governance practice suggests that policy should be based on sound evidence derived from rigorous analysis of the available facts on the issue that the policy is supposed to address (OECD 2013, p. 149)," Parkhurst, *supra* note 12, at 30. Also, Carolan, *supra* note 14 and P. Sullivan, et al., *Defining and Implementing Best Available Science for Fisheries and Environmental Science, Policy, and Management*, 31 Fisheries 460 (2006) ("One popular view is that science is simply a body of organized knowledge. . . . Science may also be viewed as a rigorous, standardized way of collecting information.").

16 For instance, the term *actionable science*, which refers to knowledge "that can inform or guide decisions in the management of natural resources," Wet al., *supra* note 4; the term *useable knowledge*, which encompasses a substantive core that makes it useable for policymakers, Holmes & Clark, *supra* note 7; etc.

17 There is no express or implied definition – in Article 1 of the UNFCCC titled "Definitions" – of the terms *science*, *scientific knowledge*, etc., which are, however, being used in the following articles of the treaty; the same applies to Article 1 of the Paris Agreement.

18 The same wording is used in the Kyoto Protocol Preamble – "being *guided by art. 3 of the Convention*" – and (indirectly) in the Paris Agreement Preamble: "In pursuit of the objective

> Where there are threats of serious or irreversible damage, lack of full scientific certainty should not be used as a reason for postponing such measures.

Against this background, it could therefore be established, by an argumentum *a contrario*[19] and in combination with Article 4.1(g) of the United Nations Framework Convention on Climate Change (UNFCCC), that "scientific certainty" – most likely another word for *scientific evidence*[20] – is whatever allows policymakers to understand, "anticipate, prevent, or minimize the causes of climate change and mitigate its adverse effects."

As a result, the broad approach of science in the climate change treaties does not tie the hands of policymakers while, at the same time, allows for fostering the use of scientific evidence in decision-making. Nonetheless, the use of science – even *lato sensu* – in decision-making is not as simple as it first sounds.

2.1 Using Science Implies Handling Scientific Uncertainty

Although using science in policy-making appears to be quite a simple task, it is observed that scientific experts may often disagree, be biased,[21] or – much common – lack full scientific certainty in regard to how to tackle a phenomenon, at the time a decision needs to be made. Such a lack of scientific certainty may be related to the characteristics of a precise environmental issue (e.g.

---

of the Convention and *being guided by its principles* (reference is therefore being made to Art. 3 of the UNFCCC titled *"Principles"*)."

19 According to the UNFCCC Article 3.3, 2nd sentence: *(l)ack of scientific certainty* cannot be used as a reason to *postpone* the enumerated measures; therefore, one may argue that *full scientific certainty* may be understood as a means *allowing the "adoption"* of such measures (Article 3.3, 2nd sentence, *a contrario*). Consequently, full scientific certainty (namely, reliable scientific knowledge) is what allows adopting measures in climate change. This approach is in line with UNFCCC Article 4.1 (g): Parties shall "[p]romote and cooperate in scientific . . . research, systematic observation and development of data archives related to the climate system and *intended to further the understanding and to reduce or eliminate the remaining uncertainties regarding the causes, effects, magnitude and timing of climate change* and the economic and social consequences of various response strategies (emphasis added)."

20 See *infra*, n. 70.

21 Scientific experts may be unintentionally, but also deliberately, biased, such as when they intend to defend their country's interests, Philippe Roqueplo, Entre savoir et décision, l'expertise scientifique (Paris INRA 1997), 14: "[. . .] quand "de façon volontaire et consciente, (ils) se donnent l'apparence de parler au nom de la science alors que leur connaissance ne leur sert en réalité qu' à construire un argumentaire destiné à tenter d'imposer la politique qu'ils ont reçu la charge de défendre (translation: "[W]hen voluntarily and consciously, (they) give the appearance of speaking in the name of science while their knowledge is only used, in reality, to develop arguments intended to impose the policy for which they stand guard)."

science is not able to provide clear and reliable knowledge to decision-makers;[22] scientific perspectives are not converging,[23] etc.), or to the fact that more than one environmental issue will have to be finally taken into account (namely, resolving the problem at stake will most likely create further ones).

To provide an example, it was announced in 2018 that scientists had further developed a plastic-eating bacteria – the *Ideonella sakaiensis* – to take advantage of an enzyme (i.e. a biological catalyst) it uses. This substance, which had been first discovered in Japan in 2016, was estimated by experts to be "capable of digesting plastic more effectively than anything else found in nature."[24] In comparison to the microorganism found in 2016, the new substance developed in 2018 was estimated to be much more efficient, due to its unique ability to strongly accelerate the degradation process.[25]

This newly discovered ability of a microorganism to digest plastic was then regarded as preparing the ground for a revolutionary "green" biotechnology.[26] Accordingly – and despite the issues raised on the strength of these conclusions[27] – the findings were presented to the public as allowing the creation

22 *Id.* Roqueplo mentions an expert's answers to a member of the French Parliament [MP] as regards the effects of air pollution on forests (*translated*):

"[MP] – What about the forests? Are they under threat or not? If so, is it resulting from air pollution?
[Expert] -It is very difficult for me to answer this question. Scientists hesitate. There are signs towards a direction, but also the contrary. Honestly, strictly speaking, we do not know.
[MP] -We need to take informed decisions. Who, if not you, an expert in this field, could provide us with this knowledge?
[Expert]-In the current situation, I repeat, science does not provide us with this knowledge.
[MP] – Can you at least tell us what you think, what you are convinced of?
[Expert] – This is a different issue. I will answer it without hesitation."

In the same line of thought, "[a]lthough it may be challenging, scientists can help lawyers, legislators, and regulators to understand the limitations of science with respect to relevant ecological thresholds and objectives," Moore et al., *supra* note 4, at 379.

23 "[T]he divide between climate scientists and meteorologists is an example of a much broader pattern in environmental law and policy: different scientific disciplines have very different perspectives and often reach very different conclusions about the state of the world and the need for policy interventions based on similar or identical information," Biber, *supra* note 6, at 471.

24 J. Gabbatiss, *Plastic-Eating Enzyme Accidentally Created by Scientists Could Help Solve Pollution Crisis*, Independent (2018) <www.independent.co.uk/news/science/plastic-eating-enzyme-pollution-solution-waste-bottles-bacteria-portsmouth-a8307371.html>.

25 Interestingly, around the same time, in 2017, caterpillars (namely, larvae of the greater wax moth, referred to as *Galleria mellonella*) likewise able to digest plastic were identified and announced to the scientific community by a scientist-amateur beekeeper in Spain.

26 The term refers, in this precise context, to biotechnologies in the service of sustainable development.

27 "We cannot rule out the possibility that the wax moth *Galleria mellonella* might indeed be capable of the chemical (rather than physico-mechanical) destruction of polyethylene but the present publication does not provide sufficient proof for this claim," Carina Weber, Stefan Pusch & Till Opatz, *Polyethylene Bio-Degradation by Caterpillars?* 27 Current Biology R744 (2017).

of a reliable new method for the recycling of plastic objects, a natural solution to be used in the recycling industry in combination with other instruments. However, it was also argued that a very large quantity of such organisms would be necessary to make a significant dent in reducing plastic pollution,[28] probably creating more risks to the environment. In this sense, the real long-term effects of a policy, based on the massive and deliberate release of such enzymes or microorganisms into the marine ecosystem, were controversial.[29]

This example shows that despite having access to science, establishing priorities in order to adopt efficient environmental policies remains a challenge. Science remains an essential input for environmental policy-making, but

> even when scientists can develop some consensus on which factors might be used to address the problems of underlying uncertainty, there is little consensus on how to prioritize those factors, retaining ample space for the use of subjective preferences and value choices.[30]

In other words, it is not always clear which sort of evidence is most trustworthy[31] or in which way this evidence should be incorporated into policy.[32]

International environmental law does not address this question in full. Instead, it establishes science (or technology)[33] as a comprehensive basis

28 Such a solution would require "billions of caterpillars, eating constantly all year round" in the case of the *Galleria mellonella*, P. Ball, *Plastic-Eating Bugs? It's a Great Story – But There's a Sting in the Tail* (The Guardian 2017) <www.theguardian.com/commentisfree/2017/apr/25/plastic-eating-bugs-wax-moth-caterpillars-bee>.

29 Clear reference was made – by the rest of the international scientific community – to the risks which would probably arise from the release of these alien species in the environment, such as: a possible devastation of bee colonies [Ball, *supra* note 28]; the potential absorption of a new food source – namely of plastic objects – for naturally existing plastic-eating microbes living in the seas and in landfills [D. Rader, *Are Plastic-Eating Bacteria the Solution to Ocean Pollution? It's Not That Simple, Science Shows*, EDF/Environmental Defense Fund (2018) <www.edf.org/blog/2018/07/13/are-plastic-eating-bacteria-solution-ocean-pollution-its-not-simple-science-shows>] like the subsurface oil-eating microbes discovered after the 2010 Gulf oil spill [D. Biello, *Meet the Microbes Eating the Gulf Oil Spill*, Scientific American (2010) <www.scientificamerican.com/article/gulf-oil-eating-microbes-slide-show/>], etc.

30 Biber, *supra* note 6, at 475.

31 Head & Brian, *supra* note 5, at 18.

32 Moore et al., *supra* note 4.

33 The terms "science" and "technology" refer to distinct intellectual assets but are sometimes used equivalently. For example: "Environmental science studies the mechanisms and processes underlying our interactions with the natural environment . . . while environmental technology allows us to apply this knowledge and take the actions necessary to prevent, prepare for, or mitigate environmental risks. . . . Today, as the terms 'environmental science and technology' are used interchangeably, or as one homogeneous phrase, the complex interactions between environmental science, technology and society are not easily recognized, rarely considered and often misunderstood," Nikolaos Voulvoulis & Mark A. Burgman, *The Contrasting Roles of Science and Technology in Environmental Challenges*, 49 Critical Reviews in Environmental Science and Technology 1079 (2019).

for risk regulation, in some respects to the detriment of non-scientific considerations. In particular, both risk assessment[34] and risk management[35] are to be based on science, but to varying degrees. Should we understand the decision-making process in environmental law as a five-step process,[36] risk assessment (a mainly fact-based phase) would be the third step, which would be principally based on the evaluation of science. Other values may also be taken into account at the end of this phase to evaluate risks, but they do not consist in what is referred to as "knowledge" basis. For this reason, the methodology being used, up to this point, has to be highly rigorous[37] to minimize, as much as possible, the range of uncertainty, at least while evaluating risks.

Following that, decision-makers will review the risk assessments to adopt policies (fourth step), now taking into account other societal values as well, since they will need to "combine the risk information they have received with information from other sources and on other topics,"[38] before deciding. At that point, decision-making will enter a predominantly value-based phase, possibly resulting either in mitigation or adaptation (despite the fact that some scientists allege a strong reliance on green technologies – instead of adaptation – would be problematic).[39]

34 Risk analysis or risk assessment is an analysis phase which consists in assessing two key factors, namely, (a) the probability that an adverse event will occur and (b) the consequences of the adverse event, R. N. Jones, *An Environmental Risk Assessment/Management Framework for Climate Change Impact Assessments*, 23 Natural Hazards 197 (2001).

35 Risk treatment or risk management is an implementation phase which aims at reducing the consequences of adverse events identified by risk analysis (or risk assessment), *Id.*

36 In environmental law, we consider that the decision-making process may well be described as follows: (1) *evidence* leads to (2) *knowledge base*, and then to (3) *risk evaluation*; following that, (4) *decision-makers review* the risk evaluation results in (5) *decision*, Terje Aven, *supra* note 10.

37 In reality, agreeing a methodology is a problem in itself, taking into account that "thresholds are location, activity- and value-dependent, and . . . a synthesis of multiple assessments is needed to diagnose levels of dangerous climate change," Jones, *supra* note 34, at 206 and 228.

38 Aven, *supra* note 10.

39 "End of pipe environmental technologies seem to be economically preferable when used at a small scale but developing carbon dioxide removal (CDR) or negative emissions technologies to a climate-relevant scale might not ever be feasible because of scientific, technical, and societal constraints," Mark G. Lawrence & Stefan Schäfer, *Promises and Perils of the Paris Agreement*, 364 Science 829 (2019). Similarly, "the broad use of desalination technologies could have a negative impact on water security (SDG6) and energy security (SDG7)," Voulvoulis & Burgman, *supra* note 33. On the pros and cons of adaptation and mitigation (which address different aspects of climate risk), see also Roger N. Jones et al., *The Relationship between Adaptation and Mitigation in Managing Climate Change Risks: A Regional Response from North Central Victoria, Australia*, 12 Mitig Adapt Strat Glob Change 685 (2007). At the same time, it is argued that only recently adaptation measures were given importance in the UNFCCC negotiations, Louis V. Verchot et al., *Climate Change: Linking Adaptation and Mitigation Through Agroforestry*, 12 Mitig Adapt Strat Glob Change 901 (2007).

However, the key challenge today remains[40] to address some of the uncertainty which remains "inherent in science"[41] (or, from a different aspect, the "contradictory certainties,"[42] the risks etc.). The reason is that scientific uncertainty is potentially present at any level of the process, as it may be related not only to climate change but also to the implementation of policies (eventually to both).[43] Hence, the difficulty in achieving scientific certainty resulted in "excluding it at first as a basis of policy, in international environmental law."[44]

In particular, the treaties endorsed the precautionary principle, "which states that action to protect the environment against the danger of severe and irreversible damage need not wait for rigorous scientific proof,"[45] precisely as a rationale for risk management.[46] The principle, adopted in the 1990s,[47] has been, in reality, criticized in a variety of ways,[48] such as for discouraging policymakers from fully using the advances in science and technology.[49]

Against this background, the explicit rule of Article 3.3. of the 1992 Convention[50] was gradually replaced by an indirect reference to the principle of precaution. Both the Kyoto Protocol and the Paris Agreement mention only

40 Aven, *supra* note 10.

41 Mary Jane Angelo, *Harnessing the Power of Science in Environmental Law: Why We Should, Why We Don't, and How We Can*, 86 Texas Law Review 1527 (2008).

42 "The reason that these 'sound scientific' procedures yield such contrasting pictures of risk is that the answers delivered in risk assessment typically depend on how the analysis is 'framed,'" Andrew Stirling, *Risk, Precaution and Science: Towards a More Constructive Policy Debate. Talking Point on the Precautionary Principle*, 8 EMBO Report 309 (2007).

43 Jones, *supra* note 34, at 688.

44 Fisk, *supra* note 14, at 4.

45 Weiss, *supra* note 9, at 137.

46 Aven, *supra* note 10, at 7.

47 In regard to international environmental law, it is alleged that the precautionary principle was first adopted in Principle 15 of the Rio Declaration ("In order to protect the environment, the precautionary approach shall be widely applied by States according to their capabilities. Where there are threats of serious or irreversible damage, lack of full scientific certainty shall not be used as a reason for postponing cost-effective measures to prevent environmental degradation" (UN, 1992)), which actually derives from German law, *Vorsorge* concept, Stephen Michael Dark & Shelley Burgin, *An Examination of the Efficacy of the Precautionary Principle as a Robust Environmental Planning and Management Protocol*, 60 Journal of Environmental Planning and Management 2122 (2017). Also, on the German roots of the principle: David Kriebel et al., *The Precautionary Principle in Environmental Science*, 109 Environmental Health Perspectives 871 (2001).

48 For example, the principle has been criticized for being vague; for opposing critically needed innovation based on unsubstantiated suspicion, etc., Weiss, *supra* note 9, at 138. On its usefulness, Kriebel et al., *supra* note 47, at 872.

49 On the basis that "sound scientific techniques of risk assessment already offer a comprehensive and rational set of 'decision rules' for use in policy (Byrd & Cothern, 2000); these science-based approaches yield a robust and practically operational basis for decision-making under uncertainty (Morris, 2000)," Stirling, *supra* note 42, at 309.

50 UNFCCC, Article 3.3: "[L]ack of full scientific certainty should not be used as a reason for postponing such measures."

the Convention's principles *in general*,[51] and priority seems to be placed now on how, in the context of policy-making, to maximize science.[52]

In addition to that, reference to scientific uncertainty was avoided in the Paris Agreement Preamble,[53] whereas member states were openly urged to promote science, by steadily increasing the production (and use) of reliable climate data. From this perspective, one may argue that the Paris Agreement established a clear *"pro-science" tone.*

2.2 *Enhancing the Development and Use of "Better Science"*

The 1992 Convention was adopted within the context of "climate scepticism," which has waned but may sporadically still be observed.[54] The climate change treaties are, in this sense, voluntarily based on the view (i.e. on the scientific opinion) that, *first*, human-induced climate change is due to greenhouse gas emissions[55] and, *second*, to be effective, the response to the threat of climate change should be based on the best available scientific knowledge.[56] From this standpoint, it appears that the scientific orientation of the treaties was a policy choice, based both on scientific and non-scientific arguments.[57]

51 Kyoto Protocol, Preamble: "Being *guided by article 3 of the Convention*." And Paris Agreement, Preamble: "In pursuit of the objective of the Convention and *being guided by its principles* (emphasis added)."

52 This appears to be a general tendency. For example: "Europe is currently at a crossroads: we need actively to develop responsible policies in a forward-looking and global perspective, or we will be confronted by policies shaped by others, in Europe and globally. The technology and its applications are developing rapidly: the Commission believes that Europe's policy choice is, therefore, not whether, but how to deal with the challenges posed by the new knowledge and its applications" in Life sciences and biotechnology – A Strategy for Europe, *supra* note 1, at para. 1.1.

53 The Paris Agreement Preamble makes no reference at all to scientific uncertainty. To make a comparison, the 1992 Convention Preamble was underlying, on the contrary, that "there are many uncertainties in predictions of climate change, particularly with regard to the timing, magnitude and regional patterns thereof."

54 Weiss, *supra* note 9, at 150. Regarding diverging views, in general, on scientific topics: "Dissenters always exist, but they become a lot more important when the political or economic stakes of a decision that might depend on science are very high," Biber, *supra* note 6, at 471.

55 "The Kyoto Protocol . . . was concluded in 1997, by which time the evidence had risen to the level of a 'clear showing,'" and "[b]y the time of the Conference of the Parties held in Marrakesh in November 2001, the IPCC report offered 'clear and convincing evidence' that global warming was a serious problem requiring international action," Weiss, *supra* note 9.

56 "As one would expect, the Paris Agreement calls on the IPCC to provide the scientific backup for the policy decisions that have already been made," Jaap C. Hanekamp & Lucas Bergkamp, *The 'Best Available Science' and the Paris Agreement on Climate Change*, 7 European Journal on Risk Regulation 42 (2016).

57 By way of illustration, this precise scientific direction is not favoured by the USA, following a different policy choice: "Of the seventeen Republican presidential candidates vying for the party's nomination in 2016, only one – Ohio governor John Kasich – believed that climate change was a serious problem caused by human activity," R. Guttmann, *The Challenge of*

Gradually, the scientific community began to distance itself from the view that science "cannot successfully reduce uncertainty in a way that will fully resolve environmental disputes" to the benefit of a "better science" solution.[58] In view of the fact that the climate change treaties are aimed at addressing a real-world global threat of an irreversible and urgent nature – explicitly recognized as such in the Paris Agreement[59] – the member states agreed to make use of the best scientific means; the critical importance of climate knowledge was clearly established as early as the 1992 Convention: "[S]teps required to understand and address climate change will be . . . most effective if they are based on relevant scientific . . . considerations and continually re-evaluated in the light of new findings in these areas."[60]

On this basis, various obligations to create and use science in policy-making were then unequivocally established: the obligation to develop the scientific information which is needed to adopt efficient environmental policies (1992 Convention, Preamble, Article 4 *Commitments*[61] and Article 5 *Research and systematic observation*);[62] the obligation to update – and foremost to use updated – climate change knowledge, results, or technologies (1992 Convention, Article 7 *Conference of the parties*),[63] and as the scientific knowledge base needs to be constantly improved, to likewise train future generations

---

Climate Change, *in* Eco-Capitalism Carbon Money, Climate Finance, and Sustainable Development 1–33 (R. Guttman (ed.), Palgrave Macmillan 2018).

58 "There are nontrivial areas in environmental science for which the evidence from the natural world cannot – at least at this point of time – resolve all reasonable uncertainty. . . . One possible solution is for 'better science' to reduce the uncertainty and the need for assumptions, inferences, and interpretations, and therefore to let the natural world resolve the political dispute," Biber, *supra* note 6, at 488. The tendency to rely increasingly on science in policy-making (instead of "hiding behind" scientific uncertainty) is the same in domestic law, such as in UK, John Holmes, Clark, *supra* note 7.

59 Paris Agreement, Preamble ("Acknowledging that climate change is a *common concern* of humankind") and Article 7.2: "taking into account the *urgent and immediate needs* of those developing country Parties that are *particularly vulnerable to the adverse effects* of climate change (emphasis added)."

60 UNFCCC, Preamble.

61 UNFCCC, Article 4: "All Parties, taking into account their common but differentiated responsibilities and their specific national and regional development priorities, objectives and circumstances, shall: a) Develop, periodically update, publish and make available to the Conference of the Parties, in accordance with Article 12, national inventories of *anthropogenic emissions* by sources and removals by sinks of all greenhouse gases (emphasis added)."

62 UNFCCC, Article 5.1: "In carrying out their commitments . . . the parties shall [s]upport and further develop . . . programmes and networks or organizations *aimed at defining, conducting, assessing and financing research, data collection and systematic observation* (emphasis added)."

63 UNFCCC, Article 7: "The Conference of the Parties, as the supreme body of this Convention . . . shall make, within its mandate, the decisions necessary to promote the effective implementation of the Convention. To this end, it shall: (a) periodically examine the obligations of the Parties and the institutional arrangements under the Convention, *in the light of* the objective of the Convention, the experience gained in its implementation and *the evolution of scientific and technological knowledge*." (emphasis added).

of climate scientists;[64] the obligation to produce and present reliable climate change data at a national and international level (1992 Convention, Article 12 *Communication of information related to implementation*),[65] etc.

Furthermore, and in line with the idea that scientific knowledge on climate change is whatever allows it to "anticipate, prevent or minimize [its] causes,"[66] the 1992 Convention adopted no limits on the nature of what should be considered as "scientific" knowledge, apart from establishing that such information should be continually re-evaluated, to ensure that the legal instruments are constantly kept up to date.[67]

Many of the obligations to develop and make use of reliable science were reaffirmed in major climate change treaties – such as in the Kyoto Protocol[68] – but the Paris Agreement did not only reassert the importance of scientific knowledge[69]; it additionally went some steps further.

First, the concept of "*science*" itself – expressly not defined, yet most probably used as a synonym for evidence or evidence-based knowledge[70] – was broadened to a certain extent so as to be potentially complemented by such

64 UNFCCC, Article 6: Parties shall promote (d) "*[t]raining of scientific*, technical . . . personnel" (emphasis added).

65 UNFCCC, Article 12: "[E]ach Party shall communicate to the Conference of the Parties . . . the following elements of information: (a) *a national inventory of anthropogenic emissions* by sources and removals by sinks of all greenhouse gases not controlled by the Montreal Protocol . . .; (c) any other information that the Party considers relevant to the achievement of the objective of the Convention and suitable for inclusion in its communication, including, if feasible, *material relevant for calculations* of global emission trends (emphasis added)."

66 See above, note 19.

67 UNFCCC, Preamble: "[S]teps required will be most effective if based on relevant scientific . . . considerations and *if continually re-evaluated in the light of new findings*" (emphasis added).

68 The importance of scientific information was reaffirmed through the obligation of the Conference of the Parties to review the Protocol in the light of the best available scientific information (Kyoto Protocol, Art. 9), through the obligation to transfer appropriate technologies (and financial support) to developing countries and to establish cooperation in scientific research and information exchange, aiming at reducing climate uncertainties (Kyoto Protocol, Article 10, reference being made there to the UNFCCC, Article 4), etc.

69 See, for instance, the obligation to rely on *"best available scientific knowledge"* set in the Preamble of the Paris Agreement; the obligation to *"share scientific information"* set in its Article 7.7 (a); the obligation to *"strengthen scientific knowledge"* set in its Article 7.7 (c); the adoption of a technical expert's review applying to all the related scientific information mentioned set in its Article 13, etc.

70 "Scientific truth making, in particular, as human beings engage in it, is always a social enterprise. It is situated in particular places and circumstances; it is context specific, purposive, and culturally embedded. As such, even scientific claims are subject to distortion, through imperfections in the very human systems that produced them." In this sense, the conclusion (for science in the courts, but potentially applying *mutatis mutandis* to the use of science in many fields of law) is that "science cannot hold itself out as simply science, the source of transcendental truths. More modestly and with appropriate caveats, it can be the source of just evidence," Sheila Jasanoff, *The Limits of Science in the Legal Process*, 34 Journal of Law, Medicine & Ethics 328 (2006). The fact that it is not "transcendental truths" which are being taken into account in policy-making results mainly from the unavoidable biases in the creation,

information as "traditional" or "local" knowledge, according to Article 7.5 of the Paris Agreement.[71] Reference to traditional or local knowledge as reliable information was an innovation in climate change law and lies on the recognition of its importance as a general trend.[72] In particular, attention is now given to the fact that rural or indigenous communities (where they exist) have often come up with efficient laws and practices to cope with natural events or resources governance, such as terracing, groundwater irrigation, etc. As these proved to be efficient tools, it is now accepted that these practices could also be incorporated[73] into "official" environmental policy, rather than replacing them.[74]

Second, and more than broadening the basis of the science input so as to include traditional and local knowledge in environmental decision-making, the Paris Agreement seems to have established a comprehensive science-based process for policy-making.

3 Main Architecture of the Science-Based Policy-Making Process

In theory, the interplay between science and policy-making[75] may consist of the following: (a) a *science-push model*, where scientific research – conducted first – results from the identification and analysis of societal needs, as well

---

selection, and interpretation of evidence, Parkhurst, *supra* note 12, at 41: "Bias and the politics of evidence."

71 Paris Agreement, Article 7.5: "[A]daptation action . . . should be based on and guided by the best available science *and, as appropriate, traditional knowledge, knowledge of indigenous peoples and local knowledge systems* (emphasis added)."

72 The same tendency is observed, among others, in International Intellectual Property law (the WIPO members established in 2000, for this purpose, the *Intergovernmental Committee on Intellectual Property and Genetic Resources, Traditional Knowledge and Folklore* (IGC)).

73 The trend across Western countries to marginalize traditional and indigenous knowledge seems to vanish, as it is being argued that this type of knowledge and practices can arguably "provide an important basis for today's efforts in dealing with even greater challenges of climate change" (Cuthbert Casey Makondo & David S. G. Thoma, *Climate Change Adaptation: Linking Indigenous Knowledge with Western Science for Effective Adaptation*, 88 Environmental Science and Policy 83 [2018]). Following these developments, the Paris Agreement considers that such knowledge *may* consist in scientific input (Article 7.5, "and, *as appropriate*, traditional knowledge, knowledge of indigenous people and local knowledge systems" [emphasis added]). In reality, these types of knowledge appear to be acceptable as an input, but they are all, before being used, assessed by the scientific bodies of the UNFCCC (on the IPCC works in reference to traditional knowledge, see, for example, Annalisa Savaresi, *Traditional Knowledge and Climate Change: A New Legal Frontier*, 9 Journal of Human Rights and the Environment 32 [2018]).

74 Harry Jones et al., *Strengthening Science – Policy Dialogue in Developing Countries: A Priority for Climate Change Adaptation* (Overseas Development Institute, 2009) <https://odi.org/en/publications/strengthening-sciencepolicy-dialogue-in-developing-countries-a-priority-for-climate-change-adaptation/>. Also, Moore et al., *supra* note 4, at 384.

75 C. Huggel, et al., *A Framework for the Science Contribution in Climate Adaptation: Experiences from Science-Policy Processes in the Andes*, 14 Environmental Science & Policy 80 (2015) and Parkhurst, *supra* note 12, at 23. Also, Dilling & Lemos, *supra* note 3.

as on guidance provided to policymakers in order to legislate;[76] (b) a *policy (or demand)-pull model*, where scientific research goals are being set by policymakers and stakeholders (in this case, the problems and possible solutions at hand are considered first at a policy level, and scientific research commissioned in the aftermath, in a specific field);[77] and finally, (c) *an ongoing two-way dialogue* between science on the one hand and policy needs and objectives on the other.[78]

The possibility that science interacted with policy-making (following one of the aforementioned options) does not necessarily mean that there will indeed be an interplay between them. In reality, scientific information is only one of the many inputs used in decision-making, since other factors – namely, national interests – have to be taken into account as well. Decisions and policies are adopted by decision-makers alone, and only the latter are accountable to stakeholders for policy-making. Further, the democratic accountability of policymakers alone (in this specific context) may even produce inertia to a certain degree, as "policy-makers . . . elected on the basis of particular policy pledges . . . may . . . feel that their democratic legitimacy rests upon supporting a particular piece of legislation, irrespective of new information."[79]

Therefore, to avoid the pitfalls inherent to this type of policy inaction, the two-way dialogue between science and policy-making was promoted as being adapted to better achieve the objective of tackling climate change.[80] In this sense, the idea behind the Paris Agreement was to eventually establish a process allowing to find – through such dialogue – a balance between the na-

76 A characteristic example of the science-push model is the UNFCCC, which was negotiated after the IPCC reported evidence for global warming, Weiss, *supra* note 9, at 150.

77 For an example of the demand-pull model, in international law: "The United Nations Children's Emergency Fund (UNICEF) has similarly produced an 'advocacy toolkit' in which one strategy promoted is to generate 'evidence for advocacy' so as to influence decisions in line with their interests in 'improving children's lives' (UNICEF 2010). The World Health Organization (WHO 2012) has also used the term 'evidence-based advocacy' to explain how analyses of local country level data can be developed into advocacy materials to 'build stakeholder commitment' for policy actions to improve reproductive, maternal and newborn health," Parkhurst, *supra* note 12, at 72. For its use in American law, Dilling & Lemos, *supra* note 3.

78 This third interplay is considered to be more efficient: "Although research may start as a direct response to a policy need, research processes can stray off the policy need as it progresses. Regular discussions and meetings may be required to check that research is still aligned to the policy problem(s). . . . Similarly, policy needs and thinking may need to change in response to scientific understandings and insights from research" and "[l]ack of coordinated planning between science and policy can lead to 'closed' thinking and a focus on immediate priorities for policy, without regard to identifying and acting on emerging and/or long-term issues," Juliette C. Young et al., *Improving the Science-Policy Dialogue to Meet the Challenges of Biodiversity Conservation: Having Conversations Rather Than Talking at One-Another*, 23 Biodiversity and Conservation 387, 395–396 (2013).

79 Jones et al., *supra* note 74.

80 Huggel et al., *supra* note 75.

tional interests at stake and global environmental needs, as identified precisely by the scientific measurement of climate change.

In reality, the adoption of nationally tailored and flexible commitments (NDCs) based on a principle of progression[81] – agreed upon by the member states as allowing them to take due account of their national interests[82] – was incompatible with the very essence of the climate change problem. Despite the fact that tackling climate change at its roots requires a dynamic coordination of responses together with the alignment of national policies, "no assessment of the ambition of individual NDCs (was established); [t]he system relies entirely on the national level determining and implementing ambitious efforts and the persuasive impact of publicity, consultations, and the so far unspecified global stocktake."[83]

In an effort to balance such flexibility with efficacy, the magnitude of the environmental problem to be addressed was underlined in a determined manner right from the Preamble of the Paris Agreement, where the climate change issue was rightfully identified as "*a common concern of humankind*" of an urgent nature.[84]

In addition to that, the precise goal of fighting climate change was, at the same time, being defined scientifically – through the incorporation of precise

81 "An important yardstick of success of the PA is thus its ability to increase ambition over time. The PA seeks to address this issue via regular updates of NDCs in what has been labeled as cycles: – parties have to submit new NDCs every five years. Each successive update of NDCs is expected to reflect a party's 'highest possible ambition' and to be stronger than the previous one ('principle of progression')," Ralph Bodle, Lena Donat & Matthias Duwe, *The Paris Agreement: Analysis, Assessment and Outlook*, 10 Carbon & Climate Law Review 5 (2016). Similarly, "Pour atteindre cette cible, l'article 4 de l'Accord de Paris organise ensuite un système d'atténuation collectif qui repose sur une triple obligation. Chaque partie est ainsi tenue: d'établir une "contributio[n] déterminé[e] au niveau national", comprenant notamment un objectif d'atténuation, et de la communiquer au Secrétariat de la CCNUCC; de prendre "des mesures internes pour l'atténuation en vue de réaliser" l'objectif énoncé dans sa contribution; et de rehausser le niveau d'ambition de sa contribution tous les cinq ans, conformément à un nouveau principe de progression qui oblige les États à transmettre à chaque fois une cible plus ambitieuse que la précédente," Lassus St-Geniès Géraud de, *L'Accord de Paris sur le climat: quelques éléments de décryptage*, 28 Revue Québécoise de droit international 27, 37 (2015).

82 A bottom-up approach – based on the common but differentiated responsibilities of the parties (Paris Agreement, Article 2) – was combined with a top-down system aiming at progression over time, through the nationally determined contributions (Paris Agreement, Article 3), leaving in this way considerable discretion to the parties and allowing to ensure a long-term global climate framework for action, Lara Lázaro-Touza, *Governing the Geopolitics of Climate Action after the Paris Agreement*, *in* Handbook of Energy Politics 460 & 487 (Jennifer Considine (ed.), Edward Elgar Publishing 2018).

83 Bodle, Donat & Duwe, *supra* note 81, at 9.

84 Paris Agreement, Preamble: "Recognizing the need for an effective and progressive response to the *urgent threat of climate change*..." and "[a]cknowledging that climate change is a *common concern of humankind*." In addition to that, Article 7.2 makes reference to the fact that adaptation to climate change is "*a global challenge faced by all with local, subnational, national, regional and international dimensions*" (emphasis added).

emission rates into the treaty[85] – contrary to the 1992 Convention, which was only making reference to the stabilization of greenhouse gas concentrations "at a level that would prevent dangerous anthropogenic interference with the climate system."[86] Concretely, according to Article 2.1(a) of the Paris Agreement, the aim was now to hold "the increase in the global average temperature to well below 2°C above preindustrial levels and pursuing efforts to limit the temperature increase to 1.5°C above preindustrial levels."

To reach this goal, member states had set aside the long-lasting scientific disagreements on the calculation of emissions that should be reduced within a specific time frame so as to efficiently tackle climate change,[87] and the rates enshrined in Article 2.1(a) were adopted on the basis of a political consensus.[88] In so doing, clear contours for national legislation and policy decisions were, at the same time, being determined in an authoritative manner.

Thereafter, having established said contours for the climate change policies, aiming at complementing the bottom-up approach, the Paris Agreement promoted the use of *common science-based tools* by the member parties (practically consisting in the methodologies and common metrics of the Intergovernmental Panel on Climate Change [IPCC])[89] to guide them in the adoption of appropriate and efficient environmental policy measures.

85 In a similar way, precise scientific information was being incorporated in comparable agreements; for instance, the Montreal Protocol on substances that deplete the ozone layer (1987), signed by the Parties to the Vienna Convention for the Protection of the Ozone Layer (1985), mentions in Annex I (group I and II) precise chlorofluorocarbons/CFCs like CFC-11, CFC-12, etc. mainly used as refrigerants, solvents, etc.; the Kyoto Protocol mentions precise greenhouse gases (CO2, CH4, etc.) and source categories (fuel combustion, etc.) in Annex A and quantified emission limitations in Annex B, etc.

86 UNFCCC, Article 2: "The ultimate objective of this Convention . . . is to achieve, in accordance with the relevant provisions of the Convention, stabilization of greenhouse gas concentrations in the atmosphere *at a level* that would prevent dangerous anthropogenic interference with the climate system (emphasis added)."

87 On the main scientific views regarding measurement of climate change: "the 2°C above preindustrial temperature target and a 0.1°C per decade maximum tolerable limit emerged from discussions at the Bellagio workshop in 1987, a workshop supported by the Advisory Group on Greenhouse Gases (AGGG – a group established by the UNEP, World Meteorological Organization and International Council of Scientific Unions) and behind them the Stockholm Environment Institute (SEI)," Samuel Randalls, *History of the 2°C climate target*, 1 WIREs Climate Change 598 (2010).

88 St-Geniès Géraud de, *supra* note 81.

89 For example, regarding accounting of emission reductions, "[p]arties have to use the methodologies and common metrics of the IPCC and ensure 'methodological consistency' between the reference levels chosen to define their NDCs and the calculations used during their implementation," Bodle, Donat & Duwe, *supra* note 81, at 13. More details are provided at *Common Metrics* (United Nations Climate Change) <https://unfccc.int/process-and-meetings/transparency-and-reporting/methods-for-climate-change-transparency/common-metrics>. See, in addition to that, as regards the role of the SBSTA, *infra*, notes 107, 108, and 125.

In particular, along with the general guidelines established in Article 7 of the treaty,[90] the Paris Agreement stipulated that member states should strengthen their efforts and cooperation, including with regard to "sharing information, good practices, experiences and lessons learned . . . as these relate to science,"[91] "strengthening institutional arrangements . . . to support the synthesis of relevant information and knowledge,"[92] and "strengthening scientific knowledge on climate, including research, systematic observation of the climate system and early warning systems, in a manner that informs climate services and supports decision-making."[93]

On this basis, and following the division of the decision-making process into phases,[94] a science-based policy-making process was established in the Paris Agreement, made up of three sequential steps: (a) a situational awareness grounded on a holistic,[95] evidence-based approach for addressing climate change, requiring the communication of any relevant scientific information; (b) a *stricto sensu* decision-making process based on the enhanced cooperation with specialized scientific experts and bodies; and (c) the assessment of climate change policies, aiming at allowing better predictions and planning in the future.

From this perspective, the most remarkable feature of the Paris Agreement decision-making process is that, in all these phases, the interplay between science and policy-making was clearly enhanced.

3.1 Situational Awareness Based on the Sharing of Scientific Information

The role of the member states pertaining to climate change awareness and understanding[96] is, in the Paris Agreement, mainly framed by the urgent need to efficiently strengthen the global response,[97] the challenge no longer being *where*, but *whether*, greenhouse gas emissions occur. Against this background, it was established that the parties should share amongst themselves scientific

90 Such as that "adaptation action should . . . be based on and *guided by the best available science*" and in a context of "support for and *international cooperation on adaptation efforts*," according to Art. 7.5 and 7.6 of the Paris Agreement (emphasis added).

91 Paris Agreement, Article 7.7 (a).

92 *Id.* at 7.7 (b).

93 *Id.* at 7.7 (c).

94 See previous, notes 10 and 36.

95 The need for a holistic approach is expressly mentioned in the Paris Agreement, precisely in relation to the implementation of the nationally determined contributions of member states (Art. 6.8: "Parties recognize the *importance of integrated, holistic . . . approaches*" [emphasis added]).

96 Member states awareness is differentiated from public awareness, which is addressed in the Preamble of the Paris Agreement ("Affirming the importance of . . . *public awareness*") and in Articles 11 and 13.

97 Paris Agreement, Article 2.1.

information on climate change, but also good practices, experiences, and lessons learned.

The scope of Article 7.7(a) of the Paris Agreement is therefore explicitly broad, encouraging member states to communicate information, not only in regard to climate change – so as to better understand the complexity of the climate change phenomenon and its impacts – but also in relation to "planning, policies and implementation in relation to adaptation actions." The sharing of such knowledge (containing, among others, scientific input) through national communications[98] was already the practice for many member states. Building further on this achievement, the Paris Agreement states that this information has to be submitted periodically[99] and recorded into a public registry maintained by the secretariat,[100] to facilitate learning, cooperation,[101] and support.

98 In particular, "[t]o date, the main international reporting channel for countries' national adaptation responses has been national communications. National communications have been reported approximately every 4 years since 1994 for Annex I countries, and much less frequently for many non-Annex I countries (see Briner & Moarif, 2016, for a summary). Recent (2015) information on countries' current and/or planned adaptation responses has been communicated via their intended nationally determined contributions. In addition, several developing countries have communicated some adaptation information via technology need assessments (TNAs) and national adaptation plans," Climate Change Expert Group, *Communicating Progress in National and Global Adaptation to Climate Change* (Paper No. 2016(1)) OECD/IEA, 2016, 10.

99 Pursuant to Article 7.11 of the Paris Agreement, such information shall be, as appropriate, submitted through, for example, a national adaptation plan, a nationally determined contribution, and/or a national communication, as a component of, or in conjunction with, such documents. The content of this communication is specified in details, such as in Ad Hoc Working Group on the Paris Agreement (APA), *Revised additional tool under item 4 of the agenda. Further guidance in relation to the adaptation communication, including, inter alia, as a component of nationally determined contributions, referred to in Article 7, paragraphs 10 and 11, of the Paris Agreement* (Informal note, Bangkok – September 2018), UNFCCC, 2018 <https://unfccc.int/documents/181806>.

100 "Modalities for communicating, submitting, and updating the adaptation communication: . . . The adaptation communications shall be recorded in a public registry maintained by the secretariat in accordance with the modalities and procedures being developed by the SBI (Subsidiary Body for Implementation)," in Ad Hoc Working Group on the Paris Agreement (APA), *Revised additional tool under item 4 of the agenda, Id.* at para. I.5.

101 "The purpose of an adaptation communication is to: . . . (c) [p]rovide input to the global stocktake; . . . (j) [e]nhance learning and understanding of adaptation by sharing lessons, experiences, evidence and good practices," in Ad Hoc Working Group on the Paris Agreement (APA), *Revised additional tool under item 4 of the agenda, Id,* at para. I.2(b).2. On this basis, both the SBSTA (Subsidiary Body for Scientific and Technological Advice) and the SBI (Subsidiary Body for Implementation, maintained both in accordance with Art. 18 of the Paris Agreement), help foster international cooperation in this field. For example, the SBI organizes the Durban Forum on capacity-building (an annual, in-session event, designed in 2011), which brings together stakeholders involved in building the capacity of developing countries to mitigate and adapt to climate change and to enhance coordination further; see *Durban Forum on Capacity Building* (United Nations Climate Change) <https://unfccc.int/topics/capacity-building/workstreams/durban-forum-on-capacity-building>.

However, such wording should not be interpreted as implying that all the relevant scientific knowledge on climate change ought to be shared.[102] In reality, the obligation to share scientific information should be read in the light of Article 10, which regulates technology transfers.[103] In particular, taking into account that a specific provision regulating the sharing of patentable climate information was adopted – namely, Article 10, governing the transfer of technologies able to improve resilience to climate change and reduction of greenhouse gas emissions – one may consider that Article 7.7(a) most probably refers to the (scientific) works of the mind, which are not protectable, either as innovations or as creative works.

In this sense, and following an established practice from previous years,[104] Article 7.7(a) of the Paris Agreement aims at first encouraging the sharing – among member states – of theoretical climate knowledge and of relevant lessons learned, to foster understanding of the phenomenon (such as in the field of greenhouse gas emissions calculation, etc.) and to allow for better-informed decision-making.

102 According to Paris Agreement, Article. 7.7, "[p]arties should strengthen their cooperation on enhancing action . . . with regard to (a) sharing information . . . including, *as appropriate, as these relate to science*," and "(c) strengthening scientific knowledge on . . . *systematic observation of the climate system and early warning systems*" (emphasis added). In this context, it is apparent that the data based on climate change observation (i.e. allowing data standardization) should be distinguished from the knowledge on the specific technologies allowing this precise type of observation. For example, early warning systems, which aim at "detecting abnormalities and indicators of flood defense failure before it actually happens, and by providing real time information during a flood event," use complex electronic sensors to this end (B. E. Pengel et al., *Flood Early Warning System: Sensors and Internet, in* Floods: From Risk to Opportunity 445 [A. Chavoshian & K. Takeuchi (eds.), IAHS Press 2013]). The scientific information that has to be shared would be the knowledge on climate change resulting from those systems, not the knowledge on the sensors themselves.

103 Paris Agreement, Article 10.2: "Parties, noting the importance of technology for the implementation of mitigation and adaptation actions . . . and recognizing existing technology deployment and dissemination efforts, *shall strengthen cooperative action on technology development and transfer* (emphasis added)."

104 On the sharing of climate information: UNFCCC, Article 4.1: "(g) Promote and *cooperate in scientific, technological, technical . . . research*, systematic observation and development of data archives related to the climate system and intended to further the understanding and to reduce or eliminate the remaining uncertainties regarding the causes, effects, magnitude and timing of climate change and the economic and social consequences of various response strategies; (h) [p]romote and *cooperate in the full, open and prompt exchange of relevant scientific, technological, technical . . . information* related to the climate system and climate change, and to the economic and social consequences of various response strategies." Kyoto Protocol, Article 10 (d): "*Cooperate in scientific and technical research* and promote the maintenance and the development of systematic observation systems and development of data archives *to reduce uncertainties* related to the climate system, the adverse impacts of climate change." Etc. (emphasis added).

3.2 Decision-Making Through Cooperation With Scientific Bodies

In the Paris Agreement, decision-making lies within the competence of member states.[105] However, at the same time, the policies and issues at stake are likewise being discussed in the context of a close collaboration and dialogue between policymakers and scientific committees, which is, in reality, not easy to achieve;[106] such scientific bodies were established from the beginning, when the 1992 Convention was adopted.

By way of illustration, a permanent scientific body[107] – the multidisciplinary Subsidiary Body for Scientific and Technological Advice (SBSTA) – was already created under the UNFCCC (Article 9), with the goal of providing the Conference of the Parties, and if necessary, other subsidiary bodies, "with timely information and advice on scientific and technological matters relating to the Convention";[108] the precise content of such information and advice

105 Paris Agreement, Article 16: "The conference of the Parties, the supreme body of the Convention, shall serve as the meeting of the Parties to this Agreement."

106 On the complexity of the scientists/policymakers collaboration: "A policy-focused assessment is more than just a synthesis of scientific information or an evaluation of the state of science. Rather, it involves the analysis of information from multiple disciplines – including the social and economic sciences – to answer the specific questions being asked by stakeholders," J. Scheraga, et al., *From Science to Policy: Developing Responses to Climate Change, in* Climate Change and Human Health: Risks and Responses (A. J. McMichael, et al. (eds.), WHO/WMO/UNEP 2003).

107 Two subsidiary bodies were established under the 1992 Convention: the Subsidiary Body for Scientific and Technological Advice (SBSTA), according to Article 9, and the Subsidiary Body for implementation (SBI), according to Article 10. Both of them were maintained to support the work of the parties under the Kyoto Protocol (CMP) and under the Paris Agreement (CMA) as well. As the SBI is competent for the implementation of the convention in general, the body specialized in scientific matters is the SBSTA. The two of them often work collaboratively and meet at least at every climate change summit, Nidahl Attia, Le guide de l'accord sur le climat 54 (Heinrich Böll Stiftung Foundation – Tunis Office 2018).

108 The SBSTA comprises government representatives which are each competent in the relevant field of expertise that is being discussed, and it is empowered to develop, among others, the guidelines for national communications and emission inventories. The body meets at least twice a year; its second session has to take place in conjunction with the COP meeting, Nidahl Attia, *Le guide de l'accord sur le climat*, *Id.* at 55. Its reports are of major interest and published at the UNFCCC (all available at *Bodies Subsidiary Body for Scientific and Technological Advice SBSTA* [United Nations Climate Change, Process and Meetings] <https://unfccc.int/process/bodies/subsidiary-bodies/sbsta>), while covering various topics such as in SBSTA, *Progress in Implementing Activities under the Nairobi Work Programme on Impacts, Vulnerability and Adaptation to Climate Change* (Pre-session document FCCC/SBSTA/2020/INF.1, 27 May 2020), UNFCCC Secretariat, 2020; SBSTA, *Summary Report on the SBSTA – IPCC Special Event: Unpacking the New Scientific Knowledge and Key Findings in the IPCC Special Report on the Ocean and Cryosphere* (Report, SBSTA 51, 22 May 2020), UNFCCC 2020; SBSTA, *Good Practices and Lessons Learned in Adaptation Planning Processes Addressing Ecosystems, Human Settlements, Water Resources and Health, and in Processes and Structures for Linking National and Local Adaptation Planning: A Synthesis of Case Studies* (Pre-session document, FCCC/SBSTA/2015/4, 20 November 2015), UNFCCC. Executive Secretary, 2015, etc.

was further explained in a detailed manner in paragraph 2 of the same article, which was making reference, amongst others, to the "state of scientific knowledge relating to climate change"; the identification of "innovative, efficient and state-of-the-art technologies" in this field; information on scientific programmes and international cooperation in research and development related to climate change;[109] etc.

The idea was further developed over the next years, and the role of the IPCC[110] as a permanent collaborator in the UNFCCC framework was likewise established,[111] pursuant to Article III of the Berlin Mandate signed in 1995.[112] Following this pattern, the Paris Agreement explicitly maintained and reaffirmed the participation of the SBSTA,[113] the IPCC,[114] and the expert review teams,[115] without necessarily increasing their (mainly advisory) functions.[116]

109 Precisely, UNFCCC Article 9.2 provided that "*[u]nder the guidance of the Conference of the Parties*, and drawing upon existing competent international bodies, this body shall . . .: (a) [p]rovide *assessments of the state of scientific knowledge relating to climate change* and its effects; (b) [p]repare *scientific assessments on the effects of measures* taken in the implementation of the Convention; (c) *[i]dentify innovative, efficient and state-of-the-art technologies* . . .; (d) *[p]rovide advice on scientific programmes* . . ., and (e) *[r]espond* to scientific, technological and methodological questions" (emphasis added). One should note that, under the Kyoto Protocol, part of the scientific information the SBSTA would provide had to be reviewed by experts before being taken into account by policymakers (Kyoto Protocol, Article 8).

110 According to its founding MOU, the IPCC was established in 1988 by the World Meteorological Organization and the UNEP; see *History of the IPCC*, IPCC <www.ipcc.ch/about/history/>.

111 *Nota bene*: the IPCC had been already entitled, according to Article 21.2 of the 1992 Convention, to cooperate closely with the interim secretariat of the UNFCCC, for a specific purpose: "[t]he *head of the interim secretariat . . . will cooperate closely with the IPCC* to ensure that the Panel can respond to the need for objective scientific and technical advice" (emphasis added). Analytically, at *Cooperation with the IPCC*, United Nations Climate Change <https://unfccc.int/topics/science/workstreams/cooperation-with-the-ipcc>.

112 Berlin Mandate, Art. III: "The process will be carried out in the light of the best available scientific information and assessment on climate change and its impacts, as well as relevant technical, social, and economic information, *including, inter alia, reports of the Intergovernmental Panel on Climate Change*. It will also make use of other available expertise (emphasis added)."

113 Paris Agreement, Article 18.

114 *Id.* at 13 par. 7 (a), which makes indirect reference to the IPCC: "Each Party shall regularly provide the following information: (a). A national inventory report of anthropogenic emissions by sources and removals by sinks of greenhouse gases, prepared using good practice methodologies *accepted by the Intergovernmental Panel on Climate Change* and agreed upon by the Conference of the Parties (emphasis added)."

115 Paris Agreement, Article 12 ("The [technical expert] review shall also . . . *include a review of the consistency of the information with the modalities, procedures and guidelines referred to* in paragraph 13 of this Article, taking into account the flexibility accorded to the Party under paragraph 2 of this Article") and Article 13.11 ("Information submitted by each Party under paragraphs 7 and 9 of this Article *shall undergo a technical expert review*, in accordance with decision 1/CP.21") (emphasis added).

116 Paris Agreement, Article 18: "The provisions of the convention relating to the functioning of these two bodies *shall apply mutatis mutandis to this Agreement*" (emphasis added). The

Precisely, as Article 18.1 of the Paris Agreement lays out that "the provisions of the Convention relating to the functioning of these two bodies [i.e. the SBSTA and the Subsidiary Body for Implementation] shall apply mutatis mutandis to this agreement" without providing any further details and without any changes, it is clear that the scientific body is considered to form part of the climate change institutional framework,[117] which should be neither called into question nor compromised.

However, together with (indirectly) reaffirming – in this manner – its support to the existing climate change scientific bodies, the Paris Agreement handed in parallel the baton back to member states. Concretely, parties were now expressly encouraged to strengthen institutional arrangements, "***including***" those under the Convention that serve the Paris Agreement (which may be interpreted to mean that the parties are, ***in fine***, encouraged to strengthen the institutional arrangements established under the Paris Agreement, but also other ones, established, for example, under their domestic law).[118]

In this sense, the idea of science-based decision-making arrangements – as established in the context of the UNFCCC – was not only being consolidated but also indirectly "disseminated" from the international to the national level, aiming at being eventually applied (as a guiding rule) to the national legislative procedures as well.

3.3 Strengthening of the Climate Change Policies Assessments

Finally, Article 7.7(c) of the Paris Agreement provides that member states should strengthen their scientific knowledge on climate in a manner that supports decision-making.[119] However, as this precise "manner that supports decision-making" is not being further explained, this should most probably be interpreted in the light of the general guidelines on science-based decision-making, as established throughout the Paris Agreement.

Following this reasoning, scientific knowledge on climate change – including systematic observation and early warning systems – should allow policymakers

---

collaboration with the Subsidiary Body for Scientific and Technological Advice had been reaffirmed in the Kyoto Protocol as well and adapted to this specific agreement pursuant to its Article 15 par. 1.

117 The institutional framework is evidently not limited to the SBSTA, the IPCC, and the expert review teams. Many United Nations specialized organizations and agencies are encouraged to support the efforts of parties (Paris Agreement, Article 7.8).

118 Paris Agreement, Article 7.7 (b): Parties should strengthen their cooperation, including with regard to "[s]trengthening institutional arrangements, ***including those under the Convention*** that serve this Agreement, ***to support the synthesis of relevant information and knowledge***, and the provision of technical support and guidance to Parties" (emphasis added).

119 Paris Agreement, Article 7.7 (c): Parties should strengthen their cooperation, including with regard to "[s]trengthening scientific knowledge on climate, including research, systematic observation of the climate system and early warning systems, in a manner that informs climate services and ***supports decision-making***" (emphasis added).

to make informed decisions but, further, to also measure their progress in addressing climate change issues: in particular, on the basis of a "synthesis of relevant information and knowledge," which is mentioned in Article 7.7(b),[120] scientific knowledge should allow adopting "an effective and progressive response to the urgent threat of climate change on the basis of the best available scientific knowledge."[121]

To allow this, the climate change treaties put forward a common (and commonly approved) methodology for assessing climate change information, before using it as a knowledge basis for policy-making. In this sense, according to the 1992 Convention, to be trustworthy, scientific information had to be "relevant,"[122] "comparable," and "agreed upon by the Conference of the Parties,"[123] having taken "into account the best scientific knowledge."[124] In practice, the SBSTA was established as the body which undertakes on a regular basis the substantive work on methodological matters, such as for reporting guidelines on annual inventories and reviewing the methodological work.[125]

120 The synthesis of knowledge is secured by institutional arrangements. In this sense, institutional arrangements or structures refer to the different rules, dynamics, roles, and interactions that enable the flowing of knowledge and shape decision-making processes, Claudia Múnera & Lorrae van Kerkhoff, *Diversifying Knowledge Governance for Climate Adaptation in Protected Areas in Colombia*, 94 Environmental Science & Policy 39 (2019).

121 Paris Agreement, Preamble.

122 UNFCCC, Preamble: "Recognizing that steps required to understand and address climate change will be . . . most effective if they are based on *relevant scientific . . . considerations*" (emphasis added).

123 UNFCCC, Article 4.1(a): "Parties shall develop, periodically update, publish and make available . . . national inventories of anthropogenic emissions . . . *using comparable methodologies to be agreed upon by the Conference of the Parties*"; one should also note that the Conference of the Parties was entitled to "[p]romote and guide (the member parties, on) the *development and periodic refinement of comparable methodologies*," according to Article 7.2 (d). The same criteria ("using *comparable* methodologies to be promoted and *agreed upon*") is mentioned in Article 12.1(a) of the UNFCCC (emphasis added).

124 UNFCCC, Article 4.2(c) ("*Calculations* of emissions . . . should *take into account the best available scientific knowledge*") and (d) ("The Conference of the Parties shall . . . review the adequacy of subparagraphs. . . . *Such review* shall be carried out *in the light of the best available scientific information*") (emphasis added).

125 "The SBSTA carries out methodological work under the Convention, the Kyoto Protocol, and the Paris Agreement, and promotes collaboration in the field of research and systematic observation of the climate change," see *Bodies Subsidiary Body for Scientific and Technological Advice SBSTA* (United Nations Climate Change, Process and meetings) <https://unfccc.int/process/bodies/subsidiary-bodies/sbsta>. For its recent work, see SBSTA, *Report of the Subsidiary Body for Scientific and Technological Advice on its thirtieth session, held in Bonn from 1 to 10 June 2009* (Session and meeting reports, FCCC/SBSTA/2009/3, 5 August 2009), UNFCCC. SBSTA, 2009, which makes detailed reference to "[m]ethodological issues under the Convention (Agenda Item 7)" and to "[m]ethodological issues under the Kyoto Protocol (Agenda Item 8)"; the SBSTA, *Summary Report on the SBSTA – IPCC Special Event: Unpacking the New Scientific Knowledge and Key Findings in the IPCC Special Report on the Ocean and Cryosphere*, *supra* note 108, based on the joint SBSTA-IPCC special event organized to generate a better understanding of key scientific findings of the SROCC (Special

The Paris Agreement took a further step in this direction. In 2015, reference was not being made to "the best available knowledge"[126] and "the best available science"[127] in general, but member states were directly encouraged to take into account the "existing methods and guidance"[128] together with the "good practice methodologies accepted by the IPCC and agreed upon by the Conference of the Parties."[129] In this sense, the "best available science" character of the Paris Agreement – a quite broad and wide-ranging concept – was, in reality, making reference to the scientific knowledge as represented in the IPCC reports (and commonly approved), though not exclusively.[130] Overall, the UNFCCC scientific bodies are the authorities entitled to put forward the best available science, on the basis of science and methodology assessments, in various fields.[131]

Report on the Ocean and Cryosphere in a changing Climate) through an open exchange of views on new scientific concepts and definitions used there, whereas also aiming at identifying research gaps and clarifying uncertainties associated with specific findings, etc.

126 Paris Agreement, Preamble.

127 Paris Agreement, Article 7.5.

128 *Id.* at 4.14.

129 *Id.* at 13.7 (a).

130 In regard to the concept of "best available knowledge," "[t]he Paris Agreement provides no definition. At a minimum, it includes the IPCC reports to which the Agreement explicitly refers. . . . By the terms of the Agreement, scientific insights and results outside the IPCC's assessment reports are not a priori excluded from competing for the label of 'best available science,'" Hanekamp & Bergkamp, *supra* note 56, at 44. At the same time, this concept of "best available science" most likely refers to science that could help attain the climate change goals, from the perspective that in precise contexts, "(i)n order to be able to *judge whether evidence is 'good,' . . . the first question we must ask is if it is relevant to the goals or purposes of the policy itself.* Graphically, we can use a simple diagram to illustrate the fact that, of the entire field of evidence available, there will be a sub-set of evidence that can be judged to be relevant in this way," Parkhurst, *supra* note 12, at 112 (emphasis added).

131 Such as the IPCC; "We will make this Synthesis Report not only a value-added document for policymakers, *providing the best available science, as did all previous synthesis reports,* but also a more useful resource for policy leaders around the globe,' said IPCC Chair Hoesung Lee, who is leading the preparation and writing of the report. . . . Over the past 12 months the IPCC, the world's leading body for assessing the science related to climate change, has released three special reports – on global warming of 1.5°C, on land use, and on the ocean and cryosphere – *and a methodology report,*" in IPCC Newsroom, *IPCC Opens Meeting in Singapore to Draft Sixth Assessment Synthesis Report Outline* (IPCC, October 2019) <www.ipcc.ch/2019/10/21/syr-ar6-scoping-opening/> (emphasis added). In fact, the key role of the IPCC (in addition to its prestige, since it uses some 3,000 scientists in the peer review of its assessments, Fisk, *supra* note 14) is based on the view that "emerging scientific approaches *whose potential weaknesses have not yet been fully quantified by the scientific community may require careful assessment regarding the weight of evidence* that these new technologies or analyses can provide. Regardless of their specific statistical approach, being comfortable with translating statistical outputs into understandable and compelling language that accurately captures scientific certainty and uncertainty is a key aspect of effectively linking science to law," Moore, et al., *supra* note 4, at 383 (emphasis added).

In addition, a completely new mechanism – referred to as the "global stocktake" – was established by the Paris Agreement to "periodically take stock of [its] implementation" and "assess the collective progress towards achieving [its] purpose . . . and its long-term goals." In the context of a science-based policy-making process, the global stocktake was created precisely to encourage member states to produce and work with scientific data, and to as well adopt measures based on scientific evidence.

Following this reasoning, the global stocktake promotes the reviewing of "the adequacy and effectiveness of adaptation and support" and "the overall progress made in achieving the global goal on adaptation,"[132] to encourage member states to learn from such scientific assessments and constantly improve their national policies and regulatory frameworks. From this perspective, this may be considered as the third and final step of the science-based policy-making process.

4 Conclusions

The central idea behind the adoption of the Paris Agreement was to essentially encourage member states to extend their commitments in relation to the reduction of gas emissions after 2020,[133] based on the view that there were still major challenges in attaining the climate change goals[134]

However, to take into account the fundamental right to development of member states, as well as the specific needs and circumstances of some member states,[135] the agreement was reached to allow member states to "pursue" – rather than to actually implement[136] – domestic actions to tackle global climate change. In reality, this approach, explained by the fact that an appropriate balance had to be found among the competing national, regional, and international interests, was clearly running counter to the objective of tackling a global problem.

In this context, the Paris Agreement – evidently not operating in a *legal vacuum* – took into account both the fact that the 1992 legal framework was unable to develop in a more binding (and therefore more efficient) instrument[137] and the urgency and scale of the climate change challenge. Above all,

132 Paris Agreement, Article 7.14 (c) and (d).

133 St-Geniès Géraud de, *supra* note 81.

134 It seems that this is still the case, United Nations Environment Programme (2023). Emissions Gap Report 2023: Broken Record – Temperatures hit new highs, yet world fails to cut emissions (again). Nairobi. https://doi.org/10.59117/20.500.11822/43922.

135 Paris Agreement, Preamble.

136 St-Geniès Géraud de, *supra* note 81.

137 "The failure of the developed nations including the U.S. and EU to practically make up to the levels as their pledges to legally binding Kyoto made the international climate actions to reach a concrete foothold," B. B. Sikder & S. Prodhan, *International Climate Change Policymaking: An Outline of the Post-Paris Framework*, 6 Journal of Pollution Effects & Control 224 (2018).

the most critical for the international community was to reach a consensus on strengthening the response to climate change.

Driven by this idea, there was, finally, an agreement to build further upon the legal and institutional framework of the UNFCCC, namely, upon the UNFCCC acquis,[138] *inter alia*, in a very specific direction. Specifically, together with being so flexible with member states in reference to the measures they would adopt to attain climate change goals,[139] the treaty established common procedural standards and efficiency indicators based on objective and reliable scientific knowledge and methodology.

In particular, member states – in principle free to determine their policies[140] – have to develop and draw on reliable scientific knowledge in reference with climate change and to avoid or diminish uncertainty.[141] On this basis, they are accordingly required to adopt measures to implement the climate change goals (which are now defined in a scientific, precise, and objective way) by means of a reliable and holistic scientific approach,[142] taking well into account the

138 *Id.*

139 This was the main critique to the treaty, due to the urgent nature of the climate change issue, St-Geniès Géraud de, *supra* note 81.

140 "Within the UNFCCC, the Subsidiary Bodies for Scientific and Technical Advice, and Implementation, develop and provide guidance for policy-makers on managing risk, but *do not advocate particular decisions.* Policy-making itself takes place in a less structured and more political environment, where structured decision analytic frameworks are less often applied. This has variously been described as a 'policy mess' where decisions can be ad hoc and short-term (e.g., Turnpenny et al. 2005), often having little impact on the initial problem of climate change," Jones et al., *supra* note 39, at 688 (emphasis added).

141 Since the Paris Agreement is *a political consensus to tackle climate change*, it implies that (1) the scientific evidence that may be used will be the one approved upon and promoted by the official scientific bodies, such as the SBSTA, the IPCC, etc. ("Parties *have* to use the methodologies and common metrics of the IPCC and *ensure* '*methodological consistency*' between the reference levels chosen to define their NDCs and the calculations used during their implementation," Bodle, Donat & Duwe, *supra* note 81, at 13 [emphasis added]), and (2) such evidence will also have to be used in a precise direction (i.e. to tackle climate change). On the one hand, there may be concerns about a perceived lack of democratic legitimation of the science-based policy-making process (on the "input legitimacy," Parkhurst, *supra* note 12, at 149); but on the other hand, the Paris Agreement, which has established a close "control" of the scientific evidence and methodology, leaves no room for decisions annulling the treaty's goals.

142 "[M]any issues are of an international nature and can only be addressed in a meaningful way through collaboration between countries. Such collaboration can take many different forms, ranging from simply sharing of experiences to the establishment of very large multi-level organizations, such as the Intergovernmental Panel on Climate Change (IPCC)," see OECD, Scientific Advice for Policy Making: The Role and Responsibility of Expert Bodies and Individual Scientists – Policy Papers, No. 21. 13 (OECD Publishing, Paris 2015). At the same time, it should be pointed out that advising policymakers, and "translating" raw data and science knowledge into usable science for policymakers, is not always easy to achieve, P. Spruijt, et al., *Roles of Scientists as Policy Advisers on Complex Issues: A Literature Review*, 40 Environmental Science & Policy 16 (2014); on the barriers to incorporating knowledge in decision-making processes in general, C. Cvitanovic, J. McDonald & A. J. Hobday, *From*

opinion of the competent scientific bodies,[143] and with the view to constantly step up and improve efforts.

From a practical perspective, responding appropriately to climate change is not only a matter of adopting (and/or implementing) a scientific approach:

> Delivering a low carbon economic model worldwide – in line with the consensus of limiting mean temperature increases to well below 2°C above pre-industrial levels – will require restructuring global production, distribution and consumption models that have fuelled economic growth since the Industrial Revolution, largely through the use of fossil fuels.[144]

In this sense, taking more into account the assessments of science in the context of environmental decision-making is nothing more than an efficient strategy; it has to result in determined economic (mainly) measures, to produce effects.

Thus far, surveys show that support to the INDCs implementation will be a key concern in the future,[145] but blaming a technical mechanism – aiming at strengthening the science input – for the results of the whole decision-making process amounts to reducing the responsibility of policymakers; they are the only entitled to finally adopt the policy measures (by taking into account the scientific knowledge, *inter alia*). From this perspective, it may be argued that, in fact, science often comes in a second position, in comparison with economic considerations. It is therefore clear that through the incorporation of scientific values and concepts in the climate change treaties,[146] the aim was to encourage

---

Science to Action: Principles for Undertaking Environmental Research that Enables Knowledge Exchange and Evidence-Based Decision-Making, 183 Journal of Environmental Management 864 (2016), etc.

143 Interestingly, it is at the same time argued, on behalf of the scientists, that: "Engaging with the policy process and communicating the current level (and limits) of scientific understanding will lead to more effective policy-making than merely providing clear statements of state of the science in terms familiar to the scientists themselves," Leonard A. Smith & Nicholas Stern, *Uncertainty in Science and Its Role in Climate Policy*, 369 Philosophical Transactions of the Royal Society A 4818 (2011).

144 Lázaro-Touza, *supra* note 82, at 455.

145 "However, there is a clear signal from respondents voicing concerns for the future as they see political support and buy-in from public and private stakeholders as key challenges going forward . . . preparing an NDC requires good coordination between ministries, agencies, and other stakeholders, including ensuring timely input. Our evidence suggests that time constraints and delays were common in the NDC preparatory process of which some may be explained by coordination challenges," Frauke Röser, et al., *Ambition in the Making: Analyzing the Preparation and Implementation Process of the Nationally Determined Contributions under the Paris Agreement*, 20 Climate Policy 415, 420 (2020).

146 In this context, the reference to particular scientific concepts and rates gives a precise contour to the international commitments arising from the climate change treaties (*supra* note 88) and balances the fact that there is no common view of science, climate thresholds, etc.

parties to first agree on the evidence of climate change[147] and, following that, to adopt the tackling of climate change as their principal priority[148] as well.

In order to achieve all these global climate change objectives, a science-based decision-making process was established in the Paris Agreement, though without being binding on member states, in its entirety; it does, however, comprise quite a few mandatory rules, such as the obligation to *present sound information* supporting the nationally determined contributions, the obligation to *create the global stocktake*,[149] etc.

Overall, it is clear that the general tendency to increasingly rely on science-based policy-making is also reflected in international environmental law. In this context, fostering the use of science in decision-making should allow, on the one hand, for policymakers to rely on rational arguments while negotiating and introducing measures to tackle climate change and, on the other hand, to avoid political inertia. Given the methodological support provided by the Paris Agreement, it would be difficult to justify any absence of initiatives.[150]

(*supra* note 14). At the same time, it should not be forgotten that the scientific terms and values which have been adopted are the result of political decisions, as it appears that scientists and scientific bodies were arguably *not* established to finally decide, interpret, evaluate, etc. instead of policy-makers (but only to provide rational opinions). The pitfall of scientists openly "substitut(ing) their own values for the policy choices needed at the trans scientific junctures and characterize the final science-policy decisions as the result of scientific experimentation and scientific judgment" was eventually avoided, Wagner, *supra* note 3.

147 The adoption of divergent environmental policies is visible proof that policymakers are, sometimes, not even convinced of the key influence of human activities on climate change (e.g. Lázaro-Touza, *supra* note 82, at 468: "3.2 The United States"); it is in this connection precisely that the Paris Agreement science-based decision-making process could provide useful support. At the same time, it is also clear that (accepting the evidence of, and following that) fighting climate change is, from a certain angle, highly threatening key economic interests; this is what is reflected in the diverging programs of the different governments (on the respective agendas of Democrats *vs.* Republicans, in the United States, *idem*, p. 475 for the reasons of the Trump administration for pulling out of the Paris Agreement). See also n. 57 ("Donald Trump . . . had referred to the climate threat alternately as 'nonexistent' . . . before promising to cancel the Paris Climate Change Agreement of December 2015 if elected president," *idem*).

148 Also, on the ground that the costs of environmental inaction would be far greater adopting measures, from a precise perspective (e.g. "the European Commission (2016) estimates that the size of the global market for green goods and services is €4.2 trillion, a significant market opportunity for the business sector") Lázaro-Touza, *supra* note 82, at 457.

149 St-Geniès Géraud de, *supra* note 81. "The Paris Agreement is also legally binding on reporting emissions and progress towards meeting NDCs," Lázaro-Touza, *supra* note 82, at 488.

150 In the same line of thought, B. Taebi & A. Safari, *On Effectiveness and Legitimacy of 'Shaming' as a Strategy for Combatting Climate Change*, 23 Science and Engineering Ethics 1289 (2017). In particular, "*a scientific consensus of 'a clear showing' of serious and irreversible environmental damage*, while it cannot force sovereign states to support intervention if they do not wish to do so, *does generate major diplomatic pressure for action*," Weiss, *supra* note 9, at 150 (emphasis added).

In this sense, the establishment of a science-based decision-making process – providing, eventually, the ground for "an effective climate communication"[151] – should at least *work as an incentive* (another word for *diplomatic pressure for action*)[152] for member states to finally adopt efficient[153] measures to combat climate change.

151 Sikder & Prodhan, *supra* note 137.
152 Weiss, *supra* note 9, at 150.
153 In the long term, the law seems to be fashioned by objective information, such as this provided by science: "Dans ce conflit, il est loin d'être sûr que le droit ait le dernier mot – quelles que puissent être les apparences –, car il est loin d'être sûr qu'il dispose, devant les pressions et le conditionnement exercés par les sciences, d'un véritable libre arbitre. Croyant décider, il risque fort de ne faire qu'entériner ce que les scientifiques lui auront indirectement dicté (translation: In this conflict, it is far from certain that the law will have the last word – whatever the appearances – due to doubts about its real autonomy in the face of pressures and conditioning exercised by sciences. Under the illusion to decide, it is likely that the law will only endorse what has been dictated by scientists)," M. Castelli, *Sciences et droit: relation et rapports de force*, 37 Les Cahiers de droit 93 (1996).

13 The Intersections Among Science, Technology, Policy, and Law

In Between Truth and Justice

Paolo Davide Farah and Justo Corti Varela***

Science and law are abstractions (i.e., social constructs), that make sense only by the meaning attributed to them. While science delivers "objective truth," law determines justice. Yet both aim for the attainment of a particular truth by an approach that, in the Western tradition, begins with Socrates's method of distinguishing between truths and opinions. Both also follow a procedural method based on evidence and rationality.[1] The "truth" achieved is one of the multiple possible outcomes, depending on the inputs introduced. Like trials, it is a truth-as-agreement, recognized as such because a procedure accepted by a consensus has been followed. Since evidence can vary, the social acceptance of this method depends fundamentally on the exercise of rationality, which, as Aristotle said, is a "habit" or behaviour and not something that depends on our will. If rationality is a social practice, it changes over time, and with it, the idea of truth. Truth-as-an agreement is common in law, where judges resolve conflict and determine "truths" based on evidence that has previously risen to the status of facts through a legal proceeding. In the Western legal tradition, this method migrated from law to the natural sciences during the Enlightenment.[2] However, during this shift, the distinction between things

* Paolo Davide Farah, Full Professor, West Virginia University, Eberly College of Arts and Sciences, John D. Rockefeller IV School of Policy and Politics; Founder and Director of the West Virginia University, Energy Justice and Just Transition Lab; Founder and Coordinator of the Eberly College Interdisciplinary Research Collaborative on Global Challenges and Local Responses Initiatives; Visiting Professor of Law, University of Pittsburgh, School of Law; Founder, President, Director, Principal Investigator and Senior Research Fellow, at gLAWcal – Global Law Initiatives for Sustainable Development (United Kingdom). Email Addresses: paolofarah@yahoo.com; paolo.farah@glawcal.org.uk

** Justo Corti Varela, Associate Professor, National Distance Learning University (Spain), Deputy Dean on Quality and Innovation of the Law School. Former visiting professor at Paris Ouest La Defense Nanterre University (France) and visiting scholar at University College London. Chair of the Jean Monnet European Climate Law project. Corresponding Author: jcorti@der.uned.es

1 For a review of how rationality has been framed in the Western legal tradition focusing on Weber concept of rational legal authority, *see*: Sebastian Guzman, Rational Legal Authority (2007) < https://doi.org/10.1002/9781405165518.wbeosr026.pub2>.

2 To gain insights on the difficult relations between science and law emphasizing the role of rationality, see: Ronald N. Giere, Science Without Laws (University of Chicago Press 1999).

DOI: 10.4324/9781003472421-13

(simple evidence), juridical facts (contrasted evidence considered valid by the legal system, which requires a preponderance of the evidence for a civil case and "beyond a reasonable doubt" in a criminal case), and knowledge (contrasted evidence considered truth after passing a rational method) disappeared in natural science, once identified, "things" were automatically regarded as scientific "truth."

As Junker explains,[3] the "mathematization" of knowledge production and the specialization that followed during the Enlightenment reduced the qualification of "science" to activities that studied quantifiable "things." This eliminated the necessity of checking whether they really happened (facts) and equated science with knowledge. When the scientific method returned to social science, including law, where things are social constructions, facts were automatically understood as reality. It was not until sociologists, particularly those in sociology of knowledge, started to study science as a socially constructed reality,[4] and philosophers and lawyers began to see science as a cultural phenomenon, that other truths (post-truth) and other rationalities (post-rationality) became possible. Firstly, digitalization, then the internet, and nowadays social networks have exponentially increased the amount of information available. Therefore, it is becoming even more challenging today to distinguish facts from lies. This saturation of information makes us more prone to forget the "habit of" fact-checking and subsequent reasoning. Intuition, or even belief judgements (truthiness), becomes the approach used for assessing the truth in several cases. Belief judgements reaffirm each other by repetition, which, at best, multiplies the creation of more information that is impossible to process, and at worst, leads to the formation of a distorted perception of reality. Irrationality is no longer a source of shame as it was in the past, but is now seen as a reasonable option. This confusion between information and knowledge exacerbates the democratic deficit in Western societies, which may no longer be capable of rebuilding consensus agreements.

Hence, the acceptance of well-meaning beliefs, or even malicious alternative facts arises from the anthropological demand for certainties in an uncertain context where "mathematized" science can no longer guarantee truths due to information overload. Communication is replaced by interaction, experience-based memory by database storage, and physical "corporeity" by virtualization and referentiality. By contrast, law and its courts use the evidence-gathering process to distinguish facts from opinions and apply

3 Kirk W. Junker *Facts Are the Moveable Furniture of the Legal Mind, Not Stones of Science, in* Science, Technology, Policy and International Law (Justo Corti Varela & Paolo Davide Farah (eds.), Routledge 2024).

4 For a general introduction, see: Peter L. Berger & Thomas Luckmann, The Social Construction of Reality: A Treatise in the Sociology of Knowledge (Penguin 1991); On the relations between science and knowledge: Vojin Milić, *Sociology of Knowledge and Sociology of Science*, 23 Social Science Information 213 (1984); H. M. Collins, *The Sociology of Scientific Knowledge: Studies of Contemporary Science*, 9 Annual Review of Sociology 265 (1983).

presumptions and premises (for example, the burden of proof) to achieve a truth. This truth is not the only possible truth but the best of the possible options. It remains a source of knowledge rooted in rationality, which seeks to deliver justice.

The evidence-gathering process, however, is not immune to the social context of the discrediting of science. In EU case law, according to the advocate general's conclusions, it is necessary to create different methods for integrating scientific evidence into trials, sometimes through procedural means and other times through a more substantive approach. In the first method, scientific evidence is admitted based on the method by which it was produced, and it can be qualified as sound scientific evidence. This approach, though easier to implement, may lead to an overreliance on experts and the sciences, narrowing the standard of review to the mere assessment on the production of scientific evidence. In the second approach, the scientific method of production is not essential; rather, the research result itself is assessed and compared with the other available scientific conclusions to check its accuracy. This review may reveal epistemic difficulties, methodological limitations, inaccurate determination of facts, or alternative interpretations among the compared conclusions. Consequently, the substantive approach often leads to judges resolving scientific uncertainty by determining what the truth is for the specific case. Legal principles, such as the precautionary principle,[5] should be created to address this lack of certainty.

Besides aiding decision-making in these contexts where scientific evidence is partial or contradictory, the precautionary principle could be integrated into trials through the analysis of evidence and could also change the judicial procedure itself. According to Corti Varela's analysis of international case law,[6] the precautionary principle could be "proceduralized," which would alter the burden of proof and the standard of review. *Actori incumbit probatio* is no longer an immutable rule. For example, in interim orders, a shift of the burden is admissible in cases where the threat of environmental damage is proven. When this occurs in the main proceedings, it reduces the standard of proof by using presumptions to accept mere *prima facie* cases as proven facts.

5 The precautionary principle emphasizes the need for taking preventive actions in the face of uncertainty, particularly when public health is involved. It guides legal interpretation in several countries and has been subject of extensive literature, especially regarding its role in environmental protection. For an overview of the principle and its application in environmental law, *see*: David Kriebel & others, *The Precautionary Principle in Environmental Science*, 109 Environmental Health Perspectives 871 (2001); Per Sandin, *Dimensions of the Precautionary Principle*, 5 Human and Ecological Risk Assessment: An International Journal 889 (1999); Kenneth R. Foster, Paolo Vecchia & Michael H. Repacholi, *Science and the Precautionary Principle*, 288 Science 979 (2000).

6 Justo Corti Varela, *The Precautionary Principle and the Burden of Proof in International Risk Regulation Trials*, *in* Science, Technology, Policy and International Law (Justo C. Varela & Paolo Davide Farah (eds.), Routledge 2024).

This statement leads us to conclude that the integration of science into judicial proceedings does not always reinforce the legitimacy of judicial decisions. In the past, science contributed to the legitimization of sentences because it was a socially accepted method for identifying truth. However, it is now increasingly perceived as a source of uncertainty. Hence, judicial decisions based on science are often discredited by the public. Moreover, judges can no longer rely solely on science; they need to confront those who attack it (e.g., distinguishing between science and religion in intelligent design trials) or compel governments to apply scientific criteria in their policy management (e.g., climate change and climate justice litigations).

Beyond litigation, science has always been a stable base of support for international law, especially regarding the eternally difficult issue of defining the source of law. For example, science was integrated into the decision-making process of the UNFCCC.[7] However, it was necessary to establish a "depoliticization" process before incorporating science, a duty assigned to the Subsidiary Body for Scientific and Technological Advice. In the Paris Agreement, the integration of science into decision-making was based on exchange of information, the inclusion of experts in *strictu sensu* decision-making, and the impact assessment of its policies. This integration process was designed to compensate for the lack of consensus on which measures should be adopted to fight climate change and, consequently, a failure of the law as such. At the end of the day, it is international law's last call for legitimacy in the face of the uncertainty emanating from the loss of its traditional supports. The hard paradigm, based on the classical model of state and rule of law, where the principles of international law and their implementation in international customs were the main sources of law, has shifted to a more pragmatic model. In this new model, truth is no longer a universal aim, but rather an effort to achieve more than just a contextual description of reality. It also prevents the law from becoming merely a "regulation," a normative technique for achieving circumstantial agreements (such as international treaties). More recently, within the post-modern framework, truth is no longer the guiding principle of international law; it has been replaced by narrative(s) model(s) of truths. In that model, science-based decision-making is just one narrative among others, and there is space for multiple narratives to emerge through argumentation. Therefore, it is not surprising that scientific arguments could be politicized. Within this framework, international law does not regulate liquid societies; it manages them through "multilevel governance."

Multilevel governance states are no longer the sole actors in international society.[8] The reduction in its importance parallels its diminishing legitimacy,

7 On the mechanisms used within the UNFCCC to integrate science within policy and decision-making, see: Dagmar Lohan, *Assessing the Mechanisms for the Input of Scientific Information into the UNFCCC*, 17 Colorado Journal of International Environmental Law and Policy 249 (2005).

8 On the crisis of multilateralism within the international community, see: Jutta Brunnée, *Multilateralism in Crisis*, 112 Proceedings of the ASIL Annual Meeting 335 (2018); Lukasz

which, in Western societies, was synonymous with democracy. While information technologies, whether through deliberative or direct democracy tools, could facilitate the democratic process, it would be a form of technological utopianism to believe they could reverse the trend of delegitimization. Smartphone applications, as noted by Stojanoski and Vukovich,[9] could indeed play a role in the democratic decision-making process. These applications enable voters to access electoral information and compare policy preferences with the programs of candidates. Moreover, in some countries, smartphones are utilized for e-voting, providing an alternative method of casting votes. However, concern about the reliability of these technologies remains. Blockchain technology is one of the most promising options, but, of course, there are pros and cons.[10] Smartphone applications raise concerns about the protection of fundamental rights, such as freedom of expression and speech. For example, voters publicly stating their voting choices on social media could undermine the electoral process.

Earlier, we discussed how information overload hampers the search for scientific truth through rational processes and proceedings. Statute law is also affected by this information overload, especially when it regulates technology. The abundance of information slows down the decision-making, which is why the law often lags behind technological transformations.

Hobcraft[11] provides a good example of the challenges posed by timing difficulties, using the case of the UK Human Fertilisation and Embryology Authority. To address information overload, this authority adopted a proactive or reactive approach, depending on the circumstances, in the constantly

---

Gruszczynski & others (eds.), The Crisis of Multilateral Legal Order: Causes, Dynamics and Consequences (Routledge 2021). For regional perspective on multilateralism focusing on EU and the United States, see, for Europe, Christian Leffler, *Championing Multilateralism, in* The European Union's New Foreign Policy (Springer 2020); Mike Smith, *The EU, the US and the Crisis of Contemporary Multilateralism*, 40 Journal of European Integration 539 (2018). On China, see: Jingyuan Zhou, *A New Multilateralism? A Case Study of the Belt and Road Initiative*, The Chinese Journal of Comparative Law cxaa022 (2020); Jianfu Chen, *Tension and Rivalry: The "Belt and Road" Initiative, Global Governance, and International Law*, 8 The Chinese Journal of Comparative Law 177 (2020).

9 Mihail Stojanoski & Lilla Vukovich, *Use of Smartphone Applications in the Democratic Decision-Making Process, in* Science, Technology, Policy and International Law (Justo C. Varela & Paolo Davide Farah (eds.), Routledge 2024).

10 For an overview of how blockchain technology is being used by local government, see: Shaonan Shan & others, *Research on Collaborative Governance of Smart Government Based on Blockchain Technology: An Evolutionary Approach*, 2021 Discrete Dynamics in Nature and Society 1 (2021); Paolo Davide Farah & Marek Prityi, *Public Administration in the Age of Globalization and Emerging Technologies from Theories to Practice Symposium Issue: Blockchain Technology and the Law*, 88 UMKC Law Review 397 (2019).

11 Gemma Hobcraft, *Assessing the Soundness of Science to Determine Reactive and Proactive Regulatory Change. Human Fertilisation and Embryology Authority, Mitochondrial Donation, Treatment Add-ons and Future Challenges for Regulation, in* Science, Technology, Policy and International Law (Justo C. Varela & Paolo Davide Farah (eds.), Routledge 2024).

evolving field of new fertilization techniques. The proactive approach involved establishing regulation before the technology became available to the public, implementing strict and ethically sensitive oversight, and facilitating the development of mitochondrial donation. This demonstrates that, even in complex and information-overloaded contexts, it is possible to regulate scientific development effectively. However, as the author suggests, this regulatory management of science is only feasible at the national level. At the international level, implementation becomes significantly more challenging.

This difficulty poses a real problem when the regulation of technology is necessary on a supranational scale, either due to its scale or implementation.[12] This is particularly true in the case of information technologies (IT). In such cases, law has no alternative but to resort to soft paradigms, which are more closely related to the idea of governance and distant from classical concepts such as sovereignty and the rule of law. Regulation through norms becomes impractical, and the law must suffice with a set of technical rules that impose isolated limitations in contrast to the vast freedom of technological development.

The precautionary principle serves as a notable example of how law attempts to grapple with uncertainty. Its adaptability, stemming from its interactive and evolving nature, enables it to function across a variety of contexts. However, this adaptability can only be realized through constant negotiation in each specific application. The need for continuous negotiation and the presence of limited accountability are characteristics that render the practical implementation of the precautionary principle challenging.

In addition to the precautionary principle, there exist other flexibility mechanisms in international law aimed at addressing technological and scientific advancements. As suggested by Ibrahim and many other scholars,[13] Article XX of the GATT could serve as one of those mechanisms. This GATT article was a crucial tool for reaching agreements in disputed cases involving sovereign sensibilities during the previous century. Other examples include compliance mechanisms, frequently utilized in the Paris Agreement, which

12 For a successful case of transnational regulations, see the case of anti-corruption: Régis Bismuth, Jan Dunin-Wasowicz & Philip M. Nichols, The Transnationalization of Anti-Corruption Law (Routledge 2021).

13 On the use of Article XX in the protection of human rights, see: Rachel Harris & Gillian Moon, *GATT Article XX and Human Rights: What Do We Know from the First 20 Years?* 16 Melbourne Journal of International Law 432 (2015); Salman Bal, *International Free Trade Agreements and Human Rights: Reinterpreting Article XX of the GATT*, 10 Minnesota Journal of Global Trade 62 (2001); Paolo Davide Farah, *Trade and Progress: The Case of China*, 30 Columbia Journal of Asian Law 51 (2016). On its use for environmental protection, see: Christopher Tran, *Using GATT, Art XX to Justify Climate Change Measures in Claims under the WTO Agreements*, 27 Environmental and Planning Law Journal 346 (2010); Steve Charnovitz, *Exploring the Environmental Exceptions in GATT Article XX*, 25 Journal of World Trade 37 (1991); P. D. Farah & E. Cima, *Energy Trade and the WTO: Implications for Renewable Energy and the OPEC Cartel*, 16 Journal of International Economic Law 707 (2013).

represent another instance of substituting international norms with soft regulation. Financial technologies, including digital currencies, do not even fall under the category of governance utility, yet they are included in a "global sandbox program" aimed at facilitating international cooperation. Lastly, the mechanisms within international water law are not merely tools, but rather open regulatory frameworks where governance is in a constant state of flux, depending on the regulatory requirements of science (and not vice versa). Flexibility is not always a means to balance societal and economic concerns within the legal system but also, as in the case of conscientious objection, moral ones.

Antonio Quirós Fons[14] develops a parallelism between conscientious objections in cases of abortion, contraception, assisted reproduction, or sex reassignment surgery, which were once based on ethical reasoning but are now grounded in beliefs of reasonable doubt concerning issues of sound science. Consequently, belief alone can question scientific arguments. These doubts merit protection, based on human rights protection systems in particular cases, but it is challenging to assert that they alone could delegitimize regulation based on science.

In this new method, technological accountability replaces technological regulation, and when supported by international governance, it can occur without sovereignty. Besides the legitimacy question mentioned before, there is a naïve element in the narrative of neoliberal deregulation ideology. Deregulation is based on confidence in technological progress; however, technology is never neutral. A new technological elite could exploit this regulatory deficit, steering Western societies towards a neo-democracy that is favourable to authoritarian regimes beyond our borders.

Democracy is challenged both by a classical view and a broader perspective. Climate change is making the limitations of the Anthropocene and globalization irrefutably apparent.[15] Ecological modernization – neoliberal adaptation to climate change aiming to reduce its velocity, but not reverse the trend of degradation – does not guarantee true climate justice. Intergenerational equity calls for more engaged action founded on the imperative of responsibility as the ethical foundation of climate justice. These actions must surpass

14 Antonio Quirós Fons, *The Precautionary Principle and the Burden of Proof in International Risk Regulation Trials*, *in* Science, Technology, Policy and International Law (Justo C. Varela & Paolo Davide Farah (eds.), Routledge 2024).

15 The Anthropocene has garnered significant attention in the past decade, being framed and analyzed as the epoch in which human activities have led to radical environmental changes. For more on the relationship between climate change and the Anthropocene, see: Christophe Bonneuil, Jean-Baptiste Fressoz & David Fernbach, The Shock of the Anthropocene: The Earth, History and Us (David Fernbach transl., Verso Books 2017); Paolo Davide Farah & Alessio Lo Giudice, *Climate Justice in the Anthropocene and Its Relationship with Science and Technology: The Importance of Ethics of Responsibility*, Connecticut Law Review (2023) <https://opencommons.uconn.edu/law_review/572>.

the synchronic and anthropocentric vision and should correct not only the damages produced by science subjugated to predatory productivism but also account for historical and geographical differences between the past and the present, the Global North and the Global South, and between human and non-human subjects, including, foremost, nature.

Going deeper into each chapter written by our book authors and contributors, one could wonder about the real impact of the overall issue and its significance for future research. Junker,[16] for example, highlighted that interplay between law, science, and technology does not necessarily result in the betterment of society. This is because, in our "post-truth" era, facts, logic, and reasoning – including legal reasoning – and information have lost their importance to citizens who are isolated in their own social media bubbles and inundated with a high volume of information, making it difficult for them to assess the quality or correctness of this information. Currently, citizens are prone to believe information that supports their own ideals, regardless of its validity, even using terms like "my truth," despite the fact that there can only be one truth. Given this reality, one could question the actual relevance of the technological and scientific developments within the general framework of the Fourth Industrial Revolution and the role of law in regulating these advances. It seems that individuals are becoming less capable of processing facts and information as technology evolves, perhaps out of laziness but certainly out of an unwillingness to do so. This trend is noticeable across generations and varies with the amount of time a person spends on social media. Thus, despite all the achievements in science and technology, once entangled in politics, they have been used to establish new realities and protect echo chambers, rather than as a means to reach political consensus. This is a dangerous phenomenon, where truth and facts are claimed to be subjective, leading to situations where people deny climate change or assert that vaccines like those for COVID-19 have severe negative consequences, despite a lack of scientific evidence.[17] Scholars are examining this topic, addressing issues of post-truth and the impact of the internet and social networks.[18] This is crucial, as irrationality and anti-science sentiments have gained ground in recent years.[19]

Bombelli and Farah[20] preferred to focus on the interconnection between science, technology, society, and law. The deconstruction of the classical link

16 Junker, *supra* note 3.
17 Jamie L. Vernon, *Science in the Post-Truth Era*, 105 American Scientist 2, 2 (2017).
18 Anna Visvizi & Miltiadis D. Lytras, Politics and Technology in the Post-Truth Era (Emerald Publishing Limited 2019).
19 Michael Lynch, *We Have Never Been Anti-Science: Reflections on Science Wars and Post-Truth*, 6 Engaging Science, Technology, and Society 49, 49 (2020).
20 Giovanni Bombelli & Paolo Davide Farah, *The Interlinkages Science-Technology-Law: Information and Communication Society, Knowledge-Based Economy and the Rule of Law*, *in* Science, Technology, Policy and International Law (Justo C. Varela & Paolo Davide Farah (eds.), Routledge 2024).

between information and knowledge, mainly due to the inability to process the vast amount of information in complex data societies, leads to a deepening democratic deficit and a weakening of the law. However, technology does not necessarily undermine legal structures. New spaces created, for example, in cyberspace or cryptocurrency environments, aim to establish their own order based on different preconditions and consensus. There is little resistance to this process, primarily due, to the political-institutional crisis of mediators (such a political parties) and the individualization of the deliberative process, which has led to a decline in political legitimacy and consensus mechanisms. The confusion between information and knowledge and the fragmentation of discourse in the post-democratic (or neo-democratic) age facilitate the spread of political demagogy and populism in Western society.

Ibrahim[21] addresses the constant technological and scientific changes occurring in society and the appropriate legal response to these developments. He suggests that law struggles to keep up with these changes and that only through the use of flexibility mechanisms can it catch up. Flexibility mechanisms can both stifle innovations and provide regulators with the needed space to manage constant technological and scientific uncertainties. In this context, Ibrahim[22] focuses on specific examples of flexibility mechanisms: (1) Article XX of the GATT Agreement, (2) compliance mechanisms within the Paris Agreement, (3) regulatory sandboxes for the regulation of financial technologies, and (4) flexibility mechanisms within international water law. Such mechanisms are necessary to address scientific and technological developments, making law more attractive and efficient and increasing the likelihood of compliance by various actors. However, flexibility mechanisms also have downsides, such as noncompliance due to economic and political pressures[23] and other limitations.[24] Indeed, flexibility is the only potential means of tackling the challenge of ever-evolving technologies and sciences, especially considering the expected problems in these fields. Such mechanisms allow for addressing unforeseen issues[25] through cooperation, both nationally and globally.[26] Despite their shortcomings, these mechanisms have been incorporated

21 Imad Antoine Ibrahim, *Using Flexibility Mechanisms for Addressing Technological and Scientific Developments: Examples from Selected Global Regulatory Frameworks*, *in* Science, Technology, Policy and International Law (Justo C. Varela and Paolo Davide Farah (eds.), Routledge 2024).

22 *Ibid.*

23 Jeffrey L. Dunoff & Mark A. Pollack (eds.), Interdisciplinary Perspectives on International Law and International Relations: The State of the Art 175–176 (Illustrated ed., Cambridge University Press 2012).

24 Sia Spiliopoulou Akermark & Olle Marsater, *Treaties and the Limits of Flexibility*, 74 Nordic Journal of International Law 509 (2005).

25 Christopher Marcoux, *Institutional Flexibility in the Design of Multilateral Environmental Agreements*, 26 Conflict Management and Peace Science 209 (2009).

26 Jeffrey Kucik & Eric Reinhardt, *Does Flexibility Promote Cooperation? An Application to the Global Trade Regime*, 62 International Organization 477 (2008).

into international agreements, such as the Kyoto Protocol.[27] This trajectory reflects the direction that international environmental agreements have been taking for some time.[28]

Drawing upon the concept of post-modernism and its implications for science, technology, and international law principles, Donati[29] examined its impact on post-truth and post-modernism, highlighting similar roles to flexibility mechanisms. In this analysis, the precautionary principle is viewed through both positive and negative lenses. While it can play an important role in furthering science and technology, it may also increase confusion and lead to multiple scientific and technological innovations. The *precautionary principle* is a long-standing term in international law, gaining prominence mainly during the 1970s, and has since been subject to extensive analysis and interpretation in the literature and within specific fields, such as international environmental law.[30] It is not surprising that this principle was examined in the context of science and technology, given its focus on anticipating and preventing damage from occurring,[31] as such harm may arise due to the uncertainties inherent in these fields. In this context, the principle serves as a guide for the decision-making process of states seeking to regulate scientific and technological developments.[32] Indeed, the concept itself serves as a reminder that science and technology have limitations that must be considered within the realm of political debate.[33]

27 Fanny Missfeldt, *Flexibility Mechanisms: Which Path to Take after Kyoto*, 7 Review of European Community and International Environmental Law 128 (1998).

28 Peter H. Sand & Jeffrey McGee, *Lessons Learnt from Two Decades of International Environmental Agreements: Law*, 22 International Environmental Agreements: Politics, Law and Economics 263 (2022).

29 Alessandra Donati, *The Precautionary Principle Under EU Law: A "Post-Modern" Principle in a "Post-Truth" Era*, *in* Science, Technology, Policy and International Law (Justo C. Varela & Paolo Davide Farah (eds.), Routledge 2024).

30 Arie Trouwborst, *The Precautionary Principle in General International Law: Combating the Babylonian Confusion*, 16 Review of European Community & International Environmental Law 185 (2007); Claudia Saladin, *Precautionary Principle in International Law*, 6 International Journal of Occupational and Environmental Health 270 (2000); Aline L. Jaeckel, The International Seabed Authority and the Precautionary Principle: Balancing Deep Seabed Mineral Mining and Marine Environmental Protection, vol. 83 (Brill 2017); Sonia Boutillon, *The Precautionary Principle: Development of an International Standard*, 23 Michigan Journal of International Law 429 (2001); Owen McIntyre & Thomas Mosedale, *The Precautionary Principle as a Norm of Customary International Law*, 9 Journal of Environmental Law 221 (1997).

31 Mary Stevens, *The Precautionary Principle in the International Arena*, 2 Sustainable Development Law & Policy 7 (2010).

32 Meinhard Schröder, *Precautionary Approach/Principle*, Max Planck Encyclopedia of Public International Law – OUP (2014) <https://opil.ouplaw.com/oxlaw/entryview/viewoxlawoxchap/10.1093$002flaw:epil$002f9780199231690$002flaw-9780199231690-e1603;jsessionid=BDD5A38E425A3B703381A5670AC31905>.

33 Jacqueline Peel, *Precaution: A Matter of Principle, Approach or Process?* 5 Melbourne Journal of International Law 483 (2004).

The precautionary principle was also examined by Justo Corti Varela,[34] who suggested that it is used as a risk management choice by policymakers seeking a higher level of protection. Legal scholars have not fully addressed states that do not apply this concept in cases of scientific uncertainty, which affects the ability to consider it as an adjudication principle. Indeed, upon an examination of the literature, the focus has mainly been on the risk management approach, rather than on one of adjudication.[35] Hence, this book provides two different methods for the application of the precautionary concept within the general framework of science and technology. The decision-making process in uncertain situations does complicate the use of science in policy-making.[36] Risk management in this context involves risk assessment to determine whether uncertainties are well-understood or familiar and, if not, to take precautionary measures.[37] Criticisms regarding this focus on risk management primarily support other critiques made against this principle, particularly that it ignores science and hampers innovation.[38] Regardless of the validity of these arguments, further research is needed to ensure that this concept serves to better disseminate science and technology, considering all the factors and stakeholders involved.

The role of science and technology in the context of sexual and reproductive rights is examined by Quirós Fons.[39] This is a delicate topic, as the definition of sexual and reproductive rights, and their extent, particularly concerning abortion, has been subject to significant controversy over the decades.[40] This controversy is especially pronounced in the United States, where Republicans and Democrats hold different opinions on these issues.[41] The

34 Corti Varela, *supra* note 6.

35 On the precautionary approach, see: Terje Aven, *The Cautionary Principle in Risk Management: Foundation and Practical Use*, 191 Reliability Engineering & System Safety 106585 (2019); Julian Morris, Rethinking Risk and the Precautionary Principle (Butterworth-Heinemann 2000); Ronnie Harding & Elizabeth Fisher, Perspectives on the Precautionary Principle (Federation Press Sydney 1999).

36 European Commission, Future Brief: The Precautionary Principle: Decision-Making under Uncertainty (Issue 18, September 2017) <https://ec.europa.eu/environment/integration/research/newsalert/pdf/precautionary_principle_decision_making_under_uncertainty_FB18_en.pdf>.

37 Marco Martuzzi, Joel A. Tickner & World Health Organization Regional Office for Europe, The Precautionary Principle: Protecting Public Health, the Environment and the Future of Our Children (World Health Organization Regional Office for Europe 2004) <https://apps.who.int/iris/handle/10665/346211> accessed 18 September 2023.

38 Sven Ove Hansson, *How Extreme Is the Precautionary Principle?* 14 NanoEthics 245 (2020).

39 Quirós Fons, *supra* note 14.

40 Renu Addlakha, Janet Price & Shirin Heidari, *Disability and Sexuality: Claiming Sexual and Reproductive Rights*, 25 Reproductive Health Matters 4 (2017); Elaine Reis Brandão & Cristiane da Silva Cabral, *Sexual and Reproductive Rights under Attack: The Advance of Political and Moral Conservatism in Brazil*, 27 Sexual and Reproductive Health Matters 76 (2019); Wanda Nowicka, *Sexual and Reproductive Rights and the Human Rights Agenda: Controversial and Contested*, 19 Reproductive Health Matters 119 (2011).

41 Françoise Girard, *Implications of the Trump Administration for Sexual and Reproductive Rights Globally*, 25 Reproductive Health Matters 6 (2017).

recent overturning of *Roe v. Wade* has further underscored this divide, sending shockwaves across the country and the entire Western world.[42] Quirós Fons[43] provides specific guidelines for addressing this topic, considering both sides of the debate and taking into account human rights, the roles of each stakeholder involved, the responsibilities of public institutions, and even an environmental approach to human life. These guidelines benefit from the progress made on the technological and scientific front. In the future, we can expect further development of guidelines and regulations, leveraging advancements in science and technology. Still, this much is certain: these advancements do not change the core debate associated with morality, philosophy, and human rights.[44]

According to Stojanoski and Vukovich,[45] who examined the use of smartphone applications in the pre-vote, vote, and post-vote stages, technology and science have affected the democratic decision-making process. They found that such applications resulted in the propagation of fake news and hampered freedom of expression and human rights in general. The use of blockchain technology in this context presents a questionable solution, while the Council of Europe Recommendations on online voting are seen as an adequate first step in regulating this issue. The use of smartphones in the democratic decision-making process is a serious concern that warrants further evaluation, especially given the need to ensure their use for the promotion of good governance in the context of rampant globalization.[46] To this end, suggestions have been made for the establishment of an innovative digital democracy that benefits from a user-centric design.[47] Authors like Buchstein have introduced concepts such as net optimism, net pessimism, and net neutralism when discussing the potential of digital information for democracy.[48] Another relevant term is the concept of "e-democracy," which posits that democracy can be practiced through information and communication technology.[49] Smartphones, in this regard, are a key aspect of e-democracy. The Arab Spring is often cited as the first smartphone revolution, where citizens challenged nondemocratic regimes

42 Nicole Huberfeld & Linda McClain, *Is the End of Roe v. Wade Near? Leaked SCOTUS Brief Says Yes* (BU Today, 2022) <https://scholarship.law.bu.edu/shorter_works/150>; Mary Ziegler, *The End of Roe v. Wade*, 22 The American Journal of Bioethics 16 (2022).

43 Quirós Fons, *supra* note 14.

44 Jaime Todd-Gher & Payal K. Shah, *Abortion in the Context of COVID-19: A Human Rights Imperative*, 28 Sexual and Reproductive Health Matters 1758394 (2020).

45 Stojanoski and Vukovich, *supra* note 9.

46 David Simmonds & others, *Decision-Making on the Go: Smartphones and Decision-Making in Early 21st-Century Workflow*, 36 Business Information Review 164 (2019).

47 Janne Berg, Jenny Lindholm & Joachim Högväg, *How Do We Know That It Works? Designing a Digital Democratic Innovation with the Help of User-Centered Design*, 26 Information Polity 221 (2021).

48 Olaf Winkel, *The Perspectives of Democratic Decision-Making in the Information Society*, 8 International Journal of Computer Science and Information Technology 1 (2016).

49 T. M. Vinod Kumar (ed.), E-Democracy for Smart Cities (Springer 2017) <http://link.springer.com/10.1007/978-981-10-4035-1> accessed 18 September 2023.

through its use.[50] Therefore, including this chapter in the book was highly relevant.

Hobcraft[51] delved deeper into this topic within the context of the Human Fertilisation and Embryology Authority (HFEA), exploring mitochondrial donation, treatment add-ons, and their regulation. The focus was specifically on the United Kingdom (UK) HFEA and its efforts to regulate assisted reproduction, providing examples of proactive regulation regarding treatment add-ons and contrasting them with reactive regulation concerning mitochondrial donation. The UK has developed various regulations in this area, resulting in a substantial body of literature on the subject. The questions raised in this chapter are highly complex, necessitating thorough examination of the role of the law. In this context, science and technology play an essential role, providing crucial evidence for regulators aiming to minimize existing risks and address complex moral and philosophical questions. Despite extensive literature on the topic,[52] it remains unclear whether the legal response is adequate or sufficient, not only in the UK but also globally. The focus on the UK in this chapter stems from the relevance of its adopted laws. However, while Hobcraft's assessment[53] of the situation in that state is thorough, further research is necessary on a global scale, particularly in developing countries,[54] where laws may not be as well-developed due to a lack of technological, scientific, and human capacity to address these issues.

Molitorisová and Burke[55] addressed the issue of scientific evidence through the opinions of the advocates general, examining the procedural versus substantive approaches. They highlighted the increasing complexity of incorporating science in the court system. Despite this complexity, science remains essential in the production of proof. Therefore, the advocate general needs to develop a new, sound scientific approach to ensure fair decisions that benefit from current technological developments.[56] Examples of science used include forensics, a field recently scrutinized by the legal community.[57] Indeed, not all

50 Omer Karasapan, *Social Networks and Cell Phones in the Aftermath of the Arab Revolutions* (World Bank Blogs, 8 February 2013) <https://blogs.worldbank.org/arabvoices/social-networks-and-cell-phones-aftermath-arab-revolutions>.

51 Hobcraft, *supra* note 11.

52 See for a comparative study: Chokri Kooli, *Review of Assisted Reproduction Techniques, Laws, and Regulations in Muslim Countries*, 24 Middle East Fertility Society Journal 8 (2019).

53 Hobcraft, *supra* note 11.

54 Frida Simonstein, Reprogen-Ethics and the Future of Gender (Springer Science & Business Media 2009).

55 Ciarán Burke & Alexandra Molitorisová, *Procedural versus Substantive Approaches to Scientific Evidence in the Opinions of Advocates-General, in* Science, Technology, Policy and International Law (Justo C. Varela & Paolo Davide Farah (eds.), Routledge 2024).

56 Stephen Breyer, *Science in the Courtroom*, 16 Issues in Science and Technology 52 (2000).

57 Éadaoin O'Brien, Niamh Nic Daeid & Sue Black, *Science in the Court: Pitfalls, Challenges and Solutions*, 370 Philosophical Transactions of the Royal Society B: Biological Sciences 20150062 (2015).

legal experts see science as beneficial in court; some argue that mere junk science is being used in many instances.[58] This is especially concerning as science and technology become more complex, making it increasingly challenging for lawyers and judges to make informed decisions based on them. Efforts are being made to improve this reality, but these fields are evolving rapidly.[59] This topic has been addressed every decade since the last century, given the routine scientific and technological developments,[60] leading some scholars to label the role science plays as "disappointing."[61] This chapter represents another attempt, this time from the legal community, to understand the best ways science and technology can be used, based on the practice and experience of the advocate general.

Farah and Lo Giudice[62] tackled the interplay between climate justice in the Anthropocene on the one hand and science and technology on the other, emphasizing the relevance of ethics and responsibility. These authors argued that ethics of responsibility, within the framework of Hans Jonas's philosophy, can serve as a rationale for climate justice and as a means of addressing the relationship between science, technology, and society. Climate justice as a concept has gained traction globally in recent decades, despite the need for further clarification about its status and how it intersects with morality, philosophy, and power politics.[63] It falls under the general framework of environmental justice developed in previous decades.[64] Science and technology have played an important role in advancing justice for human-caused global warming.[65] Through technological development and scientific progress, the Intergovernmental Panel on Climate Change (IPCC) has been able to prove that climate change is occurring.[66] Philosophy and morality remain necessary, as some still

58 Joseph M. Price & Gretchen Gates Kelly, *Junk Science in the Courtroom: Causes, Effects and Controls*, 19 Hamline Law Review 395 (1995).

59 Kelly Servick, *Reversing the Legacy of Junk Science in the Courtroom*, Science (7 March 2016) <www.science.org/content/article/reversing-legacy-junk-science-courtroom> accessed 18 September 2023.

60 Arthur Tompkins, *Science in the Courtroom: Is There, and Should There, Be a Better Way?* 49 Australian Journal of Forensic Sciences 579 (2017).

61 Jim Hilbert, *The Disappointing History of Science in the Courtroom: Frye, Daubert, and the Ongoing Crisis of Junk Science in Criminal Trials*, 71 Oklahoma Law Review 759 (2018).

62 Paolo Davide Farah & Alessio Lo Giudice, *Climate Justice in the Anthropocene and Its Relationship with Science and Technology The Importance of an Ethics of Responsibility*, *in* Science, Technology, Policy and International Law (Justo C. Varela & Paolo Davide Farah (eds.), Routledge 2024).

63 Chukwumerije Okereke, *Climate Justice and the International Regime*, 1 WIREs Climate Change 462 (2010).

64 David Schlosberg & Lisette B. Collins, *From Environmental to Climate Justice: Climate Change and the Discourse of Environmental Justice*, 5 WIREs Climate Change 359 (2014).

65 Rashmi Verma, Role of Science, Technology and Innovation in Addressing Climate Change (Science Policy Forum, 2020) <https://thesciencepolicyforum.org/articles/perspectives/role-of-science-technology-and-innovation-in-addressing-climate-change-a-perspective/>.

66 Shardul Agrawala, *Context and Early Origins of the Intergovernmental Panel on Climate Change*, 39 Climatic Change 605 (1998).

deny its existence.[67] Additionally, technology and science are currently being used for climate change adaptation and mitigation, guided by moral and philosophical considerations.[68] This context makes the chapter highly relevant, especially for future debates on climate change developments driven by science and technology.

Finally, Koskina[69] examined the science-based decision-making process of the Paris Agreement. Given that it requires parties to the convention to implement its provisions, the drafters included specific measures defining scientifically how governments should fulfil the treaty's obligations. This was the result of years of scientific research, leading to clear and defined commitments in which technology played an important role. The agreement specifies that the best available science is to be used to ensure a rapid decrease in global emissions and to measure the progressive realization of the convention. Indeed, the agreement establishes science-based processes for reporting, assessing developments, and increasing the ambitions of signatory states.[70] Already, scientific expert bodies established in the context of the treaty provide much-needed scientific advice and facilitate information exchange with treaty-making bodies,[71] in this case, the Conference of the Parties. This emphasis on the role of science in the agreement is not surprising, given its overall significance in the broader field of climate change, as highlighted earlier.[72] What is currently happening is that this role is being properly legislated within the provisions of conventions, with the Paris Agreement as progenitor. This approach, adopted by the international community, represents a new way of thinking, based on which innovative mechanisms for compliance and implementation of climate change agreements are being put in place.[73] Only time will tell whether this new strategy is truly effective.

67 "Global Warming: How Skepticism Became Denial – Spencer Weart, 2011" <https://journals.sagepub.com/doi/full/10.1177/0096340210392966> accessed 18 September 2023.

68 Wai Chee Dimock, *What AI Can Do for Climate Change, and What Climate Change Can Do for AI* (Scientific American, 5 April 2022) <www.scientificamerican.com/article/what-ai-can-do-for-climate-change-and-what-climate-change-can-do-for-ai/> accessed 18 September 2023.

69 Anthi Koskina, *The Science-Based Decision-Making Process as Established in the Paris Agreement (2015)*, *in* Science, Technology, Policy and International Law (Justo C. Varela & Paolo Davide Farah (eds.), Routledge 2024).

70 World Meteorological Organization et al., *Systematic Observations and the Paris Agreement: Report of the Task Team on the Paris Agreement* (2018) 6 <https://wedocs.unep.org/20.500.11822/32141>.

71 Joseph Orangias, *The Nexus between International Law and Science: An Analysis of Scientific Expert Bodies in Multilateral Treaty-Making*, 25 International Community Law Review 60 (2022).

72 Candice Howarth & James Painter, *Exploring the Science – Policy Interface on Climate Change: The Role of the IPCC in Informing Local Decision-Making in the UK*, 2 Palgrave Communications 1 (2016).

73 Imad Antoine Ibrahim, Sandrine Maljean-Dubois & Jessica Owley, *The Paris Agreement Compliance Mechanism: Beyond COP 26*, 11 Wake Forest Law Review Online 147, 26 (2021).

A brief overview of these different contributions highlights that each topic is extremely relevant to the interplay between law, science, and technology, and that each issue deserves an entire manuscript to be addressed properly. The goal of this book is to continue the ongoing debate by posing a new set of topics, questions, and analyses that require further examination in future research endeavours. It is worth mentioning that the topics addressed are non-exhaustive, and the editors had to carefully select each subject and tailor it for the book, acknowledging that through this research they are merely scratching the surface of an ocean.

Index

For Product Safety Concerns and Information please contact our EU representative GPSR@taylorandfrancis.com
Taylor & Francis Verlag GmbH, Kaufingerstraße 24, 80331 München, Germany

www.ingramcontent.com/pod-product-compliance
Lightning Source LLC
LaVergne TN
LVHW021119300926
849160LV00010B/778
* 9 7 8 1 0 3 2 7 5 1 1 3 9 *